EASTER ROSS 1750-1850:
the Double Frontier

EASTER ROSS 1750-1850: the Double Frontier

IAN R. M. MOWAT

JOHN DONALD PUBLISHERS LTD
EDINBURGH

Printed in Great Britain by Bell & Bain Ltd., Glasgow
Phototypesetting by Burns & Harris Ltd., Dundee

Preface

THE eastern districts of Ross and Cromarty probably have figured more prominently in the national consciousness in the twentieth century than at any time since Macbeth rose from his traditional position as Mormaer of Ross in the eleventh century to become King of Scotland. The importance of the Invergordon naval base in two World Wars has been succeeded by the arrival of industrial development in the shape of aluminium smelting and, even more notably, oil and its related concerns. At the same time, there has been an increasing awareness that the area, as part of the larger, inner-Moray Firth region, is one of the last, relatively unspoilt parts of the United Kingdom hospitable to human settlement. The debate about the ways in which the area can be developed already has engendered as much heat as light and no crystal ball is required to see that contention is far from being stilled.

Oil, aluminium and twentieth century warfare may seem to be far removed from the concerns of a pre-industrial society but, if history does not repeat itself, certain historical problems most certainly do. The threat of exploitation, the need to face the challenge of change and the balancing of private and local desires against public and national interests were dominant issues in the eighteenth and nineteenth centuries as they are today. While they are dealt with here at a local level, they have indeed a universal relevance.

This study of Easter Ross in the eighteenth and nineteenth centuries was conceived originally as a topic suitable for an undergraduate dissertation and has grown through a post-graduate thesis to its present form as a book. Despite its academic origins and its treatment of fundamental issues the book, above all, is a study of local roots. No doubt the author has displayed bias in one or more directions but it is open to question if true historical objectivity is ever achieved. So far as possible the evidence has been allowed to speak for itself.

In preparing this book I have become indebted to large numbers of people: to Mr R. G. Cant and Mr B. P. Lenman for their guidance in the past; to the large assembly of archivists and librarians who have helped me to obtain the necessary evidence; to my former colleagues Mr A. Anderson, for his encouragement and support, and Mr I. Brown for triggering the final phase of development; and to Mr A. Fenton who gave early advice on sources and latterly has done much to further the cause of publication. Thanks are due also to Mrs E. Innes, who typed the original manuscript, Mrs J. Durham, without whose enthusiastic support the book would never have been and with whose interest at an earlier stage much more might have been done, and to my wife for sharing an alien enthusiasm, for bearing with the text through its various transformations and for helping to reduce to a minimum the number of errors remaining.

Ian R. M. Mowat
Glasgow, 1981

Contents

Abbreviations

N.R.A.	National Register of Archives (Scotland)
N.S.A.	New Statistical Account of Scotland
O.S.A.	Old (First) Statistical Account of Scotland
P.P.	Parliamentary Paper
S.G.M.	Scottish Geographical Magazine
S.R.O.	Scottish Record Office
S.S.P.C.K.	Society in Scotland for the Propagation of Christian Knowledge

1
Introduction

The area of Easter Ross[1.1] which is the subject of this book is that portion of the eastern coastal plain of Scotland lying within the boundaries of the present-day District of Ross and Cromarty. The eastern coastal plain extends almost without interruption from the central belt round the north-east shoulder of Scotland and as far north as the Dornoch Firth. There it narrows into insignificance before burgeoning forth again to form a northern pendicle in Caithness.

With the exception of the Caithness section, which has a highly individual history and character, the Ross-shire stretch represents the northernmost significant portion of the plain. It lies at the head, and forms part of the northern littoral of the Moray Firth, having a closer geographic affinity with the remainder of the Moray Firth sub-region than with the rest of the coastal plain.

The exact boundaries of the region which will be most intensively examined have been drawn to include the parishes of Tain, Tarbat, Fearn, Nigg, Kilmuir Easter, Logie Easter, Alness, Rosskeen, Kiltearn, Dingwall, Urquhart and Logie Wester, Resolis, Cromarty, Rosemarkie, Avoch, Knockbain and Killearnan, comprising a total area of just over 376 square miles and covering most of Easter Ross proper (i.e. the peninsula between the Cromarty and Dornoch Firths), the Black Isle and Ferindonald. These parishes do not exactly coincide with the limits of the coastal plain, for within them lie several areas of high land while beyond them the plain extends up the valley of the Conon and its tributaries into the parishes of Fodderty and Contin, across to the western end of the Black Isle in the parish of Urray and along the shore of the Dornoch Firth in Edderton parish. An accurate picture of the true character of the area is obtained, however, by paying the closest attention only to the parishes listed above.

The peripheral areas cannot be readily distinguished, at least in quantitative terms, from the remainder of the parishes in which they lie. Those parishes are, overall, quite definitely Highland in character and, as such, clearly distinct from the area to the west.[1.2]

At one time the identity of the western peripheral areas was very much clearer. The western area of the Black Isle, now in Urray, was formerly the separate parish of Kilchrist and much of the plain to the west of Dingwall, now in Fodderty, the parish of Kinnettas. Both of these parishes had been merged with their larger neighbours well before the middle of the eighteenth century.[1.3]

The inclusion of some of the parishes forming the northern shore of the Cromarty Firth is perhaps more questionable than the omission of the districts mentioned above. Kiltearn, in particular, is closer to the parishes of the west than to most of the other parishes bordering on the North Sea. In size, topography and, to a considerable extent, history there is little to distinguish it from most 'typical' Highland parishes. Alness and even Rosskeen could also be similarly considered but in these parishes the coastal plain has been of major significance in terms both of area and history. Despite their differences, therefore, they and Kiltearn have been included, in order to give a more complete picture of the area as a whole.

The general character of the region is to a large extent determined by its topography, for, as might be expected of a coastal plain, the area is low-lying and relatively gently contoured. The uppermost limits of cultivation in the North-West Highlands may never have gone much beyond the seven hundred foot contour[1.4] and this height is only exceeded in the centre of the Millbuie (the ridge running the length of the Black Isle) and where the hills start rising to Mid-Ross in the west.

Easter Ross generally has been thought to be an area of considerable fertility[1.5] although by no means all the region is fertile and even some of those parts which have been so considered are not naturally of the highest quality.[1.6] The fact remains, however, that there are some soils of considerable value and that compared with the Highland average most of the area could be considered rich.

The contrast between Easter Ross and the surrounding Highland districts with respect to topography and fertility is heightened by climatic differences. The area of the North-West Highlands is one of heavy rainfall (a precipitation of forty inches is general, rising to well over eighty inches in the west), high and frequent winds and low temperature. Easter Ross benefits from the shadow effect of the hills to the west. Nowhere is the rainfall higher than thirty inches (except in the marginal areas on the western border) while winds are fewer and more gentle, and temperatures, at least in summer, are somewhat higher. The relatively mild climate is encouraged by the moderating influence of the Moray Firth.

As a result of the low rainfall and favourable topography there are few large inland lochs in the area.[1.7] Most of those which do exist are to be found in the more Highland west. Rivers, too, are generally short and carry no great volume of water. The only river of any size, the Conon, only touches the south-western limits of the area although it has significantly influenced the historical development of all the country to the north of it.

In contrast with the lochs and rivers, the firths form a major feature of the area's geographical structure and have, in consequence, been of some importance. As previously indicated, both Easter Ross proper[1.8] and the Black Isle front on to the Moray Firth. The two peninsulae are respectively separated from Sutherland by the Dornoch Firth and Inverness by the Beauly Firth and from each other by the Cromarty Firth.

The absence of major rivers[1.9] allowed the relatively easy development of land transport within the region (those rivers which do exist were all fordable or bridgeable without great effort), although the Conon for long acted as a barrier to communication with the south and the Oykell with communication to the north. The firths, on the other hand, enabled water transport to grow in sheltered conditions.

With such geographical advantages over neighbouring districts it is hardly surprising that Easter Ross is an area with a long history of settlement. The Picts and their successors in the 'Dark Ages' left evidence of their occupation in the Pictish place names and in the great carved stones at Nigg, Shandwick and Rosemarkie.[1.10] By the end of the eighth century a new element, in the shape of the Vikings, appeared on the scene in the North of Scotland and the Scandinavians in their turn settled the area, leaving traces of their occupation behind them in place names.[1.11] Their settlement appears to have been particularly heavy on the eastern side of the Black Isle although their political significance was only of a temporary nature.[1.12]

The Celtic element in the population remained dominant and in the twelfth century Easter Ross, as part of the greater province of Moray, served as a power base for several claimants to the Scottish throne opposed to the modernising and Normanising trends of the Caenmore dynasty. The twelfth and thirteenth century kings had good reason, therefore, to carry their policy into Moray itself and settle loyal Anglo-Norman barons and their supporters in place of the indigenous but insurgent natives. Easter Ross did receive an infusion of new blood in this way but the greater part of the area remained unaffected and most or all of the new settlement was concentrated at the eastern end of the Black Isle.[1.13]

From the Anglo-Norman settlement until the eighteenth century there were no major new elements introduced to the population. There were, however, minor variations which may have been of some significance in affecting the balance between the different existing language groups. The Gaelic-speaking element in the population may have been strengthened when the Macdonalds of the Isles inherited the Earldom of Ross and possibly gained further reinforcement following the re-distribution of lands after the Reformation.[1.14]

Just as the basic elements of the population of the area were established by the thirteenth century so, by the same period, were laid the foundations of much of the social structure of that population. The basic organisational division of the church into parishes was made at this time although considerable changes were made in the number and size of the parishes in subsequent centuries. The legal basis of land-holding was established and towns made their appearance for the first time as corporate bodies with particular functions and privileges. Law and local government went hand in hand with the creation of sheriff-doms. Cromarty and the enormous sheriffdom of Inverness, in which Ross was included until the seventeenth century, date from this time. An abortive attempt was made to create a separate sheriffdom of Ross in 1503 but not until 1644 did this actually come into being.[1.15] Then, of course, it included the island of Lewis, the west coast and the central mountains as well as Easter Ross.

One section of Easter Ross, comprising the estate of Ferintosh, was actually in the county of Nairn because of the longstanding connection of its owners with that county.[1.16] In the later seventeenth century the local government situation was further complicated. In 1685 George, Viscount Tarbat procured an act annexing his estates to the sheriffdom of Cromarty. This act was replaced by another of the same tenor in 1698.[1.17] In its original form the shire of Cromarty consisted only of the parish of Cromarty and part of the adjoining parish of Resolis (then two parishes of Kirkmichael and Cullicudden). The effect of the acts was to create a patchwork of Cromartyshire enclaves within the broad mass of Ross-shire. Until 1748 the three counties involved in the area functioned as independent units.[1.18]

While the period of the twelfth and thirteenth centuries was as important for the establishment of legal principles of landholding as it was for the creation of other elements of the social structure, it did not see, as was the case, for example, in the neighbouring county of Sutherland, the introduction of a number of families destined to retain their property until the eighteenth century and beyond. Indeed although some families retained their possessions with remarkable tenacity throughout the centuries, the degree of turnover of property is surprising in the light of accepted myths of highland clans and families of ancient pedigree.

Throughout the middle ages the area was dominated by the power of the Earldom of Ross. Shadowy early earls were followed by Farquhar Macintsaggart who was created earl in 1236 and founded a dynasty which lasted until the end of the fifteenth century. Macintsaggart was traditionally the descendant of the hereditary abbots of Applecross and of Celtic origin although he aligned himself firmly with the monarchy. His descendants built on his work and by the fourteenth century the earls held extensive property along the southern shore of the Moray Firth as well as the greater part of Ross and the Lordship of Skye. The last male descendant of Farquhar died in 1357[1.19] and, after an unsettled period during which disputed claims to the title resulted in the battle of Harlaw in 1411, the Lords of the Isles established their rights to the earldom.[1.20]

The forfeiture of the last Macdonald earl in 1476[1.21] led to the rise of the lesser gentry of the region. Those who had previously held from the earls now became direct vassals of the Crown. Some of these lesser families were long settled in the area, including scions and supporters of the earls of Ross. The Rosses of Balnagown and the Munros of Foulis on the north and the Urquharts of Cromarty on the south shore of the Cromarty Firth were established in their lands before 1400. Such families represented the new elite, but below them were many lesser lights — often cadets of the leading families. Amongst these smaller proprietors there was a considerable turnover and while certain families such as the McCullochs and the Dunbars held some land in the region for centuries, they rarely held the same land for lengthy periods.[1.22]

While the earls of Ross were the greatest secular landowners in Ross in the middle ages, they were closely rivalled by the church for, in addition to the endowments of chaplainries and military orders,[1.23] both the bishopric of Ross and the Abbey of Fearn held extensive properties.[1.24] The Reformation led to the disbursement of these lands. While some of the church land was obtained by local landlords,[1.25] much of it was gained by incomers from the south and west. In 1597, for example, Sir Patrick Murray obtained a grant of the Abbey of Fearn. Former priests, too, were amongst those obtaining property at this time such as Robert Graham, Archdeacon of Ross, in 1573, and a descendant of the first earl of Montrose, who purchased Drynie.[1.26]

Undoubtedly, however, it was the Mackenzies who gained most from the disturbances of the late sixteenth century. Although gradually they had been moving east from their original centre of Kintail during the preceding century, their presence had hardly been felt on the east coast before the Reformation. Once established, they quickly rose to a dominant position. In 1644 in the presbyteries of Chanonry and Dingwall twenty-nine of the ninety-seven proprietors were Mackenzies, while in the mid-eighteenth century, even after some decline, landlords of the name of Mackenzie were said to hold twelve parishes on the east coast of Ross.[1.27]

It was not only from the church that the Mackenzies made gains in the period after the Reformation. The various branches of the family obtained land from both local gentry and other landowners from outside the area owning property in Easter Ross.[1.28] These acquisitions continued for almost two centuries until nearly the middle of the eighteenth century.

The Mackenzie gains were only part of a greater turnover of property in the seventeenth and eighteenth centuries. Although the major families such as those of Balnagown and Foulis continued to establish cadets in small properties, many of the older cadet branches died out or were bought out.[1.29] Increasingly, too, restrictive entails limited the division of estates and created problems of succession.[1.30] While the creation of estates for younger sons may have become less prevalent, newcomers to the area continued to acquire land in Easter Ross.[1.31] Throughout the centuries under review, however, it is noticeable that the number of absolute newcomers to the area, of people with no connection at all with the region or immediately surrounding districts, is very small. Even more striking is the general absence, in contrast with some other parts of Scotland, of land acquisition by status-seeking burghers.[1.32] Also in contrast with many other districts was the fact that the great majority of landowners by 1750 held directly from the crown. This was largely because of the earlier assumption by the crown of rights previously held by the church and the earldom of Ross, but the individual proprietors were still purchasing the superiorities of their estates throughout the seventeenth and early eighteenth centuries.[1.33]

If the length of tenure of estates by particular families varied considerably, the size of estates varied no less. The fragmentation resulting from the disappearance of the earldom of Ross and the church as landowning entities led by 1644 to a situation where there were 164 proprietors in the Ross-shire section of Easter Ross alone. In an area the size of Easter Ross where some landowners held large estates there were inevitably also a number of very small properties.[1.34] If the main feature of the immediate post-Reformation period was the division of property into smaller estates, the pattern after the mid-seventeenth century was one of aggregation.[1.35] By 1756 the number of landowners in Easter Ross had fallen to ninety-four, partly as a result of purchase, partly by inheritance.[1.36]

From the middle ages a number of the estates in Easter Ross formed only a part of the total property of the landlords who owned them. The Earls of Ross had held extensive lands in the counties on the southern shore of the Moray Firth and, after the accession of the Macdonalds, in the western isles. After the fall of the earldom the smaller landlords who succeeded it were no less restricted, and in particular, the links with the southern shore of the Moray Firth were retained. A number of those who held lands in Easter Ross had their principal estates elsewhere, while some proprietors centred in Easter Ross had additional properties in other parts.[1.37] If property owning was not entirely a local matter, however, it was largely regional, for there are few instances of families with even small estates in Easter Ross holding any substantial property outside immediately adjoining territories.[1.38]

Within the various estates the land was divided according to a long-established pattern. The davoch, a unit of productive capacity rather than a measure of area in its original sense, remained the unit of division — though sometimes no more than nominally — and land continued to be held, in the main, on the old runrig system of strips of land annually re-allocated to small tenants. There is some evidence that tacksmen, in the Highland sense of leaseholders on a large scale, sub-letting most or all of their land to tenants at will or on short leases, may have existed in the area but, towards the middle of the eighteenth century, Easter Ross, as a whole, seems to have been occupied by small tenants holding directly from the owners of the land, either at will or on short leases of from three to five years which were regularly renewed.[1.39] Farms usually were worked jointly by the tenants and their families with, depending upon the size of the holding, a number of servants.[1.40]

The apportionment of land in this way resulted in the absence of any identifiable middle class outside the towns. In theory the gap between the upper and lower sections of society was lessened by kinship, a sense of community and a generally low standard of living but the gap was, nevertheless, a very real one and was in no way diminished by the attitude of the landlords towards their tenants. Despite the backward nature of farming in the area, the low yields and poor returns on investment by the tenants, the landlords regularly charged high rents. In the parish of Nigg in 1794 it was said that the rent of a large part of the parish had not been increased for two hundred years 'and yet at present it is as high as the land can possibly bear'.[1.41] Rack-renting seems to have been the general rule so far as the Mackenzie lands were concerned, while the landlords around Tain were themselves prepared to admit in 1783 that they had indulged in two centuries of extortion.[1.42]

If rents were too high, they could also be too restrictive. The necessity to pay in kind may have stifled initiative although it is equally true that the farms were usually too small to provide a yield large enough to be independently marketed. In at least one instance the obligation to pay in kind was stretched to its absolute limit, however.[1.43]

Leases, almost without exception, were granted for too short a period — when they were granted at all. As late as 1782 in Resolis only one lease had ever been given for longer than seven years.[1.44] On the other hand tradition and inertia before the mid-eighteenth century may often have been sufficient to ensure that tenants could retain their holdings indefinitely. Certainly, in one well-known instance, the Logan family had been tenants of Drumderfit for three hundred years by 1750.[1.45]

Because of the exactions of their landlords most tenants were unable to rise above a very low standard of living. This is most clearly evident in the condition of their homes. Houses in the highland part of Kiltearn in 1791, which were certainly no worse than those in the more low lying parts for many years previously were

> built of earth, and are usually razed to the ground once in 5 or 7 years, when they are added to the dunghill. Indeed, they [the tenants] cannot afford to build them of better materials, not even with clay and stone.[1.46]

The main crops grown by the tenants were oats, barley (or more usually bear) with smaller quantities of pease and beans. Wheat was grown occasionally by the landlords and usually only for the needs of the grower, while root crops were scarcely known until shortly before 1750.[1.47] The crops were raised by the old infield-outfield system, whereby a relatively small area of the best land received all the manure and the remaining area was cropped without manuring until soil exhaustion necessitated a period of fallow. Even in the infield yields were low as there was but little understanding of the value of rotation.

The farm implements which were used were primitive in the extreme. Ploughs were heavy, unyieldy and badly made and required large numbers of animals to pull them, and properly fashioned spades, harrows and other tools were not to be found.[1.48] A major problem with regard to implements was the scarcity of iron, and this in large measure explained the poor quality of the tools used.

The need for large plough teams and the dependence on garrons (or even, on occasion, men) [1.49] rather than carts for transporting goods meant that farms generally were overstocked. This in turn created considerable problems over feedstuffs. Traditionally, owners of Easter Ross estates either possessed Highland estates as well or leased farms on other Highland estates to pasture their animals in summer. Donald Macleod of Geanies leased a farm at Rhidorroch near Ullapool in the later eighteenth century, for example. In winter, however, the beasts were let loose on the fields of the low country farms in order to obtain what they could by scavenging amongst the stubble. As the whole countryside was regarded as a common pasture this meant that enclosure was much opposed and the lack of enclosure prevented the introduction of crops which would provide winter feeding for the animals.[1.50]

While the overall level of agriculture in Easter Ross before 1750 was low,[1.51] there were signs of improvement even from a relatively early date. In 1735, for example, Balnagown tenants were given leases to encourage improvement,[1.52] but it was the landlords themselves who were the prime movers in improvement, and during the first quarter of the eighteenth century Gordon of Invergordon and Ross of Balnagown introduced new techniques such as draining and fallowing.[1.53] The most significant and widespread indication of improvement was in forestry. As early as 1550 it is said that John Mackenzie, 9th of Kintail, planted Spanish chestnuts at Castle Leod, and by the eighteenth century planting had become widespread on both sides of the Cromarty Firth.[1.54]

Agricultural produce represented almost the entire output of the area before 1750. The other major natural resource — the fisheries — was even less exploited than the land. There were boom periods when fishing made a major impact on local economies but there was no strongly organised industry. Backward organisation and primitive equipment made the fishers largely dependent upon inshore fishing. Unfortunately, the herring which was the mainstay of the industry was fickle in its affections and tended to move from one area to another, providing no certainty of income for those who pursued it.[1.55]

Quarrying occupied a small number of men but the only industry to make a noticeable impact on the region before 1750 was whisky distilling. The main distilling centre was on the estate of Ferintosh whose owner had been granted the privilege of producing duty-free whisky in 1690 as compensation for the losses he had suffered there at the hands of the Jacobite rebels. The industry had prospered and provided a steady market for local farmers but organisation remained sadly defective. Outside Ferintosh the vagaries of government policy over excise duties did not encourage the growth of a major industry. Nowhere did distilling reach the status of a major employer of labour or become much more than a cottage industry.[1.56] The manufacture of linen, which was to dominate the industrial scene in Easter Ross after 1750, while in existence before that date did not make a major impact on the local economy.[1.57]

With little activity or growth in other fields it is not surprising that there was not much agricultural improvement. Timber was in demand for fuel by the eighteenth century as the peat mosses became exhausted and before coal became common,[1.58] but there was no such local market for increased agricultural produce other than the stills. That agricultural produce was exported may be assumed from the positioning of estate girnals or granaries — where rents were collected in kind — by the sea shore, and by the building of a pier at Portmahomack by the first Earl of Cromarty.[1.59] Until the rapid population expansion of the later eighteenth century, however, external markets were not extensive.

Trade both internally and externally was hampered by poor communications. As the roads in the area were not so bad after 1750 as southern critics made out, it may be that the same holds true for earlier periods and there certainly were a number of roads, however badly made, in the parish of Tain by 1750.[1.60] But land transport was undoubtedly difficult and movement beyond the boundaries of the region was restricted by the absence of bridges over the Oykell and, more especially, the Conon. Water transport proved the best medium for the conveyance of goods[1.61] but the effectiveness stopped short at the sea shore. While a postal system was in operation by the early eighteenth century, its activities were subject to political hazards as well as to the more obvious difficulties arising from inadequate transport.[1.62]

In such an environment the towns could be nothing but small, serving largely local needs, but their role should not be undervalued. Their lack of size and wealth was not untypical of Scottish burghs as a whole. Some idea of the relative standing of the royal burghs of Easter Ross may be gained from the amount of tax paid by each burgh, compared with the sums paid by other burghs in Scotland. The accompanying table shows how many burghs paid less and how many (in brackets) as much tax as the Easter Ross burghs. Cromarty is included in 1690 although it already had ceased to be a royal burgh by that date. There is a noticeable decline in the position of the Easter Ross burghs from 1690 to 1737, perhaps in part as a result of competition from the recently established non-royal burghs and other, non-burghal local markets and fairs.[1.63]

	1690	1697	1707	1737
Tain	25 (3)	24 (2)	25	19 (3)
Cromarty	19 (2)	—	—	—
Fortrose	19 (2)	15 (3)	17	9 (9)
Dingwall	5 (2)	0 (14)	7	9 (9)
Total number of burghs	66	65	65	67

The region held both royal burghs — answerable only to the crown and with extensive trading privileges, including, until the seventeenth century, a monopoloy on foreign trade which was upheld by the royal burghs' own central organ, the Convention — and burghs of barony and regality — dependent upon local landowners and with much more limited rights.

The oldest, fully established royal burgh, Dingwall, received its charter in 1227. Although it subsequently lost its status on being granted to the Earls of Ross, its privileges were resumed on the forfeiture of the earldom. Fortrose and Tain were both ecclesiastical in origin, the one growing up around the episcopal centre of Ross, the other at a pilgrimage shrine. Although both had trading privileges from an early date, neither was fully recognised as a royal burgh before the sixteenth century. Cromarty was another early erection, but after losing all its lands to the neighbouring family of Urquhart it was finally removed from the list of royal burghs in 1685.

In the same year it was recreated as a burgh of barony for Viscount Tarbat and it was at this period that the other non-royal burghs came into being. Indeed the later seventeenth century appears to have been a time of relative prosperity, or at least buoyant expectations, for no fewer than eight burghs (including Cromarty) were founded in Easter Ross between 1677 and 1699. While none of these ever achieved the status of self-governing communities and therefore lapsed after 1748 they were, for a time, a significant feature in the local economy. Cromarty, Milntown and Culbockie retained some significance, if not status, for a longer period.[1.64]

The primary function of the burghs of whatever status was local trade. The royal burghs in theory had the right to a more extensive trade but in practice depended almost exclusively upon Inverness and Elgin for non-locally produced goods.[1.65] The lack of distinction between the two categories is clearly seen in the plight of Dingwall from the late seventeenth century onwards and in the contrasting, if temporary, prosperity of Cromarty before 1707.[1.66] However small they may have been, these markets fulfilled an essential role and stood in sharp contrast to the situation prevalent over much of the Highlands.

Additionally the towns acted as focal points for services and administration while their function as cultural centres became increasingly important as the eighteenth century progressed.[1.67] Unlike many other burghs in Scotland, however, none of the burghs in Easter Ross appears to have served as a social centre for the local gentry to any notable extent. The neighbouring proprietors often owned property in the towns but seem to have preferred enriching themselves at the burghs' expense to living in them.[1.68]

That other attraction for greedy landlords (at least at the time of the Reformation), the Church, wielded considerable power in almost all aspects of life. This influence was of long standing as, although most of the great centres of the Celtic church were in the west or south, Christian influences penetrated the area from an early date. Indeed the monastery at Rosemarkie was of some importance during the lifetime of St Boniface.[1.69] Little is known, however, of the position before the introduction of Roman Catholicism in the twelfth century. The reforms of that period led to the area being reorganised, in common with the rest of Scotland, into a system of parishes and dioceses. In Easter Ross there were, in the middle ages, at least twenty-one parishes[1.70] and these, with the remaining parishes in Ross, were gathered, by the reign of David I, into the diocese of Ross centred at Rosemarkie.[1.71]

Apart from the cathedrals and parish churches, the Highlands as a whole were largely bare of ecclesiastical foundations in the middle ages. Easter Ross, however, more closely resembled the Lowlands in this respect, for in addition to the cathedral at Rosemarkie (later transferred to Fortrose), the area sustained a Premonstratensian foundation at Fearn and a collegiate church at Tain.[1.72] The abbey of Fearn never achieved any great distinction — its one claim to fame being that the pre-Reformation martyr Patrick Hamilton was abbot for a time — but the collegiate church of St Duthus at Tain was of some renown as a pilgrimage centre. James IV was a regular visitor, making seven trips to the church between 1493 and 1514.[1.73]

The Reformation swept away much of the old structure. Fearn Abbey and the college at Tain ceased to exist as functioning organs of the church. The episcopate continued for a time but was greatly diminished in stature. With the changes following from the 1688 Revolution came further upheavals. Episcopacy was replaced by Presbyterianism. The new structure was to last but it remained rudimentary for a number of years. In 1707 there were only ten ministers for the whole of Ross and Sutherland as compared to over fifty in 1688.[1.74] Manpower shortages resulted at first in the new presbyteries being extended to cover vast areas,[1.75] but by the early eighteenth century most of these temporary difficulties had been overcome and the Synod of Ross had emerged with its three presbyteries covering the area of Easter Ross.[1.76]

During the seventeenth century struggles between Episcopacy and Presbyterianism the North of Scotland seems generally to have inclined towards the episcopal party, while in the most conservative areas Catholicism remained supreme and neither of the reformed communions made headway. In Easter Ross, however, the situation was not quite so clear cut. Most of the Black Isle and much of Easter Central Ross were major centres of Episcopacy, and remained faithful to the cause well into the nineteenth century. Easter Ross proper, however, diverged sharply from the standard pattern, and evinced considerable enthusiasm for the Presbyterian cause from at least the period of the Restoration.[1.77] Indeed the area was to prove the forcing ground for the Presbyterianism of the entire North-West Highlands and to set a standard of puritanical zeal and devotion much envied elsewhere.[1.78] The evangelical enthusiasm of the local population manifested itself in the period before 1750 in a number of religious revivals possibly unparalleled north of the central belt of Scotland, while the parish of Nigg was the centre of one of the few secession movements to appear in the north of Scotland in the first half of the eighteenth century.[1.79]

It is tempting to see the split between Episcopacy and Presbyterianism in the area as part of a more general conflict between the Gaelic and English-speaking sections of the population, but Episcopacy was widely supported by both language groups in the north of Scotland in general, and although in Easter Ross Episcopalian strength did tend to lie in the Gaelic west it was by no means confined there.[1.80] A more satisfactory explanation of the divergence in belief between the two portions of the area may lie in the attitudes of the local gentry. The Mackenzie lairds on the Black Isle were active advocates of the Episcopal cause.[1.81] The gentry in Easter Ross were no less keen supporters of Presbyterianism,[1.82] and it may be assumed that tenants and dependants on both sides would generally be prepared to take a lead from their landlords in such matters, whatever their own views. At the same time Easter Ross Presbyterianism seems to have been essentially a popular movement and tenants were not always of the same belief as their landlord.[1.83]

Although the church's main concern was with the spiritual welfare of the people, spiritual welfare, in the definition of the times, could be extended to cover a wide field, including most things cultural. In particular the church dominated education. The parish schools, of course, were practically an extension of the church,[1.84] while before the later eighteenth century almost the only other educational presence in Easter Ross was the Society in Scotland for Propagating Christian Knowledge, which was primarily a religious institution and whose schools were regularly supervised by the ministers of the presbyteries in which they lay.[1.85]

The S.S.P.C.K. schools offered only the mere rudiments of education but the parish schools, some of which were functioning in the area from the middle of the sixteenth century at least,[1.86] gave instruction in the traditional classical grammar as well. More important was the emphasis that all schools placed upon the value of English as the language of instruction. Only in 1739 was a Gaelic-English vocabulary published for use in S.S.P.C.K. schools.[1.87] Initially this emphasis on English restricted the value of the education offered to the English-speaking elements of the population, and in the long term the bias was probably a major cause of the decline of the Gaelic language.

In the early eighteenth century Gaelic was undoubtedly the dominant language in most of the area. The three eastern parishes of the Black Isle, Avoch, Rosemarkie and Cromarty, with their history of settlement by Scandinavians and Anglo-Normans, were largely English-speaking, but in the remaining parishes English speakers were in a minority.[1.88] Even in the towns English was restricted to the middle classes. However rich in poetry and song the Gaelic language was, the exclusion of the greater part of the population from the well-developed literature (scientific as well as imaginative) of the English tongue was, in the circumstances of the time, culturally impoverishing.

Easter Ross was not, however, an area of complete cultural deprivation. In addition to the education offered by the schools, some attempt was made in the early eighteenth century, as part of a wider scheme, to introduce a number of public libraries into the area. Although the provision made for their maintenance was insufficient, there appears to have been some demand for their stock. Amongst the English-speaking sections of the population even some of the less well to do were sufficiently educated to build up their own collections of books.[1.89]

Evidence that the upper classes, at least, were in touch with the outside world is most clearly seen in the architecture of the area, particularly the domestic architecture. What little remains of the mediaeval ecclesiastical architecture of Easter Ross is enough to suggest that the stylistic fashions common in the south of Scotland were followed.[1.90] While the seventeenth and early eighteenth centuries were not especially propitious for the development of ecclesiastical architecture in Scotland, the churches erected at this time in Easter Ross were little different in character from those found elsewhere and, although the majority were simple and unpretentious, some aspired to a greater elaboration.[1.91] From the sixteenth century, at least, contemporary standards of taste and design were in evidence in the castles erected for the proprietors of Easter Ross, while from the later seventeenth century these standards were transferred to the sometimes imposing if rather conservative mansions which replaced the earlier seats.[1.92]

For what reasons then should an area such as Easter Ross be studied in depth? Quite apart from the value of local studies in building up a detailed knowledge of Scotland as a whole, there are particular reasons for choosing this area at this time in its history. The brief introduction to the early history of Easter Ross in the preceding pages has, it is hoped, shown that the region was particularly distinctive. Although it is geographically located in the north of Scotland the area was not typically Highland. The strong Gaelic element in its population was countered by an arable-based economy supporting small towns, more closely related to the Lowlands. Even within the area there was considerable diversity in outlook and culture as evidenced by language and religious belief. While the frontier character of the district is worthy of study in itself, the interest is heightened by the history of strong individualism most evident in the religious tradition of the seventeenth and eighteenth centuries.

The peculiar attraction of the period lies in the fact that it, too, was something of a frontier. While it has been shown that change was not absent in the area before 1750, it remains true that in terms of day-to-day living, existence in the early eighteenth century differed very little from that of a hundred years earlier and probably not so very much from periods long before that.[1.93]

The 1745 Jacobite rebellion made little impact politically in Easter Ross,[1.94] but the legal and social reforms stemming from it affected the area as much as any other part of Scotland, while the acceleration of economic activity generally known as the Agricultural and Industrial Revolutions first made a significant impact in the region from about this time. The century from 1750 to 1850 saw the complete transformation of agricultural practice, a revolution in transport, the rise and decline of the textile industry and, as a consequence of these and other changes, a major social upheaval.

In the course of this study most aspects of the life of the district are touched upon. Politics, being essentially a national rather than a local concern, has been the one major area of interest to be excluded from detailed consideration but it should not be forgotten that even politics, particularly politics before the Reform Act, can be viewed from a local standpoint. So much politicking was bound up with the day-to-day concerns of the populace that total exclusion would be not only inadvisable but also almost impossible.

The rest of this book is devoted to an examination of the nature of the economic and social changes which took place in Easter Ross during the period — a frontier in time between old and new — and to a consideration of the frontier position, spatial and cultural, of the district, poised, as it was, between the Highlands and the Lowlands.

2
The Economy: The Land and the Sea

a. The Ownership of Land

The failure of the Jacobite uprising of 1745 and the subsequent measures taken by the goverment did not have the immediate and overwhelming effect on Easter Ross that popularly they are supposed to have had on the Highlands at large.[2.1] Nevertheless the changes consequent upon the events of 1745-6 did play their part in altering the structure of society in the region. The landowning classes were the most obviously affected both as individuals and as a group. While support for the rising was slight in Easter Ross as a whole, several of the gentry participated and amongst these was the Earl of Cromarty whose family had dominated much of the area for the previous half century and more.[2.2] The Cromarty estates were forfeited to the Crown and their management by the government for the succeeding four decades is an interesting example of state intervention in an area which had been, in most respects, far removed from normal government interest and control. The only other estate forfeited as a result of its owner's activities was soon regained by the owner's representatives.[2.3] More generally the result of government legislation was to assist the transformation of the gentry from a ruling elite still tied to a feudal past to a more strictly economy-orientated landowning class.

Many of the gentry of the mid-eighteenth century were related to families with long connections in the area. Twenty-four of the one hundred and nine proprietors in 1756 were Mackenzies, twelve were Munros, thirteen were Rosses (excluding the Balnagown Rosses whose link with the original family was extremely tenuous) and five were Urquharts.[2.4] Such a list gives a rather false air of continuity to the ownership of land, for by 1756 less than 40 per cent of the landowners belonged to families who had been represented continuously in the area since 1644, and amongst that number only about a half had held substantially the same property over the century.[2.5] Nevertheless the links with the past were strong, for the majority of property owners in 1756 were descended directly or indirectly from landlords of an earlier age and almost all had connections of some description with the region. The majority of the new landowning families were scions of the old and were often initially established by the splitting off of sections of the main estate. Some new families, however, were from outside the area such as the Macleods of Cadboll and Geanies.[2.6]

While in most cases the wealth involved in the creation of these new families was derived from the land, there were instances where landed income was replaced, or at least supplemented from other sources. In particular, wealth was derived from military service (either in the British armed forces or, as, for example, in the case of Captain Urquhart of Cromarty, who made money as a privateer in the service of Spain, in the employ of a foreign power) or from a professional career.[2.7] Both lawyers and ministers made enough to enable them to purchase small estates, while in one instance the factor on one estate became in time a fairly large proprietor in his own right.[2.8] There remained a notable absence of landlords deriving their existence from a merchant fortune, although the first Matheson of Bennetsfield raised the money to buy his estate by droving.[2.9]

Property was acquired not only in the hope of pecuniary gain but also for prestige and political purposes.[2.10] Landlords took care to exact the maximum possible rent from their existing tenants but otherwise cared little for intensive economic exploitation. A number of proprietors regularly were absent in London or elsewhere and some of these took little interest in their northern possessions.[2.11] Prominent amongst the absentees were those landlords who were in the army or in a profession, or whose major property was elsewhere.

There were, in fact, few landlords in 1756 with major properties in other parts of the country. Twenty-seven proprietors — from a total of one hundred and nine — owned estates beyond the confines of the region but of these the additional property of fifteen was situated entirely in the five adjoining parishes of Ross-shire and much of it belonged geographically to Easter Ross. Of the remainder, eight held other estates in Wester Ross or the adjoining areas of Inverness and Sutherland, while only four owned land in the more distant parts.[2.12]

The properties themselves varied considerably in size from the holdings of Sir John Gordon of Invergordon valued at £3345.16.10 Scots to those of Widow Simson in Rosemarkie valued at £0.10 Scots. Seventy per cent of the estates were valued at less than £500 Scots, although their total valuation at 27 per cent of the complete figure was only marginally greater than that of the combined figure for the six largest estates.

It was, on the whole, the larger proprietors who held estates elsewhere. Colin Mackenzie of Kilcoy held extensive estates in mid-Ross while Sir James Ross of Balnagown had even more extensive properties in the parishes of Edderton and Kincardine, as well as an original base in Lanarkshire. Several of the middling-sized estates and one or two of the smaller properties belonged to landlords whose main interests lay elsewhere. Forbes of Culloden, for example, held Ferintosh and Rose of Kilravock lands in the parish of Nigg. The Dingwall lands of the Mackenzies of Seaforth were no more than the easternmost extremity of their estates to the west.

The great majority of Easter Ross estates were held by small landlords, with little or no property elsewhere and, consequently, with limited funds at their disposal. On the other hand, because of the extent of their holdings, the greater landlords had a disproportionate influence on land development.

Many landowners, especially the larger ones, did not hold their possessions in one consolidated estate but in a number of parcels of land scattered throughout the area. This division of property was less evident in the Black Isle but it occurred everywhere to some extent and varied in form from proprietors holding several distinct estates of roughly equal value to properties where the greater part was consolidated but had associated with it a number of pendicles of small size.[2.13]

In the former category were landowners such as Sir John Gordon of Invergordon, with separate baronies in the parishes of Tarbat and Rosskeen and a third estate in Resolis, while in the latter were lairds like Sir Lewis Mackenzie of Scatwell, whose main holdings, valued respectively in 1756 at £1233 Scots and £1058 Scots, lay in the parishes of Urquhart and Avoch, but who held also land in the parish of Resolis worth £100 Scots.[2.14]

The gentry of the mid-eighteenth century were a mixed bag, providing great variety in the sources and amount of their income and in their connections, or lack of them, with the wider world outside the region. While the general tone of the proprietary may have been conservative, there were some who were familiar with, and interested in, modern ideas. Their influence was all the greater in that they were generally amongst the largest and richest of the landlords.

As the century progressed some changes occurred in the general pattern of landholdings. The concentration of property, which had been taking place for some time past, continued. In part this was a result of accidents of inheritance inevitable when a small community regularly had intermarried. Of these accidents potentially the most significant was the death, without leaving a son, of Sir John Gordon of Invergordon. His estates passed to his nephew, Lord Macleod, heir to the Mackenzies of Cromarty. If Lord Macleod had not chosen almost immediately, in 1786, to resell the Invergordon estates to the Macleods of Cadboll, the Mackenzies of Cromarty would have regained, at a stroke, their position as the dominant landowners in the area.[2.15]

To some extent concentration of property was due also to the enlargement of some estates by purchase. There was a continued inflow of capital from outside sources and, to the traditional staples of the armed services and the professions, was added the gold mine of colonial service. At the turn of the century, for example, John Mackay, a native of Sutherland, who lost his sight in consequence of his employment as a clerk to the Commissioners for India, bought and maintained the estate of Little Tarrel with the proceeds of his pension and the fortune he inherited from his brother, a captain in the Madras Native Cavalry and, infinitely more profitable, agent for carriage and draught horses to the Indian army.[2.16]

Marriage with suitably endowed heiresses was another means whereby local lairds were enabled to redeem their debts or extend their possessions. John Mackenzie of Allangrange, for example, received a substantial dowry on his marriage to the sister of the wife of Sir James Colquhoun of Luss.[2.17]

Although most property coming on the market was bought by existing landlords, there was, in the later eighteenth century, an increasing number of Easter Ross exiles who, having made their fortune elsewhere, found the idea of purchasing estates in the area attractive. Amongst these can be numbered some of the most prominent figures in the development of the area at the time, such as Davidson of Tulloch and Ross of Cromarty.[2.18]

By 1802 the concentration of property had resulted in a situation where the smaller proprietors (those valued at under £500 Scots) had dropped in number, as compared to 1756, from eighty-two to forty-six, whilst the larger properties remained the same at twenty-eight.[2.19]

Compared with the rest of Scotland, Easter Ross had, at this period, a far smaller proportion of small estates, while it had twice the national average of middle-sized, and almost twice the average of large estates.[2.20]

The concentration of property is also evident with regard to estates held outside Easter Ross. The percentage of owners holding estates in other districts actually increased from 24.7 per cent in 1756 to 27 per cent in 1802 but the actual amount of land held probably fell quite sharply. Only two proprietors held property on any scale outside the counties of Ross, Cromarty, Inverness and Sutherland in 1802, while seven held additional estates only in the parishes immediately adjoining Easter Ross. Most of the external holdings were in the hands of the larger landlords, for only five of the twenty landlords involved were valued at less than £500 Scots on their Easter Ross estates.

The reasons for sale and purchase are hard to determine. Occasionally lairds overdid the borrowing, which was a standard feature of the economic life of the gentry, and went bankrupt. The estate of Redcastle, for example, was sequestrated in 1788, after years of financial mismanagement had culminated in the final burden of debt incurred by Kenneth Mackenzie, in an effort to mend his fortunes, by raising the Highland Independent Company of which he was captain.[2.21]

In other cases estates passed to heirs with little interest in possessions so far north, or who saw the chance of bettering their fortunes by investing elsewhere the money to be realised from selling these properties. Among the former may be included James Stuart Mackenzie of Rosehaugh, who sold lands in the parish of Avoch to George Mackenzie of Avoch in 1796. The Rosehaugh superiorities were useful politically throughout the eighteenth century but Stuart Mackenzie appears to have had little enthusiasm for the lands themselves as his interests lay further south.[2.22]

Handley[2.23] has argued that those who made money in the colonies bought estates mainly for commercial reasons, and there is a certain amount of evidence to support this theory in the improvements undertaken by Grant of Redcastle and Hugh Rose Ross of Glastullich towards the end of the eighteenth century. Besides, there were, at this time, few more attractive forms of investment for surplus wealth. But the satisfaction derived from demonstrating new-found wealth was also important and, in those instances where already established gentry used money gained in the colonies to enlarge their estates, prestige may have been the dominant motive. Whatever the reasons for sale or purchase, by 1802 only about half of the estates were held by descendants of those who had owned them in 1756. Even where the original family were still in occupation there were few cases where the estate boundaries of 1802 were exactly the same as in 1756.

The ninetenth century saw an increase in the number of incomers to the area. Although there is little specific evidence to support the hypotheses, it may be conjectured that the increasing integration of the Northern Highlands with the rest of Britain, the increased sales potential of improved estates and the growing numbers of people of wealth wishing to purchase estates, wherever situated, for reasons of finance or prestige, all made Easter Ross more attractive to outside purchasers than it had been before, particularly when these estates could often be obtained relatively cheaply when compared to estates in the south. The acquisition of the Redcastle estate by Sir William Fettes, recorded in the Sasines in 1829, is an outstanding example of a southerner, with no previous connection with the area, using his surplus wealth to invest in land on the market.[2.24]

At the same time this movement of outsiders should not be exaggerated, and compared to the Highlands at large the number of incomers probably remained quite small. The largely arable estates of Easter Ross did not have the pasturing or sporting potential of the truly Highland estates. The greater number of those purchasing estates in Easter Ross in the first half of the nineteenth century continued to be people with some connection with either the area itself or with its immediate surroundings and, as before, the sources of wealth remained the land, the professions and the services. In addition, however, local merchants provided a new source of wealth and, for the first time, made a significant impact on the property market. The Murray family, merchants and bankers in the burgh of Tain, having acquired land in the immediate environs of the town over a number of decades, went on to become lairds of Pitcalzean (renamed Westfield) in Nigg in 1832; and even more successfully made its mark by purchasing Geanies on the death of the last of the Macleods in 1838.[2.25] Several merchants who had prospered in the south or abroad also invested in Easter Ross estates. The most notable of these was Sir James Matheson of the Lews, who purchased property in the parishes of Avoch and Dingwall and elsewhere towards the middle of the century from profits made in the Chinese trade.[2.26]

While the aggregation of estates continued, with the larger estates swallowing up the smaller, a reverse process gradually began to show itself. At the lower end of the property scale there began to appear small holdings feued from the original owner of the property. This process began on the lands of the burghs in the eighteenth century and was in time to cover much of the land surface of the area.[2.27]

Over the century from 1750 to 1850, although particularly in the period before 1800, the landed gentry of Easter Ross constituted a closely knit group of individuals tied together by bonds of blood and interest. Close relationships made the day-to-day organisation of life much easier as, for example, when Munro of Meikle Allan handled legal business in Edinburgh for his near neighbour and friend Robertson of Kindeace, while Robertson in his turn supervised the day-to-day running of Meikle Allan in Munro's absence.[2.28] Such integration was undoubtedly of importance in facilitating the spread of new ideas throughout the period.

b. Agriculture — The Old System

Estates differed widely in their internal arrangement as well as in their sizes and distribution, and within each estate there could be a considerable variety of holdings. It is difficult to be confident about the role of tacksmen in Easter Ross society but such evidence as exists suggests that, as a class, they were less important than in the Western Highlands. Tacksmen were found on a number of estates but in some cases they were simply leaseholders of mills or pasture land.[2.29] Occasionally tacksmen in the Highland sense existed but, even on estates where they held land, their influence was considered to be less than on West Highland estates.[2.30] The general absence of any discussion of tacksmen and their position in contemporary documents suggests further that their importance in the region was limited.

The bulk of the arable land seems to have been held directly from the landlords by tenant farmers. Some subtenants undoubtedly existed and it would be easy to underestimate their numbers because of their non-appearance on rent rolls; but when the Newtarbat estate was surveyed in 1755, only two of the sixteen agricultural holdings are recorded as having subtenants and there is no evidence that subtenants held land on any substantial scale.[2.31]

The labour required to work the farms was provided for in two ways when subtenants were not available to render services. Either the tenant farmers kept the necessary men and women as servants (as seems to have been largely the case, for example, at Newtarbat) or the labouring population was provided with crofts, either intermingled with the farms, as at Drumcudden, or concentrated on the poorer land on the moorland fringes, as at Findon.[2.32] Labour for the demesne farms of estates was still, at least in part, supplied by services in kind. Whether labour was provided by crofters or servants, the average for the number of labouring families per tenant seems to have been about four.[2.33]

Although most farms were held directly, the type of holding varied from estate to estate. On the Cromarty estate, farms were held jointly by a number of tenants but the runrig divisions appear to have been permanently allocated. The same holds true for Newtarbat, although it may be that on some other estates the land on joint farms was regularly re-allocated in the traditional manner. On the estate of Findon permanent allocation had taken a step further by 1769, at the latest, for in that year a plan shows the estate divided into a number of individually held farms.[2.34] While this arrangement may have been unusual for so early a date, the average number of tenants to a farm was not high compared to that prevalent over the Highlands at large. At Newtarbat in 1755 and at Meikle Allan in 1786 there were less than two tenants per farm, while at Cromarty in 1763 and at Aldie in 1774 there were under four.[2.35]

Farm sizes too were varied, although in most cases the variations occurred within certain limits and the great majority of farms were very much less than one hundred acres in extent. Home farms were often amongst the largest on an estate but even they could be comparatively small. It is true that in 1781 the mains at Invergordon extended to six hundred acres, that at Geanies to four hundred acres and that at Tarlogie to three hundred acres, but in the mid-century period the mains at Newtarbat were rented for only sixty-two bolls while the Tulloch home farm covered eighty-three acres (only fifty-six of which were arable) and the mains at Findon extended to a mere forty-four acres arable.[2.36] Daniel Mackenzie, tacksman of Blackhill, Finnach and Riach's Croft on Newtarbat estate, had a total holding rented at ninety-three bolls[2.37] but the majority of ordinary tenants occupied much smaller possessions. At Findon the average holding of the twenty-five major tenant farmers with arable holdings was just over fifty-three acres (including thirty-three acres arable) while on the estate of Meikle Allan in 1756 the ten arable farmers held sixty-one acres on average, of which again only thirty-three acres were arable.[2.38]

The crofting system in the Highlands is often said to date only from the late eighteenth and early nineteenth centuries[2.39] but the crofter, in the sense of a tenant of an agricultural holding too small to sustain a single family without supplementary support, was a feature of the agricultural landscape from a much earlier date. Tenants of such holdings in Easter Ross went by a number of appellations, of which the most common were mailers and cottars, but the term 'crofter' has been used in this book as the one which is most easily recognised today.

The crofters' holdings were very small indeed. At Findon in 1769 approximately one hundred crofts occupied two hundred and forty-three acres and twelve years later Wight reported three-acre small-holdings on the Invergordon estate.[2.40] Although at Findon the farms of the major tenants and the holdings of the crofters were very largely separated, the pattern of distribution at Meikle Allan and at Drumcudden, where the crofters were interspersed amongst the farms, may have been more common.[2.41] It must certainly have been more convenient on larger estates, where crofters would be suitably situated for the farms on which they laboured.

While, in most cases, there was an obvious distinction between the holdings of tenant farmers and of crofters, there were a number of very small farms which were little larger than crofts and it is probable that the average size of holding was diminishing. Certainly there was considerable pressure on the land from a population which felt that every farmer's son not destined for a profession should be settled on his own piece of land; and which would subdivide existing holdings whenever allowed. This pressure can be clearly seen in the settlement of small-holders on disputed boundary lands between estates.[2.42]

Few tenants, whether crofters or more substantial farmers, were given leases of any length, although three, five and seven-year leases were not uncommon. Some of those who were given longer leases were more substantial farmers than the average tenant, if not of the lower gentry class associated with Highland tacksmen, but amongst the mass of small tenant farmers there was a general insecurity of occupation.[2.43]

Despite this, and the generally poor quality of farming, rents were high in the pre-reform era and had been consistently so for many years.[2.44] To some extent, the actual amount charged may have depended on the fertility and productivity of the soil. Rents on the estates of Cadboll and Glastullich in 1781 were charged at the rate of ten shillings per acre, whereas on Meikle Allan, lying between the other two, they rose to as high as twenty-five shillings. On the Tarbat estate of Sir John Gordon, at the same time, the range was from one to two bolls, or approximately ten to twenty shillings.[2.45] For a district without major markets or centres of population these rents were high especially when compared to the rents exacted in other parts of Scotland.[2.46]

Most rents continued to be paid in kind, although some money rents were found, particularly amongst those with tacks.[2.47] On top of the basic rent there were substantial contributions to be made in customs, services and multures. On the estate of Cromarty in 1763 these represented an additional burden of 17½ per cent above the basic rent,[2.48] and although the amount would be less when services were rendered in kind, this was even more exacting in real terms to the tenant who found himself called to give service just when his own farm needed most attention.

It is not possible to calculate exactly what proportion of the tenant's income was deducted in rent — Sinclair estimated about a sixth in 1795[2.49] — but the effect of high rents on small farmers was to deprive them of the minimal surplus they were able to produce after feeding themselves, their families and their servants, preventing them from attempting any capital accumulation and keeping the general level of life little above that of basic subsistence. In many cases the trouble started even before the rent was paid, as too many became farmers without the necessary capital to stock their farm. The increasing burden of rent, on top of accumulated debts, forced many farmers to give up after years of labour in conditions where it was said that the common servants were often better off than their masters.[2.50]

In such a situation it is not surprising that the agriculture practised was generally of a very primitive nature. Insecurity of tenure made the effort of improvement too much for the great majority, although it is true that where conditions were more promising there could be a response from the most enterprising tenants.[2.51]

Pre-improvement farm implements were primitive in the extreme. The old Scotch plough was in general use and, whatever its potential merits may have been, the lack of iron in the area ensured that the variety in use in Easter Ross, made almost entirely of wood, left a great deal to be desired.[2.52] Other tools were either totally absent or, again largely because of the lack of iron, but poor copies of those in use in the south. The quality of the implements in use was also affected by the absence of sufficient skilled craftsmen, many of the tools being made by the farmers themselves.[2.53]

Largely because the ploughs were inadequately constructed, the plough teams required to pull them, of horses, or oxen, or both species indiscriminately mixed, were large, which resulted in farms being overstocked.[2.54] Apart from the additional cost burden imposed on farmers, this practice helped to retard the spread of enclosure, as tenants eagerly sought the stubble on the fields after harvesting and required that the land be kept open in common for ease of pasturage.[2.55] In general, animal stock was ill-bred, over-numerous and underfed.

Despite the effort put into farming the land the net result was small. In common with the rest of Scotland the arable land was divided into infield and outfield, the infield being regularly manured and cropped continually, the outfield being cropped until it was exhausted and then left fallow to recover by itself. Large areas of the region were totally uncultivated, especially on the Black Isle, although even in the more fertile areas to the north of the Cromarty Firth, as much as three fifths of a farm might be waste.[2.56] Much of the land was too damp for existing methods of drainage to cope with, and even in the most fertile areas the arable land consisted of irregularly shaped oases amongst the wastes, where weeds grew in profusion and the baulks, or unploughed strips, between the ridges were heaped with stones.[2.57] Despite this the land was relatively heavily cropped, for the proportion of infield to outfield was high. On the estates of Findon and Meikle Allan the infield occupied well over eighty per cent of the total arable area, while even on the relatively infertile farm of Novar, infield amounted to just under seventy per cent of the total.[2.58]

This land received what manure there was, although the quality of manure, like so much else, left much to be desired. Near the coast, lime could be obtained by burning sea shells, while seaweed was also used by some farmers, but elsewhere middens consisted of soil cut from outlying fields and mixed with the dung of horses and cattle. Dung itself was less plentiful than it might have been because of the widespread practice of transhumance, or summer movement of stock to hill pastures, often miles away.[2.59]

Constant successions of grain crops were raised on manured land, the standard rotation being bear, two crops of oats and then a return to bear. The better tenants used pease instead of the second crop of oats but scientific rotations were almost unknown and it says much for the underlying fertility of the soil that returns of three and a half times the seed sown for barley and two and a half for oats were obtained.[2.60] Rye and flax were also grown to some extent while potatoes, introduced in mid-century, gradually became prominent.[2.61] Although no other crop was sown generally by tenant farmers, the gentry were somewhat more adventurous, experimenting with grasses and, despite the difficulties arising from the lack of suitable mills, growing an ever increasing amount of wheat. In later years much scepticism was expressed about the wheat grown in Easter Ross in the eighteenth century but it is clear that, amongst the gentry, it was a not uncommon crop and that, although much of it may have been grown for local use, it could on occasion be marketed very profitably.[2.62]

c. Agriculture — The Spread of Improvement, 1750-92

The overall standard of farming amongst tenant farmers remained low while there was little incentive to improve. Except in years of bad harvests, there was already a surplus available for export and, as long as markets were limited and the marketing organisation in the area operated at its historically low level, no advantage could be gained easily by increasing, to any great extent, the quantities for sale. But there were signs of improvement, particularly amongst the gentry. These signs had appeared well before the middle of the eighteenth century, although it was only from about 1750 that the gentry as a whole, as opposed to leading individuals, began to take an interest in innovative agriculture.

While it is not possible to determine with certainty the causes of the spread of interest in the subject, there are several pointers which suggest the probable motives. Although the extent and width of experience of earlier landlords should not be underestimated, it may well be that only in the eighteenth century did the majority of landowners in Easter Ross begin to travel widely enough to appreciate what was being undertaken elsewhere. A number of later eighteenth-century landlords had a wide acquaintance with the south of England in several capacities. Duncan Davidson, the purchaser of Tulloch in 1763, was a solicitor in London, Sir John Gordon of Ivergordon was a politician of some importance, Admiral Sir John Lockhart Ross of Balnagown was stationed in the south when not at sea with the fleet, and Sir Harry Munro of Foulis, after being educated in the Midlands and London, represented Ross-shire in parliament for some time, while his son actually inherited an estate in the south of England in 1788.[2.63]

Such close associations with London remained the prerogative of the few, but many more had connections in Edinburgh, which, in the later eighteenth century, became the centre of the most advanced area of farming in Great Britain. Lawyers in particular were prominent in introducing new methods, and the fact that many of the lesser Easter Ross lairds were at one time or another active in the legal profession as judges, writers or agents must have increased their chances of coming into contact with the leading figures of agricultural improvement.

Charles Robertson of Kindeace, a figure of far greater importance than his rent roll would suggest, had been an Edinburgh lawyer in his youth. His neighbour and friend, David Munro of Meikle Allan, who was one of the first lairds locally to grow wheat for export, continued to practise law until his death in 1767, while David Ross of Ankerville successfully combined the careers of agricultural innovator and Senator of the College of Justice into the nineteenth century. Significantly, the greatest concentration of landed lawyers was to be found in the estates of the parishes near Tain, where much of the early improvement took place.[2.64]

Even those lairds who travelled less extensively must have had their outlook broadened, for in a society as closely knit as that of Easter Ross, the experiences of one landowner would be transmitted quickly to another. Obviously, when a major and influential figure such as Sir John Ross of Balnagown began to improve, his neighbours would take note of his actions; but a relatively minor though highly respected figure such as Charles Robertson of Kindeace could be equally influential.[2.65]

The efforts of these innovators were backed up by the increasing number of publications devoted to the practice of agriculture which described the most approved methods in the leading agricultural areas. Such publications appear to have had a fairly wide readership amongst the Easter Ross gentry throughout the later eighteenth century. Indeed, on occasion, local landowners could figure prominently in the subscription lists for books of this sort.[2.66]

It has been suggested that the Commissioners of Forfeited Estates made a major contribution to improvement in the north of Scotland[2.67] but, although government agencies controlled Newtarbat — one of the most centrally situated estates in Easter Ross — for four decades, their contribution to improvement in this area was of questionable significance. While the last Earl of Cromarty had been a member of the Society of Improvers,[2.68] Newtarbat remained largely unimproved at his forfeiture in 1746 and the Forfeited Estates Commissioners undoubtedly made some major changes. Pruning was abolished and enclosure commenced, while an attempt was made to improve the quality of craftsmen on the estate. But overall the Commissioners' impact was small, not only in the area at large but even within the confines of the estate. The Commissioners objected to the division of farms but did nothing to encourage more satisfactory farm sizes; indeed one major scheme which failed completely was the settlement of cottagers on the policies of Newtarbat House on holdings of very limited size. While prepared to consider longer leases, the Commissioners seem to have been content to maintain the pattern of short leases already prevalent, and although they rapidly stripped the estate of its existing timber their plans for replanting proved less successful. Just as Charles II is reputed to have said that his words were his own but his actions were his ministers', so it could reasonably be suggested that the Commissioners' joint heart was in the right place and that their plans were frustrated by circumstances (largely a lack of finance) beyond their control, but on the whole they failed to win the confidence of the tenants and antagonised the neighbouring gentry with lawsuits over thirlage rights and boundary disputes. Although the Commissioners' contribution to the industrial growth of the area was of considerable importance, their impact on agricultural development was, all in all, slight.[2.69]

The dictates of fashion, the experience gained from travelling and the knowledge obtained from books happily coincided with an increasing demand for agricultural produce which made innovation a potentially profitable venture. Although marketing techniques remained primitive Easter Ross had the advantage of relatively easy access to water transport and from the estate girnals by the shores of the firth it was possible to send the surplus crops to the growing population centres in the central belt of Scotland, the North of England and London and to the corn starved districts of the West Highlands. Closer at hand the garrison at Fort George and the town of Inverness provided new or expanding markets for local produce.[2.70]

But to embark on any major undertaking it was necessary to have considerable capital resources, especially before 1770 when Montgomery's Act allowed heritors of property held under strict entail to burden the estate with part of the cost of improvement.[2.71] Although agricultural improvements promised long-term rewards, the initial costs were high and early returns on capital expenditure low. The fate of John Cockburn of Ormiston and Maxwell of Arbigland was a salutary reminder to any who might be tempted to spend too freely on improvement.[2.72] In many cases this must have restricted landlords to minor improvements and it was, in the main, only those lairds with large fortunes acquired from non-agricultural sources who were able to undertake the heavy commitments involved in major schemes of agricultural improvement. A roll call of the leading improvers in Easter Ross shows hardly one without financial backing from some non-agricultural source. Davidson of Tulloch made his fortune as a solicitor in London before buying the Tulloch estate, Sir Hector Munro of Novar ransacked much of India to pay for his improvements, the Gordons of Invergordon had been amongst the few who benefited from the South Sea Bubble, Sir John Ross financed his improvements from prize money obtained while in the navy, George Ross used his position as an army agent to build up the resources which he later applied to modernising the Cromarty estate, and so on.[2.73]

Before the last decade of the eighteenth century improvement on any scale was largely restricted to the landlords themselves. The great majority of tenants continued in the old ways and showed no inclination to adopt improved methods. It would have been difficult for them to do otherwise. Their landlords increasingly castigated them as lazy and useless[2.74] without making any great effort to alleviate the harsh conditions under which they lived or to encourage them to change their ways. It may be that the limitations on heritors' capital often prevented them from improving more than their own home farms initially, but when Sir Hector Munro of Novar spent over £100,000 on his estate — much of it on improving the poor-quality land around his mansion house and on a variety of follies in the policies — there must be a strong suspicion that to him and others like him improvement was to some extent a fashionable pursuit divorced from the realities of economic life. As Southey put it: 'Sir Hector Munro expended [on his estate] the whole wealth which he acquired in India, so that he was obliged to go to India again and make a second fortune for the purpose of enabling him to live upon it.'[2.75] Such an option was not available to his tenants.

Most of the local tenants were ignored by the heritors in their plans for improvement, and for the task of supervising operations on home farms the gentry turned instead to southern-trained factors and grieves. Some of these came from as far afield as England but the majority were natives of the Lothians, reared on the advanced agriculture practised there. By 1792 all the gentlemen's farms in Kiltearn were managed by people either from or trained in the south.[2.76] Shortly before the Napoleonic wars the practice began to be extended to the tenanted farms as well, although on occasion a native farmer with the necessary capital and initiative would be given the chance to prove his worth.[2.77]

The two main aims of the improvers were to improve the land that was already cultivated and to bring into cultivation land that, until then, had been waste. Before either aim could be fully achieved a great deal of preliminary work had to be done, and throughout the latter half of the eighteenth century Easter Ross lairds were much occupied with dividing up commons and straightening march boundaries.[2.78] The acreage of arable land was increased by improving the drainage on wet, low-lying lands — Davidson of Tulloch even going so far as to reclaim land from the sea — and by breaking in previously barren moorland.[2.79]

In this latter activity the landlords were prepared to make use of the surplus population amongst the native tenantry and, in much of Easter Ross, crofters were settled on barren ground with easy leases and considerable assistance in the way of tools and seed.[2.80] So far as the landlords were concerned this proved a relatively inexpensive method of adding to their rental while, at the same time, relieving population pressure on existing arable land. Progress, however, was painfully slow. It took ten to twelve years for each crofter to reclaim up to three acres and there was an understandable tendency amongst the crofters to turn after a time to more lucrative pursuits such as smuggling and poaching, especially when it became clear that eventually the landlords would be tempted to take over the newly reclaimed land, turning it into large farms and re-settling the ejected tenantry on further areas of unreclaimed moor to begin the whole cycle all over again.[2.81] Despite the drawbacks, many landlords continued to use this method to improve the fringes of their estates, especially as a side benefit was the large pool of surplus labour which was available for harvest work.

When it came to improving land that was already cultivated, progress tended to be piecemeal, as different proprietors laid different emphasis on the various improved techniques. While Munro of Allan in the 1750s, Munro of Culcairn in the 1760s and Rose of Dam in the 1770s concentrated on drainage, Sir John Ross of Balnagown devoted considerable efforts to the improvement of livestock, especially sheep, and Davidson of Tulloch and Macleod of Geanies specialised in crops and crop rotations. Many of these processes were interdependent, of course — it was because Hugh Rose of Dam wished to dig drains in 1778 that he requested the essential first step of straightening the march between his own property and that of Cadboll — and the leading improvers carried on more than one process at a time; but, when money was scarce, priorities had to be determined and, even with the best of intentions, some of the early work which was done did not meet the more exacting standards of a following generation. It is clear from the surviving documentation that David Munro of Allan was an enthusiastic drainer of his lands, but within three decades of his death Andrew Wight found cause to criticise the ground at Meikle Allan for want of drainage, and David's successor in 1784 committed extensive resources to further drainage of the estate.[2.82]

The abolition of runrig and the extension of enclosure were two of the earliest advances to be attempted on a widespread scale by proprietors.[2.83] Even before 1750 enclosures were found in the area although they were restricted in almost all cases to the home farms of estates. Soon after the middle of the century many of the lairds and a few of the leading tenants undertook more extensive enclosure and by the time of Wight's visit in 1781 a great deal had been done. Stone dykes and hedgerows seem to have been used in almost equal numbers, while hedgerows with trees were also found. The size of enclosures varied from two to eighteen acres or more but by the end of the century most enclosures covered from six to sixteen acres.[2.84]

Many of the early enclosures were intended not for agriculture but for silviculture, for afforestation was greatly favoured by many of the leading improvers in the area. Such an interest was, perhaps, not surprising in sailors like Sir John Ross of Balnagown or Captain Urquhart of Cromarty, but at a time when there was an increasing fuel shortage there were equally strong reasons for others to pursue the same policy in an area where there were few natural woods and where many of the peat mosses were becoming exhausted.[2.85]

While the practical aspect was uppermost in most instances, trees were also used decoratively and relative exotics like walnut, lime and poplar were introduced, especially in the immediate environs of country seats.[2.86] Even amongst the larger plantations of fir and pine an appreciation of aesthetics was evident. When the Hill of Cromarty was planted, for example, avenues were left through the wood to give views of the surrounding countryside.[2.87] Aesthetics and use were combined too in the laying out of orchards. Although only one of any size was developed in the region before 1800 — that of David Urquhart of Braelangwell, extending to thirteen acres — other estates planted orchards on a smaller scale, introducing greengage plums, nectarines, cherries, peaches and apricots.[2.88]

Most of the leading landowners and a number of their lesser brethren continued this interest in forestry throughout the eighteenth century, and while efforts were made to extend arable acreages in the low country, large areas on the fringes and in the foothills were planted.[2.89] Although none of the heritors were innovators in the field, they were willing to accept new developments. Sir Hector Munro of Novar, for example, was the first person to introduce the larch to Easter Ross, acquiring three young trees from the Duke of Atholl — a pioneer in their introduction to Scotland. A larch at Scotsburn is said to date from this period also, suggesting that an enthusiasm for a new species was shared by the smaller landowners. Most of the plantations were filled with fir and pine but there were smaller quantities of a large number of other varieties. Amongst these oak was probably the most popular, being found in Ferindonald, the Black Isle and Easter Ross proper, while plane, ash, elm, beech and birch were also common.[2.90]

Although planting was pursued with enthusiasm, the management of plantations was not always effective. The only commercial nursery in the area was that owned by Kenneth Mackenzy of Cromartie at Newtarbat. Some of the larger estates had their own nurseries but many trees had to be acquired from the south, especially if they were uncommon varieties.[2.91] Commercial exploitation varied considerably, depending upon demand. In mid-century the construction of Fort George provided a ready market for large quantities of timber, and towards the end of the century the trade in supplying pit props to the North-East of England was commenced,[2.92] but for much of the period in between demand was slack and the standard of maintenance tended to drop. Already by 1762 John Adam had to warn Sir John Ross that the Balnagown plantations were in great need of pruning and thinning and, while a further thousand acres were planted at Balnagown in 1774-5, only the more accessible parts were maintained, the remoter areas being left without any after-management.[2.93]

In the main arable areas widespread efforts were made not only to increase the acreage and to arrange it more systematically but to improve the overall quality of the agriculture practised. The soil was enriched with dung and vastly increased quantities of fertiliser. Near the towns dung was obtained by letting land to townspeople for potatoes, on condition that they provided the manure, while fertiliser was at first obtained from seaweed, shells and marl (there being a marl pit near Culcairn) and later from lime imported from Portsoy and Sunderland.[2.94] The treated ground was worked with improved implements derived from the south either directly or as copies made by local craftsmen. By 1795 Small's chain plough was widely used by owners and major tenants and was beginning to be adopted by the smaller tenants.[2.95]

Better working helped to increase yields which were further improved by the adoption of scientific rotations. Initially rotations suited to totally different situations were slavishly imitated with poor results, as when Macleod of Geanies had to abandon Norfolk husbandry after only six years, but, with experience, systems more suited to the needs of the locality were adopted.[2.96] New crops and improved strains of old crops were introduced. Turnips and carrots were first seen soon after the period commenced, while sown grasses which had been introduced a few decades earlier became far more widespread.[2.97]

Many of the new crops were intended primarily for stock feeding, as this had been a major problem in the past. The provision of adequate feedstuffs made the introduction of improved breeds worthwhile and much was done to improve the quality of horses, cattle and sheep. Sir John Ross bought extensively in England and kept a herd of one hundred and thirty cows for breeding in an attempt to improve his stock — though with little success initially. Other landlords imported improved breeds of cattle from Moray and Fife, and Galloway horses were introduced to take over carting and ploughing from the oxen and Highland garrons which had formerly been used.[2.98]

While sheep were not so important in the economy of Easter Ross as they were later to be in that of other areas of the North-Western Highlands, southern breeds made an early appearance. Sir John Ross's farm manager brought in English sheep in 1763, while Sir John himself bought sheep at the Linton market from 1774 and introduced them to one of his Highland farms. Although mismanagement and local opposition forced him by 1781 to give up direct control of the experiment, he rented the farm with its stock to a sheep farmer from Perthshire. In 1782 another sheep farmer from Fort William took a lease of a highland farm of Munro of Culcairn, while, by the 1790s, the Munros of Foulis and Novar had both turned over part of their upland estates to sheep, displacing, in the one instance, deer and, in the other, existing cattle rearing tenants. The last innovation produced a riot amongst the displaced tenantry and their supporters but this was the only incident of the sort to occur in the area, for arable farming and afforestation continued to occupy the greater part of the usable land surface.[2.99]

d. The Impact of War, 1792-1815

By 1792, despite the impressive achievements of the preceding half-century, the greater part of the countryside remained largely untouched by improvement. The start of the wars with France, however, revolutionised a process that already had been gaining momentum in the prosperous conditions following the end of the American War of Independence. With the restriction on imports of grain from abroad and the increased market provided by a greatly enlarged army and navy, prices rose steeply. In the years from 1750 to 1790 victual prices in Easter Ross had risen gradually from eight or nine shillings per boll to fourteen to sixteen shilling per boll. There had been a temporary upsurge in the years 1782-3 when a major famine caused by the failure of the corn crops had more than doubled prices, but by 1784 they had returned to near normal.[2.100] From the early 1790s, however, there was a rapid escalation, with barley passing one pound per boll in 1796 and reaching a staggering fifty shillings in the bad year of 1800.[2.101] In the early years of the nineteenth century there were major fluctuations, but after each drop in price the succeeding rise was higher than the previous peaks. During the last years of the war barley regularly fetched forty to fifty shillings per boll and sometimes even more. Although gluts were not uncommon, the demand exceeded anything that had previously been experienced and Ross-shire grain frequently fetched the highest prices on the London and Leith markets.[2.102]

Whereas, before, the landlords had engaged in improvement as much in the spirit of eighteenth-century enlightenment as in the hope of any short-term gain, they now saw the possibility of making considerable profits. Increasing absenteeism encouraged a change in attitude amongst many landlords. In the past even those who had been engaged on business elsewhere had taken a keen interest in the running of their estates, being concerned with their embellishment and interested in everyday minutiae.[2.103] The increasing attractions of London life increased the economic value of estates to proprietors but lessened their personal concern in the affairs of their tenants. Easter Ross landlords in the past had not been noted for any especial benignity towards their tenants but much of even the limited paternalism evident in the eighteenth century disappeared when attacked by the pressures of a changing economic situation.[2.104] As one Ross-shire farmer put it in 1807,

> There are tenants from the improved southern counties, who do not pay from the same lands in Ross-shire, a higher rent than the poor tenants did before them, who, on an average, did not raise more than two-thirds of the produce which these strangers do. And yet these south country tenants have their difficulties. I therefore conclude, that the rental of the Lowlands of Ross-shire is not a fair one . . .[2.105]

At the same time rising rents around Edinburgh had accentuated the difference in values between the Lothians and Easter Ross, making the latter district, with its inherent fertility, an area of great attraction to the tenant farmers of the south.[2.106] The landlords took the opportunity offered to them of having their lands improved by tenants with the capital to do it themselves and, with the prospect of increased rents to entice them, began to throw the smallholdings on their estates into large farms.[2.107] Very few of their sitting tenants had the capital to bid for these new farms and so, within a few years, the majority of the tenants occupying large farms in Easter Ross were southerners, usually from the Lothians, who brought their own systems and ways of life, even down to their servants, with them.[2.108] A further step forward in the process of land improvement was the widespread feuing of burgh lands to those wishing to improve. Feuing had begun in the middle of the eighteenth century, but reached a peak about 1800. Although the towns involved may have lost their rights, the area in general gained by the additions to the total arable acreage.[2.109]

The landlords gained doubly by the influx of southern farmers, for in addition to the prospect of higher rents to be paid by the incomers they were able to settle far greater numbers of the evicted smallholders than ever before on unimproved moorland and set them to work on reclamation.[2.110] Not all who were evicted were given, or desired, this opportunity and numbers emigrated. A residue moved to the towns in the area, to work in the factories or to act as a pool of readily available labour to be hired during periods of heavy workload such as the times of the hay and corn harvests.[2.111]

As early as 1792 in Fearn farm enlargement was resulting in the displacement of from four to ten old tenants by one newcomer. The small farms had rented at anything from sixteen to fifty bolls whereas the new reached from seventy up to even one hundred and thirty bolls.[2.112] There was no regular pattern in the size of the new farms and they ranged widely from one hundred to six hundred acres and more.[2.113] Where suitable tenants could not be found, landlords increasingly took the land into their own hands — at least until it had been improved.[2.114] Even when they returned much of the improved land to tenant farmers, the home farms in many cases may have remained of a larger size than they had been in the past.[2.115] At the same time as the enlargement of some farms took place, the process of division amongst the smaller farms seems to have continued. While farms in the middle of the eighteenth century had ranged up to fifty acres or more in extent, the native farmers in the first decade of the nineteenth century were restricted to holdings of seven to thirty acres.[2.116]

The smallholders continued as before in most respects, obtaining short leases only, if leases were granted at all. The only people to gain from the increasing disposition of the landlords to give longer leases were the incoming large farmers who regularly obtained nineteen-year leases and could on occasion be encouraged to improve with very much longer leases.[2.117] The distinction between the two classes of tenants was apparent in most aspects of life. Whilst the new farmers followed the proprietors in importing southern ploughs and harrows, the native tenants stuck largely to old and inefficient implements. The new farmers speedily changed over to horses for pulling ploughs and generally attempted to improve their stock, whereas the smallholders stuck to the oxen which had been used for generations and continued to rely on garrons, black cattle and native Highland sheep, although even amongst smallholders the improvement of stock was hastened by the loss of Highland lands, previously used for transhumance, to sheep farms.[2.118]

The most marked difference of all was to be seen in arable farming. Not only were the fields of the large farms enclosed and drained with scientific rotations in operation as compared to the open, wet, stony and overcropped holdings of the others, but there was even a difference in the type of crop raised. The smallholders had never produced enough to benefit fully from exporting directly and continued to rely on barley sold to distillers, legal or illegal, as their chief marketable crop, although, by the end of the eighteenth century, up to two thirds of the oat crop, including the quantities paid as rent in kind to the estate girnals, handily situated for export by the shores of the firths, was being sold to Inverness and Leith as well as to Cromarty.[2.119] Potatoes increasingly figured as the main subsistence crop rather than oats, partly perhaps because farms were no longer large enough to give a sufficient yield of oats and partly because potatoes were easy to grow and provided high returns.[2.120]

The incomers, in contrast, were able to profit from the increased demand in the south and the ability of their enlarged holdings to produce marketable quantities and turned their attention to the cultivation of wheat. That wheat was a viable crop in Easter Ross had already been widely demonstrated but its wide-scale cultivation for export began only at the very end of the eighteenth century. George Middleton, an Englishman who had settled in the parish of Cromarty, is credited as having been the first to export wheat in commercial quantities from the region in the period after 1798. In 1802 two thousand bolls of wheat were grown in Ross. By 1806 twice as much was being grown as had ever been grown before (the previous year excepted), while by 1812 a yield of as much as ten thousand bolls was confidently expected and it was felt that there could be much more. Wheat was now the staple crop and although barley was still produced in large quantities its relative importance had declined.[2.121]

In 1806 a major step forward was taken in the improvement of marketing channels when a corn market was opened in Dingwall with the intention of attracting agents from Inverness and elsewhere. Previously the agents had travelled round the country making individual agreements with farmers and it was widely felt that this system had prevented the farmer from getting the full market value for his crop.[2.122]

To some extent this change may have benefited the small tenants as well as the large farmers and, despite the disparity between the two groups, there is some evidence that the former were able to learn from the latter. In the eighteenth century the landlords had maintained close relations with each other and knowledge of agricultural advances had been transmitted in the ordinary way through social intercourse, although a number of the more prominent improvers had widened their outlook by joining nationwide agricultural societies.[2.123] The main means whereby tenant farmers could learn of each other's progress were at church and at fairs and markets. In 1794, however, at a time when local farming associations were burgeoning throughout Scotland, the Ross-shire Farmers' Club was founded with committees at Tain, Dingwall and Fortrose and with the purposes of encouraging improvements in agriculture and regulating wages and prices. It had a membership at first of only just over fifty (some of whom were clergymen) and the fees of one guinea to join and one shilling per quarter thereafter must have discouraged the adherence of small farmers.[2.124]

At the first meeting of a successor society, the Easter Ross Farmers' Club, in 1811, the ten farmers present were almost exclusively large farmers, including newcomers such as the Dudgeons of Fearn and

Arboll, as well as longer-established major tenants such as George Sackville Sutherland of Rives and George Mackenzie of Meikle Tarrel. The number of landlords who were members was limited at first but more joined as time went on. Indeed membership as a whole rose quite substantially over the years but active members represented only a small proportion of the total. From 1832 to 1835 the average attendance at sixteen meetings was only twelve; and at the meeting in August 1835 the Praeses, or chairman, expressed his regret that so few members attended meetings and stated that the object of the Club would be completely frustrated unless there was an improvement.

Despite such difficulties, the work of these societies set an example for all to follow. Premiums were offered, talks were given, livestock shows and ploughing matches were arranged, and a co-operative venture with the Moray Farmers' Club succeeded in obtaining a stallion for breeding purposes.[2.125] More insidiously, farms of members were visited and reported on. Such reports helped to spread ideas and good practices and it is likely that, although surviving reports are, in the main, favourable, the prospects of an official visitation would have spurred the more lethargic members of the societies into action. By 1811 the Farmers' Club of the day had a small circulating library to which additions were made annually. At least one common tenant was influenced by all these activities to commence improvements and others were no doubt impressed by what they saw.[2.126]

For the first time the profit motive clearly could be seen to be the only reason for undertaking improvements. Smallholders who had been suspicious of proprietors who 'generally improve more from pleasure than profit'[2.127] were willing to learn far more from commercially practising farmers and even to look with fresh eyes at the work of the proprietors, although the differences in income and knowledge prevented a widespread adoption of all new techniques.

The gradual conversion of rents in kind to money rents which took place during this period was also, to some extent, a by-product of the influx of large farmers accustomed to paying in cash which benefited the smaller tenants financially and which allowed them to diversify their crops from the endless succession of victual which had been necessary to pay the rent. In the same way the commutation of thirlage after 1799 helped both rich and poor.[2.128]

Rents rose rapidly in cash terms especially on land that had been improved. The average rent of arable land on the Black Isle in 1795 was sixteen shillings per acre and probably much the same figure prevailed over the rest of Easter Ross, although in the proximity of towns payments in excess of thirty-five shillings per acre could be made.[2.129] Soon after 1800 the farms of Cullis and Rarichies on the Shandwick estate were let at rents which were triple those that had obtained prior to improvement, and although this increase may have been exceptional, by 1808 good arable land was letting at thirty or forty shillings an acre.[2.130] Thereafter the increase became even faster. In 1809 rents were thirty per cent above those prevailing two years previously owing to the influx of big farmers from the south, and by 1814 arable land fetched two to three pounds per acre.[2.131]

Although these were major increases, rents in Easter Ross still lagged behind those paid in the most improved areas of Scotland, and in real terms they had not advanced so very much beyond the level charged fifty years earlier. In 1781 the rents on the Tarbat barony of Sir John Gordon of Invergordon had varied from one to two bolls an acre at a time when a boll of victual was converted at approximately twelve shillings, while enclosed land near Cromarty was already priced at forty shillings an acre. The rents of 1814 compared with prices of forty-three and fifty shillings charged the previous year for bolls of barley and with the even higher prices which wheat was fetching on the London and Leith markets. In effect the rent of land remained at between one and two bolls per acre and real increases in landlords' rent rolls were attributable to the increased extent of arable land more than to any real rise in the value of existing arable.[2.132]

By 1814 improvements were in progress on a far wider scale than ever before. Easter Ross was as active in agricultural developments as most other areas of Scotland and its produce had gained an enviable reputation, but a great deal remained to be done. Much of the land was still undrained bog or marsh and a large proportion of the area actually in cultivation remained unimproved. In the parish of Tarbat, for example, the acreage of improved land rose from four hundred acres in 1800 to fourteen hundred in 1811, yet this latter figure represented only about half the arable land in the parish.[2.133] Work had progressed as quickly as possible in some areas in the boom conditions of the war economy but a general shortage of capital slowed down the rate of improvement. After 1790 there were, for the first time, a large number of tenant farmers with the capital to finance their own undertakings but this was to some extent balanced by the diversion of capital belonging to the landlords from agricultural investment to other purposes.

It is true that some heritors continued to spend heavily on improvements. Hugh Rose of Glastullich used much of the fortune he acquired in the West Indies to modernise his estate, and Sir Charles Ross of Balnagown spent almost eight thousand pounds on his Easter Ross properties (as compared to only fifteen hundred pounds expended by Sir John Ross between 1770 and 1778). But Robertson of Kindeace was persuaded to invest his surplus wealth in property speculation in Edinburgh while John Mackenzie of Strathgarve, an estate on the fringes of the region, became closely involved in iron works in the west of Scotland.[2.134]

While proprietors like Kindeace and Strathgarve were at least investing their money usefully, there were some who preferred to use the income from their estates to meet the bills for heavy personal expenditure. The last Earl of Seaforth had to pay the inevitable costs associated with being a close companion of the Prince Regent, while Sir Hugh Munro of Foulis left Ross-shire soon after his succession in 1781 and spent much of the remainder of his life stripping his estate of its assets, partly to pay for his London life and partly to deprive the nearest male heir of the advantages of succession.[2.135]

e. The Post-War Period

The great era of expansion came to a sudden halt with the end of the Napoleonic wars in 1815. Foreign grain flooded the markets and prices tumbled from their war-time peaks. Distilleries closed and banks restricted their credit so that farmers were forced to sell at any price. The markets for all kinds of farm produce were at their most depressed state for twenty years.[2.136] Easter Ross suffered with the rest of the country and may indeed have felt the slump worse than most. Certainly to one commentator things looked very black as he wrote:

> At no period, in our remembrance, did matters wear so gloomy an aspect for the corn farmers of Scotland in general, as they do at present; and in counties situated at so great a distance from market as this, as may be naturally expected, in a proportionable degree is felt the depression of price and stagnation of the Corn trade. The farmers here are much at a loss what to do with their corn; they have no opportunity of selling it at home, and to ship it, either for Leith or London, in the present glutted state of these markets, holds out the miserable prospect of sales being forced at extremely reduced prices, such as are altogether inadequate to meet rents, taxes, and other expenses; or of their grain being put in a granary, where, so far as can be foreseen, from the immense quantity of foreign corn on hand, and daily arriving, it may lie for months before it can be converted

> into cash . . . Many bankruptcies have already taken place in this county; and almost every one concerned in corn farming is at present verging towards it . . . a stop being put to draining, liming, reclaiming of waste lands, and other matters of a like kind . . .
>
> We do not hear of such a thing as a reduction of rent by any of the landlords of this county.[2.137]

Wheat which had been fetching up to three pounds per boll in the last years of the war dropped to between one and two pounds while barley and oats suffered similar declines. Black cattle fell in value by 100 per cent in fifteen months. The immediate situation was exacerbated by an occasional inability to sell corn at any price, but even when the market had recovered and grain was once more in demand in the south, prices remained well below the level they had reached in 1814. Oatmeal fell to a low of sixteen shillings and sixpence in 1829, while as late as 1838 wheat was selling at no more than twenty-four shillings.[2.138]

The landlords, however, were in constant need of money and were reluctant to give rebates of rents to those who had promised so much in the way of increased income but a few years before. An increasing number of heritors joined the ranks of those whose only interest in their estates was a pecuniary one. By 1850 almost all of the greater landowners in Ferindonald and Easter Ross were absentees, and even as early as 1820 it was said that many of the landlords did not visit their estates even once a year.[2.139] The evidence laid before the Royal Commission investigating the Poor Laws in 1844 was generally in agreement on this point, and almost all the parishes in the region had only a minority of heritors in residence — although some of those technically non-resident lived on their estates in neighbouring parishes. This was the case in Rosskeen where only one small heritor was actually resident. Although several others lived elsewhere in Easter Ross, the bulk of the heritors of the parish lived as far afield as Italy, London and Liverpool.[2.140] The situation was made worse by a crop of minorities and disputed successions. While the tutors and judicial factors who managed such estates could be expected to be honest and responsible, the conditions of their management were generally such as to prevent a useful reaction in times of crisis.[2.141]

As late as 1831 it was written that 'although grain and cattle, which rose then [during the war] with rents, have now fallen to their original standard, rents have scarcely suffered any diminution'.[2.142] In these conditions many farmers failed to survive and it was only when farms coming on the market failed to find tenants that landlords began to move. In 1818 Macleod of Cadboll gave a twenty per cent discount to his tenants on the rent of the 1816 crop, and by 1823 there was a general if slow reduction of some ten to fifteen per cent. Only Davidson of Tulloch was regarded as fully meeting the needs of the times by giving reductions of twenty-five to fifty per cent. At the same time the financial ruin of some tenants was accelerated by those heritors who by 1824 were taking legal measures to recover arrears of rent.[2.143] Even amongst those who survived the collapse the continuing drain of high rents on a greatly reduced income depleted the stocks of capital which had, in better times, been used for improvement. It is not surprising that Easter Ross farmers should have been solidly against free trade and from 1814, when the first recorded meeting to express opposition took place, they continued to support protection up to the middle of the century.[2.144]

Amidst all the gloom, however, there were some brighter prospects. Although the export market for grain crops had collapsed and wheat was often unsaleable, there was a boom in local sales of barley. Licensed distilleries began to expand again from 1818, but more importantly there was an upsurge in the amount sold to illegal stills.[2.145] Licensed distillers on the whole preferred the better quality, lower-priced barley from Angus but smugglers, who did not have to meet such stringent requirements, were content with the local produce and were willing to pay highly for it. As Sir George Mackenzie of Coull confessed in 1822, 'the highest class of farmers and even proprietors are under the necessity of indirectly encouraging this traffic [smuggling] because they have no other means for disposing of the produce of their farms'.[2.146]

Despite the risks of total loss if stills were seized and although credit was more frequent than cash payments, farmers could obtain prices from smugglers which were one third higher than those obtainable elsewhere — even on the Edinburgh market.[2.147] For many years the small farmers with limited retail outlets had relied upon the illegal stills as their main market. Now the larger farmers and even the proprietors followed suit and took advantage of the opportunity to retrieve some of their losses.[2.148] It is perhaps less surprising that landlords were unwilling to reduce rents in the light of this source of income, although it by no means wholly compensated for the collapse elsewhere. At the same time improvements did continue, if on a more limited scale than before, and the general spirit of improvement was still strong enough for a Horticultural Society to be founded at Invergordon in 1820.[2.149]

Although livestock prices fell too during the recession, some progress was made in stock farming. With the unusual prospect of immediate gain as an enticement, the owners of the hill districts of Kiltearn converted them to sheep farms in 1811-21[2.150] and, although at no time before 1850 was Easter Ross a major area for stock breeding or rearing, the post-war period did see the growth of several cattle markets. That at Muir of Ord rapidly achieved pre-eminence in the North of Scotland with sales rising from three to four hundred beasts in 1820 to three thousand (or a turnover of ten thousand pounds) in 1824. The rise of Muir of Ord was aided by the decision in 1820 to reorganise the dates of stock markets in the North of Scotland so that drovers and dealers could attend them in order.[2.151]

From 1825 revival became more general although the boom conditions preceding 1815 were never repeated. It may be that, by that time, the increase in demand was once again outstripping supply, for the market was at its best for eight or nine years. At any rate farmers in Easter Ross were in a better position than ever before to send their produce to the major markets of the south as steam navigation became general and the system which had begun in times of hardship of farmers shipping grain on their own account and consigning it to factors in Leith or London became widespread.[2.152] This practice must have adversely affected the Dingwall grain market which would never have been needed for local markets alone, and by 1836 it had ceased to exist.[2.153] By 1828 wheat production was estimated to amount to twenty-eight thousand quarters as the big farmers attempted to make up for lower prices by growing more and even smallholders entered the field to cater for the home market which the others had neglected.[2.154]

This concentration tended to be counter-productive. By the end of the 1830s every farmer in the parish of Cromarty was growing wheat for export but over-production was causing the price to fall below that of barley and oats. Attempts to boost output even further by abandoning a five-shift rotation for one of three shifts inevitably led to soil exhaustion and the evils of overcropping.[2.155] The post-war period saw a temporary decline in the production of grain crops with the exception of wheat. Turnips had been recognised as early as 1815 to be a profitable crop when grown as feedstuff for swine, and there was a general shift to root and green crops in common with much of the rest of Scotland.[2.156]

With the revival of the 1820s the smallholders' contribution to improvement possibly reached a peak. To the numbers that already existed were added many who had been evicted from Highland estates in Mid Ross. As late as 1840-50 evictions from the Highland area of Easter Ross to make way for deer forests provided further reinforcements.[2.157] Much of the reclamation undertaken by these crofters took place on the Black Isle. After the failure of several earlier attempts at division, notably in 1764, the last and greatest of the commons of Easter Ross, the Millbuie, was finally portioned out amongst the neighbouring heritors in 1828 and a whole new area was opened up for development. At the same time, the landlords in the south-west of the Black Isle developed a tardy interest in improvement. Partly, perhaps, because any other form of improvement was too expensive, and partly, at least on the Kilcoy estate, from humanitarian considerations for those displaced from elsewhere, the mode of improvement adopted was that of settling smallholders. The Gairloch estate in Urquhart was one of the most active in this field, settling smallholders who had been evicted from Strathconon some years previously.[2.158]

For the first time long leases for these smallholders became general and with the confidence of security they too, so far as they could, began to adopt the improved methods in use elsewhere. Indeed, by mid-century, the only areas where long leases were not the standard practice were in the immediate environs of the towns where high rents could be obtained even on land leased annually.[2.159]

For many crofters, however, security of tenure came too late. In areas where smallholders had already reclaimed the land upon which they were settled, the process of enlargement continued and in some parishes it would appear that the limit of economic reclamation had been reached, for the evicted crofters were not resettled on new fringe moorland.[2.160] Not all reclamation, of course, was undertaken by crofters, for larger farmers were involved too. Using improved methods farmers were able to obtain yields of up to eightfold from the newly broken-in land in contrast to the decreasing yields which were resulting from overcropping in the more settled areas.[2.161]

More improvement may have been financed directly by the proprietors than had been common during the war period, presumably because tenants with the necessary capital were no longer so readily to be found.[2.162] As boom conditions were no longer in evidence, even those tenants who did undertake their own improvements may have done so on a smaller scale than at the start of the century.

One of the greatest improvements throughout the area in these years was the widespread adoption of tile drainage. Hugh Rose of Glastullich led the way and built a tile works on his estate which supplied much of Easter Ross.[2.163] Other improvements during this period were merely continuations of processes initiated at an earlier stage. Planting revived and the commercial exploitation of existing forests reached new levels; rents in kind, which were still in the majority in 1815, were rapidly converted; the changeover from hired servants to a system of day labour was largely completed and the replacement of the few remaining joint farms by unified holdings continued.[2.164]

By 1850 the next stage in agricultural development was just beginning to make itself felt. The rural population which was already being stabilised or cut back in some areas because of the absence of more moorland worth reclaiming was, for the first time, seriously threatened by the introduction of advanced technology. Steam threshing machines and wire fences heralded a new age when the numbers required to maintain the farms of the district would be considerably reduced.[2.165]

f. The Fishing Industry

Easter Ross was primarily an agricultural area with all other economic activities playing a secondary role to the land as sources of income and employment. But some of these other activities were significant and the fishing industry was one of the most prominent of these. The industry never assumed the importance in Easter Ross that it held on the west coast but it was well established by the middle of the eighteenth century and made a valuable contribution to the local economy throughout the period.

In the eighteenth century the fishing industry in Easter Ross was a primitive affair scarcely affected by various government attempts to encourage its growth. The fishers were scattered in small communities all the way along the shores of the firths and concentrated upon inshore fishing, rarely venturing more than a few miles off shore and often relying on the shoals making their way into the inner firths. White fish, herring and salmon were all plentiful and were pursued within these limits but herring, possibly the most important of these, could not be relied upon to re-appear yearly at the same spot, and such uncertainty combined with the fishers' inability to pursue the fish at any distance made the growth of a stable and prosperous fishing community more difficult. The fishermen based in the Cromarty Firth seem to have been particularly timid — partly, at least, because the easy availability of fish within the sheltered waters of the firth prior to 1774 had made it unnecessary to learn to face the rougher conditions out in the Moray Firth — while those of Tarbat and Fearn were rather more willing to venture from home waters to secure a catch.[2.166] Only at Avoch were the fishermen sufficiently organised to pursue the fish to distant waters. The Avoch fishing fleet grew from one craft in 1700 to nine fully employed boats and a number of others fitted out for the herring season only in 1795. The fishermen of the village spent from October to March in the upper reaches of the Beauly Firth after herring and the following month moved after cod, skate and haddock to the coasts of Moray and Caithness. In May and June, while some continued with haddock, others caught lobsters off Tarbat Ness. In mid-July the whole fleet sailed for six to eight weeks to Caithness and Lochbroom before returning for the home herring season.[2.167]

With the exceptions of Avoch and Cromarty the fishing hamlets were all very small. There were only two boats at Hilton of Cadboll in 1781, while even towards the end of the century Inver had no more than four, and the twelve boats fishing from Tarbat parish belonged to no fewer than five fisher towns.[2.168]

The standard boat was a low, open, clinker-built craft about twenty-six feet long, sometimes with two big square sails but often relying solely on oars for propulsion.[2.169] It was easily beached and harbours, therefore, were not necessary. The six-oar boats which were most common in the Moray Firth in the later eighteenth century carried a complement of up to seven men and a boy but a number of boats fishing from Easter Ross were crewed by a smaller number. Those at Hilton in 1781 had only five men, while some of the smaller boats from Tarbat which were only occasionally used for fishing were manned by no more than two or three.[2.170]

Fisher families tended to live in closed communities. As late as 1842 it could be said that

> intermarriages with the rural population are very uncommon; and it is seldom that the children deviate from the perilous craft of their fathers. They are characterized by peculiar notions and practices; and they have a certain feudal spirit, or pride of order, which tends to preserve them as a separate community.[1.171]

They were economically integrated with the rest of Easter Ross society, however.

In Easter Ross proper the industry was financed by the landlords. On the Newtarbat estate the landlord furnished both boat and dwellings with gardens for the crew, who provided sails, masts, oars and tackle and were responsible for maintenance. In return the estate received a fifth of the catch as rent. In addition the crew had to provide services of an agricultural nature, as well as making their boats available for trips to such places as Dingwall and Inverness when required.[2.172] Even prior to 1750 the rent on the Newtarbat estate had been converted and by 1793 conversion was becoming common, with a rent of four pounds being paid yearly for larger boats and three pounds for smaller ones. It was the practice in Tarbat parish towards the end of the century for the proprietor to replace the boats every seven years.[2.173] At Avoch commercial firms were involved. The Falls of Dunbar were for many years the principal concern in the village before their bankruptcy in 1788. The Northumberland Fishing Company then took over and supplied the capital for the local fishers.[2.174]

Fishing was rarely a full-time occupation. As has been noted, agricultural services — providing shearers, making hay and carrying peats — were exacted and most fishers had crofts to supplement their winnings from the sea. In the early eighteenth century the fishermen of the area had been noted for their reluctance to go out and fish at all when not impelled to do so and the preference for a diversity of occupation continued, with some fishers using their boats for freighting lime and peats for a good part of the year.[2.175]

In 1749 an act of parliament established the Society of the Free British Fishery with the promise of bounties to encourage the growth of the industry and with proposals to set up Fishing Chambers in any places where ten thousand pounds could be raised to promote local enterprise. By 1759 over eleven and a half thousand pounds had been raised for the creation of a Fishing Chamber at Inverness and fifteen of the ninety-three subscribers belonged to Easter Ross, including eleven landowners, a merchant and a Cromarty shipmaster.[2.176] Very little seems to have come of this venture, however. The bounty played little part in the encouragment of fishing in Easter Ross, being designed for other purposes, and the Fishing Chamber failed to make any noticeable impact on the region. This lack of success was fairly general, and when the Society's charter expired in 1771, it was not renewed. Only Macleod of Geanies amongst the Easter Ross subscribers could have had more than a marginal interest in the promotion of fishing and none of those other heritors who already participated extensively in the industry bothered to subscribe.[2.177]

Another attempt to promote the industry was made by the Commissioners of Forfeited Estates who settled ex-sailors at Newtarbat, intending that they should become fishermen. The boats that the Commissioners supplied, however, were too small and the sailors soon gave up and left the area along with the rest of the proposed colony.[2.178]

While the fishermen of Easter Ross proper were largely content to provide fish for the immediate neighbourhood, those on the Black Isle, being more commercially organised, supplied a very much wider market. The fishermen of Avoch, in particular, supplied the London market as well as Inverness, Fortrose and the western Black Isle.[2.179] Backward organisation and technology prevented any great expansion in the export of fish. Curing especially left a lot to be desired and when, for example, in 1787 a good year of fishing drew buyers from all the towns on the east coast of Scotland, shortages of barrels and salt led to much of the catch being ruined.[2.180]

The early nineteenth century saw very little change in technique. The continued reliance on small open boats left fishermen very much at the mercy of the changing habits of the fish they sought to catch, while even when a catch was successfully made, bad curing could cause widespread damage. The quality of salt was poor and the proportions used often wrong, while the results of faulty processing were compounded by the use of badly made barrels. Poverty and bad judgment kept many fishermen partially tied to the land and unable to take full advantage of the opportunities the sea offered.[2.181]

At the same time the post-war period saw a considerable increase in the fishing population. The end of the Napoleonic wars meant that the fear of press gangs was considerably reduced, while the introduction of a four shilling per barrel bounty in 1815 encouraged the growth of many herring fishing stations around the Moray Firth.[2.182] Several good seasons led a company to set up business in Cromarty in 1819 on a larger scale than ever before. Within three years Cromarty rose to become the eighth largest centre for herring curing in Britain. By 1824 twenty thousand barrels of herring were being exported and two years later it was reported that two hundred women were employed in cleaning and salting the fish and that twenty-nine masted vessels lay in the firth waiting to carry away the finished product. While Cromarty was the greatest success story, there was a general increase in activity in this period and several fishing villages were encouraged by the construction of harbours.[2.183]

Over most of the area, however, the boom was short-lived. Although the fishing industry in Scotland as a whole survived the end of the bounty system in 1830, the villages on the Cromarty Firth were badly hit, for the cessation of bounty payments coincided with the disappearance of the herring from the immediate environs of the Firth.[2.184] While large shoals of herring were still to be found on the Guilliam Banks in the Moray Firth, directly opposite Cromarty, these were inaccessible to fishermen who had been accustomed to venture no further than ten or twelve miles out into the open sea. Their boats were not constructed to enable them to go fifty miles to sea and return with fish in a curable condition, even if it had been profitable for them to do so, and the profitability of the industry suffered with the decline in fish prices. The fishermen of Nigg who had made profits of twenty pounds and more in good seasons while the herring boom lasted had neglected the ordinary fishing and run up debts. When the boom collapsed they were left in poverty. As late as 1843 Cromarty fishers were still attempting to catch herring but with almost no success, although at that time the harbour was being used by larger French boats which were able to cure the fish on board.[2.185]

At either end of Easter Ross, at Avoch and at Portmahomack, the picture was a great deal brighter. The regular fleet at Avoch grew to nine boats, each manned by ten men, by 1840. Although they still had a reputation for laziness they made a profitable livelihood in the white fishing off the coast of Sutherland and Caithness, being joined in mid-July by another twenty-six local boats for the herring fishing.[2.186]

The fishing grounds off Tarbat Ness had, by 1840, attracted the attention of commercial interests. Curers who engaged boats in November and December gave bounties of five to eight guineas as well as about ten pounds each May to assist in fitting out. The number of boats fishing from Tarbat parish rose to over one hundred, and many of the fishermen had good houses while a few were comparatively wealthy. In addition, a further two hundred boats from elsewhere arrived during the main fishing season and each year the population of Portmahomack temporarily doubled with people from all over the Highlands arriving to assist with the herring curing.[2.187]

In addition to the major fisheries discussed above, the waters of Easter Ross had a number of minor attractions. Salmon were caught near Dingwall and Fortrose and provided useful additional sources of income to these burghs. In 1750 the salmon fishings off the Ness at Fortrose were rented at one hundred marks Scots. By 1794 they were valued at seventy pounds sterling — a startling increase.[2.188]

Dingwall's fisheries had a rather more chequered history. Prior to the mid-eighteenth century the town had not charged a rent, and indeed from 1763 to 1778 the rights to the fisheries were disputed by the Commissioners of Forfeited Estates on behalf of the Cromartie estate. In 1768 the stell and yair fishings were valued at eleven pounds and the value had only increased to twenty-five pounds in 1797 when the stell fishings were let to an Inverness company. In 1825, however, the rent shot up to one hundred and twenty pounds per annum. By this time the Cromartie estate had revived its claims to the fishings and the dispute dragged on for many years before Dingwall finally won. The burgh had continued to let the fishings throughout the case but the total rental did not compare with the legal costs incurred which amounted to over three thousand pounds by 1850.[2.189]

Tain did not have the dubious advantage of a salmon fishing but it did have the rights to a mussel scalp (bed) which proved very profitable over the years, bringing in an income of one hundred and fifty pounds in 1837. By 1842, however, the scalps were in a bad way and a four-year moratorium had to be imposed to prevent them being destroyed altogether.[2.190]

It is difficult to avoid the conclusion that the fishing industry represented a wasted opportunity so far as Easter Ross was concerned. The potential was there to be exploited, despite the irregular movements of the herring, and a more substantial input could have brought significant returns. The timidity and reluctance of the local fishermen to pursue their trade wholeheartedly was encouraged by under-capitalisation, however. Lack of funding meant that boats remained too small and that the back-up services — curing, coopering and the like — were not of a sufficiently high quality to meet the demands of the market. As the fishermen, themselves, hardly earned enough to maintain their families except in the most favourable seasons,[2.191] the gentry and merchants were the only indigenous sources of funds. While the merchants made some attempt to provide support, they were not wealthy enough to provide sufficient finance. The reluctance of the gentry to commit funds to activities not directly under their control or of immediate interest to them was unfortunately typical of their attitude to industrial development in the area as a whole.

3

The Economy: Industry, Trade and Transport

a. The Textile Industry

While fishing, like agriculture, was an industry that largely depended upon local natural resources and could survive, if it could not flourish, with little in the way of technological expertise, there were also manufacturing industries in the area which required rather more in the way of technological investment. Of these the most important was the textile industry.

This industry was based almost totally on flax and its associated fibre, hemp, and had existed in Easter Ross for some centuries before 1750. Depending on locally grown flax, the spring market at Fortrose had long supplied all of the north of Scotland with the town's coarse linen, while the shoemakers and fishers of Avoch raised and manufactured hemp for their own uses.[3.1] Throughout the second quarter of the eighteenth century Ross-shire produced over eleven thousand yards of linen cloth each year.[3.2] Although it was never an important crop in Easter Ross, flax was grown throughout the period, and as late as 1850 locally raised fibre was being used to produce sheets, napkins and table cloths for domestic use.[3.3]

From the middle of the eighteenth century the industry, relying on imported fibres, expanded rapidly. After initial growth at Tain where, following on from earlier developments, the British Linen Company in the late 1740s was supplying flax and financial support to John Reid, Michael Anderson and David Munro, the new focus of development settled at the head of the Cromarty Firth, rather than at the old centre of Fortrose, although production continued there, too, throughout the eighteenth century.[3.4]

The new industry, probably unlike the old, was not indigenous, for it was, to a large extent, composed of offshoots from already established companies in the south and was given considerable financial assistance by the Commissioners of Forfeited Estates and the Board of Trustees for Manufactures.[3.5] On the other hand its success in the second half of the eighteenth century depended to a considerable extent on local entrepreneurs. Moreover, while the Easter Ross linen industry was to some extent a subsidiary of southern interests, the area in its turn served as the focal point for activity in the Western Highlands.[3.6]

William Forsyth, a Cromarty merchant, claimed to be the first to introduce the spinning of yarn to Ross and Cromarty in 1748.[3.7] This is demonstrably untrue as an average of almost eleven thousand yards of linen a year had been produced in the previous twenty years, and even in Cromarty itself, if Forsyth was the first in the field it was only by a short head.[3.8] The years immediately after the collapse of the Jacobite revival did see an upsurge in the industry, however, with branches being established at Tain in 1747, Milntown before 1748, Dingwall in 1748 and Culcairn in 1751.[3.9] In this expansion Forsyth played a leading role. He became the agent of the British Linen Company in the country north of Inverness, Cromarty, his home town, being chosen for its central position and good harbour. Forsyth imported the flax from Holland and Russia, had it prepared in Cromarty and distributed it to the spinners in his own boats. He and his contemporaries insisted upon the use of spinning wheels rather than the traditional distaff and spindle and hired spinners to teach the use of the wheel. While the bulk of activity was confined to Easter Ross, Forsyth's enterprise extended into the Highlands of Ross, possibly as far as Lochbroom.[3.10] Robert Gordon, a Cromarty manufacturer, Harry Munro a manufacturer in Tain and William Forsyth's brother Joseph, centred in Dingwall, were also active in the Highlands.[3.11]

The main competition to Forsyth and the British Linen Company came from the leading firm of William Sandeman and Company of Perth who had an establishment at Cromarty around 1750 and, after its failure, maintained connections with the area through two further bases at Milntown and Fortrose opened in the early 1760s.[3.12] The Milntown branch was managed by John Montgomery who had been spinning yarn there on his own account since 1751.[3.13] The centres at Dingwall, Milntown, Tain, Fortrose and Cromarty controlled large numbers of spinners throughout the region. As early as 1750 John Reid, the British Linen Company representative in Tain, employed about eight hundred spinners, while in 1765 Sandeman reported that his business involved almost one thousand more.[3.14]

Most of the activity was confined to the initial stages of linen manufacture. Hecklers (or flax dressers) and spinners were common enough and by 1756 spinning was said to be as much practised in Easter Ross as in any part of Scotland. Indeed ten years later the industry was so well established that it was felt unnecessary to continue supporting it with government funds.[3.15]

But there were few engaged in the more advanced stages of manufacture and little profit accrued to the.majority who were involved. By 1766 the flax dressers had gained a monopoly on the importation and selling of flax. In fact they sold very little and issued most of it for spinning at low rates of pay for the quality of work they demanded. This situation remained much the same thirty years later. The middlemen, acting as agents for the southern companies, profited but the spinners made very little.[3.16]

Cheap labour, however, proved an incentive to growth, and the manufacturers of Perth and Edinburgh were joined by those of Aberdeen and Inverness in distributing flax to Easter Ross spinners.[3.17] Production in the late 1740s and early 1750s was double that of the preceding twenty years and by 1772 it had doubled again to reach a peak of over forty-five thousand yards. Throughout the third quarter of the eighteenth century the level of production remained on average about two and a half times greater than that in the period before 1746, although there were considerable fluctuations and the peak of 1772 was not surpassed, at least before the start of the Napoleonic wars.[3.18] Easter Ross was never one of the major centres of linen production but from 1727 it maintained its share of the total quantity of linen produced in Scotland until the onset of increasing industrial centralisation in the 1780s. As late as 1783 it was said that the earnings from spinning had saved many from starvation during the period of famine.[3.19] For most of the period the combined total production of Ross and Cromarty (almost all of it concentrated on the area of Easter Ross) placed these two counties in the middle rank of Scottish counties for the quantity of linen made. It is noticeable, however, that the monetary value of the linen produced in Ross and Cromarty was below the average for Scotland as a whole.[3.20] This was largely due to the lack of finishing in Easter Ross products and also to the fact that those finished articles which were produced were of the cheapest sort.

Although the linen industry in Easter Ross largely remained throughout the eighteenth century one of partial production — articles being made up in the south — there were some instances of more advanced development. The first bleachfield in the area was established in 1751 with assistance from the Board of Trustees for Manufactures. By 1755, £83 had been spent in laying out a bleachfield owned by Munro of Culcairn. The field was operated by Robert Munro, who had been trained as an apprentice at the famous Saltoun bleachfield in East Lothian. His successor in 1782, William Tait, had been one of the Board's apprentices at Saltoun also and, by and large, the Culcairn field maintained a profitable existence until the end of the century, Tait obtaining a grant of £15 from the Board as late as 1791 for 'beetling' or beating machinery. Other fields were established subsequently, although they made little impact and had short lives.[3.21]

In addition to the usual spinning commitments, William Sandeman of Perth from 1764 also controlled a weaving establishment at Fortrose. It was supervised by Walter Provan, a weaver from Dundee, and had twelve looms, a house with a washing mill and a cylinder and heckling house.[3.22]

The major undertaking of the eighteenth century, however, was the erection in 1773, by George Ross, in Cromarty, of a factory to make sacking. Sixty-one looms were employed using hemp yarn to make flour bags, biscuit bags, wool sacks, hop bags, hammock stuff and tarpaulin stuff mostly for the London market. Ross advanced the whole money for the building, charging interest at five per cent, and the total capital outlay amounted to seven thousand pounds. Over two hundred people were employed inside the factory and there were never less than six hundred women spinning yarn for it in the surrounding countryside — mostly in the parishes of Nigg, Fearn and Tarbat.[3.23] The sharp drop in linen production from 1770 to 1779 may in part at least be due to the fact that many spinners changed to hemp. By 1781 production in Cromarty was running at the rate of one or two thousand yards of cloth per day and in 1792, in the parish of Fearn alone, the activity related to the Cromarty factory resulted in a circulation of four hundred pounds, making a significant contribution to the local economy.[3.24]

Although linen production reached its lowest point for over thirty years in 1790, the evidence suggests that the decline did not continue. Increasing competition from the south may have already begun to affect the industry in Easter Ross, but with the outbreak of the Napoleonic Wars in 1792 the situation changed for the better and certainly none of the commentators at the end of the eighteenth or the start of the nineteenth centuries saw any evidence of recession.[3.25] Indeed there were some indications of revival and continued progress. The main centres of Cromarty, Fortrose, Milntown, Tain and Dingwall all continued to participate in the industry, with work being channelled to the country spinners as before by agents for Aberdeen and Inverness companies.[3.26] By 1798 Milntown had added a weaving establishment to the existing organisation and at the same time, in the Black Isle, David Urquhart of Braelangwell erected a waulk mill and two lint mills.[3.27] There was expansion , too , in the production of hempen goods, for, during the war era, the Cromarty factory (owned since about 1787 by the London firm of Alex. Dyer, Emmett and Co., who now made up the bagging in London from the cloth manufactured at Cromarty) opened branches at Invergordon and Portmahomack. In the year 1807, 185 tons of hemp were imported and approximately ten thousand pieces of bagging, valued at twenty-five thousand pounds, were exported from Cromarty.[3.28] On a very much smaller scale, the farmers of Avoch continued to raise hemp and manufacture it into sails and nets, not only for the local fishermen but for those in Caithness and Lochbroom as well.[3.29]

The wartime boom was the last flourish of the textile industry in Easter Ross, however, and peace brought a fairly rapid decline. Linen production (apart from the Cromarty factory) in the early 1820s was no higher than that of a hundred years earlier, while at Cromarty the value of output just about halved in the fifteen years after 1807.[3.30] As late as 1831 there were still two hundred employees in Cromarty but by 1844 the number had dropped to ninety, and by that date the branch factories at Invergordon and Tarbat had failed. The mechanised production lines centralised in the large cities proved too much for local industry in the end, and whereas at the start of the period a workman had moved to Easter Ross from Dundee, towards the close some of the workers in the Cromarty factory followed their industry's geographical contraction back to Dundee.[3.31]

Throughout the eighteenth and early nineteenth centuries a number of attempts were made to introduce a woollen industry, the most interesting being the establishment of a stocking factory on the Balnagown estates by the factor in the 1770s and the construction of a mill for carding wool, and jennies for spinning it, by David Urquhart of Braelangwell around 1800.[3.32] By 1850 these lesser activities had also long since ceased.

While it lasted, the textile industry was of considerable value to the local economy. It provided the hard-pressed farming community with an additional source of revenue which could make the difference between life and death in years of really bad harvests. It was also of great importance in being one of the mainstays of the small merchant community: a community which so distinguished the area from surrounding territories.

Lack of a strong local market and of locally funded support, combined with external control and the concentration on low-quality goods, made the industry's contraction and demise almost a foregone conclusion, but the inevitability of its doom can be over-emphasised. Stronger local support might, at the least, have postponed the decline.

b. Distilling and Brewing

The other major industry to make an impact on Easter Ross was that of distilling. In some ways its history provides an interesting contrast with that of the linen industry, for, whereas linen received major government encouragement, the stills largely survived despite all the efforts of officialdom; where linen was a major employer distilling was not, but while the stills relied heavily on local produce, the linen manufacturers did not. It is not surprising then that the chronological development of the two industries should be very different.

The beginnings of Highland distilling are lost but the industry had obviously been known in the area for many centuries. The first major development in Easter Ross, however, came in 1689 when Forbes of Culloden obtained a farm of the excise duties on his estate of Ferintosh for a yearly payment of four hundred merks Scots, in recompense for the devastation to his property caused by the Jacobite rebels.[3.33] Since the local producers were no longer subject to the ordinary state controls there was an immediate boom, and as early as 1703 the privilege had to be restricted to spirits distilled from grain grown only on the Ferintosh estate because of the protests of local landowners. Attempts to charge excise on the product of imported grains was largely unsuccessful and by 1761 grain was being brought to Ferintosh not only from the neighbouring districts but even from the most distant parts of Scotland.

Although private and illegal distilling was widespread in the rest of Easter Ross in the middle of the eighteenth century, legal stills do not seem to have been common. Presumably licensed distillers could not compete with the privileged position of Ferintosh. In any event, as the century progressed Ferintosh became increasingly important and in 1781, when the average annual production was approaching twice the level of twenty years earlier, there was an outcry from Lowland distillers against the flood of whisky produced in Ferintosh which was finding its way into southern markets. For a payment of little more than seventy pounds Forbes of Culloden was making a profit of around six hundred pounds a year. In 1782 it was calculated that the hundred thousand gallons and more of whisky produced in Ferintosh would have had to pay duties of around twenty thousand pounds if these had been charged. At this time, too, there was an increasing penetration of the English market, especially in London where a warehouse specifically for Ferintosh spirits was opened. The final straw came with the construction of a large distillery at Ferintosh in or about 1782 by a company of gentlemen and merchants which, in six months, distilled well over five thousand gallons of spirits — far more than the usual small Highland stills.[3.34] Several attempts had already been made by the government to buy out the privilege and in 1786 action was finally taken, Forbes of Culloden receiving a compensatory payment of twenty thousand pounds.[3.35]

Nothing was done for the local population who had been engaged extensively in the industry. It was the normal Highland practice at this time for distilling to be a part-time occupation, largely for women, but in Ferintosh, it was said, around a thousand people had been wholly engaged in the trade and few men had been left to cultivate the land. These people suffered a serious drop in their standard of living as a result of the revocation, and although some assistance was forthcoming from the landlord, many people were forced to leave the area and seek employment elsewhere. There was a considerable demand for their skills from distillers in other parts and for a time there was a decrease in the parish population.[3.36]

This setback appears only to have been temporary, however, for by 1792 there were twenty-nine licensed stills in the parish of Urquhart and considerable quantities of barley were once more being imported. The revocation of the excise privilege, moreover, seems to have benefited the rest of the area, for in the last decade of the eighteenth century licensed stills were to be found in the parishes of Kiltearn, Fearn, Kilmuir, Knockbain, Resolis, Avoch and Killearnan. In Kilmuir and neighbouring parishes two thirds of the barley crop was distilled and the general importance of the industry lay not so much in the numbers of men employed in it but in its importance as a market for the local grain crop.[3.37]

The products of the stills also satisfied a local demand, for by the later eighteenth century spirits were the staple drink of the poorer classes. It is hard to tell for how long this situation had lasted. It has been argued that until the middle of the eighteenth century the common drink in the Highlands was ale, and it is true that in 1755 there were eight brewers and no commercial stills in Newtarbat barony, but the number of prosecutions for illegal distilling and the growth of Ferintosh even before its whisky became widely known in the south suggests that there had long been a steady market for spirits in the area.[3.38]

The mash residue from distilleries was also available as a foodstuff for stock although this was not so useful in the north, where stills were small, as in the south. The advantages of distillery refuse as a feedstuff were denied by one opponent of Highland distilleries who contended that the farmers would do far better to give the grain in its original condition to their underfed beasts. But the system as it operated, while it may have reduced the protein value of the animal feedstuffs, did allow the farmers to get a cash return on their crops before recycling them through their stock.[3.39]

Despite its considerable local importance the distilling industry was very poorly organised. Outside Ferintosh the stills were usually run as a sideline by local farmers who, in consequence, were unable to give their full attention to either occupation.[3.40] Lack of specialisation bedevilled the Easter Ross economy throughout the period, and its effects are nowhere more evident than in the production of whisky. Small farmers generally lacked the capital to run a distillery adequately — even the small stills of thirty to forty gallons which were the rule — and the constant cash shortage forced them to sell their produce at uneconomic prices. Even those who had capital were unable to take advantage of it in a market which was constantly over-supplied.[3.41]

Matters were made a great deal worse by generally well-meaning but badly misdirected government interference. Before 1786 the legislation in force made it practically impossible to operate a legal still in the Highlands because the minimum scale of operations permitted was above the level which was economic in Highland conditions of shortage of grain and limited markets.[3.42] While these drawbacks did not operate to the same extent in Easter Ross, a relatively low population was a disincentive to legal stills. At the same time legislation was not strictly enforced in the area during most of the eighteenth century and the 1784 act abolishing duty on distilled spirits and low wines made evasion of dues even easier.[3.43]

In 1786 a new system based on a theoretical maximum production was introduced with different rates in the Lowlands and the Highlands (to which latter district Easter Ross was assigned). The Highland district also benefited by the remittance of most of the duty on malt — because of the generally inferior quality of Highland grain. With the abolition of the Ferintosh privilege at the same time, the number of licensed stills in Easter Ross increased, but they were unable to take full advantage of the unusual situation in the district as an arable area in the generally non-arable Highlands because the size of stills in the Highland district was legally limited and Highland distillers were prevented from selling their produce in the south.[3.44] While these regulations could not be completely enforced, the effort involved in circumventing them was completely unproductive and the limitation on size prevented the development of specialisation in a district which was in many ways suited to the rise of distilleries.

With the start of the Napoleonic wars legislative interference became very much worse and for a couple of years from 1795-7 distilling was forbidden altogether because of a grain shortage. Greater attempts were made to enforce the law for a time, and duties were regularly increased until in 1814 all duties within Scotland and between Scotland and England were equalised. At the same time the small stills which had formerly been permitted in the Highlands were forbidden.[3.45] The Highland distillers had never had an opportunity to build up the capital necessary for large-scale undertakings even if these would have been profitable under equal competition from more favourably located establishments, and many were forced to close.[3.46]

At a time of agricultural recession, when markets for grain were hard to find, this provided a golden opportunity to smugglers who entered upon their golden age. Landlords, unwilling to see reductions in rent, seized on the only chance offered to obtain high prices for crops and turned a blind eye to illegal activities. A government commission investigating the problem reported in 1823 that

> The punishment of delinquents under the excise laws, except in cases of magnitude, is left to the justices of the peace. In this county scarcely one legal sentence has been passed during many years.[3.47]

Indeed a local farmer remarked:

> to such an extent has the evil of smuggling arrived, that I am confident the records

of the Excise can furnish instances (with reverence be it spoken) of some of our Presbyterian clergymen being engaged in the nefarious and disgraceful traffic.[3.48]

The activities of the smugglers increased to such an extent that they supplied almost the whole market in the area. Mackenzie of Gairloch, it was said, never drank any but smuggled whisky.[3.49]

Most of the illegal stills, however, were not actually located in Easter Ross, where the countryside was generally too open to afford suitable locations for their concealment, but on the Highland fringes nearby, although the Black Isle, with its tradition of small stills, seems to have been a hot bed of smuggling.[3.50] More than ever, the importance of the industry lay not in the activity it engendered but in the market it offered to farmers, large and small. Even the Sheriff of Ross was known to send carts of grain up to twenty miles to the smugglers' stills while, according to a Mr. Mackenzie of Midfern by Bonar Bridge in his evidence to a government commission, William Murray, bank agent and merchant in Tain and the factor on the Balnagown estates, benefited both ways: sending barley to the stills at Ardgay and being 'a great protector of smugglers, who are good customers to his shop'.[3.51]

Within two years of the 1814 act its obvious failure led to further legislation. Small stills were once more permitted in the Highlands but as the same rate of duties continued to be exacted throughout Scotland, strenuous attempts by local lairds to encourage licensed stills (the number rose from one in 1814 to five in 1818) met with little success and the very frequency with which the regulations were changed led to disillusionment amongst those, such as Munro of Teaninich, who had attempted to work within the law. The continuing emphasis on malt duties as opposed to spirit duties was regarded as favouring the smugglers, and the high number of prosecutions for excise offences continued. In 1820 the duties on malt made solely from bear or bigg were reduced, and additional legislation in 1822 and 1823 further reducing the rates of duty and favouring a more liberal approach to the issue went a long way to reducing the attractions of illegal stills.[3.52] The writer in 1826 who thought that smuggling had already almost ceased in the Black Isle may have been rather optimistic, for the following year an extension had to be made to the jail in Dingwall — where excise offences were already believed to be more frequent than anywhere else in Scotland — to cope with the increased numbers jailed for smuggling.[3.53] But as the alternative markets for agricultural produce increased in the late twenties and thirties the financial attractions of the smuggling trade rapidly diminished and by 1840 illegal distilling in Easter Ross had ceased to be a problem.[3.54] Although some licensed stills continued to operate — one was opened at Dalmore in 1839 and another at Morangie in 1843 — legal distillers never rose to occupy a position similar to that held by the smugglers in the early years of the century.[3.55]

Brewing was never a major industry in Easter Ross but breweries did exist throughout the period. The one at Morangie, which was converted to a distillery in 1843, was opened in 1738, while yet another of the improvements of George Ross of Cromarty was the construction of a brewery at Cromarty after 1772. The beer produced was intended to replace spirits as the local beverage but only became popular with the upper classes.[3.56]

Like the linen industry, distilling in Easter Ross never rose to a position where it could challenge the primacy of agriculture. Indeed one of its principal attractions to the local inhabitants was that it sustained and was sustained by the agricultural produce of the area, being another vital source of income to farmers struggling to make ends meet. The failure of the industry, in most instances, to rise above its part-time inheritance, condemned it to decline when the legal constraints affecting distilling throughout the country were altered. It is true that, for a time, the illegal side of the industry was a necessary prop to the local economy but distilling, as such, had little to offer Easter Ross in the way of long-term economic development.

c. Minor Industries

While linen and whisky were the only manufactured items to make a sustained impact on the Easter Ross economy between 1750 and 1850, several smaller industries rose to temporary significance. George Ross of Cromarty, who inherited the small estate of Pitkerry in the parish of Fearn and made a fortune in London as an army agent before purchasing Cromarty in 1772, was instrumental in introducing several of these lesser activities including a pig-curing station, a nail works and lace making.[3.57] After his death a rope works was opened at Cromarty and elsewhere tanning, snuff making and the manufacture of tiles were carried on, but many of these industries were short-lived and few ever expanded from supplying the local market to providing goods for export.[3.58] The processing of kelp had a longer life, lasting throughout the second half of the eighteenth century, but was pursued on a very small scale and is only of interest in that it was organised by William Forsyth, a local merchant, rather than by the landlords or southern entrepreneurs as on the west coast.[3.59] Towards the middle of the nineteenth century there was even an iron foundry opened in Tain, but by that time most of the other industries in the area had failed in competition with the output from the major centres of the south.[3.60]

Of the smaller industries only shipbuilding and quarrying became widespread in the area for any length of time. Based on locally grown timber, shipbuilding on a small scale flourished throughout the period. Construction seems to have reached a peak in the third and fourth decades of the nineteenth century but even before 1750 William Forsyth's first vessel had been built locally.[3.61] Sloops, schooners and barques all were built, with sizes ranging up to at least one hundred and twenty-three tons. Because locally grown timber was used, construction sites were scattered all along the Cromarty Firth and around the remaining coasts of the Black Isle, though not in Easter Ross proper where the coastline was less suitable and immediately accessible forests were fewer. Actual boatbuilding yards were found at a number of sites including Jemimaville, Cromarty and Avoch.[3.62]

Several attempts were made to exploit coal and iron deposits in Easter Ross. As early as 1764, John Williams was sent by the Trustees for Forfeited Estates to survey the Castle Leod estate for coal. When, to general disappointment, he found none, he extended his search throughout the county, but with an equal lack of success. Unfortunately, none of the deposits which were found, then or later, proved economically viable, and only quarrying for stone was developed commercially.[3.63] During the period of intensive agricultural improvement there was a fairly steady demand for stone for building and dyking. In addition, quarries in Avoch, Cromarty and Killearnan supplied materials for major projects, such as Fort George and the Caledonian Canal, and, on a more long-term basis, provided Inverness with most of its building material.[3.64]

Most of these minor industries are of some interest in showing how attempts were made to exploit local resources in order to broaden the economy and capitalise on local markets. They also reveal increasingly how difficult it was for local entrepreneurs to compete with larger competitors in the south as large-scale industrial techniques improved and better transport and increased commerce opened up Easter Ross to the outside.

d. Towns, Commerce and Trade

Although they all had some minor industries, the towns of Easter Ross were not, primarily, industrial centres, and, apart from being the largest local centres of population, the burghs had little to offer in the way of encouraging industrial growth. Indeed much of the industrial activity which occurred from 1750 to 1850 took place outside the three royal burghs of Dingwall, Tain and Fortrose; and Cromarty was already declining by the time that it was recreated a burgh.

The towns had more important roles to play as administrative and commercial centres and despite their small size they did contribute significantly to the general wellbeing of the area. Part of the administrative activity was self-engendered as each of the royal burghs had its town officers to serve the councils, but of more importance to the region as a whole was the role of each burgh in providing a home for the major church and civil courts. In addition, until 1839, the burgh prisons were expected to serve the surrounding areas as well as the towns themselves.[3.65] The town councils, although concerned with the internal affairs of the burgh, did provide a useful, if occasional, meeting place for the local gentry, as many lairds sat as councillors.[3.66] The attraction of councils for the landlords was largely political, for Dingwall and Tain combined with Dornoch, Wick and Kirkwall, and Fortrose with Inverness, Nairn and Forres to return members to parliament. The election of members was the responsibility of delegates appointed by the councils. So far as the towns were concerned the presence of prominent landowners on the council could be useful for prestige and for obtaining official positions for inhabitants. It was convenient, too, to have someone like Lord Ankerville, who regularly was resident in Edinburgh, on Tain Town Council, as he could represent the burgh at meetings of the Convention of Royal Burghs without the town incurring unnecessary expense.[3.67] In addition, if a landlord was on the town council he was less likely to encroach illegally on the burgh lands, as the lairds of Cadboll, Aldie and Mounteagle were accused of doing by the council of Tain in 1797.[3.68] Of course, legalised robbery of town lands was practised regularly by councillors but at least the towns got financial recompense for the loss in these instances.

In theory the landlords played a prominent role in burghal affairs. In Tain, for example, there were usually six or seven lairds on the fifteen-strong council, the number rising in 1808 to a majority of eight. But apart from the provostship the other official posts of Dean of Guild,

Treasurer and Bailies almost always were held by townsmen and, in practice, the landlords attended very few council meetings, except those involving local or parliamentary elections.[3.69] It is clear that the major despoliation of the burghs' properties carried out in the later eighteenth and early nineteenth centuries was for the benefit of townsmen as much as for the landlords.[3.70]

Normally the county town had an even more important administrative function than other burghs, but while the centres of two counties were located in Easter Ross there was not a county town as such for most of the period. The administrative centre for the county of Cromarty was Cromarty, which became a parliamentary burgh only in 1833, its earlier status as a burgh of barony having lapsed in 1747.[3.71] The act creating the county of Ross unfortunately had failed to specify which burgh would act as the county town although, from the start, Tain, as the centre of the most populous and wealthy district, and Dingwall, as the most centrally located burgh for the county as a whole, were regarded as the main contenders. For most of the eighteenth century the principal legal officers of the county were resident in or near Tain. In particular, Macleod of Geanies, the Sheriff of Ross from 1774 to 1837, had his seat only a few miles from the town, and his local partiality strengthened the existing dominance of the burgh in terms of size and wealth. From 1733 to 1826 ninety-two of the ninety-six head courts of the county were held at Tain and during that time the Sheriff Clerk of Ross had his residence in the town.[3.72] As the other districts of the county increased in prosperity and as transport facilities improved, the central location of Dingwall increased its importance and the position was finally resolved by an act of 1843 which declared Dingwall to be the county town.[3.73]

To some extent the administrative role of the burghs engendered a social function. The councils acted occasionally as a meeting place for those lairds who were elected to them, while head courts, meetings of the justices of the peace and similar occasions brought together a wider selection of the landed interest. The lower classes were attracted to the towns by the fairs and markets whose social function remained important even when their economic significance had begun to decline. As Angus Bethune commented in 1837, 'at these [fairs] the country people assemble in great numbers, partly because they still have somewhat of the character of festivals, (which the term "fèil" in Gaelic imports), but chiefly owing to the force of confirmed habit, since all that can be purchased at the fairs may be had quite as conveniently in town at any time.'[3.74]

At Tain, where a masonic lodge was in existence from at least 1761, the regularity of social events was such as to lead to the construction of an assembly room towards the end of the eighteenth century,[3.75] and Tain and Fortrose, at least, attracted as residents ex-colonials and half-pay or retired soldiers and sailors because of the educational facilities and general attractions.[3.76] But socially the burghs of Easter Ross were always greatly overshadowed by Inverness, which towards the end of the eighteenth century had such attractions as a theatre and the widely popular Northern Meeting to draw the gentry from much of the Highland area.[3.77] In consequence few of the landlords of Easter Ross ever resided in the towns of the region.

Inverness also dominated the other burghs as a service and commercial centre although its stranglehold of the seventeenth and early eighteenth centuries was gradually relaxed. In addition to the rivalry of Inverness, the three Easter Ross burghs had to face commercial competition from local villages and fairs. Cromarty was in a class of its own as a commercial and trading centre but even the small villages, such as Milntown, which had no more than twelve families in 1777, and Avoch, had some commercial activity, while completely rural areas were served by regular fairs.[3.78] The fairs were active throughout the eighteenth century but soon after 1800 their usefulness diminished as the number of shops in towns and villages increased, and by the 1830s it was only the festival atmosphere which kept some fairs alive.[3.79] Of the country fairs, only the livestock markets retained an economic value in the second quarter of the nineteenth century.[3.80]

Even with the increase in numbers of shops in towns and villages, not all needs could be met locally. Sir George Mackenzie of Coull complained that

> in Dingwall, Tain, Cromarty and almost every village, shopkeepers are established. . . . The profits demanded for this convenience are indeed considerable, granting that good weight and fair measure are given, which may be reasonably doubted. But when every article appears to be of inferior quality, it is not to be wondered at that many families supply themselves with groceries, etc., from Edinburgh and London.[3.81]

Economic changes affected villages too at the turn of the eighteenth and nineteenth centuries. Until then most of the villages had been no more than the traditional 'ferm touns', those with greater pretensions having had a past history as burghs of barony.[3.82] With the spread of agricultural improvement the old 'ferm touns' disappeared but, to replace them, new estate villages were developed. The first of these had been planned as far back as the middle of the eighteenth century.

Sir John Gordon, the first landowner to pursue the idea of a planned village, was something of a phenomenon, even in an age of eccentrics. A man who could be tetchy and litigious with his peers, he was noted at the same time for his consideration to his tenants and for his warm regard for his family connections. The vigour with which he pursued these connections manifested itself equally whether he was upholding the interests of his brother-in-law, the last, forfeited Earl of Cromarty, in the area, or wearying another of his relations, the Lord Advocate, with endless and endlessly repetitious advice on the political state of the nation. His interest in improvement was strong and deeply felt, although it represented only one aspect of a multi-faceted character which is revealed in his fascinating, but tantalisingly brief, pocket book of 1754-59.[3.83]

This pocket book details his hopes for the village at the Ness of Invergordon which he was contemplating at the same time as he was preparing for a number of other building projects. The village, which he planned probably in association with John Adam who was fresh from a similar enterprise at Inveraray, went through a number of increasingly detailed stages on paper, starting off as basically little more than a settlement for fishermen and ferrymen, and ending up, not only as a village feued out for tradesmen, fishers and ferriers, but as a community with a public house, a pier with a crane, a smithy, a common kiln, a granary, stocks and a 'well above which a balcony and cross for arms or colours or holding markets'.[3.84] The granary was to be decked out with a cupola, a vane, a clock, an enclosure, ventilators, a railed staircase and another crane, while, associated with the village were to be a lumber yard for timber, slate and coal, a stell (or fixed net) fishery and, possibly, a bleaching field and waulk mill.

As if this were not enough, Sir John envisaged, almost from the start and a mere nine years after the last Jacobite Rebellion, that the village should serve also as a holiday resort. He proposed erecting a boat house for pleasure boats and swithered between a cold bath or bathing machines based on those at Scarborough or Harwich.

Needless to say the plans proved more ambitious on paper than on the ground. Although he liked to daydream, Sir John was no fool and in 1759 he set down firmly the proposed order of activities with the aim first of having 'plans and estimates of everything propos'd and then to go on gradually as can be done without running on debt.'[3.85]

A quarter of a century later, by the time of his death, only a fraction of what he had proposed had been fulfilled. Single feus had been granted to a tailor, a ferrier and two wrights and three feus to a mariner, but of the bathing machines there was no further mention and, despite the granting of further feus in 1793, the village may not have amounted to much by the end of the century.[3.86]

After Invergordon, other villages inevitably appear as something of an anticlimax, but they were far from being devoid of interest. Milntown, a long-standing burgh of barony and, despite its small size, a centre, not only for the Newtarbat estate, for which it had a court house and prison in 1755, but, at least by the last quarter of the eighteenth century, for a much larger area of the surrounding countryside,[3.87] appears to have been re-planned in 1786, perhaps by James Maclaren, the architect of Newtarbat House. To what extent the 1786 plans were followed is now uncertain but several of the feus were taken up immediately and the existing community, a green village which is almost English in atmosphere, still has the appearance of a planned settlement, rather than a place resulting from organic growth.[3.88]

Soon after 1800 several new villages were established. Alness was laid out on nine hundred and ninety-nine year leases by Captain Munro of Teaninich. This was soon followed by Evanton which, being created to replace the old ferm toun of Drummond by the new owner of Balcony, Mr Fraser, around 1800, remains today an attractive example of a well planned, regularly laid out estate village.

If the larger and more interesting new villages were founded in Ferindonald and Easter Ross, the Black Isle was not without some representative examples. More or less contemporary with Alness and Evanton were Charlestown and Jemimaville, the latter named by George Munro in 1822 in honour of his wife Jemima Poyntz, an heiress whose money enabled him to create the village and introduce other improvements on the estate of Ardoch which, in consequence, he renamed Poyntzfield.[3.89] Conon Bridge developed as a village housing workers on the new bridge over the Conon, while Invergordon received a boost with the construction of a pier after 1818.[3.90] The old village of Culbockie was regularised and expanded before 1833.[3.91] The estate villages were intended to house agricultural workers as well as tradesmen, and following the enlargement of farms large numbers of unemployed labourers settled in the villages of the district.[3.92]

The towns, too, attracted their quota of evicted tenants, Dingwall, in particular, growing rapidly in the early nineteenth century.[3.93] But the towns had long been service centres, not only for Easter Ross but also for much of the North-West Highlands. When Ullapool was being laid out by the British Fisheries Society, for example, amongst those employed were masons from Dingwall and William Cowie, a builder and carpenter, and David Aitken, a surveyor, both from Tain.[3.94] Until towards the end of the eighteenth century banking services and purchases of fine furniture, clothes and books had to be obtained in Inverness or Edinburgh, but for more staple commodities the shops and merchants in Easter Ross sufficed and even some of the more sophisticated services were available.[3.95] Dingwall, as has been indicated, had a large band of lawyers, principally because of the business generated by infringements of the excise laws, while Tain was well supplied with surgeons. Between them the two towns offered gunsmiths, silversmiths and wigmakers whose products were purchased by the local gentry and others who could afford them.[3.96]

Despite the undoubted poverty and restricted size of the burghs of Easter Ross, the opinion of Knox in 1784 that they were 'nothing more than ruinous villages exhibiting all the symptoms of decay poverty and distress'[3.97] was not an accurate reflection of the current situation. By the last quarter of the eighteenth century, the growth of the linen industry and agricultural improvements, and the additional trade they generated, had stimulated growth in the local towns. As early as 1764 Cromarty, which was not even a burgh, was booming, as a result of linen and the herring fishing, while the Dingwall Town Council minutes reveal a state of steady if not spectacular progress. In 1765, in an attempt to improve the hygiene and appearance of the place, channels were ordered to be dug to drain away surplus water. In the 1770s drinking water was piped in, a weekly Friday market established, new roads proposed and a new steeple at the town house embellished with a clock, the gift of a Major General Scott during a parliamentary election in 1772.[3.98]

All these public works threw the burgh into debt, but activity continued into the 1780s with an extension of the water system and the feuing of forty-foot plots of land in Kirk [now Church] Street — presumably for the construction of additional housing. Andrew Wight, who seems to have been a more reliable critic than Knox, provided an alternative outside view in 1781 when he reported that Dingwall was thriving.[3.99]

A similar situation prevailed in Tain where, in 1787, Macleod of Geanies feued a new suburb on land which was built up rapidly in the following years.[3.100]

The influence of all the towns on the agricultural rents in their immediate environs, and their importance as markets for local products, are further indications of their economic importance in and to the area.[3.101]

The nineteenth century saw a marked expansion of commercial activity in the towns. Rising population, improved communications and increased wealth all encouraged growth. Branches of Edinburgh and later, Inverness banks were opened and the quantity and quality of goods on offer improved markedly so that by 1837 the commercial dominance of Inverness had largely been eroded.[3.102]

In other respects, too, improvements occurred. Although Fortrose may have made little progress, Dingwall cleansed itself of its previous dirty image, laid out a new street, renewed its pavements and water system and by 1842 had introduced gas lighting.[3.103] Tain continued to grow also. A new jail and court house were built in 1825, gas lighting was introduced in 1839 and a town constable was appointed in 1840.[3.104]

While the towns shared throughout the period in the export trade as well as in internal commerce, the burghs no longer maintained even the theoretical monopoly they had claimed in earlier times and, as with industry, trade was not restricted by administrative boundaries. Indeed Tain, hampered by the lack of a harbour, hardly participated in external trade.

Before the arrival of the railways almost all long-distance trade from the north of Scotland was conducted by sea. The only major exception was the cattle trade, the live animals being driven on the hoof to the markets in the south, but cattle exports were not a significant element in the economy of Easter Ross. To some extent trade concentrated at the best harbours — best because they offered the most shelter or because they were the most centrally situated — but from at least the early eighteenth century it was customary for any suitable beaching point to become a centre for export, as indicated by the existence of estate girnals, or granaries, at such places as Foulis Point; and, by the start of the nineteenth century a large number of small piers around the shores of the firths became focal points for trade.[3.105]

Even before 1750 William Forsyth had recognised the advantages of Cromarty and had commenced trading with the South of Scotland, England and Holland, although the level of trade remained low until a harbour was built by George Ross of Cromarty with financial assistance from the government.[3.106] By 1794 London traders alone carried one hundred thousand pounds worth of goods yearly to the four northern counties of Scotland, and much of this was deposited at Cromarty which acted as an entrepôt port for the surrounding smaller harbours.[3.107]

With the construction of harbours of Portmahomack and Invergordon in the early nineteenth century, these two ports rose rapidly to rival Cromarty.[3.108] Portmahomack was well placed to cater for the needs of the area around Tain and by 1840 had one hundred and twelve vessels totalling almost seven thousand tons using it.[3.109] Invergordon was so centrally situated that it captured much of the trade that had previously gone to Cromarty. Indeed, although the decline in the fishing and textile industries also contributed largely to Cromarty's increasing poverty, to observers at the time the main cause of stagnation was the loss of trade. In 1843 Cromarty was seen as 'a miserable place in the last stages of decay . . .' while Invergordon was 'a large village-town rising very fast into importance — as fast indeed as Cromarty is going down; it being the cause'.[3.110]

While much of the trade was organised and conducted by southern merchants using southern ships and often dealing directly with the customer in Easter Ross,[3.111] a proportion of business was won by traders operating in the Moray Firth area. In the eighteenth century, particularly, Findhorn and Portsoy appear to have been the leading centres of local trade, with the merchants of these ports purchasing and freighting local produce to external markets.[3.112] Nor were Easter Ross participants excluded. William Forsyth, who spent a year in a London counting house in 1738, was a leading businessman in the North of Scotland in the later eighteenth century, using his own ships to trade and maintaining a useful connection with Newcastle through his brother, who had settled there as a merchant. Hugh Miller has left a sympathetic and interesting pen portrait of Forsyth in his *Tales and Sketches*.[3.113] Miller's own father, who also operated a ship from Cromarty — skippering it himself — generally confined himself to trading in the Moray Firth but was known also to carry cargoes wider afield, such as kelp from the Hebrides to Leith.[3.114]

The pork trade of the early nineteenth century was revived by an Englishman, George Middleton, who settled in Cromarty around 1800 and who had a good knowledge of the London market. Indeed, well into the nineteenth century local boats were engaged in freighting goods to and from the south, although, by that time, with the advent of southern-based steam transport, their contribution to the total volume of trade must have been small.[3.115]

As the southern areas of Britain increased their control of the means of trade, so too they became more important as markets. Not only did the economy of Easter Ross become more dependent upon trade in the nineteenth century than it had been in the eighteenth, but the direction of that trade changed. William Forsyth, having initially begun trading with the continent, latterly concentrated almost exclusively on Leith, Newcastle and London, while the export of grain to Hamburg by Macleod of Cadboll, which may have been uncommon in the eighteenth century, was unheard of a century later, when the rapid expansion of urban centres in the south made it unnecessary to look elsewhere for markets.[3.116]

Throughout the period, the products traded varied very little, although the quantities of each product changed a great deal. In the middle of the eighteenth century small amounts of grain, mostly barley and oats, and a little linen constituted the greatest part of the area's output. As the century progressed the quantity of grain grown for export slowly increased, linen and other textiles expanded rapidly and some diversification took place into cured pork and barrelled fish,[3.117] but it was only after 1800 that the major boom in exports took place. The pork trade was valued at £30,000 in 1819, the amount of timber exported from 1810 to 1817 was estimated to have fetched as much again, and fish curing was undertaken on an altogether new scale.[3.118] The export of textiles, it is true, declined fairly steeply after the end of the Napoleonic wars, but the trade in grain continued to expand until the middle of the century.[3.119]

While much of this expansion was due to the increased production of wheat, sales of barley and oats were also greater than ever. Exports of grain from Cromarty and Portmahomack to other parts of Scotland alone rose from 6,214 quarters in 1827 to 25,099 quarters in 1836, and by the latter date Cromarty was the sixth largest exporting port in Scotland in this trade. Of the total exported from 1827 to 1836 wheat accounted for seventy-four per cent but in that period, while wheat exports rose by 298 per cent, barley exports increased by only a little less at 256 per cent and oats by a staggering 709 per cent.[3.120]

In contrast to the basic commodities and roughly finished processed articles exported, the imports always consisted of high-quality manufactured goods and luxury articles, plus commodities which were not available in Easter Ross itself. In bulk these commodities were the greatest imports, at least in the nineteenth century. By 1800 Sunderland lime was being widely used and coal was greatly in demand due to the exhaustion of local supplies of fuel and the repeal of transport duties.[3.121] As the North-East of England, which supplied most of the lime and coal, needed timber for pit props and grain for a growing population, a useful and substantial two-way trade developed.[3.122] While linen was manufactured, large quantities of flax had to be imported also and by 1808 one hundred and eighty-five tons of hemp a year were being brought in for the factory in Cromarty.[3.123]

At the start of the period wines, fine clothes, high-quality furniture and other manufactured articles were regularly imported for the upper classes.[3.124] With the spread of large farms and the increasing wealth of the towns, demand was increased for these items and for improved agricultural implements from the south, while by 1850 mass-produced goods from the large conurbations had largely displaced the locally made goods even amongst the lower classes.[3.125]

e. Transport

Much of the economic advance of Easter Ross from 1750 to 1850 could be attributed to improvements in transport, for during the century a great deal was done to better communications both internally and externally. Contemporary accounts of the state of the roads in the area around 1750 differ quite markedly, although to some extent the differences may be more important than real. If Burt is to be believed, there were no roads at all in the Highlands north of Inverness in the 1720s, while an inspector for the Commissioners of Forfeited Estates found in 1766 that there was very little in the way of road-making in Ross-shire because the common people regarded statute labour as an oppression.[3.126]

Yet roads are clearly marked in Roy's map of the area in 1747, and in 1755 the factor for the Commissioners of Forfeited Estates at Newtarbat found the roads in Easter Ross good and communications between Milntown and Tain easy. In Cromarty statute labour was regularly used, even if it was opposed in Ross.[3.127]

To some extent the contrast in the evidence may be explained by the fact that the commentators criticising the state of the roads were speaking of a far wider area than Easter Ross and in consequence made generalisations which may not have applied uniformly — it is even possible that Burt did not consider part, or all of, Easter Ross to be in the Highlands. It is also true that while the roads that did exist may have been good by the standards of the time there were not nearly enough of them. Those who lived near the main post road from Beauly to Tain, or the few other major thoroughfares, were well served but the farmers in the straths of Ferindonald, for example, had no roads within miles.

Overall, however, the standard of communications in the area seems to have been better than might have been expected. As so often is the case, reports from a distance exaggerated the awfulness of northern conditions and Bishop Forbes was warned about the dreadful condition of Ross-shire roads before he set off on a pastoral visit to his Episcopal congregation in 1762. It was with pleasurable surprise, therefore, that he was able to record that the roads in the area though 'only natural [were] extremely good.'[3.128] The maintenance of the roads is even more surprising as the area was not one which received attention from the military following the Jacobite rebellions. The only military road in Ross-shire was that running from Poolewe to the east coast. It is first mentioned in 1761 and was officially known as the Contin to Poolewe road. Pennant, however, refers to it as the Inverness to Poolewe road and it may be that military assistance on the road from Inverness to Dingwall, mooted in 1757 and promised in 1764, was forthcoming.[3.129] However this may be, the road to the west of Contin was not maintained for long. Annual repairs, using statute labour, were made for a decade from 1770, but after 1780 nothing further was done.[3.130]

In 1771 the Commissioners of Supply for Ross-shire began a major expansion of the roads in the county which, in the course of the next thirty years, led to the construction of six hundred miles of roads.[3.131] While some of this mileage may have been located in Wester Ross, the greater part of it would appear to have been in Easter Ross and, although no new techniques may have been adopted, the initiative begun in 1771 radically altered the communications system in the region.

Critics remained and John Knox, the London bookseller turned economic expert, was particularly scathing, claiming that on the east coast of the Northern Highlands 'the want of good roads and bridges proves an insurmountable impediment to the improvements of the country, particularly in agriculture; keeps the natives at a distance from each other, in a state of nature, and the most abject poverty.'[3.132] Knox's main interest, however, was in the west coast and much of his information about the east coast may have been secondary. Secondary or not, it was evidently inaccurate. In 1781 a more thorough observer, Andrew Wight, found the roads on which he travelled in Easter Ross to be well made and generally good, and by 1795 Sir John Sinclair was of the opinion that there were few roads in Britain which, lacking the benefits of turnpikes, were better made.[3.133] Roads in some districts remained poor but major surveys were made of some of the leading roads in the last decade of the eighteenth century and by 1806 improved highways were fairly general.[3.134]

Much of the credit for this improvement must go to Macleod of Geanies, the Sheriff of Ross, who was noted for his enthusiasm for road-building and whose own road-building activities on occasion led him into dispute with his neighbours.[3.135] He was active not only in the promotion of public roads but also in the construction of private ones and it was the improvement of private roads that was most necessary for a general advance. The major through routes might be well kept, but until the local inhabitants had ready access to them they served little purpose. Indeed one reason why the main roads generally were well maintained was probably because of the limited amount of traffic using them. The old private roads were mere tracks and that from Geanies to Fearn and Cromarty was described in 1774 as 'no other than so many ridges of arable ground which the late Cadboll secured'.[3.136] By 1771 Geanies was making these roads fit for wheeled traffic and while, even by 1797, this was not yet general, there was an undoubted increase in the number and quality of private as well as public roads.[3.137]

The construction and repair of public roads in Easter Ross during the eighteenth century was financed solely by a small levy on property owners. The standard rate in Cromarty was ten pence sterling for every hundred pounds Scots of valued rent, which brought in the princely sum of five pounds six shillings sterling.[3.138] The county of Ross was rather better provided, for when, in 1771, the roads programme was begun, fifty pounds sterling was devoted to the Black Isle alone and it was agreed to spend twenty pounds sterling a year thereafter on the same area until roads were made over every part of it.[3.139]

This money was used to pay for the tools used by the statute labourers on the roads and for the wages of the overseers who supervised them. William Forsyth who was, amongst so many other things, a superintendent of the Cromarty roads, spent the 1766 levy, for example, on the purchase of four new wheelbarrows mounted with iron, four pick axes mounted with steel and twelve strong double spades.[3.140]

No record remains of exactly how the roads were made but certainly the parish roads did not receive much attention, and prior to 1807 none of them in Ross-shire had ever been metalled.[3.141] They were formed only by small ditches thrown up on either side, but although they could be almost impassable in wet weather they generally served the limited needs of the area well enough before agricultural improvements took place.

Greater care was obviously taken with the major roads, Sir John Sinclair recommending the methods used in the Black Isle to people in the south, and at least one overseer was enthusiastic enough in the improvements of 1771 not only to attempt to straighten the line of his road but also to make it twenty-four feet wide instead of the statutory twenty.[3.142] By 1801 it was not only the road surfaces which were receiving attention. Almost every crossroads on the Black Isle was marked with a direction post, a practice which was unusual outside populous areas and not standard even within them.[3.143]

Towards the end of the eighteenth century increasing pressure on the roads put an even greater strain on the statute labour system. Before 1790 almost all statute labour had been exacted in kind, but in 1794 a general county scheme of commutation was adopted with rates of one shilling and sixpence sterling for each man liable for labour per year and two shillings more for each plough of eight bolls rent and upwards in lieu of carts, carriages and horses. Once again the moving spirit was the Sheriff of Ross, but within a year the rates of conversion were found to have been fixed too low and the conviction grew that an Act of Parliament would be needed to tackle the problem.[3.144]

Whilst traffic remained light, the main hazards for maintenance were the elements, and in particular water. Numerous streams flowed from the rain-soaked hills of the west, causing problems of upkeep even when they were not large enough to make passage difficult. But once again the region was surprisingly well provided from an early date, although communications between Easter Ross and the rest of Scotland were made difficult by the absence of bridges over the rivers Beauly and Conon and the Dornoch Firth. Within the region itself the only major river which needed bridging in 1766 was the Aultgraad in the parish of Kiltearn and this was, in fact, tackled in 1777.[3.145] Elsewhere even minor streams were bridged, although on parish roads there were often only 'miserable wooden bridges put across the rivulets or water runs . . . which were frequently breaking down'.[3.146] Further bridges were built as part of estate improvements, and by 1791 existing bridges were being widened for the convenience of carriages.[3.147] All the public bridges were built and kept in repair by the counties as an additional charge upon the landowners and, unlike the roads, the bridges were attended to by skilled workmen.[3.148]

While the traffic which used these roads was light, it was not as small as might be expected from comments such as those by Knox. Agricultural produce generally was carried in bags on horseback in the eighteenth century — amongst the small farmers at any rate — a procession of seven or eight horses tied in a row being the standard means of carrying corn to the mill.[3.149] In January 1778, however, Mackenzie of Ardloch warned that even horses might not be available. If his request for victual were not met quickly, the grain, when it was supplied, would have to be carried on men's backs, as horses would be too weak after the winter to travel to the low country.[3.150]

This dependence on human and animal transport was partly because the road network was not extensive enough, but it was also due to the primitive nature of the carts used by the tenant farmers. There were three types of cart in common use. The most primitive was merely a sledge with a basket on top, while only a little better was the type in use at Culrane in the latter part of the century. Its wheels consisted of three six-inch diamater sticks fixed at the centre by the axle. Probably the commonest carts in use were those with solid wheels of about two and a half feet diameter. These carts were capable of carrying only very small quantities — less than a common wheelbarrow, it was said — and were used largely for the carriage of manure and peats.[3.151]

Increasingly, however, larger carts came into use. In 1791 in Kiltearn there were ten oxen wains and thirty box carts — more than double the number in use twenty years earlier — and by 1795 the large farm carts as used in the south were common amongst the gentry and large farmers.[3.152] To some extent this may have been due to the improvements on the roads carried out after 1771, although such carts could be used where there were no roads and represented part of the general improvement in agricultural practice then being introduced.

Well before the end of the century wheeled transport was causing difficulties in the towns. As early as 1766 all riding on horseback either with or without carts was forbidden in Fortrose.[3.153] Twelve years later the town cross in Tain had to be dismantled as it was proving to be an impediment to traffic, although by 1783 the council found parking a problem as they ordered the town officers to seize and destroy any carts found blocking the streets.[3.154]

More striking than the gradually increasing use of carts is the relatively rapid, if small-scale, growth in the number of carriages in the area. In 1740 an attempt by Lord Lovat to travel from Beauly to Edinburgh by coach had ended in the complete disintegration of the vehicle after a number of earlier breakdowns.[3.155] Few, if any, carriages were to be found in Easter Ross at that time, but from about 1770 they became more popular in the area. In that year a chaise was booked at Inverness to come to Ardullie in Kiltearn one day and return the next.[3.156] Only three years later the roads around Invergordon were good enough for Sir John Gordon to go for a ride in his chaise, merely to take the air. While such a journey might be dismissed as no more than another example of Sir John's eccentricity of character and concern with health, there was a reasonably extensive use of chaises by others in this part of the district in succeeding years.[3.157] Indeed by 1779 it was suggested that as an alternative to crossing the Moray Firth by boat, Robertson of Kindeace return from Nairn to Cadboll by chaise.[3.158] It is true that only fifteen wheeled carriages existed in the whole of Ross in 1785 but it may be reasonably assumed that all, or almost all, of these were in the Easter Ross area, and to that number must be added any belonging to residents of the county of Cromarty.[3.159] It is also clear that there was some use of carriages even by those who did not personally own one. Towards the end of the century the more intrepid explorers from the south were beginning to arrive by carriage and by this time local use was fairly widespread. In 1801 carriages were reported to cross Kessock Ferry regularly.[3.160]

The nineteenth century saw a major advance in road-building policy and techniques. Government assistance was given for the main routes and the maintenance of lesser roads was organised on a more efficient footing. In response to Telford's reports on the Highlands the government established in 1803 a Highland Roads and Bridges Commission to assist in the construction of roads. Local landlords could apply to the Commission for new roads and the Commission would then undertake a preliminary survey. If this proved favourable the landowners would deposit half the cost and a full-scale survey would be made, the Commission meeting all the remaining costs.[3.161] Under this system new roads were built and improvements were made to existing roads over much of the area, but the most important of the Commissioners' undertakings for Easter Ross was the construction of bridges across the

Conon in 1809 and the Beauly in 1811.[3.162] Along with the work done on improving roads south of Inverness, this opened up the region to the south. From 1812 to 1819 a total of over thirty-two thousand pounds was spent on the parliamentary roads, as they were called, a sum far in excess of any previous allocation.[3.163]

The original remit to the Commission was concerned only with the construction of roads and bridges, but in 1814 a further act was passed for the preservation and repair of these roads and bridges. Three quarters of the expense of repairs was to be met locally, but as this was likely to be too heavy for some counties a maximum assessment of one and a half pence in the pound was fixed.[3.164] The parliamentary roads were maintained under this system for the remainder of the period.

Before the county could raise the money for this level of expenditure, an act had to be passed in parliament. This was obtained in 1805 when it was stipulated that an assessment not exceeding four pence sterling and not less than three pence sterling in each pound Scots of valued rent could be levied in Ross and Cromarty (including Ferintosh), with life renters and heirs of entail having the right to charge the estate for payment. Within two years it was found that the revenue raised by this act did not allow the commencement of many works at one time, and in 1807 a further act was at last secured for the conversion of statute labour.[3.165] The act appointed a number of trustees and divided the county into nine districts, six of them covering the Easter Ross area. It was also decided to make the Dingwall to Tain road a turnpike with toll gates every six miles. Amendments were made to the act in 1810 but the tenant farmers remained dissatisfied with the whole conception for, whereas in Inverness half and in Moray one quarter of the assessment for roads was defrayed by proprietors, in Ross the whole payment was met by the tenants.[3.166] A proposal to double the assessment on farms rented at over one hundred pounds in 1813 was objected to, not because the tenants were opposed to the increase in principle but because they felt that the proprietors should pay a share of the total cost. The objection was unavailing, however, the levy being raised to six pence on all farms rented at over twenty pounds, and the tenants continued to pay the full assessment without having any say in the disposal of the monies raised.[3.167]

Further changes were made by the acts of 6 Geo IV c 110 and 9 Geo IV c 102, and the revised legislation continued to regulate the conduct of affairs until the close of the period. Rates were levied on proprietors to the extent of not less than four pence and not more than nine pence sterling in the pound Scots, with a further assessment of from two pence to nine pence to pay existing debts. Landlords were allowed to recover some of this outlay from their tenants to the extent of three pence in the pound sterling of real rent. Assessments were made by District Boards who also determined, with the final approval of the County Trustees, which roads to make and repair. Money raised in one parish could be spent in another and this was regarded as being superior to the system of parochial assessment prevalent in the south.

Although this arrangement was considered to be satisfactory in 1836,[3.168] and while there can be no doubt that it was a major improvement on any previous scheme, it was not a complete solution to the problems of road construction, because the county could not raise sufficient funds to undertake all the improvements desired. As early as 1812 a shortage of funds prevented the third district (comprising the parishes of Logie, Kilmuir and Rosskeen) from starting any new roads, and in the succeeding years much of the annual assessment went towards paying off interest on debts already incurred.[3.169] Shortage of capital amongst the tenants during these years meant that they often fell into arrears with their rates and at times they could only clear their debts by reverting to statute labour.[3.170] For those who were unable to work there was no escape, and it is recorded that in Resolis 'the blankets have been often taken off the beds of the old bed-ridden by the merciless exactors'.[3.171] Even towards the end of the period the road network was not complete and some parishes had few or no roads worthy of the name, while where parish roads did exist some remained unmade in the eighteenth century manner.[3.172]

Methods of road construction were greatly improved on the parliamentary and possibly some of the other major roads. The old twenty-foot width, including side drains and the green margin, was retained but the roads themselves were now made up of a foundation of four inches of unbroken stone and ten inches of gravel.[3.173] By contrast with most of the other Highland counties, it was found unnecessary to quarry for stone in Ross, the stones and gravel being obtained by or near the roads.[3.174]

While the improvements may have been limited and imperfect, they were substantial enough to allow a further growth in transport and, for the first time, regular services were provided by carriers. In 1808 the first carrier to begin a service further north than Dingwall started on the route between Inverness and Tain, and in the following year a diligence began the same journey.[3.175] With the completion of the parliamentary road through Caithness a mail coach began to run from Inverness to Thurso in 1819, and by 1821 a conveyance was running between Cromarty and Inverness once every ten days for the convenience of passengers going to London by sea.[3.176] A number of other coach services soon sprang up, although some of them operated only in the summer or at busy periods. By 1842 there was even a coach hire service at Kessock Ferry.[3.177] Private transport also increased. Munro of Allan had two carriages in 1814 as compared to one in 1785.[3.178]

Roads, even in an unimproved state, were not solely of economic value, particularly so far as the gentry were concerned. Joseph Mitchell recalled that the road from Dingwall to Tain

> facilitated social intercourse and Highland hospitality among the families, and no doubt in this limited circle there were many happy and jovial re-unions. Indeed, at the gates of Brahan Castle and Novar, and I believe at Foulis Castle, there were public houses called 'Talisaughs', for the accommodation of the retainers and horses of the guests.[3.179]

Economically the transport revolution facilitated agricultural developments both by improving internal farm efficiency and by allowing easier access to markets, while commercially it led to a considerable enlargement of the areas served by the towns. Dingwall, in particular, had its role as the market centre for the greater part of Wester Ross considerably enhanced, although it also was easier now to get from the small towns of Easter Ross to the far larger centre of Inverness.

The main impact of road improvements was on internal communications, but the links between Easter Ross and the rest of Britain were also improved as a result of changes in sea transport. Water had always been an important means of communication both between the various parts of the region and between the region as a whole and other districts, but before the nineteenth century the organisation of sea transport was very primitive. A pier had been built at Portmahomack by the first Earl of Cromarty but this had fallen into decay and there was no other man-made harbour in the region before the one at Cromarty was constructed in 1785 with a capacity for vessels of three hundred and fifty tons.[3.180] Vessels using other landfalls had to be beached at the most suitable point. This was bad enough for trading ships but at least they were only occasional callers.

The ferries which operated all the time (even, it appears, on Sundays) had to put up with the same conditions, and while this created few problems where the terrain was suitable, it meant at Invergordon, for example, that passengers sometimes had to mount their horses nearly quarter of a mile from the shore.[3.181] Despite such hazards numerous ferries continued to operate. In 1766 there were six within the bounds of the Presbytery of Chanonry and at least one other existed at Meikle Ferry near Tain.[3.182] None of them was satisfactory. That at Chanonry Ness could not take the passengers, horses and a chaise all in one journey in 1762, while in 1780 Sir John Gordon of Invergordon was forced to abandon the Invergordon ferry and go to Cromarty directly by boat. George Ross of Cromarty, whom Sir John intended to visit, had sent his carriage to Balblair, on the south side of the Invergordon ferry, to save Sir John the trouble of crossing and recrossing in his own carriage, but this plan had to be put aside as the ferry could not operate due to unfavourable winds and tides.[3.183] In 1795 all the ferries were considered to be in a wretched condition — a state which was attributed to their being in private ownership — and, even in the nineteenth century, accidents were liable to occur because of the inadequate state of the ferries then in use.[3.184]

On the other hand similar reports were made on ferries throughout the country and in 1819 Kessock Ferry, even in its unimproved state, was actually considered to be the best in Scotland.[3.185] Some improvements took place after 1800. Piers were built at Invergordon after 1818, and in the 1820s a steamboat ferry was introduced and piers and an inn were constructed at Kessock, but as late as 1825 passengers on the Cromarty ferry had to be carried ashore on a woman's back at the Nigg side.[3.186]

Improvements in other spheres were more marked. An act of 1806 transferred to the Commissioners for Highland Roads and Bridges the thirteen thousand pounds remaining from the restoration of the forfeited estates to their owners, and this money was used to build harbours in the Highlands.[3.187] In Easter Ross piers or harbours were financed at Portmahomack, Fortrose, Avoch, Chanonry and Invergordon. There was even a canal constructed at Dingwall in 1815, to allow small vessels to make their way through the mud flats at the head of the Cromarty Firth and up the River Peffer to Peter's Bridge, conveniently close to the centre of the town.[3.188] An eye-witness account of the laying of the foundation stone of the principal pier of the canal splendidly recaptures the excitement of the day. Miss Mackenzie, Inchvanie, whose life spanned the nineteenth century, recalled that

> It was a beautiful summer afternoon, and I think every man woman and child in the town turned out. Great numbers of people from the surrounding districts

> flocked to Dingwall, for it was understood that the making of the Canal was to benefit the trade of the whole district. . . . The Provost, Sandy Hilton (Alexander Mackenzie of Hilton), delivered a splendid speech, and I particularly recollect the tremendous cheering that followed the neat compliment he paid to the ladies, with their beautiful dresses and bonnets. The band of the Militia was there, and the Bailies. . . . In the evening there was great jollification. The leading gentlemen dined in James Ross's house, and you could hear the cheering at the other end of the town.[3.189]

The high hopes of the onlookers, sadly, were not to be realised. As early as 1819, Southey observed that the canal, which was little more than a mile long, had cost £3,800 to build and was being used at that time to export timber and grain and to receive lime and coal, 'has been finished about four years; but already thro' neglect the sea wall shews symptoms of decay, and the mud has lessened the depth of water three feet'.[3.190] Decline continued and the canal, being little used, never justified the expectations of its builders.

Rather more successfully, at the same period, private piers were erected at many other points to serve the interests of fishermen and traders. While many fishing boats and some trading vessels continued to use beaches rather than harbours, by 1850 the greatest number of the ships found in the area made use of the many harbours and piers available, particularly those of Invergordon, Cromarty and Portmahomack.[3.191]

Harbours had become more necessary as the number and size of ships visiting the area increased. In the middle of the eighteenth century the numbers were very small, and even in the 1770s small vessels from London arrived only once in every four or five weeks. Boats engaged in local trade were more frequent, of course. The construction of Fort George from 1747 to 1769 generated a quite considerable amount of activity, with boats being used to carry stone and timber for the building of the Fort itself and local produce for the soldiers engaged on the work of erection. When the boats were not being used for official purposes they could be diverted to carrying local grain or other goods to and from the south. John Adam claimed in 1758 that he had used between eighty and a hundred open boats, since work began on the Fort, in carrying 'to Fort George from different places along the Moray Firth large quantities of stone, lime, timber and other materials'.[3.192]

As trade with the south increased, so longer-distance coastal traffic grew and, from 1804, smacks began to trade between Inverness and London once every three weeks, the service increasing to once every ten days in 1814. At first only occasional calls were made at Cromarty but later the service began from there. In 1804 also an Inverness to Leith service running once every ten days was established.[3.193] By the 1830s, with the introduction of steam, this service was running once a week, while one of the three steamers sailing through the Caledonian Canal from Glasgow to Inverness came on to Cromarty and Invergordon.[3.194] Connections were also established with Aberdeen, Dundee and Newcastle, and as early as 1824 a packet boat sailed daily in summer between Nairn and Cromarty. There were even occasional visits by vessels from Ireland and Russia.[3.195]

Although the coasters carried a varied mixture of passengers and cargoes, which cannot always have been very enjoyable for those travelling on them, the improvement of sea transport greatly facilitated the increase in trade between Easter Ross and the rest of the country. In 1811 it was difficult to find space for produce on board the London traders, but within nine years there were five vessels regularly sailing to London and eight to Leith, while the introduction of steamships was already being mooted, holding out the prospect of sending fresh butcher meat to London.[3.196] It is unlikely that this prospect became much of a reality by 1850, for the journey from Invergordon to London still took nine days as compared to ten to fourteen at the start of the century, but the regular services allowed the arable farmers to ship their grain to the markets at Leith and London where the highest prices could be fetched.[3.197] At the same time increased shipping enabled southern manufacturers, for the first time, to make a major penetration of the Easter Ross market, all but destroying the locally based rural industries and greatly increasing the area's dependence on the outside world.

This trend was to be accelerated with the arrival of the railways. A line was first proposed from Inverness to Tain in 1845, but the railway actually reached Inverness only in 1854 and did not progress northwards until the following decade.[3.198]

Postal services in the region were much better than in the remainder of the North-West Highlands and dated from at least the early eighteenth century.[3.199] Revenues suffered because so many in the North of Scotland could send mail free under the privilege of soldiers' letters, and postal agents were liable to suffer financially, but increasing use led to the revenue in Ross and Cromarty rising from four hundred pounds in 1780 to two thousand pounds in 1808.[3.200] The number of offices also increased, rising from six in 1791 to eight in 1817 (as compared to only fourteen others in the whole area north of the Caledonian Canal) and nine in 1853, while in 1836 a free town service was established in Tain.[3.201]

Communications within Easter Ross, and between Easter Ross and the rest of the world, were never incapable of further improvement and always lagged behind the best practice in more prosperous parts of the country. Nevertheless, to anyone accustomed to regarding organised civil transport in the North of Scotland as non-existent before the nineteenth century and hardly thick on the ground even after 1800, the level of communications in the area, even in 1750, must come as something of a surprise. Good communications were a vital factor in encouraging economic growth and in leading to improvements in the standard of living.

4

The Rich Man in His Castle: The Poor Man at His Gate

a. The Standard of Living

While the gentry enjoyed the highest standard of living as a class in Easter Ross, there were wide variations between the individual landowners with regard to both the sources and the amount of their income. The majority of proprietors throughout the period derived most of their wealth from the land but a substantial minority had other sources of income and, in a few instances, these other sources were of more importance than the produce of the estates. Such evidence as there is suggests that the importance of outside sources of income increased fairly substantially in the latter half of the eighteenth century but that this increase was not sustained and that by 1850 landed wealth was more significant than it had been for at least one hundred years. Even in 1850, however, wealth derived from the professions, government service or trade added significantly to the incomes of a considerable number of landowners, and on many occasions in the preceding years large-scale injections of outside capital had brightened the financial outlook of local families.

While outside incomes were important, they were generally transitory. Fortunes were easily made in war or trade, but they were as easily spent and succeeding generations might have to depend entirely upon the revenues of the estate or at best add the supplement of the income of a half-pay officer. For most families profits obtained from sources other than their estates, while occasionally high, were not relied upon as a source of regular income.

Because the remaining evidence is so imprecise it is impossible to estimate with any accuracy variations in the total income of proprietors over the century but it is clear that revenue derived from estates rose quite substantially. Even before the great period of inflation at the end of the eighteenth century there were major increases. The Balnagown rental, for example, jumped from £1,327.17.4 in 1765 to £1,695.0.10¼ in 1777.[4.1] It is not clear, however, how far this notional increase in monetary terms mirrored a real increase in wealth or how widespread any such increases were. The rental at Meikle Allan showed a drop in the number of bolls of victual received from 1751 to 1792. Both Balnagown and Meikle Allan were extensively improved during this period and both estates lie in the same part of the region, but their revenues obviously had a different history. While statistical evidence is lacking, it would seem reasonably clear that more landlords resembled the owner of Balnagown than the owner of Meikle Allan in this period.[4.2]

Whatever the position was before the 1790s, from the time of the Old Statistical Account until 1815 the value of Easter Ross estates almost trebled, from just under £18,000 to just over £50,000.[4.3] Much of this increase may have been attributable to inflation but the Easter Ross performance was at least as good as, and probably better than, that of Scotland as a whole.[4.4] Although the post-war period saw no further dramatic increases, a steady improvement was maintained for, by 1853, the value of landed property in Easter Ross exceeded £59,000.[4.5]

Expenditure rose as quickly as, or more quickly than, income. Instances of landowners getting into real financial difficulties were not too common. From time to time, it is true, landed families, such as the Bains of Tulloch at the commencement of the period and the Mackenzies of Redcastle at the end of the eighteenth century, went under, as their mounting debts grew too large for them to cope with. Temporary embarrassments caused by extravagant expenditure could also lead to estates being placed under the care of trustees for a time, as happened to Davidson of Tulloch in the mid-nineteenth century. In general, however, lairds kept within the limits of their income, if only just.[4.6]

A major commitment for most landowners was the maintenance of their establishment or establishments. The greatest landlords had not only a number of country houses but residences in Edinburgh and London as well.

By 1750 London was the main centre of interest for the major proprietors, but a presence of some sort was also maintained in Edinburgh and it was in the latter city that the small and medium-sized gentry were most likely to congregate.[4.7] Direct evidence of the possession of town houses by Easter Ross lairds has been found in only a few cases but the numbers living in Edinburgh may have been increased by those who took lodgings for the season only. It is known that Lord Seaforth died in his Edinburgh house in Charlotte Square in 1815 but it is probable that he had maintained an establishment in London also, as befitted his rank in society, and as an earlier head of the Mackenzie clan, Lord Fortrose, had done before his death in 1761. Sir John Gordon of Invergordon's pocket book not only reveals his residence in the capital but also gives details of the contacts and purchases which such a residence enabled him to make.[4.8] It is uncertain how many lairds had town houses in the eighteenth century but by the middle of the nineteenth few of the Easter Ross gentry resided permanently on their estates.[4.9]

While residence in London or Edinburgh involved considerable expenditure, the maintenance of mansions on estates was also a heavy commitment. For reasons of comfort, fashion or prestige there were few mansions in the years from 1750 to 1850 which were not improved to some extent, while many were significantly altered or totally rebuilt.

Reconstruction to meet higher standards was no new phenomenon, of course, but until the middle of the eighteenth century some of the smaller lairds remained content with single-storey dwellings, and even the major lairds continued to reside in tower houses which were one, two or three centuries old.[4.10]

Two sketches on a plan of the estate of Findon in 1769 show that, whilst the mansion house of Kinbeachie was a typical mid-eighteenth century, two-storeyed, five-windowed, gable-ended small laird's dwelling, that of Culbo was a much more modest affair altogether, consisting of a single-storey, two-windowed cottage. The house of Meikle Allan was only a slightly larger version of Culbo when depicted on another plan, ten years earlier. These were the homes of small lairds but even Macleod of Cadboll, the third largest landowner in the area, according to the valuation of 1756, was reported by Bishop Forbes in 1762 as having but 'a very indifferent house to live in'.[4.11]

Even before the boom conditions of the early nineteenth century, a spate of building resulted in vastly improved accommodation for the majority of landlords. Indeed much building activity seems to have been concentrated into the three decades immediately following the Jacobite Rebellion of 1745, and before the collapse of the Ayr Bank and the start of the American War of Independence introduced a temporary recession. Almost all of the wealthiest gentry, in particular, were accommodated in elegant mansions. The best of these, designed by architects of national rather than local importance, were comparable with all but the finest architectural achievements elsewhere.

Few of the largest houses in the area have an adequately documented building history. Cromarty, the finest of them all, clearly shared the same architect as Culloden House near Inverness; though whether this was Robert Wright, the possible designer of the Episcopal chapel in the Cowgate in Edinburgh, as has been suggested, or some other, better known figure, is not clear. Cromarty can be dated more or less precisely to 1772, when George Ross bought the estate, but a considerable amount of work had already been undertaken by that date in Easter Ross by the Adam family.[4.12]

In the 1750s one of the Adams, probably the eldest brother, John, prepared plans for the reconstruction of Invergordon Castle for Sir John Gordon. The plans proposed a three-storied mansion, probably in the standard Palladian tradition with advanced quadrants leading to service wings. Although the details of reconstruction have been lost, work was completed in 1781.[4.13] In the early 1760s John Adam prepared designs, based on his own work at Dumfries House, for a new villa, at a cost of £5,000, for Sir John Ross of Balnagown. Work on this project never started but a more modest alteration to the old castle was in progress in 1763 and the ceiling of the Trophy Room at Balnagown may date from this period, as it is similar in appearance to other Adam work of the time.[4.14]

John's more famous brother, Robert, may have been responsible for the additions to Tulloch Castle at the same time, as he was the author of the designs for the interesting little folly of Caisteal Gòrach, up the hill to the north-west of the castle.[4.15]

Foulis was building in stages for about twenty years from 1754, Novar was enlarged at about the same time — possibly by the same architect, as both buildings share, with John Adam's design for Balnagown, similar semi-octagonal projections at each end — and further reconstruction took place at Balnagown in 1780.[4.16]

Wartime profits after 1792 encouraged some of the smaller lairds to get in on the act and Shandwick, Knockbreck and Mountgerald all seem to have been built around 1800 by the same architect — probably a local man. Shandwick, which, it was said, was fated because it was built from the stones of the Secession Chapel at Ankerville, had been planned as offices in the first instance but was expanded in a somewhat grandiose manner with a central projecting bow, two smaller side bows in the wings and a new court of offices at the back. Whoever was responsible for Shandwick, it has been established that a local architect, James Smith of Inverness, designed the new house of Newhall, constructed in the early years of the nineteenth century and containing some of the finest plaster work in the district.[4.17]

Most of the gentry were housed adequately by the end of the Napoleonic wars. Those who were not, such as Mackenzie of Ardross, who, as late as the middle of the nineteenth century, chose to reside with his mistress in the squalor of a thatched Highland cottage — it is not clear whether it was the mistress or the fact that he had gone native which most scandalised his neighbours — often had reasons unconnected with financial inability for not embarking on a building programme. In particular, as the century wore on, increasing absenteeism may have lessened the interest in refurbishing rural residences. A new wing in the latest Gothic Revival style was added to Balnagown by Gillespie Graham in the 1840s but it is significant, perhaps, that Ardross Castle, one of the few other major building projects being undertaken at this time, was built merely as a hunting lodge, not as a residence.[4.18]

The quality of furnishings improved with the advance in accommodation. Although high-quality products from the south were available to even the lesser gentry from at least the middle of the eighteenth century, both the quality and the quantity of the furniture improved over the years.[4.19] It is clear that at the start of the period much of the furniture was simple in style and of Scottish, possibly even locally produced materials. Ash, fir and wainscot were the woods used in the furniture at Meikle Allan in 1767, for example.[4.20] Gradually a certain degree of opulence crept in. Native woods were replaced by exotics such as mahogany and rosewood, bare floors were covered by carpets and rugs, the old hard chairs were supplemented by easy chairs and couches, and by the end of the period pianos, card tables and bidettes were found in addition to the everyday items which had been standard in the previous century.[4.21]

In general the landlords were not tied to local sources in the same way as their tenants, and this freedom is seen in their choice of fuel, food and clothing. Although for most of the eighteenth century the gentry, like everyone else, remained largely dependent upon local supplies of peat and timber for heating, from around 1750 there was a steady increase in the import of coal brought in by sea from the

Lothians and, more particularly, from the North-East of England.[4.22] Coal from the mine at Brora, in Sutherland, was also used and after the repeal of the duty on seaborne coal in 1794 the use of the fuel (wherever derived) amongst the better off became standard.[4.23]

The diet of the gentry was doubly superior to that of the mass of the local population for, in addition to the variety of imported goods available, only the lairds and those closest to them economically could afford the full range of local produce. Wheat was locally grown for gentry needs at a time when it was largely unknown as a general crop.[4.24] Proprietors' gardens produced a selection of roots and greens such as kidney beans, white turnips, lettuces, cucumbers, pease, beets, cauliflowers, spinach, parsnips and broccoli; and orchards, which were found on some estates, also contributed their share to the lairds' tables.[4.25] The full range of locally available meats was also generally restricted to the upper classes. Even at the start of the period the local produce was supplemented by a large variety of imported items such as tea, sugar, mustard, vinegar, spices, rice, hops and raisins, and as the range of foods available in Britain as a whole increased, so no doubt did the number of items on Easter Ross tables.[4.26]

Many of the clothes worn by the upper classes in Easter Ross were made at home, large quantities of cloth, buttons and thread being purchased for the purpose, and local craftsmen may have supplied much of the remainder.[4.27] Somewhat surprisingly, even as late as 1779 kilts were being made for the children of Robertson of Kindeace, despite the laws against the wearing of Highland dress[4.28] but there can be little doubt that when occasion demanded, the gentry of Easter Ross would dress in all the finery of the day, and those with homes in Edinburgh and London would have had ready access to the latest fashions.

While it was not uncommon for the lower classes to have some experience of the wider world, only amongst the gentry was foreign travel the rule rather than the exception. Although the amount of foreign travel undertaken purely for education and pleasure may have been limited, the opportunities for employment open to the gentry ensured that many of them travelled extensively, not only in Europe but also in America and the Far East.

Exceptionally, David Urquhart of Braelangwell, who was born in 1805, received his early eduction in France, Spain and Switzerland before going on to St John's College, Cambridge; but in most cases the gentry only went abroad, if they went at all, to complete their education at some continental university of international renown. Sir

Harry Munro of Foulis, who succeeded to the estate in 1746, spent some time at that favourite stamping ground of expatriate Scottish youth, the University of Leiden, while, a century later in 1849, Sir Kenneth Mackenzie of Gairloch proceeded from the University of Edinburgh to the University of Giessen in Germany. There is no evidence that either of these baronets, or any of their contemporaries from the area, undertook the Grand Tour in the approved eighteenth century manner but, on the other hand, it is not difficult to imagine that such a typically eighteenth century figure as Sir John Gordon of Invergordon may have spent a year or two in his youth exploring the continent.[4.29]

Certainly, many of the local gentry pursued careers far from their native shores. Lord MacLeod, the forfeited heir to the Earldom of Cromarty, rose high in the ranks of the Swedish army before receiving his pardon and doing equally well in the British army. Francis Mackenzie, Lord Seaforth, served as Governor of Barbados in the early nineteenth century and his son-in-law, James Stewart Mackenzie, as Governor of Ceylon from 1837 to 1840. Quite the most interesting of the natives of the area to make their name abroad was David Urquhart of Braelangwell, who, after his early peripatetic education (already mentioned) and a spell of duty in the Greek War of Independence, went on to establish his reputation as a distinguished diplomat and expert on Turkish affairs in the middle of the nineteenth century.[4.30]

The clergy of the established church in some ways formed a distinctive social group but their standard of living probably more closely resembled that of the gentry than that of any other group. Their incomes were far below those of the great landlords but compared favourably with the smaller proprietors. In 1755 the average stipend for the clergy of the area was just over £58, with a range from £34 to £72.[4.31] By the time of the Old Statistical Account the average stipend was probably worth closer to £90, and by 1837 it exceeded £245.[4.32] On top of their stipends the clergy had their glebes, manses and offices and, perhaps, especially in the last quarter of the eighteenth and first quarter of the nineteenth centuries, they supplemented their clerical income on occasion by renting farms from neighbouring landowners.[4.33] Indeed in the eighteenth century it was not unknown for a minister to be a landlord in his own right.[4.34]

Clerical incomes rose in two ways. In the first instance, as the price of victual rose so too did stipends, which were based on victual prices, and revenue from the sale of agricultural produce. This increase, however, no more than kept pace with inflation if it did that. If it is true that grain prices increased more slowly in the eighteenth century than did the price of other commodities, then the clergy may have fared rather badly before the start of the Napoleonic wars.

The hope of obtaining real rises in income lay mainly in obtaining augmentations of stipends from the teinds (tithes) which had remained in lay hands since their expropriation at the time of the Reformation. Although the right of ministers to reclaim teinds was undisputed, until the issue was finally settled at the start of the nineteenth century there was some doubt as to whether more than one augmentation was permitted in any parish. An act of 1808 allowed an augmentation to be made twenty years after the previous one, and the local clergy made much use of the legislation to enhance their incomes.[4.35] Even before the rapid inflation of the last years of the eighteenth century some augmentation had taken place, and in the 1790s a number of stipends were enlarged by this method. The process continued into the nineteenth century, with the result that by 1811 nine of the seventeen stipends were greater in real terms than they had been at the time of the Old Statistical Account.[4.36] Thereafter the rate may have slowed down but most of the parishes in Easter Ross were still in a position to enable considerable further augmentation to take place. Indeed the livings in the area appear to have been considerably richer than the average for Scotland as a whole. Acts of 1810 and 1825 stipulated a minimum stipend of £150. Four hundred and two parishes throughout Scotland (or more than 40%) had teinds which were either inadequate or did not permit a further augmentation. None of the teinds of Easter Ross were inadequate and only three were exhausted. Most of the remaining parishes had large untapped resources.[4.37]

The manses of the clergy were provided by the heritors (landowners) and, although the latter could, in the opinion of the former, be parsimonious on occasion, the general standard of accommodation was high, with homes being built which were at least equal to those of the lesser gentry. At least twelve manses were rebuilt or radically altered in the second half of the eighteenth century.[4.38] Of these, six were again rebuilt or added to between 1800 and 1850, while at least another four dating from before 1750 were reconstructed during the same period.[4.39] The late eighteenth century manse of Alness is a particularly fine small pedimented classical mansion while that at Rosemarkie, dating from 1833, although perhaps a little old-fashioned, is equally impressive.[4.40]

While the clergy had a higher income than any other rural group apart from the gentry, they were closely rivalled in the towns by the better off tradesmen and merchants. Although the burghs had generally been in recession in the early eighteenth century, the post-Jacobite period saw an economic improvement which led to a rapid rise in the standard of living of the ruling elite. It is not so clear whether or not the rest of the urban population enjoyed a similar improvement, although to some extent they must have benefited from the urban improvements of the time.

It is clear that the opportunities for enrichment open to the few increased considerably after 1750. Stimulated by improvements in agriculture and transport, trade expanded to the obvious benefit of the merchants, while new avenues to wealth opened up for those who had obtained bank agencies and factories or who participated in industrial ventures.[4.41]

William Forsyth, who settled in Cromarty in the first half of the eighteenth century after a year away in London, certainly was the most successful of the eighteenth century merchant community, carrying on trade with England and the continent and diversifying into such activities as linen and kelp manufacture. But he was not unique. Amongst his successors, the wily William Murray of Tain used every opportunity successfully to enhance his income and, in Dingwall, Hugh Innes Cameron, appointed agent for the National Bank in 1834, rapidly rose to fame and fortune as county clerk, provost and factor for several estates, before a social scandal in the early 1840s forced him to leave for London, where, subsequently, he was imprisoned for dishonest banking practices.[4.42]

Ranking with these new rich were the older-established professionals. In 1792 Dingwall had six lawyers, while in 1825 it could be said that the town 'swarms with lawyers'.[4.43] Most of these lawyers made a profitable living as a result of prosecutions concerning infringements of the excise laws; but lawyers in Dingwall, as elsewhere, rarely have had problems in finding either business or profit. More limited in number were the physicians. There was at least one surgeon in Tain in the eighteenth century, and by 1844 there were four medical men in Dingwall and two in Fortrose. Despite the generosity of these doctors in attending the poor, free of charge, their income and general standing in society seem to have been not insubstantial.[4.44]

The standard of housing erected in the late eighteenth century was much superior to that prevailing in earlier periods. At Cromarty, in particular, the homes which the local merchants, such as William

Forsyth, erected compared favourably with the lairds' houses in the surrounding countryside. In Dingwall it could be reported in 1792 that 'the town has of late been greatly enlarged, as well as improved in the appearance of its houses'.[4.45] Improvement, of course, was relative and what was acceptable in 1792 did not remain so, for, in 1837, it was recorded that 'most of the better sort of houses have been built within the last twenty years'.[4.46]

Even before the mass-produced clothing of the south became widely available, towards the middle of the nineteenth century, the townsfolk must have benefited from the close contacts in trade, for in 1803 it was said that many of the people of Cromarty were 'as well and as fashionably dressed as any in the city of London'.[4.47]

While the gentry may have had the greatest opportunity for recreation, the townsmen too had a chance to broaden their horizons or improve their physique. It can be no coincidence that golf is mentioned in connection with both Tain and Fortrose in the eighteenth century, while in the early nineteenth century it was even possible in Cromarty to see theatrical performances by groups of strolling players.[4.48]

If the standard of living amongst the wealthier merchants and professional men in the towns was such as to compare with the lesser gentry, and was maintained, if not improved, throughout the period, the same could not be said for the urban poor. Despite the favourable impact which the better type of housing made, most visitors to Dingwall were not impressed by what they saw. Southey has left his impression that the town was 'a vile place'.[4.49] Botfield, just as succinctly, in 1830 commented that it was 'a dirty old town'.[4.50] Much of the squalor could be attributed to the desperate housing conditions of the poor for, as Spence noted in 1817, the town was 'mean, and some of the houses wretched; those of the cottagers quite of the Glenburnie description'.[4.51]

The better off townspeople and the rural rich never constituted more than a small proportion of the total population; and, while the urban poor may have represented a larger element of society, the general standard of living was determined by the conditions of the farmers, cottars, servants and labourers who occupied and worked the land. The tenant farmers constituted the most important element in this society but cannot be considered as a single group. The great majority of tenants were smallholders whose ancestors had held land in the area, sometimes for centuries. Indeed, for most of the later eighteenth century very little land was held by any other type of tenant. In the middle of the eighteenth century these small farmers were oppressed and poverty-stricken, despite the nostalgic memories of later generations, but the very slow rate at which society changed may have cushioned most of the effects of the theoretical insecurity, and the strong community spirit may have helped to prevent individuals from being overwhelmed in times of need.

As the century progressed conditions probably worsened, at least in some respects. While the cost of living possibly doubled by 1790, the income of the tenants did not keep pace.[4.52] The price of grain, which was the principal source of income for most farmers in the area, did not rise, it has been suggested, as rapidly as other commodities, while the increasing subdivision of holdings meant that each tenant had a smaller crop to sell. Crop failures of 1782-3 not only brought much of the population to the brink of starvation but led to arrears of rent which took years to pay off and hastened the descent of many into bankruptcy. In 1796 it was claimed that the thirty-acre farmers of Killearnan had not cleared £2 per annum on average in the previous twenty years, and although the income from farms was often supplemented by the profit from spinning and distilling, by the end of the century the native tenant farmers were often in a worse position than not only cottars but even some servants.[4.53] Their housing was appalling, consisting, even as late as 1806, of single-roomed hovels 'made up (not built) of stone and feal [turf]', with entry by a common door to the space shared by the family and their animals.[4.54]

Within the farmhouse there was little evidence of household goods or furniture. In 1795 Sir John Sinclair estimated that an average small farmer in the Black Isle would have no more than a bedstead, a press, a meal chest, a clothes chest, three chairs and three stools, two spinning wheels, a reel, four wooden dishes and four cogs (wooden cups), three pots, a pan, ten horn spoons, tongs, a crook or chain for the fireplace, a table, eight blankets and three rugs.[4.55]

On the other hand, the small farmer appears to have been decently, if unostentatiously dressed. Knee breeches were standard apparel for men for most of the second half of the eighteenth century, although some young men wore the kilt. Towards the end of the century some favourite sons of small tenants began to be kitted out with trousers, and by the middle of the nineteenth century trousers were as commonplace as breeches had been a century earlier.[4.56]

Sir John Sinclair listed the clothing of his average small farmer as consisting of a bonnet (the universal headgear, even amongst large farmers), a coat, waistcoat and breeches of home-made cloth, three pairs of home-made coarse worsted hose, one pair of brogues and one pair of shoes, linen, a great coat and a long coat of shop cloth and a pair of corduroy breeches for Sunday.

According to Sir John, the farmer's wife would have a gown and coat of blue-dyed woollen stuff, aprons, stockings, a pair of shoes, linen, a printed cotton gown (possibly a relatively recent innovation) or a linsey-woolsey (a coarse fabric of linen with wool filling) dress and a cloak of shop cloth or tartan plaid. While the farmer's clothes cost £3.9.6 and his wife's £2.14.6, Sir John allowed only 2/6 for the clothing of a child.[4.57]

Even in the eighteenth century there were some larger tenants in the area, but before the last decade most of these were more directly comparable with the small gentry in status than with their fellow farmers. The introduction of improved agriculture, however, led to the arrival of large tenant farmers from the south. They took over much of the land from the previous tenants and established themselves as a rural middle class. Although some small farmers had begun to experience an improvement in their living conditions in the 1790s, the arrival of the southerners finished them as a class. Those who were not completely evicted were as often as not resettled as cottars. By 1853 only a small part of the total arable land was left to old-style small farmers.[4.58]

In 1806 a writer in the *Farmers' Magazine* was able to report concerning large farms that, despite earlier, misleading rumours, 'there were more handsome farm houses and manses in Ross-shire than in most other places.'[4.59] Although the post-war depression, with low prices and continuing high rents, ruined many of the new tenants, recovery must have been fairly rapid, as the construction of large new farmhouses was resumed in the fourth and fifth decades of the nineteenth century.[4.60]

While small tenant farmers occupied most of the land in the second half of the eighteenth century, they were probably greatly outnumbered by cottars. Although some cottars held their crofts as subtenants on large farms the majority were direct tenants. The crofts were not large enough to provide a living for their occupants who were additionally almost all either day labourers or tradesmen. Cottars who had obtained long leases of unreclaimed moorland on favourable terms and who had succeeded in improving their land may well have attained a standard of living which compared favourably with the small farmers because of their ability to supplement their income with the produce of their land and because of their freedom from a heavy rent burden, but more often than not the strain of improving moorland proved too much and extra wealth had to be obtained from the uncertain profits of smuggling.[4.61] Cottars on longer-settled land did not have the benefit of low rents or secure tenure, although they may have had more opportunity to pursue other occupations.

It is not obvious, however, that either tradesmen or day labourers benefited greatly from the increased output of the area. The wages of tradesmen certainly increased, rising, for journeymen masons, from eleven pence per day in 1734 to one shilling and three pence in the 1770s and, at best, one shilling and sixpence in the early 1790s. This represented an increase of only sixty-three per cent compared to a possible one hundred per cent rise in the cost of living.[4.62] Wrights do not appear to have fared any better. A sharp rise in money wages might have been expected as a result of inflation during the Napoleonic wars, but the rate of wage increase actually slowed down. By 1837 masons were earning no more than two shillings a day on average, which represented only a thirty-three per cent increase on the figure for the 1790s. While these statistics may not be exact, there seems to be little reason to doubt their general validity.[4.63]

While some rural craftsmen may have had fairly continuous employment, others, such as masons, worked only for about nine months in the year. It may be because of this that masons' daily rates were rather higher than, for example, those of wrights. Shortage of work also forced masons into a peripatetic existence. In the early nineteenth century they moved from job to job, spending their nights in ramshackle bothies with neither privacy nor comfort.[4.64] Hugh Miller has left a vivid account of his days as a mason when he experienced the privations of this desperately inadequate accommodation:

> These barracks or bothies are almost always of the most miserable description. I have lived in hovels that were invariably flooded in wet weather by the overflowings of neighbouring swamps, and through whose roofs I could tell the hour at night, by marking from my bed the stars that were passing over the openings along the ridge: I have resided in other dwellings of rather higher pretensions, in which I have been awakened during every heavier night-shower by the rain-drops splashing upon my face where I lay a-bed. . . a neighbouring laird, when asked why he left a crazy old building standing behind a group of neat modern offices, informed the querist that it was not altogether through bad taste the hovel was spared, but from the circumstance that he found it of great convenience every time his speculations brought a *drove of pigs* or *a squad of masons* the way.[4.65]

Although, even in the 1820s, masons' diet remained based on meal rather than potatoes, little else could be said in its favour. Hugh Miller's reminiscences included the recollection that in the masons' barracks

> the food is of the plainest and coarsest description: oatmeal forms its staple, with milk, when milk can be had, which is not always; and as the men have to cook by turns, with only half an hour or so given them in which to light a fire, and prepare the meal for a dozen or twenty associates, the cooking is invariably an exceedingly rough and simple affair.[4.66]

Over the century from 1750 the differentials between craftsmen and day labourers were, to some extent, eroded but this was more to the detriment of the craftsmen than to the advantage of the labourers. Labourers' wages certainly rose, but in many respects their conditions worsened. In the third quarter of the eighteenth century most of the agricultural labour had been undertaken by cottars or permanent servants but towards the end of the century two major changes began to take place. The displacement of so many of the old small tenant farmers created great pressure on the land. Numbers were accommodated on unimproved crofts and emigration provided an escape for those with some capital, but many became landless casual labourers resident in the towns and villages. At the same time the practice of hiring servants by the half-year began to give way to a greater dependence on day labour.[4.67] Although the widespread introduction of improvements initially generated many job opportunities for the new labour pool, the adoption of more efficient methods meant that, in the long run, there would be a reduction in the numbers required to work the land. The hidden labour surplus was revealed when the post-war depression brought improvement to a halt, resulting in widespread unemployment, and, although improvement was renewed in the 1830s, the introduction of mechanisation towards the middle of the century posed a new and more permanent threat to the livelihood of the rural labouring classes.[4.68]

While the rise in rates may to some extent have satisfied those who remained crofters, it can hardly have compensated the landless labourers for the increasing insecurity of their existence. For forty years from 1750 the daily wage rate for casual labourers remained at six pence. This rate was increased at harvest time, but employment was not continuous and for much of the winter no work was available. Only in the last decade of the eighteenth century did wages increase. By

1795 the standard rate had risen to eight pence and by this time the adoption of piece work resulting in even higher earnings was becoming common. In the early years of the nineteenth century rates reached one shilling and sixpence a day and even, exceptionally, one and ninepence before falling back by the late 1830s to one shilling or one shilling and three pence.[4.69] Some were able to earn more than this by going south in the summer to work for higher wages on lowland farms or on the railways, but if sufficient work was available in Easter Ross few were tempted by such temporary employment.[4.70]

Evidence is lacking as to the changing costs of working class furniture and clothing but neither would have compared with those of even the small tenant farmers. In 1795, for example, when a farmer's shoes were estimated to cost five shillings, those for a man servant cost only three shillings and, whereas a farmer's wife might have linen to the value of twelve shillings, a woman servant had to make do with linen worth three shillings.[4.71]

There is little indication in the diet and housing conditions of the labouring classes that they experienced any increase in purchasing power over the century. Quite the contrary, in fact, for while, in 1750, oatmeal was the major item of consumption, by the 1790s potatoes were as important, and in the nineteenth century they were the staple food of the common people.[4.72] It appears, however, that labourers in Easter Ross consumed more meat than their fellows in the west during the nineteenth century.[4.73]

Working class homes in the eighteenth century were universally rude constructions. Some improvements took place in the first half of the nineteenth century and, by 1842, James Cameron, a surgeon in Tain, felt able to give a reasonably optimistic report on working class housing conditions. The houses of farm servants, he wrote,

> are built in the immediate proximity of the farm-steading, in a line with each other, forming as it were one side of a short street: some of these houses have immediately in front a pavement or causeway. On many of the large farms the houses are roofed with tiles or blue slate; the more common practice, however, is to thatch them with straw and clay; and they are generally kept water-tight. Their site is, in general, dry, though frequently too near the fold or court of offices. Most of them have pigsties either before or behind; bur rarely immediately attached to them. The dwelling houses are usually constructed of stone or mud-work. The flooring is made of a mixture of earth and clay, wood flooring being seldom used. The fireplace and chimneys are well constructed. All the rooms ordinarily are used as dormitories. They are generally kept clean and in good order, the walls being whitewashed with lime. The furniture consists of a few chairs, a

> cupboard, a table, and a bed; curtains are often seen in the best apartment, but in general they are closely shut up with boards — a practice detrimental to health. Their bed-ticks are stuffed with straw or chaff; feather-beds are not used in such houses.
>
> The houses of crofters and day-labourers are generally inferior to those of farm servants. They are also less cleanly in their habits: in many cases they and their cattle enter through the same door with the inmates, and the 'domestic' fowls, strictly so called, perch themselves on the rafters or couples above the heads of their lords. This description, however, is happily applicable only to the minority, and the more ancient of these dwellings. The houses of artisans and shopkeepers depend for their comfort and accommodation, in great measure, on the industry, character, and success of their occupiers.[4.74]

Where Cameron felt that some progress was being made, another commentator in the same year, viewing the same evidence, was less hopeful, expressing horror that the peasantry were still too commonly 'sheltered by dingy turf or dry stone huts, with bare earthen floors; than which it is impossible to conceive abodes for human beings more squalid and wretched'.[4.75]

In 1848, an official report on destitution in the Highlands went even further, condemning the housing in Portmahomack, 'which, this day, presents a scene of misery and neglect such as society has rarely witnessed or been startled by the recital of in Scotland — houses presenting such pictures of damp, filth, stench and putridity, as makes any other result than the present fever, which has existed for a year, impossible, and as I before never in my experience beheld in any country . . .'[4.76]

There is no evidence of any dramatic improvement in working conditions either. Women were employed in large numbers as farm labourers — on the farm of Tarlogie in 1829, for example, there were five women labourers and only one male labourer — and, although some of the heavier duties, such as trenching dung, seem to have been reserved for men, women were expected to undertake a wide range of tasks, from cutting broom for thatching and making straw ropes to hoeing root crops and filling carts with stones. As late as 1844 children of eight and nine were being sent out to herd.[4.77]

In 1781 work commenced in summer at four or five in the morning and ended at seven or eight at night with two hours for meals. During the winter, daylight hours were worked with only a one-hour break. An attempt towards the end of the eighteenth century to restrict the working day to ten hours between six in the morning and six in the evening proved impractical because of local climatic conditions, and in

1811 working hours were as long as they had been thirty years earlier. It is true that by 1842 working hours at long last were said to be restricted to the period between five in the morning and six at night, again with two hours for meals, but, as the only regular holiday was New Year's Day (Old Style), it is hardly surprising that the only recreation of the working classes was reported as being 'absolute cessation from labour'.[4.78]

While the condition of servants did not improve noticeably, they may have fared rather better than other rural employees, especially in the first half of the period. Money wages, at least, rose fairly quickly from one pound ten shillings a year in 1750 through three pounds in 1781 to six pounds in the early 1790s. Increases in the nineteenth century were not so great, but for much of the first half of the century the better servants received between seven and eight pounds.[4.79] Throughout the century servants received the greater part of their wages in kind: the proportion of money to kind probably did not vary greatly from 4:6. In some cases servants were kept in the farmer's home. In the eighteenth century this may have made little difference to their general comfort, as farmers' cottages were notoriously ill-kept and within the cottages servants were not even provided with blankets for their beds, but as the living standards of tenant farmers rose in the nineteenth century the living-in servants benefited from improved accommodation and a more varied diet.[4.80]

Servants who did not live with their employers received in lieu allowances of victual and fuel, a house and other extras. Such allowances did not suffer from rises in the cost of living and the number and amount of benefits seems, if anything, to have increased. The overall value of servants' wages actually increased from twelve pounds in 1793 to from twenty to twenty-two pounds in 1837.[4.81]

Information on servants' clothing in the eighteenth century is scanty and uninformative, but by 1842 it could be said that farm servants

> are in general well and warmly clothed, the males in corduroys, or coarse woollen stuffs; the females in flannel petticoats and cotton-prints. The females go bare-headed, or wear 'mutches', which they take a particular pride in keeping neat and clean. Most of them also are provided with warm blue cloaks. The men always wear strong worsted stockings and thick shoes, or half-boots.[4.82]

It may or may not be an indication of some improvement in standards that corduroy, a material which had been kept as Sunday best by tenant farmers in the eighteenth century, had become an ordinary item of clothing for servants in the nineteenth.

Servants' attire — particularly when it consisted of cast-offs from their masters and mistresses — probably was superior to that of most of the working class, although the local fishermen too were 'well and warmly clad in blue woollen stuffs. The men always wear stout shoes or tall sea-boots; the women, except in winter, or on Sundays, generally go barefooted.'[4.83]

Throughout the century, the upper and middle classes benefited from a significant rise in living standards. Their horizons broadened and their expectations increased; and goods and standards from the south which, for long before, had been considered desirable, increasingly came to be regarded as the norm.

Although sections of the working classes, notably farm servants, may have seen some improvement in their lot too, the urban poor, the crofters and the landless labourers ended the period under review no better, and, in some respects, possibly even worse off than they had been at the start. As the material divisions in society increased, with the better off winning out at the expense of the poor, so these divisions were reflected in, and reacted upon, the social and cultural structure of that society.

b. Social Welfare

Although the provision of assistance by the community to those in need was a long recognised duty and although legislation as far back as the sixteenth century had created an organisational framework for the distribution of such assistance, the system as it operated in Easter Ross in the middle of the eighteenth century was not designed to meet the real needs of those requiring aid. It was held that such relief as was given should be made available only to those who were unable to provide for themselves — the young, the old and the disabled — while, even for people in these categories, distributions were intended to be usually no more than supplementations of funds obtained from other sources. All official relief in the area was of the outdoor variety, and before 1850 the only provisions of any kind for indoor relief seem to have been the almshouses founded in Dingwall by Robertson of Blackwells in the eighteenth, and by Gladstone of Fasque in the nineteenth century. As the Gladstones and the Robertsons were connected by marriage, it is possible that the nineteenth century foundation was only a refoundation, with additional funding, of the original Robertson institution.[4.84] Legislation had created the basic system but its successful operation depended upon a continuing belief in the moral worth of paternalism and Christian charity, rather than upon obedience to the letter of the law.

Existing legislation in the eighteenth century permitted parochial assessments to raise funds for the poor but, whatever the situation in other parts of the country, in Easter Ross assessment does not appear to have taken place and voluntary contributions remained the major source of finance. Most of these contributions were received from the weekly church collections and the income was handled in the rural parishes by the kirk sessions and heritors. Until a legal judgment of 1835 ruled that only in parishes which were wholly burghal were the magistrates allowed to handle the poor funds, some burghs in Scotland were responsible for much of the poor relief within their bounds, but on the basis of the surviving evidence it would appear that none of the burghs in Easter Ross were involved regularly in social welfare.[4.85]

The church collections were supplemented from a variety of other financial sources, varying in importance from parish to parish. Some kirk sessions administered the funds from mortifications — property endowed for charitable purposes — left by previous generations for the benefit of the poor. The burgh of Fortrose benefited from a number of mortifications, valued in total in 1843 at £31.12.8½, while, in Cromarty, mortified lands left by McCulloch of Goodtrees in 1656 yielded nine bolls, six and a half pecks of victual yearly. Several Easter Ross parishes were the legatees of a mortification from an Earl of Cromarty, which allowed for the distribution of relief in kind to those in need.

Additionally, some parishes added to their funds such small sums as were forthcoming from the hiring out of parish mortcloths and bells and from fines administered to those who had transgressed against church discipline. To these regular sources of income were added, from time to time, donations from the wealthier members of the community. When a surplus existed, the capital might be lent out to a local landlord and the resulting interest used to supplement the payments to paupers. In addition to paying for social welfare, the funds collected by kirk sessions had to meet the salaries of session clerks, precentors and other parish officers and incidental expenses incurred by members of the session. These commitments were usually met first, and when funds were low there was little left for distribution to the poor.[4.86]

The funds distributed through official channels represented only a small fraction of the total amount of charity provided. In the small, relatively closed communities of eighteenth century Easter Ross most of the necessary relief came from the friends, relatives and neighbours of those in need. To some extent this charity was integrated with the official system, as kirk sessions issued badges to indigents on the poor roll, licensing them to beg, but even when such badges were not issued it was generally accepted by the community at large that it should look after its own.[4.87] The badges, in fact, were introduced in 1754 in an attempt to control unlimited begging by vagrants or able-bodied poor for whom there was no legal provision. In this they were unsuccessful, and vagrancy declined only towards the middle of the nineteenth century after the county constabulary came into being.[4.88]

Some mortifications were privately administered, while, from time to time, landlords would make provision for the needy on their own estates. Only exceptionally did the gentry feel that their private charity might be extended to the poor at large, and at times of national disaster more general assistance had to be obtained from external sources.[4.89] In the famines of 1782-3, for example, the government purchased supplies of grain and shipped them to the area, while in the nineteenth century the growth of national charitable organisations provided similar assistance.[4.90]

Private charity was often, probably usually, given in kind as the need dictated but the official system was mainly financially based.[4.91] Relief of three kinds was given. The major effort went into the distribution of funds to allow paupers to buy food and other necessities. It was a standard practice to distribute the relief at times of the year when provisions were at their cheapest, so that the limited sums given could be stretched as far as possible. Towards the end of the eighteenth century it became common to divide those on the poor roll into different classes according to need and allocate different sums to each class.[4.92]

In addition to this financial relief, provision was made from 1803 for the free education of children whose parents were paupers, and while there was no systematic medical relief before 1845 an attempt was made in some parishes to provide medical care for those on the poor roll who were ill.[4.93] Such attempts were woefully inadequate and much depended upon the willingness of the local doctors to spend freely of their time and money. As late as 1844 nineteen out of twenty in Easter Ross died without medical attention.[4.94]

Regular relief was provided only for those on the poor roll, but despite the fact that existing funds were generally inadequate even for that, kirk sessions also attempted to assist the occasionally needy — those who, through no fault of their own, had suffered from a natural disaster or who, because of some temporary illness, could not provide for themselves.

In 1771, for example, the Session of Kiltearn made exceptional payments to an Englishwoman and someone by the name of Stewart, both on the recommendation of the Presbytery of Dingwall, to an old man, by order of the Synod, to a reduced gentleman from Glasgow and to Donald Eagle's daughter, her house and means of livelihood having been destroyed by fire. Money could be made to go further by being lent rather than given. Usually money was lent to individuals who were temporarily down on their luck — such as William McPhee, a weaver in the parish of Tarbat, who was given a loan of six shillings in 1796 — but occasionally the need for such a practice became more widespread. In 1783, for example, two pounds, two shillings and eightpence was lent to the parishioners of Tarbat to help them to buy bread during the time of famine.[4.95]

Just as national assistance was forthcoming on exceptional occasions, so it was felt necessary to contribute, in some instances, to charitable causes on a wider scale than that of the parish, presbytery or synod. Although such contributions might be met from the regular income, it was more common to have special church collections for a particular cause. Collections of this nature were most frequent for medical reasons, as it was impossible to provide all the necessary facilities at a local level. In 1766, for example, the Synod of Ross decided to make annual contributions to the Aberdeen Infirmary in return for the treatment of poor people from the area of the synod at the Infirmary.[4.96]

The treatment of the insane was also regarded as being worthy of special attention, either in the form of a voluntary assessment of heritors, or as another type of case meriting separate collections. Such treatment was restricted only to the troublesome insane, those who were merely feebleminded being left at large to cater for themselves so far as they could. It is possible that the Roderick Mcfarquhar, who spent at least six weeks keeping crows from the wheat at Tarlogie farm in the winter and spring of 1829-1830, may have been one who was not intelligent enough to be trusted with any more demanding task, but who was given this useful duty to keep him gainfully employed.[4.97]

Although the amount of relief available was insufficient to prevent hardship, within the limits of the expectations of the period the system may have worked in the middle of the eighteenth century, especially in the towns were there was always a better provision for the poor. At any rate it was possible for a number of parishes to build up quite substantial surpluses before altered circumstances towards the end of the century began to create intolerable strains.[4.98]

The increase in population began to outstrip the increase in resources towards the end of the eighteenth century. Additional wealth, of course, there was, but not enough of it was being channelled into poor relief to meet an increasing need, for the numbers of poor rose with the general rise in population. Indeed poverty probably became more rather than less severe and the demands which were made upon funds greater rather than lesser.

The philosophy behind the poor relief system began to break down towards the end of the century as attitudes changed at both ends of the social scale. Increasing absenteeism restricted the opportunities for landlords to give generously to the poor, just as paternalism waned and was replaced by a more strictly economic interpretation of landowning rights and obligations. The breakdown in social cohesiveness was hastened by the wholesale introduction of large farmers from the south who did not regard themselves as being of the same community as those they replaced. The small tenants, who were resettled to make way for the southern farmers, increasingly became disenchanted with the situation. They had previously given as generously as they could but the feeling grew that their church contributions were intended merely to 'save the landlords from bearing the burden which is by law thrown on the land'.[4.99]

The crop failures of 1782-3 and the legacy they left of impoverished tenants sliding into bankruptcy created a new demand for aid, while the Napoleonic wars added substantially to the number of widows, a class which had always constituted an important element amongst those on the poor roll. After the wars further problems arose. To the numbers of unemployed created by the recession in agricultural improvement and the decline of rural industries were added those soldiers who had lived to return to the district without much prospect of gainful employment. Many of these new poor did not even qualify for aid under the law.[4.100]

To some extent the situation improved with the revival of agriculture in the late 1820s but by this time the changeover from regularly employed servants to casually employed day labourers was widespread. Many of these casual labourers were unemployed for much of the time and hardly earned enough when they did work to tide them over for the rest of the year. Formerly farm labourers had been able to supplement their earnings with produce raised on smallholdings but increasing numbers in the nineteenth century were resident in the towns and villages and had, at best, only small gardens.[4.101]

In the nineteenth century also the welfare problems arising from religious secession increased considerably. As long as the great majority in each parish belonged to the established church the weekly collections were a major contribution to the relief of poverty. Weekly collections in secession churches, however, usually were required for other purposes — particularly the maintenance of the minister — and the greater the number who participated in secession, the greater was the strain on those who remained so far as the provision of poor relief was concerned.[4.102]

The existing system of poor relief could not cope with these new problems and the position worsened steadily. Kirk session funds available for distribution hardly kept pace with the rising cost of living in the second half of the eighteenth century and, although in the nineteenth century the amount given to each pauper may have increased more rapidly than before, this was to some extent due to the fact that the numbers being admitted to the poor roll were being more stringently supervised. Supervision was the more necessary as the poor gradually lost their feelings of shame on applying for relief.[4.103]

As a result many parishes adopted the system of requiring anyone admitted to the poor roll to agree to leave all his goods to the poor fund. This practice usually had an immediate effect on the numbers on the roll. When the rule was introduced to Resolis in 1793 there was a reduction from ninety to thirty-four, and in Tain, where the numbers had risen gradually from about ninety in the 1760s to well over one hundred and fifty by the start of the nineteenth century, the adoption of the rule halved the number of applicants. But such expedients, besides being no more than temporarily successful — by the 1830s the poor roll in Tain was once again over one hundred and fifty — merely concealed the problem. Those whose need was temporary rather than permanent may have been dissuaded from seeking relief by the new measures, but their distress was in no way lessened.[4.104]

There was an increase in formal private charity in the nineteenth century. Friendly societies came into being in some parishes (the Guildry Society in Tain which existed chiefly for the benefit of widows had been founded as early as 1738) and, in Cromarty at least, had some success. But the benefits of such self-help organisations were restricted, as few earned enough when they were in employment to put much aside for time of depression. The friendly society at Avoch, founded in 1830, had ceased to exist by 1844 because of this inability to save, but by the latter date nine societies were functioning in the Easter Ross area.[4.105]

The clergy and gentry continued to oppose compulsory assessment on theoretical and financial grounds but the inevitability of its introduction became more and more obvious.[4.106] Voluntary assessment was practised from time to time for the benefit of lunatics, and in the 1830s the heritors of Dingwall, under threat of an application to have compulsion introduced, agreed for a time to extend this voluntary assessment to some of the old and bedridden.[4.107] Such half-hearted measures did little to alleviate the situation and even when, as in Cromarty, existing funds were deemed practically sufficient, the uncertainty in their collection and the multitude of sources whence they were derived made reorganisation necessary. In most places funds were only too obviously insufficient and the poor lived in squalor and degradation.[4.108]

In 1845 the poor state of social welfare in Scotland as a whole led to the introduction of new legislation. The kirk sessions were replaced by parochial boards. There was even a minority of elected members on these boards, although most of the power rested with the appointed chairmen. For the first time legal provision was made for medical care and an attempt was made to provide for indoor relief.[4.109]

In Easter Ross the first poor house, catering for the Tain district of parishes, was opened in 1850. Despite its attractive appearance, however, it was greeted with something less than enthusiasm by the local inhabitants, and the new act in general seems to have done little before 1850 to improve the situation.[4.110] It was, of course, unfortunate that the new system was hardly established before it faced the most extreme of tests in the potato famine of the later 1840s. In 1847 the poor of Evanton were reduced to living on turnips and, if the distress experienced was not as severe as it was on the west coast, the whole area still suffered badly. During the year of famine 15.78 per cent of the total population of Rosskeen were forced to go on the poor roll, while in Tarbat the figure was 17.72 per cent, in Kilmuir 18.57 per cent and in Fearn 19.21. These figures are all the more striking when it is remembered that, unlike the west, Easter Ross remained a basically prosperous district and that, at the same time as up to a fifth of the population were being reduced to beggary in their search for sustenance, the exports of grain from the district were reaching levels previously undreamt of.[4.111]

By 1848 Easter Ross had recovered from the worst effects of the famine but the poor remained in a state of destitution which had changed little in a century. There had been little or no material improvement and as the standard of living of the more prosperous sections of the community improved, the paupers' relative position had actually worsened. At best the new Poor Law held out only some hope of future improvement in relief.

5
Churches and Cultures

a. Religion

As the economic life of Easter Ross was dominated from 1750 to 1850 by one major element, agriculture, so the social life of the area was similarly dominated by religion, which exercised a major influence on the development of education, culture and social welfare. For most of the period the Church of Scotland maintained an almost total control of the allegiance of the population of the area. Catholicism presented no challenge at all. From 1732 to 1827 the nearest Catholic priest was located in Strathglass and only in the latter year was one settled as close as Inverness.[5.1] Webster's census recorded a total of only eight Catholics in the whole district and six of these were in Cromarty where the landlord of the time was a Papist. By 1851 even this small number had disappeared, for the census of that year listed not one Catholic in all of Ross and Cromarty.[5.2]

The Episcopalians had presented a far more serious challenge to the Presbyterian ascendancy after 1688, but the failure of the Jacobite rebellions had been a double blow in failing to establish a government favourable to Episcopacy and in antagonising the existing government which had previously been sympathetic. By 1750, as a result, Episcopalian congregations remained strong only in the southern Black Isle.

After 1707 there was no resident bishop in the North of Scotland, and the visit of Bishop Forbes after his consecration in 1762 was the first to the area for many years. Ministers, too, became scarcer and non-resident and although there was a regular series of lay Episcopal catechists in Rosemarkie until 1826 the absence of a firm ecclesiastical establishment weakened the hold of the church in Ross. When the two ministers in charge of the presbyteries of Dingwall and Chanonry died in 1765 they were not replaced for two years, and then only by one individual who had to cover Appin and other areas in the West Highlands as well as Ross. This minister's successor at Arpafeelie, the church in Knockbain which had become the Episcopalian centre in Easter Ross, served a district including all of Ross and Skye, while the minister who followed in 1817 was centred at Strathnairn.[5.3] As late as 1770 Bishop Forbes could preach to a congregation of over five hundred at Arpafeelie and even in 1813 there were about three hundred Episcopalians in the parish of Killearnan.[5.4] But in the absence of regular Episcopal services many adherents attended the parish churches and gradually they lost their old allegiance.[5.5] The high quality of some of the Presbyterian clergy in the area may have hastened the decline. By the middle of the nineteenth century, only in the parish of Knockbain did Episcopacy retain a large element of popular support.[5.6] Elsewhere Episcopal congregations consisted largely of the upper classes. Several of the gentry had been Episcopalians in the eighteenth century, particularly active supporters of the Jacobite cause, such as McCulloch of Glastullich, or passive sympathisers, such as Macleod of Cadboll. Cadboll was an interesting individualist, whose antiquarian sympathies were much in evidence, both in his personal pursuits — he had a noted coin cabinet and library and took his interest in history so far as to christen his son Robert Bruce—and in his political beliefs, which were in favour of Scottish independence under a different king from England. Even amongst the gentry who were not tainted with Jacobitism, however, Episcopal adherents were to be found.[5.7]

It is probable that, as popular support for Episcopacy dwindled, adherence amongst the landed classes increased. As late as 1843 Major General Munro of Teaninich was ordained as an elder in the Church of Scotland but, by that time, many of the gentry had at least split allegiances, attending Church of Scotland services in Scotland and Church of England services in England. Conformity with the Church of England, at a superficial level at any rate, was a prerequisite for advancement in many spheres and, as the lairds increasingly were educated in England and in other ways were absorbed into the culture of the dominant elite in the south, so their adherence to Episcopacy became a matter of belief as well as convenience.[5.8]

Although the Church of Scotland was without a serious rival by 1750, it had internal problems, some of which were not satisfactorily resolved a hundred years later. In particular the constitution of the church courts caused difficulties. The lowest court of the Church of

Scotland was the kirk session, comprising the parish minister and an unspecified number of elders. In the seventeenth century the lay representation in the church had been dominated by the gentry, but in Easter Ross by 1750 the eldership was in a sorry state. In some parishes there was no properly constituted session. In seems unlikely, for example, that the inclusion of two women in the Tarbat kirk session in 1750 had received official sanction.[5.9] In other parishes, the elders who were appointed lacked authority. The minister of Edderton, in opposing an elder nominated to act as a delegate to the General Assembly in 1772, 'regretted that so few people of consequence or influence within the bounds have accepted the office of the eldership. This, perhaps, is owing to their not being willing to associate themselves with those whom necessity obliged our predecessors to bring into the eldership. And as many of these are illiterate, they are too easily led to act according to the dictates of designing men, who have their own purposes to serve.'[5.10]

On the other hand, amongst the four elders who were present at that very meeting, one was a farmer and merchant descended from a clergyman, another was a substantial farmer and a third a tailor who had for many years been precentor and session clerk of the parish of Fearn. It is also true that while the gentry no longer dominated the church, a number remained active in its government. In fact, although the lack of weight amongst the elders continued to trouble ministers into the nineteenth century and could cause difficulties in disciplining the more powerful members of the community, it reflected to some extent the populist nature of religious support in the area.[5.11]

As the number of major heritors actively participating in church affairs declined towards the end of the eighteenth century, so problems arose with regard to the attendance of lay members at the higher church courts. Small farmers, millers and tailors found it difficult enough to find the time to attend the meetings of presbyteries and synods when they were not held in their own parish, but it was quite impossible for them to make the annual trip to Edinburgh for the General Assembly. In the middle of the eighteenth century landlords like Sir John Gordon of Invergordon represented the area in Edinburgh, but when the gentry became increasingly Episcopalian in sympathy the church in Easter Ross had to rely on people with Easter Ross connections who were already resident in Edinburgh. Kenneth Mackenzie, a writer in Edinburgh, represented the Presbytery of Dingwall almost continuously from 1794 to 1820 and William Paul, an Edinburgh accountant, the burgh of Tain from 1836 to 1841.[5.12] That this was a problem shared with other areas of Scotland is evident from the statement by Paul that 'It has been said publicly that a considerable part of the Assembly is Composed of Lawyers and Men of business in Edinburgh . . . there can be no more effectual way of putting an end to such a statement than by the Burghs and presbyteries sending up Elders from their different localities . . .'[5.13] But there was no one else to send and the continuation of this procedure was to lead the strictly evangelical presbytery of Dingwall to have as their representative in the 1830s the arch-moderate, John Hope, whose successful advocacy of the rights of patrons to present to parishes despite the opposition of parishioners was a major factor in persuading evangelical ministers that they had no future in the Church of Scotland, and in leading them to secede at the Disruption in 1843.[5.14]

One problem which was of relatively little importance in Easter Ross was that of an insufficient ecclesiastical establishment. Indeed, up to 1750 the opposite was more probably true for, for several centuries, the number of parishes had been dropping because of amalgamations. Although the population increased after 1750, expansion was not rapid and was in most cases easily met by rebuilding or extending existing churches. Only in the towns were more extensive measures needed. Largely as a result of the industrial activity of George Ross of Cromarty, the town of Cromarty expanded rapidly in the later eighteenth century and Ross found it necessary to get government help to establish a Gaelic chapel to cater for the immigrant workers in 1783. Robert Adam's interesting design for a church at Cromarty may have been for this chapel, rather than for the parish church, although, in the event, a simpler but still pleasing design was preferred.[5.15] Tain, too, grew considerably over the century from 1750. A new church built in 1815 only partly alleviated the situation because it was felt that the congregation was too large for one minister, but nothing further was done before the upheaval of 1843.[5.16] In Fortrose the situation was rather different. Population remained relatively stable but a mortification which had been left in the seventeenth century to provide for a burgh preacher finally grew sufficiently large to allow an appointment to be made in 1841.[5.17]

The main functions of the kirk sessions were to administer poor relief, to maintain church discipline and to supervise education. The two latter responsibilities, in particular, were shared with the higher church courts. Poor relief and education are considered elsewhere in this book. Church discipline, as a more exclusively religious aspect of the church's role in society, can be dealt with here.

The degree of emphasis on the maintenance of discipline varied from place to place and from time to time. It is easy to see why the opposing literary schools of the Kailyard and of writers such as George Douglas Brown and John MacDougall Hay — both schools dominated by Presbyterian ecclesiastics — should have sprung from, and fed on, the same tradition.

In Easter Ross, parishes such as Kiltearn and Tarbat provide marked contrasts in the manner in which they approached common disciplinary problems. Kiltearn maintained a standard of strict puritanism comparable with the approach of the Ayrshire churchmen against whom Burns wrote. If Tarbat was hardly a Scottish Elysium, it did at least approach more closely to the rural idyll to which nineteenth century commentators, depressed by the problems of industrialisation and urban squalor, so often looked back.[5.18] In 1754, for example, a £10 fine, which had been paid to the kirk session by Alexander Denoon, was repaid on account of his poor health and reduced circumstances, while, in 1779, a maidservant found guilty of fornication was excused from paying the standard fine of £5 Scots as she, like so many others, was unable to raise such a sum. In the light of a high incidence of illegitimate births and the problems these created for rural communities, it is less surprising that the church should have continued to fight the problem of extra-marital sex with vigour than that, at least on occasion, the vigour should have been modified by mercy and charity.[5.19]

The other disciplinary issue regularly to trouble the church courts was that of Sabbath observance. The mid-eighteenth century is sometimes pictured as a time when a subservient population, cowed into submission by harsh church discipline, rigorously observed the fourth commandment. As usual such a simplistic picture is a distortion of reality. The church certainly took a greater interest in everyday affairs than it has been allowed or encouraged to do in more recent times but, conversely, everyday affairs impinged upon the workings of the church. The request, in 1762, that a notification to the effect that 'If you want any horses, oxen and cows young and old you cannot be better served than at Newhall, and if you know any of your friends that want such acquaint them of the Roup' be read in church on Sunday reveals the intrusion of secular affairs into the sacredness of the Sabbath.[5.20]

Indeed, in the middle of the eighteenth century respect for church discipline appears to have been astonishingly low. William Glass in Meikle was far from being exceptional when he confessed in 1751 that 'being the Lord's day, he through forgetfulness and inadvertency was employed for a considerable time in dressing and grinding corn with a quearn mill'.[5.21] Loss of memory, in fact, was an illness which seemed to be particularly virulent on a Sunday amongst the local population!

Far worse was the case, heard at the same diet of the session, of John Fraser, a fisherman in Seafield, who gathered bait during divine service and compounded his offence by being insolent to the kirk session when he appeared before them.

The church service itself was far from sacrosanct. In 1753 John Macdonald not only had to be rebuked for falling asleep but had the contumacy to reply insolently to the minister on being awakened. Worst of all was the fracas five years later when Thomas Denoon rose up and struck John Macallan in the gallery of Tarbat Church. In justification he claimed that he was but retaliating against Macallan and his cronies who had been spitting and throwing dust down at him.[5.22]

Even in parishes like Kiltearn, the nineteenth century brought an element of moderation into the proceedings of kirk sessions, but it is true also that in the preceding half-century the church had won this particular battle as the number of more serious instances of Sabbath transgression had diminished. Certainly, scandals continued to rock the community. Thomas Dudgeon, who first appeared in the Tarbat kirk session records in 1803, charged with fornication with his servant, continued for at least seven years to battle with the session and the presbytery of Tain, insulting the minister and his parishioners, behaving with levity during divine service and even, for a time, ignoring the ban of lesser excommunication laid on him by the presbytery.[5.23]

But such *causes célèbres* were, by this time, quite exceptional. From a purely materialistic standpoint it is not to be wondered at that the population as a whole should have been willing to fall in with demands for a strict observance of the Sabbath. Having only one official holiday a year, farm servants and labourers must have welcomed Sundays and fast days for the rest they provided. The Culcairn Farm Labour Book recorded in December 1829 that 'This being a day of thanksgiving throughout the presbytery no work is done in consequence',[5.24] and it is almost possible to hear the writer's teeth being ground together as he observes the fruitless passing of a 'Fine frosty day'.[5.25] There can be little doubt that, without the sanctions of the church courts, many employers — landlords and tenants — would have been even more thorough in exploiting their employees.

Such materialistic considerations were not the only, and perhaps not even the principal, reasons for the growing acceptance of church discipline, however. From the 1730s, when a series of religious revivals in the area renewed the sterner traditions of the covenanting period, Easter Ross steadily gained a reputation for evangelical piety. In 1762 Bishop Forbes, despite his natural eagerness to stress the strength of Episcopal support in the area, recognised the puritanical inclinations of the majority of the population.[5.26] Indeed, as early as 1752 the parishioners of Cromarty, involved in a patronage dispute, were called zealots, and well into the nineteenth century the fervour of religious enthusiasm was distasteful to outside observers.[5.27] A visitor in 1803 found the people of Tain 'wholly absorbed in metaphysical notions and doubts', but he doubted if this piety was more than skin deep, for

> With the love, charity and joyful hopes inspired by the genuine doctrines of our Saviour they seem to be unacquainted.
>
> Ross-shire, . . . may be called the Holy Land of Scotland, but a few days was long enough to convince me that religion does not influence the hearts of the people here more than in other parts of the country where their public devotions do not occupy above one half the time.[5.28]

While some of this criticism might be attributed to Episcopalian prejudice, a local minister in 1797 had to confess 'that some of them [the local people] do not distinguish as they ought, between the means and the end of religion; an error not uncommon where religion is most professed',[5.29] and in the 1820s the moderates of the south still looked on Easter Ross as 'the hot-bed of fanaticism'.[5.30] It was still the common people rather than the middle classes, who by now were largely of southern origin anyway, who were strongest in their enthusiasm and it is possible that it was the common element in religious observance which, to some extent, alienated the respectable middle class observers from the south. The religious zeal of the area manifested itself most obviously in the great communion services which were held only twice a year in most parishes but which were attended by large numbers from all over the district, in the opposition to Catholic emancipation, and in attitudes to church government.[5.31]

If support for the attitudes taken on these issues came from the common people, the lead was taken by the ministers who were generally strong members of the evangelical party. This common accord ensured that the voluntaries — supporters of disestablishment — within the church won little support in the area.[5.32]

When discord did arise it was over the contentious issue of patronage. While the local people were in favour of establishment, they objected to the controls which resulted from the state connection. There was no significant dispute over patronage before the middle of the eighteenth century, as many patrons did not choose to exercise the right given to them by the Patronage Act of 1712 and the choice of ministers remained with the heritors and heads of families.[5.33] By 1750, however, the religious revivals had hardened the opposition to patronage amongst the people, while during the later eighteenth century the Crown seems to have decided to take a stronger line in the assertion of its rights to patronage. As the Crown held the patronage of twelve of the seventeen parishes in the area in the eighteenth century (this was reduced in 1814 when a House of Lords' decision gave the patronage of Killearnan to Mackenzie of Cromarty), its attitude to such matters inevitably was important.[5.34]

The first major clash, however, involved not the Crown but a private patron, Urquhart of Cromarty, whose presentee to the vacant parish of Cromarty was opposed by the majority of parishioners with the backing of the presbytery of Chanonry. Indeed the presbytery used the Crown to back their opposition, claiming that the patronage of the parish had devolved from the Bishopric of Ross to the Crown. Although the Court of Session found in favour of Urquhart, the case was finally resolved in favour of the Crown and the parishioners' nominee was presented. It is clear that much of the opposition was due to the fact that Urquhart of Cromarty was a Catholic, for the parishioners' candidate was deposed for immorality in 1755 while the original presentee was presented to Avoch in 1756 and ministered there without trouble for thirty years.[5.35]

The next dispute followed almost immediately. In 1752 the heritors and heads of families in Nigg called a Mr. Bethune to fill the vacancy there, but for the first time the Crown intervened and put forward a presentee. When this presentee withdrew, another was put forward and, despite continued opposition from the parishioners and the presbytery of Tain, the General Assembly confirmed the presentation in 1756. Nigg had been a major centre of the revivalist movement only a decade before and much of the spirit still survived so that, when they lost their case, the parishioners seceded *en masse*.[5.36]

For some time thereafter relative quiet prevailed, although the first

J

minister presented by the Crown to Kiltearn in 1770 soon lost his early popularity because of his acceptance of a pulpit gown gifted to him by his brother-in-law Sir Hector Munro of Novar and within five years was forced to leave the parish.[5.37] Renewed opposition to the exercise of patronage broke out in 1783 when members of the congregation of Rosskeen obtained presbytery permission to attend other churches because of their hostility to the newly presented minister. Thereafter there were more or less serious incidents at Avoch in 1787, Knockbain in 1791, Fearn in 1802 and Kiltearn in 1816. At Avoch and Kiltearn the opposition again resulted in mass secessions from the Church of Scotland.[5.38] There was again a respite in the 1820s, partly, perhaps, because most of the ministers inducted at that time were strongly evangelical and much to the liking of the parishioners. But from 1831 there was increasing opposition to both the practical and theoretical aspects of patronage. The practical opposition clearly was directed against the principle of patronage but, inevitably, individual battles involved also clashes of personality and the combination of the two led to a number of demeaning squabbles. In 1837 Mr. Hay Mackenzie of Cromarty, the patron of the parish of Logie Easter, made clear his desire not to appoint to the vacancy in the parish against the wishes of the parishioners and the presbytery, but the parishioners, far from welcoming his moderation, objected vigorously to all the names he put forward. The nominees were all men of the highest credentials and the opposition to them reflected the bitterness of feeling on the subject. The local church courts added their opposition in the number of petitions they forwarded to the General Assembly opposing patronage and, where appropriate, congratulating or sympathising with the various parishes where the bitterest battles of the campaign were being fought.[5.39]

Although opposition to patronage was very strong throughout the period, until the middle of the nineteenth century actual secession from the church was strictly limited. The three main centres of dissent all originated in particularly violent struggles over patronage. After the parishioners of Nigg lost their contest in 1756, most of them refused to attend the services of the new minister, but there was considerable reluctance to make a final break with the church. Some attended services at Kilmuir, and it was the minister of Alness who procured the services of a dissenting preacher. Within five years the preacher was forced to leave because of financial difficulties — always a major factor in the maintenance of secession churches in the Highlands — and it was only when a minister of the General Associate Synod, or Anti-Burghers — a sect opposed not only to patronage but also to the taking of burgess oaths committing individuals to uphold the 'true Protestant religion' — was inducted, with support from the synod, in 1765 that the last links with the Church of Scotland were snapped.[5.40]

The next major split, at Avoch, exhibited another problem which faced breakaway movements — the difficulty of maintaining the original enthusiasm when there was no preacher to hold the congregation together. Although major opposition was expressed to the settlement in 1787, by 1795 only fourteen seceders regularly attended services in Inverness and Nairn, and probably only the construction of an independent Chapel linked with the Congregational Union of Scotland in 1819 prevented a gradual drift back to the Church of Scotland.[5.41] The same inability to maintain the initial drive affected the followers of the Haldane brothers, whose magnificently successful tour of Easter Ross in 1797 had no long-term results.[5.42]

The secessionists at Kiltearn had no problems over ministers, being supplied by the United Secession Church, but even in 1839, from the regular attendance of one hundred and seventy only two or three families were real seceders. The remainder were merely continuing to protest about the intrusion of an unwanted parish minister. Indeed the minister in question believed that there would have been no disruption at all in 1816 but for the arrival of five secession families from the south.[5.43]

The only other large body of people to leave the Church of Scotland before 1843 belonged to Tain, where the high seat rents in the parish church persuaded some parishioners to build their own chapel in 1836, with assistance from the United Associate Synod.[5.44] Apart from a small congregation of Baptists in Rosemarkie, a tiny scattering of varied dissenters in other parishes and, of course, the Episcopalian remnant, the rest of the population remained firmly attached to the Church of Scotland until 1843.[5.45]

The continued adherence of the greater part of the population of Easter Ross to the Church of Scotland through all the upheavals of the century after the Jacobite rebellions made the events of the Disruption all the more cataclysmic. When the break finally came at the May Assembly of 1843, fourteen of the nineteen Church of Scotland ministers in the area demitted their charges and the minister of Fearn might well have made a fifteenth if he had not been dying. Numbers of parish teachers followed suit and the greater part of the general population joined the new Free Church.[5.46] In parishes like Tain, where the congregation were following their minister, over eighty per cent of the population seceded, and in Tarbat only about half a dozen people remained in the Church of Scotland. In some parishes where ministers did not resign there was a more mixed response. In Alness, although the native farmers seceded, the southern incomers did not and in Dingwall, while only half the English congregation joined the Free Church, two thirds of the Gaelic one did so.[5.47] In general the populist evangelical allegiance transferred to the Free Church, and in the period after 1843 the great bulk of the population remained as true to their new national church as they had done previously to the united Church of Scotland.

b. Education

In 1750 the main, indeed almost the sole, element in the educational structure of Easter Ross was the parish school. By 1750, almost all of the parishes had their own schools. The school of Kiltearn was said, in 1838, to have been established in the sixteenth century, while those of Cromarty, Kilmuir and Tain all claimed a seventeenth century origin. The small parish of Logie appears to have been without a school in 1755 — though whether this was a recent loss or a long-term deprivation is not clear — but the school of neighbouring Kilmuir was regarded as serving both communities.[5.48]

By contrast, in the Highlands as a whole, there were up to one hundred and seventy parishes without parish schools in 1758.[5.49] Although, from time to time, there could be difficulties in filling vacant posts, partially at least because of low pay, most of the schools seem to have functioned fairly continuously from the mid-eighteenth century.[5.50] In most parishes the parish school was the only official educational institution, but in each of the three royal burghs there were also, throughout most of the later eighteenth century, female schools supported by the town council while Tain, in addition, financed an English school.[5.51]

The only other opportunity for education for most of the population of the area was that offered by the Society for the Propagation of Christian Knowledge, which had established a school in the parish of Cromarty as early as 1732 and which subsequently opened further schools in a number of other parishes. The Society would support schools only in parishes where a parish school was already established and where at least some financial assistance was forthcoming. Neither of these conditions created many difficulties in Easter Ross, and the number of Society schools on the first patent doubled from 1760 to 1796.[5.52]

Towards the end of the century these facilities were recognised to be insufficient and attempts were made to improve both the quality and quantity of the education available. The most important move was the introduction of academies, the first, at Fortrose, being founded in 1791, the same year as the Royal Academy at Inverness was opened.[5.53] Plans for another academy, at Tain, followed before 1800. A royal charter was given to the Tain institution in 1809 and it finally opened its doors in 1813.[5.54] Support for both academies was readily forthcoming. The initial finance for Fortrose academy came from a century-old endowment, but large sums were also provided by the local gentry. In Tain there was no original endowment, but the town council had a traditional interest in education and carried this over into support for the academy. The local gentry again provided enthusiastic support. Both schools also received large sums from the colonies. In 1811, for example, Fortrose academy received gifts of over six hundred pounds from Bombay, one hundred and twenty-five pounds from Calcutta and two hundred and ten pounds from the island of Grenada with the main fund-raising efforts in Bombay and Grenada being led by two former pupils, Sir James Macintosh and George Gunn Munro.[5.55]

Although the fortunes of both academies fluctuated — Tain even had to close for a time in 1843 because of a shortage of funds while in the first decade of the nineteenth century Fortrose had two poor rectors who almost ruined the school — for most of the first half of the nineteenth century they set new standards in the education they offered.[5.56] So effective was Tain that an academy education came to be considered quite sufficient by itself and by 1837 the numbers of pupils in the area going on to university had actually diminished as a result.[5.57]

Although the academies and parish schools provided most of the education required by the middle classes there was, after 1800, an increase in the number of private or adventure schools. Some of these were founded to make up for the temporary absence of a parish school — as at Rosemarkie — or to make good the geographical, numerical or scholastic deficiencies of existing schools. At Knockbain the farmers living at a distance from the parish school supported an itinerating school, while in Cromarty, during the 1820s, some of the wealthier tradesmen, being dissatisfied with the quality of the education locally available, secured a schoolmaster of their own. Although some of these schools were supported on a more or less formal basis, the greater number existed solely on the income from fees and there was a great variety in the standard of education on offer. In all there were eleven private and adventure schools operating in the region in 1838.[5.58]

While much of the effort of the official and private systems was directed at the relatively well to do, there was, too, a considerable improvement in the education offered to the bulk of the population. Before 1800 the only major charitable organisation involved in education in Easter Ross was the Society for the Propagation of Christian Knowledge, but soon after the turn of the century several other societies became active in the region. As early as 1806 there existed a 'Society for extending the benefits of education to the children of the poor within the counties of Ross and Cromarty', but little seems to have been done by this body and the first major initiative was taken by the Gaelic School Society of Edinburgh founded in 1811, followed closely in 1812 by the Glasgow School Society. Both societies established ambulatory schools which stayed only for a maximum of two or three years at one place.[5.59] A more useful contribution was made for a time by the Inverness Society for the Education of the Poor, founded in 1818. By 1826 it was the only Highland society concerned with the general education of the people, but its usefulness was limited by a lack of funds and support for it was not as strong in Easter Ross as it might have been. Only six of the ninety-two directors by donation and subscription came from the area, including the Mackenzies of Seaforth, Gairloch (both of whose interests lay mainly in the west) and Kilcoy, Munro of Novar and Fraser of Inchcoulter.[5.60] In 1826 there were eight Society for the Propagation of Christian Knowledge schools, three Edinburgh Society schools and one Glasgow society school. Apart from the first of these, all the societies were hampered by limited finances, and after reaching a peak in the 1820s they fairly rapidly declined as funds were diverted to the General Assembly scheme for schools which was established in 1824. In 1839 the Inverness Society handed over its schools to the General Assembly Education Committee but the Committee's dominance in educational provision lasted only until 1843 for, after the Disruption, the Free Church made a major effort to provide their own schools in each parish.[5.61]

The nationwide charitable effort was supplemented by local endeavours on a smaller scale. To cater for the needs of the Episcopalian community in Killearnan the wife of the proprietor of Redcastle supported a school in the parish in 1844, while a few years earlier Sir Francis Mackenzie of Gairloch had provided a salary, accommodation and a garden for a teacher at the west end of the parish of Urquhart.[5.62] In the towns, too, local initiatives took place. A Cromarty Society maintained two schools in the town in 1836, while ten years later the 'Industrial School Association' formed by a group of townswomen opened a female school in Tain.[5.63]

In addition to the increasing number of day schools, the nineteenth century saw the rise of Sunday schools catering largely for children who were unable to attend during the week and for adults who had missed all other opportunities of acquiring an education. The first recorded Sunday school in Easter Ross was founded in 1787 at Tain by Lady John Ross of Balnagown, who provided a salary and an allowance for coals and candles in the winter as well as free books for the scholars and detailed instructions on how the school was to be conducted. Another Sunday school was established by Charles Grant of Redcastle in Knockbain before 1794 and he too met the cost of books for the pupils.[5.64]

But prior to 1800 there was a general dislike of Sunday schools, and although by 1818 there were at least five hundred such schools in the whole of Scotland, they were still almost unknown in the Highlands. Some, at least, considered Sabbath schools to be discreditable to the parents and only poor substitutes for a better education, and there was at times considerable opposition to their establishment. The children of the poor were unlikely to obtain any other form of instruction, however, as they had to work during the week, and Sunday schools grew in number to meet this need. As in so many other fields Easter Ross, despite local opposition to Sabbath schools, more closely resembled the pattern in the south of Scotland than that prevalent in the rest of the Highlands, for, in addition to those at Tain and Knockbain, further schools were opened either shortly before or shortly after 1800, and by 1840 many parishes had several in operation.[5.65]

Towards the middle of the nineteenth century the area was served by parochial schools in every parish except Rosemarkie, twenty-nine other day schools and a considerable number of Sabbath schools, but within that total there were great variations in the quality of teaching available.[5.66] Throughout the period it was common for the teachers in parish schools to have had at least some university education. Many teachers intended to become ministers and in some cases they would accept a teaching post until they secured a living, while in others they would become teachers to finance their way through university on a part-time basis. Of the nine parish teachers in the presbytery of Tain in 1842, five had completed their literary and philosophical studies at university and had enrolled as students of divinity, three had just completed their literary and philosophical studies and one had attended only three sessions at college.[5.67]

But a good education did not necessarily mean an ability to teach and as there was no enforced retirement, those teachers who did not wish, or failed to become ministers could reach senility and still retain their posts. On some occasions, when a teacher considered himself unable to continue he would hire, at his own expense, an assistant to help him but this was not obligatory.[5.68] The academies generally attracted high-quality teachers — the third rector of Tain academy, William Ritchie, eventually became Professor of Natural and Experimental Philosophy at London University — but even in the academies bad appointments were made. The second rector at Fortrose academy was so strict a disciplinarian that many parents withdrew their children from the school, while both academies suffered along with the parish schools the problems of intemperate staff.[5.69]

Although the educational standard amongst the teachers in the schools of the Society for Propagating Christian Knowledge may not have been as high as those in the academies and parish schools, the Society did emphasise the importance of teaching ability. It is not clear, however, how successful the Society was in practice and, at least in the nineteenth century, there were a number of Society teachers who proved to be unsatisfactory.

In 1827, for example, it was reported that Daniel Bremner, the teacher at Davidstone, near Cromarty, who was aged seventy and had been with the Society for twenty-two years, was not very efficient. Nine years later Mr. Mackenzie, the teacher at Kinkell in Urquhart, who was about eighty years old and infirm, was held to be unable to teach, except to give a few pupils religious instruction.[5.70]

Standards of competence varied greatly in the other schools in the area. While some teachers had received an academy and even, occasionally, a university education, the majority had only attended a parish school themselves and had had no training at all in teaching methods. The lowest schools might be taught by widowed women with only the very rudiments of an education.[5.71]

Throughout the period, in all schools, very little attention was paid to methods of presentation or to ensuring that the pupils understood what they were taught. Mere rote learning was the standard practice until well into the nineteenth century, and as late as 1833 only half the schools submitting replies to a government questionnaire admitted to using methods calculated to enable the pupils to understand their tuition.[5.72]

The problem was exacerbated in Easter Ross as in the other Highland regions by language difficulties. Even amongst the English-speaking population in the middle of the eighteenth century there could be problems when all instruction in the higher classes in parish schools was conducted in Latin, but matters were very much worse for the Gaelic speakers in the area.[5.73] Official disapproval of the Gaelic language ensured that no adequate instruction was given in that medium in the eighteenth century. No official policy appears to have been laid down for parish schools but few gave any teaching in Gaelic, while the Society for the Propagation of Christian Knowledge schools were positively forbidden to teach Gaelic from 1753 to 1766, and even when this ban was lifted the emphasis on English continued.[5.74] Only with the arrival of the Gaelic School Societies was a major effort made to penetrate the language barrier.

The Gaelic spelling books they produced in 1811 were adopted by the Society for the Propagation of Christian Knowledge in 1817.[5.75] But the teaching of Gaelic was superficial and the emphasis on English remained. An Inverness writer claimed in 1837 that he

> could find thousands in the Highlands of Scotland who will read the English Bible tolerably well, but cannot understand more than 'yes' or 'no'; and being thus obliged to continue reading a language completely unintelligible to them, it gives them no pleasure, but rather disgust; and the moment they leave school, if they remain at home in those districts where nothing but their mother tongue is spoken, they lay their books aside and never look at them more.[5.76]

His recognition of the futility of this type of instruction bore fruit gradually as the teaching of Gaelic spread slowly to even the parish schools, but in 1842 a government inspector was still able to report of the schools in the Presbytery of Tain that

> It seems extraordinary that when the importance of the explanatory method has been recognised, and where its partial introduction has been followed by the very best results, many of the children, whose vernacular tongue is Gaelic, should be able to read English with facility, without having the slightest notion of the import of the words which they perfectly articulate.[5.77]

Low standards of teaching were not improved by the conditions in which most schools operated. Only the academies were provided from the start with reasonable accommodation.[5.78] The burgh school in Dingwall occupied a room in the tolbooth in the eighteenth century, while even when separate buildings were provided they were no better than the hovels occupied by so many of the local people.[5.79] In 1808 even a school as important as that at Cromarty was merely a low long straw-thatched building open from gable to gable, with a mud floor and an unlathed roof.[5.80]

By the middle of the nineteenth century parish schools generally were accommodated satisfactorily, although several were over-crowded, but the other schools remained in a poor state. While all the Society for the Propagation of Christian Knowledge and General Assembly schools were considered to be highly unsatisfactory, the General Assembly school at Scotsburn was possibly the worst, being damp and in bad repair.[5.81] Although accommodation was provided for all Society for the Propagation of Christian Knowledge, General Assembly and parish teachers in the nineteenth century, this was often in not much better condition than the schools. At Balintore in 1826, for example, the Society for the Propagation of Christian Knowledge teacher was provided with accommodation above the school which was very cold, badly furnished and, because of a mistake by the builder in not raising the walls high enough, almost uninhabitable.[5.82] Within the schools the provision of equipment was at a low level. The academies, it is true, were well off, Tain even having an observatory (removed in 1826 because it proved too heavy for the roof), but elsewhere, even as late as 1844, a blackboard was a luxury and other pieces of equipment almost unknown.[5.83]

Just as the conditions in the different types of schools varied widely, so too did the curricula, although within each type of school and throughout the period there was remarkably little variation. The teachers of the grammar schools in Tain and Fortrose were expected in the eighteenth century to offer English, Latin, Greek, French, Writing, Geography, Arithmetic, Bookkeeping and some of the practical parts of Mathematics and, at least towards the end of the century, this constituted the standard range of subjects offered by the country parish schools as well. Occasionally additional subjects would be offered, such as church music at Avoch.[5.84] Whatever the faults of the teaching system, the possibility existed of acquiring some knowledge on a wide range of subjects, even in the smaller schools, and in a more important school, such as Cromarty, in the early nineteenth century, the pupil who was interested had the opportunity of becoming acquainted with the *Tatler* and the *Spectator* as well as the more usual Virgils and Ovids.[5.85]

The opening of the academies increased the number of subjects taught, as well as the depth to which they were studied. History, Geometry, Algebra, Navigation, Natural Philosophy, Drawing and Natural History were amongst the subjects introduced, and for the first time teachers began to specialise. Whereas the parish and society schools had been, and remained, one-teacher schools, where the teacher was expected to be equally proficient in all subjects, the masters in the academies restricted their teaching to a limited range. At Tain the rector taught the scientific disciplines and the second master languages and grammar, while at Fortrose the humanities were the preserve of the rector and the sciences were handled by the second master. In both establishments the third master took rudimentary classes in English and Latin. Although dancing may have been too frivolous to include in the academies' curricula, dancing masters were available in both Tain and Fortrose from the later eighteenth century and academy pupils could attend as part of their education.[5.86] Some of the additional subjects offered by the academies were adopted by the parish schools in the nineteenth century — Avoch offered navigation in 1840, for example — but the standard subjects remained as they had been in the eighteenth century.[5.87]

The better private and adventure schools offered fully as wide a range of subjects in the nineteenth century as the parish schools, one female school in Tain even offering Italian, but the poorer schools concentrated on the basics of reading, writing and arithmetic.[5.88] The charity schools, too, offered only a very limited education. The main duty of teachers appointed by the Society for the Propagation of Christian Knowledge was not to educate children in their care but to further their religious instruction and although, as a by-product, some basic instruction was given, the main books used were the Bible and the Catechism. Even when the Society had some other books translated into Gaelic, they chose heavy religious tracts hardly calculated to arouse interest or enthusiasm amongst schoolchildren. In the middle of the eighteenth century pupils in Society schools were examined for their knowledge of the Bible, Testament, Proverbs, Catechism, Writing, Arithmetic and Music and even a century later, although some history had crept into the syllabus, the emphasis was still on religion.[5.89] The Gaelic School societies, too, regarded the spreading of scriptural knowledge to be their main aim and many of the Sabbath schools had no other object than the memorising of the Catechism and passages from Scripture.[5.90]

While it is reasonably easy to ascertain what sort of education was on offer, it is more difficult to determine how many were educated. Figures for school attendance are unreliable indicators in so far as many of those attending apparently gained very little from their time at school, while others, who were never in a position to attend school, picked up a rudimentary education at home. It is impossible to make any reliable estimate for the eighteenth century, but on the evidence available it is clear that for most of the century educational opportunities were very limited. None of the eleven King's Cottagers who petitioned the Commissioners of Forfeited Estates in 1765 could write, and illiteracy was widespread amongst the labouring classes.[5.91] Nor was it restricted to the one social class. None of the elders in the parish of Tarbat could read with understanding in 1735, and in 1770 four of the five elders in Alness were unable to write. Elders were not usually drawn from the lowest classes but were tenant farmers or even tacksmen.[5.92] From the evidence of estate rentals it would appear that far fewer than fifty per cent of the total population were able to write in the middle of the eighteenth century.[5.93]

It may be, however, that larger numbers were able to read. Certainly in the nineteenth century many more learned to read than to write, but even if this was the case, in earlier years the total numbers with any education at all must have remained small. Even in the nineteenth century it is unwise to place too much reliance on the sometimes exaggeratedly optimistic claims of local ministers. The Inverness Education Society found in the 1820s that almost two thirds of the population over eight years old could read (as compared to only just over fifty-one per cent for the whole Highland area). Even if, as seems unlikely, the figure represents only those who could read with understanding, no great improvement in educational facilities took place in the following decade and a half to justify the opinions expressed in the New Statistical Account that almost all could read.[5.94] Again, the numbers writing were very much smaller than the numbers reading. In a petition from the Gaelic speakers of Avoch in 1831 only sixteen of sixty adults subscribing could write, and in Tain six years later four hundred and eighty-six children were being taught to read whereas only two hundred and twenty-four were being taught to write.[5.95]

There were a number of reasons why only a limited number received education, and of these probably the most important, especially in the eighteenth century, was poverty. While the children of people on the poor roll might be educated free of charge in the parish schools after 1803, the rest were expected to pay the fees. Society schools were more generous in their attitude but hoped that parents would pay fees where possible. Even when fees were not exacted, as was increasingly common with the increase of charity schools after 1800, many families could not afford to lose the economic value of their children by sending them to school when they could be bringing in money by acting as herds or at least helping to work the family farm.[5.96]

Distance, too, created difficulties before 1800, particularly for the population of the Highland straths in Ferindonald, but clearances for sheep farms and the increasing number of schools in all districts reduced the problem to one of minor importance except in a few localities. By 1824 over eighty-six per cent of the population lived within two miles of the nearest school and only a quarter of one per cent were further than five miles from a school. This compares very favourably with the Highlands as a whole, where only sixty-eight per cent of the inhabitants were within two miles of a school and almost eleven per cent were over five miles distant.[5.97]

There was also lack of interest amongst the lower classes, who saw little purpose in education except as a means to obtain greater knowledge of the Scriptures. The language barrier increased this apathy amongst the Gaelic-speaking element of the population, and there is some evidence that the numbers of people eager to have their children educated declined as the nineteenth century progressed as a result of secession and the introduction of uneducated labourers and smallholders from the Highlands. On the other hand it may be that some parents became more eager to have their offspring instructed in English as realisation of the limitations of Gaelic spread.[5.98]

Even those who attended school did not always do so on a regular basis. Quite apart from the parents who could afford to send their children to school only occasionally, a considerable number of country children were required to work on the land in summer and attended only in winter. The largest number attending schools in the area from Michaelmas 1833 to Lady Day 1834 was about seventy per cent higher than the same figure for the period Lady Day to Michaelmas 1833, and in general only the town schools maintained their attendances with any regularity throughout the year. Irregular attendance was not conducive to concentrated efforts by the pupils and, so far as the teachers were concerned, it made more difficult the introduction of improved methods of instruction.[5.99]

It might have been possible for the pupils to make up in part for irregular attendances by extending the number of years they went to school and, as the age of pupils ranged up to twenty in the 1830s, some may well have done this, but the average number of years' attendance at school did not exceed six in any type of school at that time and is unlikely to have been longer at any earlier period.[5.100]

There were, of course, wide variations within the general pattern and, in particular, class and sex seem to have been important in determining educational opportunity. The children of the gentry were in an exceptionally privileged position and can be treated separately, but even amongst the remainder there were some more privileged than others. The children of merchants, tacksmen and other large tenant farmers were less likely to have their studies interrupted during summer than the offspring of crofters, small farmers and labourers, just as they were more likely to be sent to school in the first instance. Their home background was also more probably conducive to study because of better accommodation, readier access to books and a greater probability of speaking English as the mother tongue. Moreover, it was the children of the more well to do who were sent to the better schools, as they were more expensive and only the prosperous could afford the fees for the non-elementary subjects.

When money was tight the factor of sex became important, although there may have been a basic preference for educating sons rather than daughters irrespective of any constraints. At any rate, throughout the period boys quite clearly had a better chance of receiving an education than girls, while male children were also more likely to get a better type of education. For the eighteenth century the only figures available are those for the schools of the Society for the Propagation of Christian Knowledge, but these correspond so closely with the more general figures of the nineteenth century that there can be little doubt that the preferential treatment accorded to boys was as strong, if not stronger, before 1800 as after.[5.101]

The children of the gentry were set apart from the rest of the school population in that they were far less dependent upon the local educational system, and even before 1750 it was not unknown for children from the north of Scotland to be sent to school in the south. The lesser gentry, such as the Rosses of Kindeace, might be content with schools in the Edinburgh area but the leading families were already sending their sons to England. Sir Harry Munro of Foulis was educated at the famous academy of Dr. Philip Doddridge at Northampton in the 1730s and subsequently at Westminster School.[5.102]

The majority of the local lairds, however, did not look so far afield and were still content to send their children to the leading schools in their own localities. In the third quarter of the eighteenth century the parish school of Cromarty was prominent and many of the gentry of Ross, Cromarty and Inverness sent their children to it. Subsequently the school of Mr. Strath at Nairn became noted, and the offspring of at least one Ross-shire landlord was educated there.[5.103] The opening of the academies at Fortrose and Tain proved a counter to the increasing attractions of the south and even drew children from distant counties. Indeed Tain in the early nineteenth century had children from England and the colonies on its roll.[5.104]

But the attractions of the academies were only partial and temporary. While they might be adequate for younger sons, they were not always considered to be so for the heir to an estate who was expected to get a wider education in the south. Sir Harry Munro's example was followed in the 1770s by Macleod of Cadboll who went to Eton, and after 1800 it became commonplace for the major proprietors to be educated at English public schools if a private tutor was not employed.[5.105] The practice of engaging a private tutor, which was adopted by some landlords in the later eighteenth century, became increasingly common in the nineteenth century and spread to the lesser gentry and the clergy.[5.106]

The children of landlords and clergy had a better chance of taking their education further than most of the population, and numbers went on to university but they were not the only ones to do so. Many teachers had either attended university before taking up their appointment in the area or became part-time students while working, and it is not surprising to see the sons of major tenants or factors at university such as the son of the factor at Balnagown in 1749.[5.107] But it is at least possible that some of the twelve pupils who went to university in the space of three years from Urquhart parish school prior to 1793 belonged to less well to do families.[5.108]

Provision was made to allow those in straitened circumstances to attend college. The synod of Ross operated a bursary scheme from at least 1751 giving assistance to two students studying philosophy and divinity. Five shillings was contributed from each session box and half a crown by each minister and the total sum was split equally between the two bursars. Later in the century, although only one bursary seems to have been available, the sum raised remained the same and indeed was raised to ten shillings from each parish in 1796. As time passed nominations to the bursary were increasingly restricted to the children of local clergy.[5.109] In the later eighteenth century there is also mention of a session bursar in Tain, while, after 1767, a private bursary was made available for Marischal College from a legacy left by Walter Denoon. This bursary was to be given to nominees of the presbyteries of Tain and Dornoch.[5.110]

The great majority of university students went to Aberdeen and particularly to King's College. Of the twenty-two locally born ministers from 1750 to 1850 whose place of study is known, fifteen went to King's and four of the remainder to Marischal. No diminution in this preference for Aberdeen occurred throughout the period and it extended beyond the ministers to others attending university, particularly the synod bursars. Aberdeen was obviously attractive as being the closest and perhaps the cheapest university in the country, but such constraints were less important to the sons of the gentry. While the children of farmers, factors and ministers went to the other Scottish universities in some numbers, it was far more common for the sons of lairds to do so, particularly in the nineteenth century, and as the influence of English public schooling grew, it also became more usual for the leading gentry to go to Oxford or Cambridge.[5.111]

For most of the populace education ceased as soon as school was finished, and those who wished to go further generally had to leave the area. But some attempt was made to increase educational opportunities in the area, particularly by providing libraries. As early as 1704 Kirkwood's scheme for free public libraries in every presbytery had been accepted by the General Assembly of the Church of Scotland, and in connection with this scheme several libraries were established in Easter Ross. Although religion was emphasised, history, rhetoric, literature, philology, medicine and even astrology were also covered. Some of these libraries suffered in the Jacobite rebellion of 1715, and the scheme failed because little thought had been given to the maintenance and updating of stock. By 1826 there were few libraries left in any part of the Highlands, and although both the sessional and presbyterial libraries of Tain were amongst that number, they no longer attempted to provide other than religious material.[5.112]

Private individuals maintained large and varied collections of books and the schools had libraries of one sort or another, but not until the nineteenth century were further attempts made to make reading matter generally available.[5.113] In 1821 a reading room was opened in Cromarty, taking three London, two Edinburgh and two Inverness newspapers, while round about the same time subscription libraries were opened in Tain and Dingwall, the latter receiving donations of books from several of the neighbouring proprietors and amounting by 1831 to four hundred volumes of works in history, science and literature. Although a further reading room in Tain flourished, the subscription libraries failed. The wealthier townspeople bought their own books and the poorer inhabitants either could not afford the subscriptions or were unable to read.[5.114] The need to provide literature for the poorer classes was widely recognised and there was an increasing demand, at least from the English-speaking working class, but little was done effectively to meet this demand. In 1838 the minister of Rosskeen reported on the recently established parish library that it 'seems to be already in a flourishing state. It is hoped that it will be the means of creating gradually among the humbler classes of our population a greater taste for reading than at present exists, and of this aiding in the diffusion of useful knowledge.'[5.115] How well justified his hopes were, cannot now be ascertained. Nor, despite the assertion of James Cameron, the Tain surgeon, in 1842, that the library connected with the Secession Church in Nigg, to which the poorest class had ready access, was 'acknowledged by those who have availed themselves of it to be productive of much benefit', can it be established how widely this library was used, or to what extent its contents fulfilled the non-religious needs of the population.[5.116]

The better educated sections of the community on the other hand did have increasing opportunities to increase their knowledge. The bookshops which were opened in the early nineteenth century, the reading rooms and even the subscription libraries which were opened as regularly as they failed helped to broaden the public outlook so that in 1836 it could be said that, whereas in the past the Bible had been the only way in which a man could learn to think,

> new sources of intelligence have been opened up — it is the newspaper and the magazine, not the Catechism and the Confession of Faith, that are now stereotyped on the public mind.[5.117]

While library provision was limited, it was a great deal more satisfactory than arrangements for further education which were practically non-existent. Limited industrial development and a small population base prevented the establishment of Mechanics' Institutes until the very end of the period, when one was opened in Tain. Before the middle of the nineteenth century the only individual who is recorded as having concerned himself with such matters was William Ritchie, the third rector of Tain academy, who admitted mechanics free of charge to his public lectures if they made models for use in the academy.[5.118]

c. Linguistic Culture

One of the main aims of Highland education since the seventeenth century had been the extirpation of the Gaelic language and culture, although little progress seems to have been made before 1750.[5.119] Easter Ross, however, was not a typical Highland area, for its population contained a considerable element of native English speakers. Some of the more general comments on the subject of language made by eighteenth century commentators cannot be taken literally. Burt, writing in the 1720s, claimed that the area surrounding Inverness was entirely Gaelic-speaking, and the government agent who covered most of the Highlands, including Easter Ross, reported in 1750 that Gaelic was universally spoken except in Caithness.[5.120] But the eastern Black Isle was unquestionably an exception. The parishes of Avoch, Rosemarkie and Cromarty were almost entirely English-speaking in the middle of the eighteenth century. Some English was also spoken in the burghs of Dingwall and Tain, for the council minutes were recorded in that language and accounts by local merchants were rendered in English.[5.121] Even in some of the country parishes in mid-century English was slowly gaining ground amongst the previously Gaelic-speaking population but on the whole, outside the three eastern Black Isle parishes and the towns, Gaelic was the common language of almost everyone apart from the gentry and the clergy.[5.122] In 1762 only fourteen or fifteen people from a congregation of about three hundred at a service in Knockbain knew any English, and in the following decade English services were felt to be unnecessary in Rosskeen. Indeed, until the nineteenth century Gaelic remained the first language of the preponderant majority of the population in most parishes, although there is some evidence that English was making progress and that increasing numbers were able to understand it, if not to speak it very well.[5.123]

It is hardly surprising that English made some inroads with all the weight of the government and the church behind it. The English bias of the schools has already been noted and this was regarded towards the end of the eighteenth century as playing an important part in spreading the English language.[5.124] A leading Church of Scotland clergyman, Dr. Walker, was quite clear in 1771 that 'to spread the English Language over the Highlands has always been a laudable endeavour of the Church: as it is at once the most effectual means for the Religious Instruction of the inhabitants, and the Improvement of the Country'.[5.125] It was for this reason that the Highland clergy were instructed to preach at least one English sermon every Sabbath, although, in many cases, it must have been a total waste of time. Indeed it was argued that this practice only led to the rise of a prejudice against the language.[5.126]

The influx of southern farmers, which started towards the end of the eighteenth century, as well as altering the proportion of numbers in the two language groups, no doubt also encouraged the spread of English amongst the native population, and this population may also have been influenced by the large numbers serving in the armed forces in the later eighteenth and early nineteenth centuries. It may have been possible for soldiers spending their career in the closed communities of the local regiments to avoid much contact with English, but those who were pressganged or volunteered for the navy must have had to master the language to some extent.

Yet the movement in language was not all one-way. Easter Ross was on the linguistic frontier between English and Gaelic, and while English, with the immense backing provided by the resources of the south, spread out from existing enclaves to the neighbouring countryside, Gaelic counter-attacked in its own way. The erection of the hemp factory at Cromarty attracted large numbers of Gaelic-speaking immigrants (most of them probably from neighbouring parishes) to the town so that, by 1836, some five hundred people regularly attended the Gaelic chapel there.[5.127] Increasing numbers of Highlanders were settled in Easter Ross either as servants or as crofters. While many in the former category may have been transient, they were being constantly replaced and the total effect of this influx was to strengthen Gaelic where it was still spoken and to introduce it to Avoch and Rosemarkie which had been previously almost totally English-speaking. In 1831 it was claimed that there were in Avoch three to four hundred people with Gaelic as their main language out of a total population of eighteen hundred, and five years later there was a similar proportion of

Gaelic speakers in the neighbouring parish of Rosemarkie.[5.128]

Despite the influx of Gaelic speakers, English progressed inexorably. By 1826 over thirty-six per cent of the families in Easter Ross understood English best. It is true that outside the main English-speaking areas the proportion fell to just under fourteen per cent but even this was high compared to the rest of the north-western Highlands where not even four per cent of the total population understood English better than Gaelic.[5.129] Although large numbers continued to prefer Gaelic in the country districts, there was an increasing language barrier between the generations. In the towns, especially, the children of even the lower classes began to use English regularly, and as certain a sign as any that Gaelic was in decline was the fact that, by 1840, it was no longer heard in the playground or the street. In Kilmuir, where in 1824 Gaelic had been called the universal language of the parish, the situation had changed so much by 1838 as a result of the eagerness of parents that their children should be taught to read and understand English that that language was now generally used and even most of the labouring classes spoke it reasonably well. Even in a Highland parish like Kiltearn the influence of the Gaelic Society schools was such that Gaelic was rapidly losing ground, and in most parts of the parish both languages were used indifferently. Only in Urquhart, a parish which had received one of the largest influxes of displaced tenants from Central Ross, was there no decline in Gaelic, and even there the ability to speak English increased. Gaelic continued to be widely spoken amongst the labouring classes after 1850, but by that date the battle for linguistic supremacy had long been won by English.[5.130]

6
Conclusion

a. A Frontier Province

A writer on Easter Ross in this century has suggested that it is a district which is 'in but not wholly of the Highlands'.[6.1] The same ambiguous position can be seen in the eighteenth and nineteenth centuries with regard to the relationships between Easter Ross and the areas which encircle it.

Before it is possible to determine how Highland Easter Ross may have been, however, it is necessary to define more closely the concept of the Highlands. The standard picture of the Highland area as one of natural deprivation, where climatic and geological forces have combined to produce a terrain generally unsuitable for human settlement is, by and large, accurate and the existence of cultural and economic differences between this area and the rest of Scotland has long been clearly recognised.[6.2]

But such generalised impressions conceal wide divergences. Tiree with its fertile soil and long hours of sun is as close to many Lowland districts as it is to nearby Mull, while the comparatively well-favoured, fairly low-lying coastline of Kintyre has little in common with the equally low-lying desolate wastes of much of Sutherland. Similarly in terms of economic and cultural development the burgesses of Campbeltown, for example, must have felt that they had no more in common with the small cattle farmers of Badenoch than with the townsmen of Ayr and Irvine so much closer across the Firth of Clyde.[6.3]

The problem of definition is further complicated by the difficulty in determining a suitable boundary between the Highlands and the rest of Scotland. To accept the geological boundary of the Highland fault would be to place the whole of the North-East corner of Scotland in the

Highlands. Yet in almost all respects this corner is strongly Lowland in character. Cultural boundaries have fluctuated with the centuries and have not corresponded with geographic or economic realities besides being open to a variety of other interpretations. It might, indeed, be more realistic to recognise an intermediate zone covering much of Perthshire, Angus, Aberdeenshire, Banff and Moray and including parts of several other counties, but there would then be the problem of distinguishing two frontiers rather than one, and the difficulty of relating widely divergent conditions within the indisputable heartlands of each zone would remain.[6.4] Overall it seems better to accept the standard division between Highland and Lowland, to attempt a fairly rigorous definition of the Highlands and to compare this with Easter Ross to see how far conditions prevailing in that district were similar to those in adjoining regions.

Historians of the Highlands have in general skated over the problems of the fringe districts. Some have chosen to regard them as integral parts of the Highlands while others have equally decisively treated them as far-flung tentacles of the Lowlands.[6.5] Many who have been concerned with more general themes have failed to recognise that a problem exists at all. To some extent those who have been percipient enough to recognise a distinction between the eastern and western Highlands have found themselves even more confused in their treatment of the fringe areas. In theory these areas should be more easily fitted into an eastern Highland sub-region than into the Highlands as a whole, but even Malcolm Gray — probably the most distinguished twentieth century Highland economic historian — has found the problem intractable. In his seminal work on the Highland economy he considered Easter Ross to lie within the area of his concern and treated evidence from the district as having a validity for the Highlands in general. Gray himself, however, has cautioned that some of his early conclusions were more hypothetical than proven, and in subsequent work he has revised his opinion so far as to exclude Easter Ross from the Highlands altogether.[6.6]

Historians of Easter Ross itself have faced the same difficulty but, on the whole, they have been concerned with specialised topics or have been writing for a popular market and there has been no serious attempt to come to terms with the issue.[6.7]

For current purposes the Highlands are, rather arbitrarily, considered to include in their entirety the counties of Sutherland, Argyll and (with the exception of the burgh of Inverness and its immediate environs) Inverness, plus the upland areas of Perth, Angus, Aberdeen, Banff, Moray, Nairn, Ross and Caithness. Within this area much of the land is mountainous and very little is fertile. In some parts of the region climatic conditions are sub-Arctic and even where, as on the west coast, extremes are modified by the influence of the sea, high winds and a heavy rainfall discourage human settlement in all but a few well sheltered spots. The distinction between this geography and that of Easter Ross has already been drawn and needs no amplification.

It is possible, too, to give a general picture of the Highland economy and society existing in the eighteenth and nineteenth centuries, although again with the caveat that many sub-regional differences must inevitably be lost in such a picture. The widely accepted and generally unexceptional portrait of the area as a whole in 1750 is one in which pastoral farming formed the main basis of the economy. The local population reared black cattle which were sold for the southern market. The money thus obtained was used to pay the rent and to buy such necessities as could not be produced at home. Some grain was sown on the scattered patches of arable ground but it was for home consumption only and was insufficient to meet the needs of an expanding population. In coastal areas fishing was pursued on a limited scale, although again almost entirely for local consumption, while, particularly in the east, linen spinning and whisky distilling were locally important.

In most districts, however, the cattle trade was the major, if not the only, source of money income and over the region as a whole the economic infrastructure was almost non-existent. In the indisputable Highlands there were only three incorporated towns and practically no other communities larger than clachans. The only roads were those which had been constructed for military objectives after 1715, and limited wealth and transport difficulties prevented markets from attaining more than a very local significance.

Although the material distinctions between the various elements of Highland society were restricted because of the overall lack of resources, the social gradations were more pronounced than in other parts of the country. Landlords maintained a close hold over their tenants by granting only verbal or, at best, short written leases. Most of the written leases were granted to tacksmen, who formed an intermediate group of powerful and relatively wealthy middlemen subletting their lands to tenants at will.[6,8]

Even more important than economic considerations were the

obligations of respect and obedience which tied the ordinary people to their clan chiefs and chieftains in the essentially tribal society which still existed throughout the area. When the authority of landlord and of clan chief were combined in one individual, that individual could expect absolute obedience from his tenant clansmen. When the two authorities conflicted, the power of the clan chief often proved the greater.[6.9]

This brief overview can be substantiated by reference in greater detail to specific areas. Morvern in Argyll and Strathnaver in Sutherland were both in the eighteenth century thoroughly Highland areas with a long history of Gaelic culture. By way of contrast, coastal Caithness, although not generally regarded as being an integral part of Lowland Scotland, never has been considered to be a constituent part of the Highlands either and in many respects may be thought of as occupying a similar position to that of Easter Ross in relation to the main mass of North-West Scotland.[6.10]

Lowland Caithness and the parish of Farr (which is largely coterminous with the Naver basin) cover roughly the same area as Easter Ross and have easily identifiable boundaries, and although Morvern is not much more than a third the size, it too can be regarded as an entity capable of separate treatment and bearing comparison with the other districts.[6.11] These three areas, with Easter Ross, provide some interesting contrasts in the structure and economy of their societies.

In the middle of the eighteenth century both Morvern and Strathnaver were controlled by a small number of landowners with typically large estates. The Dukes of Argyll, who were the greatest landowners in Morvern, had held their estates in the parish for less than a century but, in addition to their strong links with the surrounding area, their claims to the estate had a long history and they had inherited the principle of a single estate dominating the area. The even more dominant Sutherland family had been established in or around Strathnaver since the thirteenth century. In neither district was the major landowner resident — even when they resided on some part of their Highland estates the proprietors were so far distant as to be absentee landlords — and at no time in the following century was residence to be the norm for most of the landlords involved.[6.12]

There were few changes in property ownership in either area until after 1800, but in the second decade of the nineteenth century major developments ensued — a pattern which would appear to be fairly typical throughout the Highlands. Rising cattle prices and the wartime boom in kelp had made it possible for Highland landlords at least to attempt to keep up with their more prosperous counterparts in the south, but the post-war slump brought this to an end. In 1819 the Argyll estates in Morvern were sold to meet the gambling debts of the current Duke, and similar financial problems forced the smaller proprietors to part with their lands too. By 1850 hardly any family with Highland, far less local, connections of any length owned land in Morvern.[6.13]

Conditions were slightly different in Farr, where the major property continued in the same family throughout, but this was only made possible by the marriage in 1785 of the heiress Countess of Sutherland into the wealthiest landowning family in Britain. As early as 1813-4 the other two properties in the parish sold out and it was almost certainly only the enormous resources of the Stafford family which prevented the sale of the Sutherland estates too. Although after 1814 the whole district was owned by the one estate, the Sutherlands did not establish complete control until a number of wadsetters, the heritable holders of lands redeemable by the original owners on repayment of a debt lent on the security of the land in question, had been bought out.[6.14]

Beneath the landlords were the tacksmen, who had formerly had a military function and who after 1745 occupied a somewhat precarious position as largely unnecessary rentiers. An attempt had been made as early as 1737 to diminish their importance and subsequently they acted out a role as agents of the landlord in the area. It would also appear, despite popular mythology, that large numbers of small tenants in both Morvern and Strathnaver held directly from the landlord. Tacksmen still continued to prevent landlords from exercising full control over their estates until well into the nineteenth century, however, and remained a major element in Highland society. At the bottom of the social structure were the small tenants with few rights and many obligations. Clan loyalties remained strong in Morvern and probably in Strathnaver too.[6.15]

Neither in Caithness nor in Easter Ross did this sort of society exist. In both districts a prosperous and relatively numerous gentry class had risen on the ruins of earlier territorial magnates and, although estates in Easter Ross may have been, in general, larger than the average for Scotland as a whole, they did not compare with the typically Highland estates of Morvern and Strathnaver in size.[6.16]

The clan system had no great hold in either district and tacksmen, in the Highland sense, generally were absent, the small tenants who farmed most of the land holding directly from the landlord. In the more Highland areas of Easter Ross clan loyalties may have remained strong, but the remark made of one landlord in 1750 that he had not 'what the Highlanders call a following'[6.17] could equally have been applied to a number of the leading proprietors. If the tenants did not feel a clan loyalty towards their landlords, they did not show much enthusiasm for any other clan chiefs either. During the Jacobite rebellion of 1745 clans had come out in defiance of their landlord throughout the Highlands, but in Easter Ross the tenants of the Earl of Cromarty, who were, in many cases, also his theoretical clansmen, refused to follow his lead and stayed peacefully at home.[6.18] The same lack of clan feeling was evident amongst the nominal chiefs and chieftains. There are a number of instances in the Highlands where clan chiefs beggared themselves in order to prevent disaster overwhelming their clansmen, but such concern was notably absent in Easter Ross.[6.19] In 1829, it is true, Mackenzie of Allangrange went to some lengths to establish his claim to be chief of clan Mackenzie but this may be viewed less as a continuation of old traditions than as an exercise in the pseudo-Celticism currently fashionable through the endeavours of Sir Walter Scott and George IV.[6.20] The same spirit is evident in the reasoning which persuaded another Mackenzie to change the name of his estate from the genuinely Gaelic Clyne to the Anglo-Irish Mountgerald.[6.21]

A study of the economic history and development of the various areas also reveals wide contrasts. Although there were considerable differences between developments in Morvern and in Strathnaver, they both conformed by and large to the standard Highland pattern. In 1750 both parishes were almost exclusively concerned with the rearing of black cattle. Arable farming was pursued wherever possible, the main crops being potatoes, bear and oats, but the produce was intended for local consumption only and, because there was insufficient land to support even the thinly scattered population that existed, both districts were importers of grain. Fishing was of little value to the local inhabitants, and although one or two other activities were prosecuted on a commercial basis, none made any substantial contribution to the local economy.[6.22] In the Highlands at large it is true that there were some industries of greater importance, the furnace of Bonawe being a notable example, but very few were of more than local or very temporary significance.[6.23]

Despite major changes both districts remained essentially pastoral, the amount of arable land actually falling over the years. From the

1770s large-scale sheep farming began to displace the native tenantry in Morvern. The process was slow and was hardly completed by 1850, but by that date most of the old small scattered settlements had been cleared and the majority of the remaining population resettled in new villages.[6.24] Change came more abruptly to Strathnaver where the old order was almost entirely destroyed between 1806 and 1819, but there too incoming sheep farmers displaced the original tenantry, some of whom were settled in more compact communities at the coast.[6.25]

Some diversification was attempted, particularly in Morvern, where the rise of the kelp industry during the Napoleonic wars allowed the Dukes of Argyll to continue their endeavours to prevent hardship and eviction but, in common with similar ventures throughout the Highlands, most of the diversification remained confined to the exploitation of basic commodities. The fall in commodity prices which came with peace in 1815 hastened the crisis which had been developing throughout the later eighteenth century and which was due primarily to the increasing pressure placed by the largely inexplicable rise in the population on resources which were not expanding at a similar rate.[6.26]

In the later eighteenth century Strathnaver and probably Morvern too had been capital-exporting areas, but increasingly in the nineteenth century they soaked up the wealth of the proprietors without offering any prospect of an adequate return on investment. Evictions and sheep farming went some way to stave off financial ruin for landlords but the balance of advantage had swung against the Highlands as a whole and the necessary capital, which might have been used for investment and development but which instead had gone to support the lifestyle and ambitions of the proprietors, in the eighteenth and early nineteenth centuries became increasingly difficult to find.[6.27]

As a result the primitive economic infrastructure which had been the rule in the eighteenth century remained largely unchanged until 1850. Communications in particular were abominable. Drove roads existed to permit the movement of cattle on the hoof but there were no roads capable of taking wheeled traffic, and well into the nineteenth century even riding was impossible along the full eleven-mile stretch of the only statutory labour road in Morvern. Rivers and streams remained unbridged and only towards the end of the period did either area see made roads of the type which had been constructed in parts of the Highlands since the early nineteenth century. Morvern and Strathnaver may have been particularly poorly placed in this respect, as both were located in inaccessible corners, but even in more central areas the new roads served largely as through routes — the trunk roads or motorways of the time — and over most of the Highlands local communications remained as primitive as ever.[6.28]

Morvern had a number of rudimentary ferry connections with neighbouring districts by 1800, but only in 1822 did a regular paddle steamer service connect the parish with the south. Conditions were even worse in Strathnaver, where the harbourless, north-facing coastline made movement by sea as unattractive as movement by land.[6.29]

Transport difficulties increased the isolation of the scattered population and, combined with the general lack of trade and widespread poverty, prevented the rise of towns, villages or even satisfactory markets. The maximum population of settlements in Morvern was about one hundred until the 1830s, and although several villages were founded in the last two decades of the period, they made little significant impact on the local economy other than as resettlement areas for displaced farmers. Strathnaver again was even more backward, for no villages developed before 1850. Farmers from the upper strath were resettled on the coast but none of the new crofting communities were either sufficiently substantial or compact to form villages, nor did they perform any of the regional functions generally associated with villages.[6.30]

While the local economy in both Caithness and Easter Ross remained predominantly rural, it was based on arable rather than pastoral farming, and in neither area was it as monolithic as in most of the Highlands. Even in the middle of the eighteenth century a variety of commodities contributed to the general wealth, and as the century progressed there was increasing diversification. Trade in the major product, grain, led to the growth of prosperous trading centres such as Thurso and Cromarty, and commerce in general flourished both internally and externally. The towns which arose as a result, though small, were of considerable significance economically, culturally and even socially.[6.31]

Non-agricultural industry generally was more successful in Caithness and Easter Ross than in the Highlands as a whole. In Caithness the flagstone industry and the growth of the herring fisheries with their associated ventures ensured a continuing prosperity throughout the first half of the nineteenth century, while in Easter Ross the fairly rapid development of the textile industry and, to a lesser extent, the fisheries again gave the area a more varied economic structure than districts to the west.[6.32]

Transport, too, was much superior to that of areas such as Morvern and Strathnaver; Easter Ross had a reasonable network of roads and bridges by the last quarter of the eighteenth century, and further rapid progress was made in the following decades. While the road system in Caithness — again located at a distance from main through routes — may not have developed as quickly or as far as that in Easter Ross, there were major improvements, and in both areas a number of harbours and piers were constructed to cater for the ever-increasing seaborne trade.[6.33]

There was also a marked cultural divide between Caithness on the one hand and most of the Highlands on the other, with Easter Ross falling somewhere in between. Gaelic was practically unknown in much of Caithness until the growth of the herring fisheries at Wick drew immigrants from the impoverished west.[6.34] Similarly the eastern Black Isle remained an English-speaking province until industrialisation at Cromarty attracted an influx of Gaelic speakers.[6.35] Unlike Caithness, however, much of Easter Ross was predominantly Gaelic-speaking for most of the period, and in the western Black Isle and Ferindonald cultural affinities probably lay with the Highlands.[6.36] Easter Ross proper was rather more mixed and clearly exhibited the characteristics of a frontier province. Language affected educational opportunity to a considerable extent, so that much of Easter Ross was not so well provided as the better off districts in the Lowlands, but the area as a whole did not face the problems of scale and poverty which affected so much of the Highlands.[6.37]

While religion was an important element in the cultural make-up of Scottish society, it is difficult to use it to define the cultural status of Easter Ross. In Caithness, as in much of the North of Scotland, there was a residual sympathy for Episcopacy for much of the eighteenth century, but Easter Ross was the breeding ground for a Calvinist theology which was more extreme than that found in most parts of the Lowlands.[6.38] Frontier societies are rarely noted for their cultural impact on their adjoining heartlands — receiving rather than imparting cultural trends. Yet in this instance the influence of Easter Ross theology spread in time over most of the North-West Highland area.[6.39]

Objective comparison, however valid, does not give the complete picture, for it is clear that contemporaries had their own views on the character of the region, sometimes, it would appear, in direct opposition to the existing evidence. Outside commentators in the early and middle eighteenth century saw little if any difference between the

Highlands at large and most of Easter Ross. Burt and the government agent who reported in 1750 drew no distinction at all,[6.40] while Archibald Menzies, reporting to the Commissioners of Forfeited Estates in 1768, although distinguishing between Newtarbat and the Highland baronies of the forfeited Cromarty estate on economic grounds, expressed himself of the opinion that 'the Highland and low Country parts of these Estates [Lovat and Cromarty] are Inhabited by People of the same Character and Disposition.'[6.41] Only in one part of Easter Ross did he find a community which both he and the local population regarded as being definitely Lowland, for he wrote,

> That corner called the Black Isle is inhabited by a sett of people quite distinct as to names, manners and customs from the rest of that country. They have been from time immemorial a manufacturing people and are supposed to have been brought into that country by the Bishops of Ross.[6.42]

Even at that date, however, more general distinctions could be drawn and, as the years passed, commentators came to recognise that the area was different from surrounding districts. The economic differences were those which were seen most clearly, but these economic differences were so great as to lead at least some sections of the community to regard themselves as having a distinct identity from the country to the west.[6.43]

By the start of the nineteenth century the peculiar characteristics of the region appeared so clear to one writer on the agricultural scene in Scotland that he could claim that 'the eastern coast of Ross-shire to a short distance from the sea, . . . has at all times been considered as a part of the Lowlands of Scotland, and has been inhabited by persons who speak the English language'.[6.44] Historically inaccurate though the statement was, the fact that it was made at all suggests that Gaelic had lost some of its strength at the time it was made. Corroborating evidence can be found in the remark of Hugh Miller on a location near Lairg in Sutherland that although 'the place was not much above thirty miles from Cromarty [his home town] . . . it was in the true Highlands which I had never before seen save on the distant horizon'.[6.45]

While the easternmost portion of Easter Ross may have been thoroughly Lowland in outlook — with the original bias being strengthened by the large influx of southern farmers from the later eighteenth century — further west the situation was more complicated, but even there the local people, it was said in 1831, were 'daily losing the characteristic features by which they were formerly distinguished from the neighbouring Lowlanders, and are yielding to the influence of those sentiments and customs insensibly adopted by the nation at large'.[6.46]

On the basis of the evidence available it seems reasonable to conclude that at no time between 1750 and 1850 could Easter Ross be regarded economically as a province of the Highlands. Its development, of course, differed markedly from that of the main Lowland areas too, but closer parallels can be found with other isolated rural Lowland areas such as Caithness, and the course of development in Easter Ross can even be seen to resemble that in the more central Carse of Gowrie in many respects.[6.47] While the area's cultural character was less clear cut, it was not at any time in the hundred years under consideration fully integrated with the Highlands. In the middle of the eighteenth century it clearly betrayed signs of the clash of cultures common in frontier societies, and while the events of the succeeding years brought it more into line as an outlying province of the Lowlands, it continued to retain links with the culture by which it was surrounded.[6.48]

b. A Failure of Leadership

Easter Ross in 1750 was a traditional and largely provincial society. An authoritarian social structure was to some extent modified by a strong sense of familial relationships which extended beyond ties of blood to include employers and employees. While clan loyalties may not have been so strong as in much of the Highlands there was, as in the rest of Scotland, a strong belief in the importance of family links which bound together widely disparate elements from the small cottar to the noble landlord.[6.49] The social cohesiveness which these links ensured usually prevented dissatisfaction with the unequal distribution of privilege from expressing itself in any major action by the more deprived sections of the community and reduced the chances of change being initiated from below. Local society continued to expect the heads of the major families, the Mackenzies of Seaforth and the Munros of Foulis, for example, to take the lead in decision-making. The opportunity and desire for change on the part of these leading families, however, was strictly limited and, although change was continuous, for several centuries mutations had occurred within the confines of a generally accepted social structure.

The abolition of heritable jurisdiction after 1745 reduced the legal control of landlords over their territory but old habits died hard. The gentry continued to dominate legal processes well into the nineteenth century, and although they may have lost their powers of life and death, the landlords retained wide economic controls. In particular the absence of reasonable leases ensured that tenant farmers would think twice before acting independently of their landlord. Additionally, the gentry, with their near monopoly of wealth, and their control of patronage — both officially in the church and, unofficially, in the way that they could exert pressure to place clients in official positions or persuade friends to give supporters employment — were the natural focus of leadership.[6.50]

The tenant farmers, themselves, generally were not in much of a position to make independent judgments. Earlier generations of landlords in the Highlands in general believed that the wealth of an estate lay in the numbers of people settled upon it, rather than in the rent paid. It is not clear how far the landlords of Easter Ross shared this opinion but the evidence suggests that they, too, were happy to accept an over-numerous tenant class, settled in poverty, on holdings too small to allow for the accumulation of capital. The lack of capital made initiatives by the tenantry more difficult; and poverty and linguistic difficulties severely limited the potential benefits of education in encouraging independent thought. Indeed such education as was available stressed the importance of acceptance of and obedience to the established order.[6.51] As in most peasant societies, the farmers had a disproportionate respect for the value of holding land, however small in extent, and had very restricted views on the alternative occupations open to their children. Their unwillingness to consider alternative occupations was, in many instances, strengthened by the bonds — however nominal — which, they believed, linked them to their superiors. As Hugh Miller put it,

> There was scarce an individual, in at least the northern counties, whose claim to self respect was not involved in the honour of some noble family . . . and it was his pride and honour not that he was an independent man but that he was in some sort a dependent gentleman.[6.52]

The original tenantry, then, were unlikely to find an alternative leadership to that of the gentry from within their own ranks. They were equally unlikely to find leaders in any other section of the community.

Certainly, the large tenant farmers, who were brought in from elsewhere, could provide a more substantial opposition to the landlords than the smallholders, and the two categories of tenants may have made common cause over such issues as assessments for road repairs. But in many respects the outlook of the large tenants approximated more closely to that of the gentry than to that of the small tenants whom they were replacing; and, in any event, it would have been unlikely that the dispossessed natives would have accepted the leadership of those who had taken over their land.

Leadership of a kind, of course, was exercised by the clergy, whose evangelical zeal reflected that of their congregations. In matters temporal, however, the clergy dismally failed to provide any worthwhile guidance. The particular bias of their creed, with its emphasis on rewards in heaven for suffering on earth, may have been the most important factor but it is probable that more mundane considerations were also influential. The clergy — from the later eighteenth century anyway — usually were presented by the landlords and, while there was nothing to prevent a minister acting independently once appointed, no landlord was likely to present a clergyman who gave any indications of expressing opposition to the landed hegemony.

The wealthier townsmen were in a position of some authority but their opportunities for innovation were limited. The towns themselves, while fulfilling a useful function as local centres, were not wealthy or large enough to form real power bases. Few townsmen became rich enough to make an impact on the region and, of those who did, most remained largely dependent upon the gentry for their incomes.

William Forsyth, for example, rose to a position of some prominence, becoming a Justice of the Peace, a Superintendent of Roads for the County of Cromarty and an elder of the Church of Scotland; but much of his trade was carried out with, or on behalf of the gentry, who would have transferred their custom if they had had reason to object to his opinions.[6.53]

Although the gap between the tenant farmers and the gentry was considerable (especially in economic terms), the tenants themselves were a socially superior minority in the rural landscape, for beneath them were large numbers of servants and cottars. Economically, however, the tenants seem to have been little better off than the rest of the population, and the fact that unmarried servants generally boarded with their employer and were treated as an extension of his family limited the possibilities of social conflict.[6.54]

It is interesting that, although evangelical ministers opposed the hardships caused by farm enlargement, the most damning, because the least hostile, account of the actions of the landlords was made by the moderate Thomas Munro, the minister of Kiltearn whose congregation had rejected him because of his stand on religious matters. He wrote in 1837 that

> the decrease [in population] in the period between 1791 and 1811 was mainly owing to the enlistment of numbers of the young men in the 42nd Regiment, under the command of their countryman, the late Sir Hector Munro of Novar. Between 1811 and 1821, a new system of farming was introduced, which sufficiently accounts for the extraordinary falling off in the numbers. In 1821, when according to the annual increase of 25, the population should have amounted to 1800, it was found to be only 1454, shewing a falling off to the number of 346 persons. During that period, numbers of small tenants were ejected to make way for farmers from the south, possessed of some capital, who, by their superior management, were able to afford higher rents. The more elevated districts of the parish, which were altogether unsuitable for cultivation, were converted into sheepwalks; and numbers were thus deprived of all means of subsistence and driven to seek in a foreign land for the shelter and protection which were denied them in their own.[6.55]

At least in the eighteenth century, and even into the nineteenth, the clergy had stronger links, in many respects, with the gentry than with other sections of the community. Some of them were landowners in their own right, or offspring of landowners, while all enjoyed a standard and style of living which equated them with the lower gentry and which was far removed from that experienced by other groups.[6.56]

Lack of suitable leadership, however, did not altogether stop protests at the direction in which economic affairs were moving. When Sir John Ross of Balnagown introduced sheep farming on a large scale to the area in the later eighteenth century the combined, usually underhand, opposition of local tenant farmers and the more conservative neighbouring lairds was sufficient to prevent him from profiting from his initiative.

More seriously, the removal of small tenant farmers from their hill grazings at Kildermorie in Alness to make way for the Cameron brothers, sheep farmers from Lochaber, in 1792, sparked off a protest movement which aimed at nothing less than the removal of all the sheep in the northern Highlands. The threat posed by the small tenants of Highland Strathrusdale who took the initiative and by those in the low country who supported them created a panic amongst the Easter Ross gentry. The intervention of three companies of the Black Watch in support of the more resolute lairds led by Donald Macleod of Geanies and Sir Hector Munro of Novar — a man with considerable experience in India of quelling troublesome natives — was required before peace was restored. After a confrontation at Boath, the ringleaders were caught and sentenced to fines, imprisonment and transportation but, in a rare act of clemency combined with common sense, the government — or their local officials in Inverness — appear to have connived at the farmers' escape from prison. Clearly it was better to have chastened and powerless fugitives from justice than emotively powerful martyrs to a cause. As it was, the Boath incident retained a place of considerable significance in the folk memory of the north.[6.57]

No other affair in the succeeding half-century proved as serious as the events of 1792, but the spirit of opposition was far from dead. The Disruption of 1843, and the bitterness it provoked, led to the fear of trouble in Kiltearn and to actual clashes at Logie and Resolis when new parish ministers were inducted. Four years later trouble flared again when the continued export of grain, despite the failure of the 1846 potato crop and the ensuing destitution, resulted in meal riots at Evanton, Rosemarkie, Balintraid and Avoch. So serious were the attempts to stop the movement of grain in the Invergordon area that in March 1847 soldiers once again were drafted into the area. From Invergordon, once peace had been restored, the soldiers, of the 27th regiment, were moved to Dingwall where a midnight raid on a local grain repository had mixed up the wheat and barley stored there, rendering them unsuitable for export.[6.58]

Such actions could be temporarily successful, but essentially they were negative responses to initiatives by others and merely emphasised the lack of control which the local inhabitants exercised over their own fates.

In the later eighteenth century the social equilibrium was subjected to severe disruption. Although the concepts of the agricultural and industrial revolutions seem to have gone out of fashion in recent years, the only adjective which adequately describes the scale and effect of the changes which took place at this time is 'revolutionary'. The catalyst in the reaction was a radical reappraisal by the landlords of their approach to estate management. Although in the years before 1750 a few landowners had exhibited some interest in agricultural experiment, the majority had remained as conservative in their attitudes as their tenants. Even in the later eighteenth century a large reservoir of able-bodied males was a useful asset to a landowner in securing his position as an army officer, and there was little incentive to increase agricultural output at a time when a surplus was already being produced.[6.59] The improvers of the early nineteenth century had great difficulty in finding markets for their produce in times of glut, and sales would have been even more difficult a century earlier when rapid population expansion was only just beginning, when Easter Ross crops ripened much later than those in the south and when transport between Easter Ross and the major markets was slow and infrequent.[6.60]

That the Easter Ross gentry did not improve earlier is less surprising than the fact that they started improving when they did. The extent of their endeavours may have been more limited in the early phases than the efforts of their contemporaries in the Lothians, but the fever of improvement appears to have struck early and struck hard.

Exactly why the gentry were motivated to introduce change in the first place must remain something of a mystery. Initially, the phenomenon of a group of essentially conservative landowners changing their estates in less than half a century from an almost medieval backwardness to some of the most improved agricultural properties in the country seems totally inexplicable and, even after careful study, there appears to have been no single powerful motivating force.

Those who started improving in the middle of the eighteenth century or before cannot have been motivated primarily by economic considerations in the sense that they saw a new opportunity for profitable investment and took it. The geographical location and economic backwardness of Easter Ross in relation to southern districts still made it difficult to sell increased amounts of produce when there was already increasing production elsewhere. Indeed, David Munro of Meikle Allan, who had spent the preceding decade making extensive improvements on his estate — deep ploughing, enclosing and draining, as well as having not one but two surveys made within two years — confessed in exasperation in 1759 that 'I am concerned that I have lost by all the labourings I ever had and I am resolved to quit that trade tho I like it, except the inclosure about my house.'[6.61]

In fact his letter gives a clue as to one of the most likely motives for undertaking improvement — the pleasure to be derived from it. Long before there was a real economic incentive, some landowners at least had discovered the joys of experimentation in agriculture, either by themselves or as a result of their association with landowners in the south who already had begun to improve.

There can be little doubt that the close contacts which many of the gentry of the area, particularly those of the legal fraternity, maintained with the Lothians, was of the greatest importance. Not only did this contact suggest ways in which improvement could be undertaken and keep lairds up to date with the latest developments in a more intimate way than reading in the specialised literature, but it also reinforced their enthusiasm for the activity, particularly as the long-term economic benefits, which were little more than theoretical in the north, would have been more evident in the environs of Edinburgh.

Where some led, others, perforce, had to follow. Example and precept no doubt persuaded friends and neighbours to investigate what the fuss was all about. More practically, the economic implications of neighbouring improvements forced some lairds to consider further improvements themselves. A move to divide a common between adjoining estates by an active improver could act as a spur to a more lethargic neighbour, while, in 1778, the Cadboll trustees, acting on behalf of Robert Bruce Aeneas Macleod who was a minor, finding themselves obliged by law to meet half the bill for the construction of a march dyke with the estate of Glastullich, were considering if they should not enclose some land on the Cadboll estates as well, in order to make the cost worthwhile.[6.62]

As the century wore on there can be little doubt that the economic rewards, real or imaginary, to be derived from improvement loomed ever larger in the minds of those whose increasing integration into southern society made them aware of the differences between the attitudes current in the north and those generally accepted elsewhere.[6.63] Rostow has suggested that

> As a matter of historical fact a reactive nationalism — reacting against intrusion from more advanced nations — has been a most important and powerful motive force in the transition from traditional to modern societies, at least as important as the profit motive. Men holding effective authority or influence have been willing to uproot traditional societies, not primarily, to make more money but because the traditional society failed — or threatened to fail — to protect them from humiliation by foreigners.[6.64]

It would seem that some such motivation spurred the gentry in Easter Ross to innovate where they had previously accepted traditional practice.

With the exception of the large tenant farmers introduced from the south, whose interests tended to coincide with those of the lairds who had brought them to Ross-shire in the first place, the gentry were almost alone, as a class, in their increasing contact with the outside world. It is true that, amongst the townspeople of Cromarty, there were a number of individuals whose travels had taken them far and wide. One had acted as a supercargo and clerk from Newfoundland to Italy, while another had served an apprenticeship as a grocer in London. Others had gained experience in the armed services, but such experiences were occasional and often of limited educational value compared with the regular interchange which took place between the lairds of Easter Ross and their peers elsewhere.[6.65]

The effect on the lairds of this interchange was to alienate them from their home background. Rejecting the prejudices which they and their predecessors had held for so long, they lost sympathy with those who continued to cling to the old beliefs. Increasing absenteeism reduced the opportunities for human contact which were so important in maintaining social links, and the growing importance of external sources of income removed the landlords ever further from the concerns which worried or motivated their tenants.

The lairds indeed were keen that their tenantry should accept the new practices which they had adopted themselves, and sporadic attempts were made to persuade or force farmers to undertake improvement.[6.66] But few landlords had the patience, the energy and the resources to persevere with a thankless task. A nineteenth century commentator reflected that 'with a singular folly . . . projectors never appear to have reflected that the Highland character was to be operated upon, by the gradual introduction of better systems, not by the hasty hand of inconsiderate reform inimical to their feelings and prejudices',[6.67] and there seems certainly to have been an inability to appreciate that whereas, for example, the failure of a new experimental rotation on an estate home farm could mean little more than a loss of face to some landowners, a similar failure on the small farm of a tenant could result in bankruptcy and possible starvation. This inability is all the more surprising in the light of the examples of landlords, both locally — for example Alexander Mackenzie of Hilton — and elsewhere, who, having overinvested in improvement, went bankrupt, and in view of the uncertain return on capital actually being obtained by local landed improvers.[6.68]

It is possible, however, that the gentry retained a sufficiently paternalistic attitude at first to make them reluctant to force through change against the united opposition of their tenantry. More probably the economic inducements to force through change remained weaker than the counter attractions — both economic and social — of having a large dependant tenant population.[6.69]

The failure of the sitting tenants to respond to landlord initiatives was to be fatal to their long-term interests but it is hardly surprising. Quite apart from the initial reluctance of a conservative society to accept change, there must have seemed sound economic reasons for not participating in the new ventures. Few real incentives were offered to them to take what was after all a major risk, and it must have seemed probable in the light of experience that, without adequate safeguards, the landlords would cream off any profits which might be made. Until towards the end of the century the probability of any profits being substantial was rather remote anyway. The collapse of the Ayr bank in 1772 was an indication of the financial disasters which could result from overinvestment in agricultural improvement, and small farmers in Easter Ross were already badly placed to withstand depression without adding to their risks.[6.70]

The native farmers proved on several occasions that they were willing to innovate if innovation was to their advantage — they rapidly accepted the potato, they overcame their prejudice against swine, after some initial reluctance and, in the nineteenth century, with the security of tenure and an assured market, those who remained at last accepted the value of a wide range of improved techniques. The peasant economy in Norway was also to demonstrate that small tenant farmers could improve quite efficiently without the dubious advantages of landlord intervention.[6.71]

Historians suffer from a tendency to see the progress of events as moving inexorably and inevitably in a predestined direction. In an attempt to make sense of the past it is easy to fall into the trap of fitting events into a logical sequence which never existed. The history of agricultural development in eighteenth century Easter Ross lends itself to such a treatment and it is tempting to see the failure of the native farmers to improve as an inevitable result of their poverty, lack of security and general backwardness. While the conditions under which they laboured made it extremely unlikely that the local farmers would overcome the obstacles in the way of a successful transition to modern farming methods, such a transition was not impossible and the exceptions to the general rule proved that it could be done.[6.72]

In fact the majority of sitting tenants were never given the chance to show if they would respond favourably to economic incentives because the reaction of their landlords to changed circumstances at the end of the eighteenth century deprived them of their land just at the time when they might have been willing to benefit from the high prices for their produce then obtaining. Towards the end of the century grain prices took off as a result of the pressure on resources of a rising population, the increased needs of a wartime army and the difficulties in obtaining corn from other sources.[6.73] For the first time large-scale improvement in Easter Ross became not only fashionably but also economically desirable. At the same time there was rapid inflation, as other prices followed grain in an upward spiral. While many southern landlords were making increasing profits from mineral and industrial ventures, it seems possible that local lairds were being thrown back on their estate incomes as their primary source of wealth. Opportunities for advancement in the only remaining major external source of income, the army, were made easier because of the war, and landlords may have felt, as a result, that they had less need of the bargaining power obtained by having ready-made regiments at hand on their own estates. The continued decline in traditional loyalties at any rate made it more likely that estate management would be pursued with greater economic motivation than hitherto.

It would still have been possible to increase estate revenues in co-operation with the sitting tenants, but an easier and more profitable method of improvement presented itself. Because improvement in the south had proceeded at a faster pace, there were already in existence large numbers of substantial tenant farmers with experience of improved farming and with the necessary capital to put their ideas into practice. The latter attraction was particularly important to those landlords who, without the freedom conferred by large outside incomes, were bound by strict entails which restricted their freedom to improve as they might wish. The farmers were attracted north by the relatively low rents, and the landlords saw the chance to have their estates improved rapidly and at relatively low cost to themselves. Higher rents could be obtained from one large farmer than from several small ones, and since there were no lengthy leases tying up estate farms, the existing tenantry were displaced to make way for incomers from the Lothians and other improved regions.[6.74]

As a result of these innovations there was a substantial change in the pattern of land occupation in the area. Although poverty may have been widespread in the eighteenth century, a large proportion (exactly what proportion it is difficult to estimate as conditions varied from estate to estate) of the total population had had the security of a holding to provide for their needs. It is possible that the numbers holding land in the nineteenth century were little less than in the previous century as large-scale reclamation of moorland had been undertaken by crofters; but the proportion holding land was probably less, the amount of land held by the native tenantry certainly was, and the quality of the land itself was in most cases poorer.[6.75] Many were deprived of land altogether and were forced to emigrate or to scrape a miserable existence as landless labourers based in the local towns and villages. The loss of land led to an impoverishment in the diet of many poorer families, and although tenants at will were in theory insecure enough, those with no land at all and irregular employment were even more so.[6.76]

It is difficult to escape the conclusion that to some extent the landlords enriched themselves at the expense of the bulk of the population and that they regularly took more out of their estates than they reinvested. Easter Ross estates do not, on the whole, seem to have followed the pattern of the Sutherland property to the north, where a substantial surplus in the later eighteenth century changed to a disastrous deficit after 1800. Sir John Ross held the estate of Balnagown for thirty years from 1760 to 1790 and in that time gained an enviable reputation as a man with a driving interest in improvement, as well as a major concern for the wellbeing of his tenants. Yet in those thirty years he only invested an estimated £10,000 in estate improvement compared with a total rental which cannot have been significantly less than £45,000[6.77] and may have been substantially more. As he was regularly absent in the south or on duty at sea, not much of the excess capital would have found its way into the local economy. The proportion of investment on improvement to total estate income remained about the same on the Balnagown estates in the first and second decades of the nineteenth century and may actually have fallen thereafter.[6.78]

There were undoubtedly cases where landlords spent more on their estates than they could hope to recoup by way of rents or profits. Sir Hector Munro of Novar, for example, is said to have spent £120,000 on estate improvements.[6.79] Little of this money was used for the long-term benefit of the community, however, for much of it was expended on enlarging the mansion and on bringing into cultivation land of questionable value. Having beggared some of his tenants by clearing them for sheep, Sir Hector spent large sums for the relief of poverty by way of the erection of a number of ornamental follies — a singularly appropriate commemoration of his style of estate management.

Although Sir Hector was a scion of one of the longest established[6.80] clan chiefs in the Highlands and might, therefore, have been confident of the continued obedience of his tenants (who were also by and large his fellow clansmen), the changing relationship between landlord and tenant, as reflected by his prolonged absences and his immoderate improvement, resulted in an expression of open and forceful opposition to eviction by those who were being replaced by sheep. The tenantry, possibly for the first time, were making clear their sense of betrayal as a representative of the old order used the benefits of his position to further his own interests, at the expense of those who had been encouraged to look to him for leadership and support.[6.81]

The failure of the gentry as a whole to provide adequate leadership is made most clear by the one major exception. George Ross of Pitkerry, a minor landowner, made a fortune in London as an army agent and, unlike many other successful Easter Ross natives, used his money not only to purchase an estate in his home county but to introduce large-scale serious improvements designed to benefit the community at large. His activity in improving his land, constructing a harbour and encouraging industry was emulated later, to some degree, by other landlords; but his concern to involve his tenants and to make sure that improvement benefited them was an example that was seldom followed.[6.82] Ross, unfortunately, was regarded with distaste by at least some of the local gentry and he did not live long enough to bring all his schemes to full fruition, buying the estate in 1772 and dying in 1786. Unlike the third Duke of Argyll at Inveraray, Ross's concerns were not pursued by those who followed him. His successor, another London army agent, exhibited the usual lack of interest of an absentee landlord and, although Cromarty continued to flourish on established enterprises, no new initiatives were forthcoming.[6.83]

Indeed, one of the problems of a system whereby self-made men with an interest in improvement bought local estates, after they had established their fortunes, may have been that such men tended to be too old or unwell to devote themselves wholeheartedly to their schemes for a long enough period; while their successors, as so often with the sons of the *nouveau riche,* lacked the drive and desire to make the same mark as their fathers. In one major respect George Ross's example may have discouraged others for, although he strove to benefit his tenants, they refused to appreciate his efforts and were slow in responding to his initiatives.[6.84]

It has been argued that, although the landlords had surplus funds, these funds may not readily have been available for investment and that there were, anyway, only very limited opportunities for investment.[6.85] While for many landlords, wealth increased only incrementally so that large sums were seldom, if ever, available at one time, there were undoubtedly those who were able to dispose of considerable fortunes without serious restrictions as to amount, time or place.[6.86] That they disposed of these fortunes in ways which, in some instances, brought little long-term benefit to themselves, far less anyone else, does not necessarily mean that they could not have used the money more profitably.

Indeed in agriculture the landlords could have benefited the community merely by accepting a short-term cut in the rate at which their wealth increased. By relying more on their external incomes they would have made it possible to take less out of the local economy. Remission and conversion of rents on easy terms, an easing of the additional burdens exacted by way of service and thirlage and the enforcement of improving clauses in reasonable leases were all positive measures proprietors might have adopted to ensure that their existing tenants had an opportunity to take an initiative in improvement for themselves. Such measures would not have conflicted with the restrictive entails which continued to hamper improvement even after Montgomery's act of 1770, which allowed some of the financial burden of improvement to be passed on to succeeding generations, but obviously did run counter to the landlords' greater desire to keep up financially with wealthier gentry elsewhere.[6.87] In transport improvements, which were vital for more general agricultural improvement, the landlords again could have shared the burden of development more equally — as was done elsewhere — but failed to do so.[6.88]

Investment in local industry was another way in which the gentry could have attempted to ensure the greater prosperity of the area. There were, of course, long-term factors at work which were detrimental to the prospects of industrial prosperity in Easter Ross, and in an area without the mineral resources which were to prove the foundations of the technological advances of the nineteenth century it would be unreasonable to expect the growth of large-scale industry. Nevertheless such development as there was might have been more successful if there had been greater investment in it and if the local market for its produce had been stronger. Whether, in the face of outside competition, local industry could have had a long-term future or not, landlord investment in such industry would have been no more frivolous than many of the other expenditures the gentry incurred, and while any industrial success is essentially transient, a more prosperous local industry might have turned out to be a more solid foundation for further advance.[6.89]

As part of the eighteenth century ideal of improvement, landlords had been interested in estate industries and had accepted the growth of linen spinning, but only Ross of Cromarty took a successful initiative in encouraging large-scale industry.[6.90] Because investment was not forthcoming from local sources of capital, Easter Ross industry, particularly the linen industry, developed as a branch economy and suffered the almost inevitable decline in times of national recession. Perhaps the most obvious failure was the lack of development in the local fishing industry, at a time when, elsewhere, fisheries were being exploited as never before. Although there was a precedent set for landlord investment in fishing as early as 1759, and despite the (admittedly largely unsuccessful) example of the Sutherland family to the north, Easter Ross landlords do not appear to have been tempted to support their own fishing industry to any extent. By the second quarter of the nineteenth century this may have been partly because of a general withdrawal of the gentry from such activity.[6.91]

There were, of course, local entrepreneurs active on the industrial scene as well, but there were few of them. Partly at least because wealth was concentrated in an oligopoly, there was little scope for major commercial or industrial marketing within the area and it generally has proved difficult to build up an extensive export trade without a sound home market first. Local businessmen tended to act as middlemen for larger concerns rather than as independent operators.[6.92]

By 1850 the rural landscape was greatly changed from its state one hundred years earlier. The scattered patches of undernourished and badly cultivated arable, tended by a large body of small tenant farmers with the assistance of numerous servants and cottars, had given way to regular fields of high-quality farmland, held by a small group of wealthy farmers, employing relatively few servants and a large number of occasional workers from amongst the still numerous cottars and even more from the greatly increased population of landless labourers.

The cultural supremacy of English which had been in doubt in the years before 1750 was firmly established by 1850, and the influx of southern ideas and practices probably was greater than ever before.

As with so many revolutions, however, the century of change did little to alter the social power structure in the region. The landlords, who were firmly in control in 1750, initiated the subsequent changes and were, by and large, little less powerful in 1850. While some of the older landowning families had disappeared, their replacements came, with few exceptions, from the upper reaches of society and, although a select few had achieved some wealth and status as prominent townsmen or prosperous tenant farmers, the great bulk of the population had seen little advance in their conditions since the start of the period.[6.93]

To some extent the failure of the majority to achieve a greater prosperity can be explained by natural deficiencies. The area lacked the mineral wealth, the central location and the other geographical advantages which influenced the course of development elsewhere. It is not necessary, however, to accept, in its entirety, the Toynbee hypothesis, of man succeeding because of adversity, to believe that natural advantages were not the sole determinant of economic and social progress.[6.94] It has been well said that 'the success of the more remote areas in catching on to a new prosperity obviously related to their natural possibilities in transport, fertility or minerals, but it also had an element of chance. A few vigorous enthusiasts could make a great difference.'[6.95]

Easter Ross, unlike the Highlands as a whole, had considerable natural advantages, which were not fully exploited for the benefit of the local community, and this human failure was due very largely to deficient leadership. Earlier development had left power and authority in the region in the hands of a small group whose composition was even more strictly dependent upon birth than similar ruling castes elsewhere in Europe. When this group were faced with the choice of introducing change either to preserve traditional values or to promote their own interests, they opted for the latter course.

There was, of course, a third option: that of sitting tight and not accepting change at all; but this recipe for disaster seems to have appealed to very few. Even an eccentrically enthusiastic proponent of the old ways, Mackenzie of Ardross, had taken care, in his youth, to make a fortune in India with which to support the idiosyncratic behaviour of his old age.[6.96]

Thomas Munro, the minister of Kiltearn, expressed the underlying philosophy of the majority of the gentry when he wrote of 'the rights of landlords . . . to manage their properties according to their own pleasure'.[6.97] Few would have agreed with the analysis of James Cameron, the Tain surgeon, who argued that the gentry

> if they knew and practised their social duties, would be sparing in superfluities to

themselves, that they might supply necessities to others. It is much to be regretted, with reference to the poor especially, that so many of the landowners of the district are absentees or non-resident. It is truly much to be desired that proprietors should act in accordance with 'a sound conception of the right to property — namely as being *official*, implying and demanding the performance of commensurate duties'.[6.98]

Indeed it is because few landlords with the power of those in Easter Ross were likely ever to accept what critics like Cameron saw as their social responsibilities, leaving a vacuum which no other element in local society could fill, that the system as such, rather than the individuals within it, was inherently wrong.

Apart from the obvious selfish motives (and self-interest has probably generally been the primary motivating force in historical development), the explanation for the landlords' choice can be found in the fact that they operated increasingly on a national rather than a local scale. In national terms the gentry were successful both in maintaining their position — more or less — as compared to other landlords and in delivering the goods — agricultural and human — which the more rapidly developing areas of the country required.[6.99]

That this success was achieved, to some degree at least, at the expense of Easter Ross was symptomatic of the growing centralisation of British society. The priorities and requirements of the leading centres dominated peripheral districts. Easter Ross was increasingly confined to the southern British market; its industry fell ever more under London and other big city domination and its human talent was drawn away for the benefit of these other centres.

It is possible to see in the conditions of 1850 a concentration of industrial power which paralleled the control of the gentry in Easter Ross in 1750, and just as the unrestricted power of the landlords in that area proved to be detrimental to its interests, so the regional imbalances created by the aggrandisement of some areas at the expense of others may have been responsible, to some extent, for future economic and social problems on a national scale.

T. C. Smout has suggested that economic development in eighteenth century Scotland was supported by the landlords and the urban middle class in the common belief that it was to their own advantage but with the victory in the battle for power going to the middle class.[6.100] In Easter Ross such a battle never developed. In the absence of a sufficiently strong bourgeoisie, the gentry expanded the economy along lines of their own choosing, an expansion which was in their own exclusive short-term interests but which probably was detrimental to the area as a whole in the longer perspective.

Notes

1.1 The term Easter Ross will be used in a geographic sense only throughout this book unless otherwise specified. It covers the Black Isle and much of what is known as Mid Ross in addition to most of Easter Ross proper, but excludes the parishes of Edderton and Kincardine which are often included in the latter district. See Appendix I map 3.

1.2 Some indication of the different character of the parishes in question is given by the figures for arable acreage on the Balnagown estate in 1808. In the parishes of Kilmuir, Logie and Fearn arable land totalled approximately 27 per cent of the total. In Edderton the figure dropped to under 13 per cent despite the fact that much of the estate was concentrated in the coastal plain of the parish while in Kincardine it was only 5½ per cent; see *Plans of the Estate of Balnagown Lying in the Parishes of Killmuir, Loggie, Fearn, Eddertoun and Kincardine . . . 1808,* S.R.O., West Register House, RHP13299.

1.3 *Origines Parochiales Scotiae* (2 vols.; Edinburgh: Lizars, 1850-55), II, part 2, pp. 501, 522.

1.4 By 1888 land at the seven hundred foot level, which had been cultivated in mid-century, had been abandoned; see Roderick Maclean, 'Notes on the parish of Kiltearn', *Transactions of the Gaelic Society of Inverness,* 15 (1888-89) p. 304.

1.5 *The Highlands of Scotland in 1750* (Edinburgh: Blackwood, 1898), p. 16.

1.6 James B. Cruickshank, 'The Black Isle, Ross-shire', *Scottish Geographical Magazine,* 77 (1961), pp. 3-14.

1.7 Although there were, as elsewhere in Scotland, areas of badly drained or un-drained land which were later improved; see Alexander Sangster, *A plan of part of ye Lands of Ankervil and Meikle Allan . . . 1759,* S.R.O., West Register House, RHP239.

1.8 That is, the area covered by the parishes of Kilmuir Easter, Logie Easter, Nigg, Fearn, Tarbat and Tain.

1.9 Major rivers, that is, in the Scottish sense — rivers which while being difficult to bridge or ford on account of their size were either too shallow or too rapid to carry water transport.

1.10 For examples of place names — Pitkerry, Pitcalzean, Pitlundy and Pitogartie — see William John Watson, *Place names of Ross and Cromarty* (Inverness: Northern Counties Printing and Publishing Co., 1904), pp. XLV-LIII. For carved stones see Cecil L. Curle, 'The chronology of the early Christian monuments of Scotland', *Proceedings of the Society of Antiquaries of Scotland,* LXXIV (1939-40), pp. 98, 100-4.

1.11 For example:— Cadboll, Dingwall and Tain; see W. J. Watson, *Place names of Ross and Cromarty,* pp. 40, 47, 93.

1.12 For Danish vocabulary still in use in Avoch in 1850 see George Anderson and

Peter Anderson, *Guide to the Highlands and Islands of Scotland* (3rd ed.; Edinburgh: A. & C. Black, 1850), p. 447.

1.13 *Origines Parochiales Scotiae*, II (2), pp. 543, 561.

1.14 The large number of Mackenzie lairds who obtained property in the area may be supposed to have brought a number of retainers with them. For the possibility of an earlier influx see Ranald G. Nicholson, *Scotland: The later middle ages*, Edinburgh History of Scotland, vol. 2 (Edinburgh: Oliver & Boyd, 1974), pp. 236-7, 608-9; Earl of Cromartie, *A Highland History* (Berkhamsted: Gavin Press, 1979), pp. 117ff.

1.15 *Origines Parochiales Scotiae*, II (2), p. 495.

1.16 From *circa* 1600 the estate was owned by the Forbes of Culloden and prior to that it had been held by the family of Cawdor. (Sir John Sinclair, *The Statistical Account of Scotland; drawn up from the communications of the ministers of the different parishes* (21 vols.; Edinburgh 1791-99), [hereafter referred to as O.S.A.] V, p. 205).

1.17 Sir George Steuart Mackenzie, *A general view . . . of the counties of Ross and Cromarty* (London, 1810), p. 15.

1.18 *Ibid.*, pp. 10-19.

1.19 Francis Nevile Reid, *The Earls of Ross and their descendants* (Edinburgh, 1894), pp. 3, 5, 6.

1.20 *Origines Parochiales Scotiae*, II (2), p. 485; F. N. Reid, *The Earls of Ross and their descendants*, pp. 6-7.

1.21 *Origines Parochiales Scotiae*, II (2), p. 485.

1.22 *Ibid.*, pp. 429, 451. John Philip Wood, *The antient and modern state of the Parish of Cramond* (Edinburgh: Peter Hill, 1794), pp. 21-2.

1.23 *Origines Parochiales Scotiae*, II (2), p. 494. Cromarty was particularly well endowed with chapels; see William Mackay Mackenzie, *Cromarty: its old chapels and parish church* (Edinburgh: Scottish Ecclesiological Society, 1905).

1.24 For land formerly held by the church see Charles Fraser Mackintosh, *Antiquarian notes: A series of papers regarding families and places in the Highlands* (Inverness, 1865), pp. 252-62.

1.25 *Origines Parochiales Scotiae*, II (2), p. 439.

1.26 Charles George Macdowall, *The Chanonry of Ross* (Fortrose, 1963), p. 63.

1.27 C. F. Mackintosh, *Antiquarian Notes*, pp. 341-8; *The Highlands of Scotland in 1750*, p. 29.

1.28 Sir William Fraser, *The Earls of Cromartie: their kindred, country and correspondence* (2 vols.; Edinburgh, 1876), II, pp. 425-427.

1.29 *O.S.A.*, I, p. 273.

1.30 While the Balnagown succession in the eighteenth century was the most obvious case of complications arising from entails there were others such as the succession to Newmore; see Colonel Charles Ross, *Petition of Colonel Charles Ross, second son of the late David Ross, Esq., of Inverchassley* (n.p.: n.p., February, 1765).

1.31 The Gordons of Invergordon were a notable example; see John Malcolm Bulloch, *The Families of Gordon of Invergordon, Newhall, also Ardoch, Ross-shire, and Carroll, Sutherland* ([Dingwall]: Ross-shire Printing & Publishing Co. 1906) pp. 13-14.

1.32 In the later seventeenth century William Robertson, an Inverness merchant, bought Kindeace; see Helen Myers Meldrum, *Kilmuir Easter. The history of a High-*

land parish (Inverness: R. Carruthers & Sons, 1935), p. 95.

1.33 Alexander Ross, *Petition of Captain Alexander Ross of Calrossie, Roderick McCulloch of Glastullich, Charles Monro of Allan & David Ross of Priesthill* (n.p.: n.p., January 29th, 1777), p. 8.

1.34 The parish of Rosemarkie, in particular, had no fewer than thirty proprietors (some holding land in other Easter Ross parishes as well) in 1644, of whom only two were valued at over £400 Scots; see C. F. Mackintosh, *Antiquarian Notes*, p. 343.

1.35 It is difficult without further study of the period to give reasons for, or the exact date of the change.

1.36 *Ross Valuation Book 1756*, S.R.O. E901/28/1.

1.37 For the Ross-shire properties of such as Leslie of Findrassie and Rose of Kilravock (who also held property in Moray and Nairn) and Ross of Balnagown and Mackenzie of Kilcoy (holding land in Wester as well as Easter Ross) see C. F. Mackintosh, *Antiquarian Notes*, pp. 341-8.

1.38 For one exception see J. P. Wood, *The antient and modern state of the Parish of Cramond*, pp. 21-2.

1.39 John Walker, *An economical history of the Hebrides and Highlands of Scotland* (2 vols.; Edinburgh, 1808), I, pp. 51-2. It is probable that Mackenzie of Meddat was a tacksman of the Highland variety; see *List of Tenants . . . who possess more than one farm, or whose yearly rent exceeds £20*, (n.d.), and *List of Farms upon the Annexed Estates Possessed by Wadsetters*, (n.d.), S.R.O. E731/21.

1.40 For the distinction between farmers (who maintained servants) and mailers or crofters (who did not) see Sir John Sinclair, *General view of the northern capitals and islands of Scotland* (London, 1795), p. 9. There is some evidence to suggest that the old system was already being modified. On the Cromarty estate, at least, the rigs were permanently allocated by the middle of the eighteenth century; see J. B. Cruickshank, 'The Black Isle Ross-shire', *S.G.M.* 77 (1961), p. 8.

1.41 *O.S.A.*, XIII, p. 16.

1.42 *The Highlands of Scotland in 1750*, p. 39; *Report of Mr. Francis Grant, General Riding Officer and Inspector*, [1756], p. 33, S.R.O. E729/7; Great Britain, Commission of Inquiry into the condition of the crofters and cottars in the Highlands and Islands of Scotland, *Report* (Edinburgh, 1884) Appendix A, XC, p. 421.

1.43 Alexander Mackenzie, 'Sir Kenneth Mackenzie of Gairloch, Bart.' *Celtic Magazine*, 6 (1881) p. 28.

1.44 *O.S.A.*, XIV, p. 91.

1.45 G. & P. Anderson, *Guide to the Highlands and Islands of Scotland*, (1850), p. 443; *Judicial rental Cromarty, 1755*, S.R.O. E746/70.

1.46 *O.S.A.*, I, p. 289.

1.47 For wheat see [Edward Burt], *Letters from a gentleman in the North of Scotland to his friend in London, containing the description of a capital town in that northern country . . . likewise an account of the Highlands, with the customs and manners of the Highlanders* (2 vols.; 2nd ed.; London: Pottinger, 1759), I, pp. 302-3. For root crops see, for example, Andrew Wight, *Present state of Husbandry in Scotland. Extracted from reports made to the commissioners of the annexed estates* (4 vols.; Edinburgh, 1778-84), 4(1), p. 242.

1.48 E. Burt, *Letters from a gentleman in the North of Scotland*, I, pp. 86-90; W. Thom, 'Journal of a Tour in the North of Scotland', *New Agricultural and Commercial*

Magazine, 1 (1811), pp. 283-4.

1.49 Letter. Roderick Macleod to Charles Robertson, of Kindeace, Edinburgh, 31st January, 1778, S.R.O. GD 146/13.

1.50 Sir G. S. Mackenzie, *A general view . . . of the counties of Ross & Cromarty*, p. 127.

1.51 The lands of Mulderg, for example, yielded no more in 1768 than in 1600; see Captain John Ross, *Information . . . against the heirs and creditors of the deceased David MacCulloch of Mulderg, defenders* (n.p.: n.p., July 30th 1768), p. 8.

1.52 William Macgill, *Old Ross-shire and Scotland as seen in the Tain and Balnagown documents* (2 vols.; Inverness: Northern Counties Newspaper Company, 1909-11), II, p. 54.

1.53 Of approximately 350 members of the Society of Improvers founded in 1723, eight were connected with Easter Ross including several of the major landowners; see Robert Maxwell, *Select transactions of the Society of Improvers in the Knowledge of Agriculture in Scotland* (Edinburgh, 1743), p. XVIII). For agricultural improvements see [William Macintosh], *An essay on ways and means for inclosing, fallowing, planting . . . Scotland; and that in sixteen years at farthest* (Edinburgh: Freebairn, 1729), pp. XLVI-XLVII.

1.54 Sheila Forman, *Scottish country houses and castles* (Glasgow: Collins, 1971), p. 149; Richard Pococke, *Tours in Scotland 1747, 1750, 1760*, Publications of the Scottish History Society, vol. 1 (Edinburgh: Scottish History Society, 1887, p. 176; W. Macintosh, *An essay on ways and means for inclosing . . . Scotland*, p. XLVI; *O.S.A.*, I, p. 261; Peter Hume Brown, *Early travellers in Scotland* (Edinburgh: David Douglas, 1891), p. 175.

1.55 For the local effects of the herring fishing on Fortrose see Convention of the Royal Burghs of Scotland, *Records of the Convention of the Royal Burghs of Scotland* (7 vols.; Edinburgh: W. Paterson, 1870-1918), 5, p. 372; and on Cromarty, Hugh Miller, *Tales and Sketches* (Edinburgh: Black, 1863), p. 289; for the general attitude of the local fishermen see E. Burt, *Letters from a gentleman in the North of Scotland*, I, p. 130, and for one attempt to improve matters see Sir W. Fraser, *The Earls of Cromartie*, I, p. CCIII.

1.56 For evidence of quarrying see Walter Macfarlane, *Geographical Collections relating to Scotland*, Publications of the Scottish History Society, vols. 51-3 (3 vols.; Edinburgh: Scottish History Society, 1906-8), I, p. 205. For prosecutions against illegal distillers see W. Macgill, *Old Ross-shire and Scotland*, I, p. 119, and for a discussion on the roll of Ferintosh see C. F. Mackintosh, *Antiquarian Notes*, pp. 80-3.

1.57 Although William Forsyth's claim to be the first to introduce the spinning of linen yarn to the area was obviously false, the linen industry made little impact on the overall economy of Easter Ross before the middle of the eighteenth century: *To the Honble Commissioners for managing his Majestie's Annex'd Estates in Scotland — The petition of William Forsyth Linen Manufacturer in Cromarty* (Edinburgh, 3rd August, 1763), S.R.O. E746/138/4; Archibald Menzies, *Report . . . to the . . . Board of Annexed Estates, 1768*, S.R.O. E787/24.

1.58 W. Macgill, *Old Ross-shire and Scotland*, II, p. 106.

1.59 Sir W. Fraser, *The Earls of Cromartie*, II, p. 427; Nigg Women's Rural Institute, *The parish of Nigg (Aberdeen*, [1967]).

1.60 Bishop Forbes was surprised at the quality of the roads in Ross during his tour in 1762: Robert Forbes, *Journals of the Episcopal Visitations of the Right Rev. Robert Forbes, M.A., of the dioceses of Ross and Caithness . . . with a history of the episcopal church in the diocese of Ross . . . and a memoir of Bishop R. Forbes. Edited and compiled by the Rev. J. B. Craven* (London: Skeffington & Son, 1886), p. 150 . See also *Plan of the boundaries of the Burgh of Tain,* 1750, S.R.O., West Register House, RHP275/1-3.

1.61 William Forsyth developed a waterborne trade not only with Leith and London but also with Holland after 1739; see H. Miller, *Tales and sketches,* p. 290.

1.62 Thomas Bamford Lang, *An historical summary of the Post Office in Scotland, compiled from authentic records* (Edinburgh: privately printed, 1856), p. 11.

1.63 Convention of the Royal Burghs of Scotland, *Records,* 5, pp. 122, 236, 421-2; 6, p. 631.

1.64 The continuing importance of Cromarty and Milton is discussed in Chapter 3 d, while the later eighteenth century existence of Culbockie as a significant community is clear from a plan of the Findon estate in 1769. (David Aitken, *Plan of the Estate and Barony of Findon the property of Sir Roderick Mackenzie of Scatwell . . . 1769,* S.R.O., West Register House, RHP3513). For information on the burghs in the area see George Pryde, *The burghs of Scotland, a critical list* (London: Oxford University Press, 1965) pp. 18-19, 24-5, 28-30, 41, 76-9, but note that the burgh of Tarbat, p. 76, is actually the burgh of Milton of Newtarbat in the parish of Kilmuir and that Pryde omits the burgh of Auchterneed; see Convention of the Royal Burghs of Scotland, *Records,* 5, p. 659.

1.65 Convention of the Royal Burghs of Scotland, *Records,* 5, pp. 641, 662.

1.66 *The New Statistical Account of Scotland by the ministers of the respective parishes, under the superintendence of a Committee of the Society for the benefit of the sons and daughters of the Clergy* (15 vols.; Edinburgh & London: W. Blackwood & Sons, 1845) 14, p. 11; Convention of the Royal Burghs of Scotland, *Records,* 5, pp. 659-60; 6, pp. 16, 535.

1.67 The role of Tain and Fortrose as educational centres was particularly important; see C. G. Macdowall, *The Chanonry of Ross,* pp. 160-1, 166-7; Robert William Munro and Jean Munro, *Tain through the centuries* (Tain: Tain Town Council, 1966), pp. 104-5.

1.68 John Anderson, 'Essay on the present state of the Highlands and Islands of Scotland', *Prize Essays and Transactions of the Highland Society of Scotland, N.S.A.* (1831), p. 29.

1.69 D. P. Kirby, 'Bede and the Pictish Church', *Innes Review,* XXIV (1973), p. 17.

1.70 *Origines Parochiales Scotiae,* II (2), pp. 416-504, 522-96.

1.71 *Ibid.,* p. 568.

1.72 David Edward Easson, *Medieval Religious Houses, Scotland* (London: Longmans, Green & Co., 1957), pp. 170, 186.

1.73 *Origines Parochiales Scotiae,* II (2), p. 433.

1.74 R. Forbes, *Journals of the Episcopal Visitations of the Right Rev. Robert Forbes,* p. 68.

1.75 Colin Macnaughton, *Church Life in Ross and Sutherland from the Revolution, 1688, to the present time. Compiled chiefly from the Tain Presbytery records* (Inverness: Northern Counties Newspaper Co., 1915) p. 4.

1.76 A separate Presbytery of Sutherland was created in 1700 (*ibid.,* p. 27), and by

1707 a Synod of Ross existed (*Minutes of the Synod of Ross*, S.R.O. CH2/312/1).

1.77 R. Forbes, *Journals of the Episcopal Visitations of the Right Rev. Robert Forbes*, p. 66; Robert Bain, *History of the Ancient Province of Ross, the County Palatine of Scotland. From the earliest to the present time* (Dingwall: Pefferside Press, 1899), pp. 223-4.

1.78 John Macinnes, *The Evangelical Movements in the Highlands of Scotland, 1699 to 1800* (Aberdeen: Aberdeen University Press, 1951), pp. 28, 156.

1.79 *Ibid.*, p. 95.

1.80 Episcopal congregations continued in the parishes of Rosemarkie (English-speaking), Dingwall (mixed) and Killearnan (Gaelic-speaking) into the nineteenth century; see R. Forbes, *Journals of the Episcopal Visitations of the Right Rev. Robert Forbes*, pp. 124, 131.

1.81 For an example of an Episcopalian clergyman being protected by a Mackenzie laird see *ibid.*, p. 116.

1.82 R. Bain, *History of the Ancient Province of Ross*, pp. 223-4.

1.83 *The Highlands of Scotland in 1750*, pp. 19-23.

1.84 Many of the parish schoolmasters were licentiates for the ministry; see, for example, *Dingwall Presbytery Minutes*, November 2nd, 1797, S.R.O. CH2/92/18.

1.85 *Ibid.*, November 26th, 1800.

1.86 *Origines Parochiales Scotiae*, II (2), p. 484; Great Britain, Select Committee on Education in Scotland, *Answers made by schoolmasters in Scotland to queries circulated in 1838* (London: H.M.S.O., 1851), PP 1841 XIX, pp. 267-75.

1.87 Henry Hunter, *A brief history of the Society in Scotland for Propagating Christian Knowledge in the Highlands and Islands; and of the correspondent Board in London* (London, 1795), p. 29.

1.88 *The Highlands of Scotland in 1750*, p. 125.

1.89 Hugh Miller, *My schools and schoolmasters* (Edinburgh: Nimmo, 1869), p.51.

1.90 In contrast, for example, to Iona which followed the Irish Gothic style.

1.91 George Hay, *The architecture of Scottish Post-Reformation Churches 1560-1843* (Oxford, Clarendon Press, 1957), pp. 272-3.

1.92 Stewart Cruden, *The Scottish Castle* (Edinburgh: Nelson, 1960) p. 170; Sir W. Fraser, *The Earls of Cromartie*, II, pp. 431, 437.

1.93 Captain John Ross, *Information . . . against the heirs and creditors of the deceased David MacCulloch of Mulderg, defenders* (n.p.: n.p., July 30th, 1768), p. 8.

1.94 For the extent to which local people were involved see *The Highlands of Scotland in 1750*, pp. 20-1; *A list of persons concerned in the rebellion, transmitted to the Commissioners of Excise by the several supervisors in Scotland in obedience to a general letter of the 7th May 1746, and a supplementary list with evidences to prove the same*, Publications of the Scottish History Society, vol. 8 (Edinburgh: Constable, 1890), pp. 72-83, 328-9.

2.1 See, for example, John Prebble, *The Lion in the North. A personal view of Scotland's history* (London: Secker and Warburg, 1971), p. 301.

2.2 Sir W. Fraser, *The Earls of Cromartie*, I, pp. XXV-CCXXIV.

2.3 *A list of persons concerned in the rebellion*, p. 328; Alexander Ross of Calrossie *et al.*, *Petition . . .* (n.p.: n.p., January 29th, 1777), p. 28; Discharge, Mr. David Ross to His Majesty etc. 1755 S.R.O. E751/2.

2.4 *Ross Valuation Book 1756* S.R.O. E901/28/1; *Valuation of the County of*

Cromarty as Settled by the Commissioners of Supply at a Generall meeting held by adjournment for that purpose at Cromarty, 25th May 1765. S.R.O. SC24/21/7. Although there is a difference of nine years between the two valuations there was very little change in Cromarty in that period so that with minor modifications the data from 1765 has been related to 1756. For the Balnagown succession see Alexander Ross, *Information . . . against Master Charles Ross, second lawful son to George Lord Ross, and his curators, defenders* (n.p.: n.p., December 6th, 1739).

2.5 *Ross Valuation Book 1756,* S.R.O. E901/28/1; C. F. Mackintosh, *Antiquarian Notes,* pp. 341-8.

2.6 M. L. Macleod *et al., 3 centuries of falsehood exposed . . .* (Golspie, 1970), pp. 15, 18.

2.7 Henrietta Tayler, *History of the family of Urquhart* (Aberdeen: Aberdeen University Press, 1946), p. 188; *Discharge and Obligation. Captain Bernard Forrester to George Ross 1758,* S.R.O. GD 159/2.

2.8 It is by no means certain, however, whether the money the Baillies used to purchase Rosehall was derived from the factory at Balnagown or from another source.

2.9 Alexander Mackenzie and Alexander Macbain, *History of the Mathesons* (2nd ed.; Stirling: Mackay, 1900), p. 30.

2.10 Lord Elibank, for example, purchased the Cromarty estate in 1764 for political reasons; see William Ferguson, 'The Urquharts of Cromarty', *Scottish Genealogist,* 6, pt. 3 (1959), p. 11.

2.11 Even when a proprietor was deeply interested in estate management his absence could lead to delays in attending to routine matters; see Letter, John Adam to Sir John Ross of Balnagown, Edinburgh 16th January, 1762, S.R.O. GD129/7/7.

2.12 While it is possible that some estates held by Easter Ross proprietors in other parts of the country may have been missed, the numbers involved will almost certainly be minimal.

2.13 *Ross Valuation Book 1756,* S.R.O. E901/28/1; *Valuation of the County of Cromarty 1765,* S.R.O. SC24/21/7.

2.14 *Register of Seisins* [Ross 1781-1860]. [N.p., n.d.].

2.15 Letter, Sir John Ross to William MacCulloch, Plymouth, 19th February, 1778 S.R.O. GD129/24/81; *Discharge and Obligation, Captain Bernard Forrester to George Ross 1758,* S.R.O. GD159/2; W. L. Wallace Brown, 'Alness in the eighteenth century', *Transactions of the Inverness Scientific Society and Field Club,* 6 (1899-1906), pp. 20, 24.

2.16 *Register of Seisins,* p. 812; Donald Sage, *Memorabilia Domestica* (Wick: W. Rae, 1889), p. 66.

2.17 R. W. Munro and J. Munro, *Tain through the centuries,* p. 105; Alexander Mackenzie, *History of the Mackenzies* (Inverness: Mackenzie, 1894), p. 360; Sir Charles Elphinstone Adam, *View of the political state of Scotland in the last century* (Edinburgh: Douglas, 1887), p. 295. While there was an inflow of capital in the later eighteenth century it is by no means certain that this was a net inflow as there was a large capital outflow as well; see *infra,* Conclusion.

2.18 Sir G. S. Mackenzie, *A general view . . . of the counties of Ross & Cromarty,* p. 50; A. Wight, *Present state of husbandry in Scotland* 4(1), p. 251.

2.19 *Valuation Book of the County of Cromarty,* 1802, S.R.O. E901/10/2; [*Valuation Book of the County of Ross*], 1802, S.R.O. E901/28/2.

2.20 Sir John Sinclair, *General report of the agricultural state and political circumstances of Scotland* (5 vols.; Edinburgh, 1814), I, p. 89.

2.21 Duncan Warrand, *Some Mackenzie pedigrees* (Inverness: Carruthers, 1965), p. 78.

2.22 *Register of Seisins*, p. 493.

2.23 James Edmund Handley, *Scottish farming in the eighteenth century* (London: Faber & Faber, 1953), p. 116.

2.24 *Register of Seisins*, p. 2/605.

2.25 *Ibid.*, p. 3/72, 3/467.

2.26 A. Mackenzie and A. Macbain, *History of the Mathesons*, pp. 142-4; *Valuation Roll for the County of Ross 1855-6*, S.R.O. VR115/1-3; *Valuation Roll for the County of Cromarty 1855-6*, S.R.O. VR115/4.

2.27 *Valuation Roll for the County of Ross 1855-6*, S.R.O. VR115/1-3; Great Britain, Commissioners appointed to inquire into the State of Municipal Corporations in Scotland, *Local Reports* (2 vols.; London: HMSO, 1835-6), PP 1835 XXIX, p. 189; PP 1836 XXIII, pp. 422-3; Roger Millman, 'The Marches of Highland Estates', *Scottish Geographical Magazine*, 85 (1969), map and p. 178.

2.28 Letter, David Munro to Charles Robertson of Kindeace, Edinburgh, 12th August, 1756, S.R.O. GD146/11.

2.29 On the estate of Aldie, for example, three of the four tacksmen held either mills or pasture; see *Abstract of the Judicial Rental of the Estate of Aldie 1774*, S.R.O. SC24/21/7.

2.30 See supra, p. 7; John Forbes, *Report upon the annexed estates of Lovat and Cromarty*, 30th July 1755, p. 3, S.R.O. E729/1.

2.31 *Judicial rental Cromarty, 1755*, S.R.O. E746/70.

2.32 *Ibid.*: *State of the Several Farms on the Barony of Newtarbat . . . 1755*, S.R.O. E729/3; D. Aitken, *Plan of the Estate and Barrony of Findon . . . 1769*, S.R.O., West Register House, RHP35/3; *Plan of the Lands of Drumcudden. The property of Captain Hugh Robert Duff of Muirtown . . . 1796*, S.R.O., West Register House, RHP1469.

2.33 See, for example, *State of the Several Farms on the Barony of Newtarbat . . . 1755*, S.R.O. E729/3; D. Aitken, *Plan of the Estate and Barrony of Findon . . . 1769*, S.R.O., West Register House, RHP3513. This estimate must remain tentative without the support of a stronger body of evidence. For the continued exaction of services, even in the nineteenth century, see Sir G. S. Mackenzie, *A general view . . . of the counties of Ross & Cromarty*, p. 142.

2.34 *A plan of the Estate of Cromarty. The property of Lord Elibank . . . 1764*, S.R.O., West Register House, RHP1046; J. B. Cruickshank, 'The Black Isle, Ross-shire', *S.G.M.*, 77 (1961), pp. 3-14; *Judicial rental Cromarty, 1755*, S.R.O. E746/70; D. Aitken, *Plan of the Estate and Barrony of Findon . . . 1769*, S.R.O., West Register House, RHP3513.

2.35 *Judicial rental Cromarty, 1755*, S.R.O. E746/70; David Aitken, *Measurement of Estate of Allan . . . 1786*, S.R.O. GD71/217; *Gross rental of the Barrony of Cromarty [1762]*, S.R.O. GD159/3/2/1; *Abstract of the Judicial Rental of the Estate of Aldie 1774*, S.R.O. SC24/21/7.

2.36 A. Wight, *Present state of husbandry in Scotland*, 4(1), pp. 248, 268, 280; *Judicial rental Cromarty, 1755*, S.R.O. E746/70; D. Aitken, *Plan of the Estate and Barrony of Findon . . . 1769*, S.R.O., West Register House, RHP3513; David Aitken,

A plan of the Estate of Tulloch . . . 1763, S.R.O., West Register House, RHP1473.

2.37 *Judicial rental Cromarty, 1755,* S.R.O. E746/70.

2.38 D. Aitken, *Plan of the Estate and Barrony of Findon . . . 1769,* S.R.O., West Register House, RHP3513; *Note of acres on the Estate of Allan* [*1756*], S.R.O. GD71/217.

2.39 James Hunter, *The making of the crofting community* (Edinburgh: John Donald, 1976), p. 3.

2.40 D. Aitken, *Plan of the Estate and Barrony of Findon . . . 1769,* S.R.O., West Register House, RHP3513; A. Wight, *Present state of husbandry in Scotland,* 4(1), p. 250.

2.41 D. Aitken, *Plan of the Estate and Barrony of Findon . . . 1769,* S.R.O., West Register House, RHP3513; D. Aitken, *Measurement of Estate of Allan . . . 1786,* S.R.O. GD71/217; *Plan of the Lands of Drumcudden . . . 1796,* S.R.O., West Register House, RHP1469.

2.42 Archibald Menzies, *Report . . . to the . . . Board of annexed estates, 1766,* pp. 106-7, 113, S.R.O. E729/8; *Letter, Ja. Morison (Annexed Estates Office) to Charles Robertson of Kindeace, Edinburgh, 26th June 1766,* S.R.O. GD146/13.

2.43 A. Wight, *Present state of husbandry in Scotland,* 4(1), p. 286; *Letter, David Munro to Charles Robertson of Kindeace, Edinburgh, 10th January 1767,* S.R.O. GD146/11; Sir J. Sinclair, *General view of the agriculture of the northern counties,* pp. 54, 104.

2.44 See supra, p. 8.

2.45 A. Wight, *Present state of husbandry in Scotland,* 4(1), pp. 266-7, 271.

2.46 James Edmund Handley, *The agricultural revolution in Scotland* (Glasgow: Burns, 1963), p. 69.

2.47 *Abstract of the Judicial Rental of the Estate of Aldie 1774,* S.R.O. SC24/21/7; Archibald Menzies, *Report . . . to the Hon. Board of Annexed Estates 1768,* S.R.O. E729/10/1.

2.48 *Gross rental of the Barrony of Cromarty* [*1762*], S.R.O. GD159/3/2/1.

2.49 Sir J. Sinclair, *General view of the agriculture of the northern counties,* pp. 80-1.

2.50 *Ibid.,* p. 56; *O.S.A.,* I, p. 289.

2.51 *Report General Inspector & Factor on Estates of Lovat & Cromarty* [circa 1769], S.R.O. E729/10/2; Sir J. Sinclair, *General view of the agriculture of the northern counties,* p. 16.

2.52 W. Thom, 'Journal of a Tour in the North of Scotland', *New Agricultural and Commercial Magazine,* I (1811), p. 283.

2.53 James Macdonald, 'On the agriculture of the counties of Ross and Cromarty', *Transactions of the Highland and Agricultural Society of Scotland,* 4th Series, 9 (1877), p. 86.

2.54 Sir G. S. Mackenzie, *A general view . . . of the counties of Ross and Cromarty,* p. 28; Robert Heron, *Scotland described* (3rd ed.; Edinburgh, 1806), p. 383.

2.55 Robert Forsyth, *The beauties of Scotland* (5 vols.; Edinburgh: Constable, 1805-8), 5, p. 222; Sir G. S. Mackenzie, *A general view . . . of the counties of Ross and Cromarty,* p. 148.

2.56 Sir G. S. Mackenzie, *A general view . . . of the counties of Ross and Cromarty,* p. 91.

2.57 A. Wight, *Present state of husbandry in Scotland*, 4(1), p. 233.

2.58 D. Aitken, *Plan of the Estate and Barrony of Findon . . . 1769*, S.R.O., West Register House, RHP3513; *Measurement of Estate of Allan . . . 1786*, S.R.O. GD71/217; *Plan of the Farm and Policy of Novar . . . 1777*, S.R.O., West Register House, RHP10671.

2.59 A. Wight, *Present state of husbandry in Scotland*, 4(1), pp. 235, 240, 272; *O.S.A.*, XV, p. 619; A. Menzies, *Report . . . to the . . . Board of annexed estates 1766*, p. 110, S.R.O. E729/8.

2.60 Sir J. Sinclair, *General view of the agriculture of the northern counties*, pp. 9-10; A. Menzies, *Report . . . to the . . . Board of annexed estates 1766*, p. 110, S.R.O. E729/8; *O.S.A.*, XIV, p. 90.

2.61 J. Forbes, *Report upon the annexed estates of Lovat and Cromarty, 30th July, 1755*, p. 3, S.R.O. E729/1. It is not clear how soon before 1755 potatoes were introduced to the area but it was about this time that they became common in the Highlands at large; see Malcolm Gray, *The Highland Economy 1750-1850* (Edinburgh: Oliver & Boyd, 1957), p. 143.

2.62 W. Macintosh, *An essay on ways and means for inclosing . . . Scotland*, p. XVIII; *Petition for Sir John Gordon Bart. and other Proprietors of the County of Ross, 8th August 1774*, S.R.O. E746/148; *Letter, David Munro to Charles Robertson of Kindeace, Clelands Yeards near Edinburgh, 19th August 1761*, S.R.O. GD146/12; *Letter, David Munro to Charles Robertson of Kindeace, Edinburgh, 22nd May, 1767*, S.R.O. GD146/12.

2.63 A. Wight, *Present state of husbandry in Scotland*, 4(1), p. 233; J. M. Bulloch, *The Families of Gordon of Invergordon, Newhall*, p. 28; Letter, Sir John Ross to William MacCulloch, Plymouth, 22nd November, 1777, S.R.O. GD129/24/81; Alexander Mackenzie, *History of the Munros of Foulis* (Inverness: Mackenzie, 1898), pp. 138-9; Joseph Mitchell, *Reminiscences of my life in the Highlands (1883): A reprint with a new introduction, corrigenda and index by Ian Robertson*, (2 vols.; Newton Abbot: David & Charles Reprints, 1971), I, p. 263.

2.64 Letter, Sir Harry Munro to Charles Robertson of Kindeace, Fowlis Castle, 20th July, 1768, S.R.O. GD146/12; Letter, Geo. Balfour to Charles Robertson of Kindeace, Tarbat, 23rd January, 1780, S.R.O. GD146/14; Letter, David Munro to Charles Robertson of Kindeace, Edinburgh, 20th November, 1756, S.R.O. GD146/11.

2.65 Letter, ? Charles Robertson of Kindeace to ? Sir Harry Munro of Fowlis, Inchfuir, 4th July, 1757, S.R.O. GD146/11; Letter, Hugh Rose of Dam to Charles Robertson of Kindeace, Nigg, 27th May, 1778, S.R.O. GD146/13; Letter, David Ross of Tarlogie to Charles Robertson of Kindeace, Tarlogie, 8th October, 1781, S.R.O. GD146/14; Letter, David Munro to Charles Robertson of Kindeace, Edinburgh, 4th January, 1757, S.R.O. GD146/11.

2.66 Letter, Alex. Guthrie to William Robertson of Kindeace, Edinburgh, 1794, S.R.O. GD146/15. In one subscription list natives of Easter Ross comprised seven of a total of approximately 425 subscribers drawn from all over Britain; see William Boutcher, *A treatise on forest trees* (Edinburgh, 1775), pp. XXVII-XLIII.

2.67 John Mason, 'Conditions in the Highlands after the '45', *Scottish Historical Review*, 26 (1947), pp. 141-6; James Edmund Handley, *Scottish farming in the eighteenth century* (London: Faber & Faber, 1953), pp. 235-43. For a different point of view see Annette Macfarlane Smith, 'The administration of the Forfeited Annexed

Estates 1752-1784', in Geoffrey W. S. Barrow (ed.), *The Scottish tradition: Essays in honour of Ronald Gordon Cant* (Edinburgh: Scottish Academic Press, 1974), pp. 198-210.

2.68 R. Maxwell, *Select transactions of the Society of Improvers*, p. XVIII.

2.69 A. Menzies, *Report 1768*, pp. 3-5, S.R.O. E787/24; *Report by the Commissioners of Annexed Estates, 1769*, S.R.O. E723/2; Archibald Menzies, *Report . . . to the . . . Board of annexed estates 1766*, p. 106, S.R.O. E729/8; *Note of Improvements proposed to be made on the annexed estate of Cromarty, Summer 1773*, S.R.O. E787/25/2; *List of Married disbanded Soldiers settled on the . . . estate of Cromarty, 1764*, S.R.O. E787/27/3; *List of disbanded soldiers settled on the Annexed Estate of Cromarty as Tradesmen and Day Labourers under the denomination of Kings Cottagers — Newtarbat 1764*, S.R.O. E787/28/5; Letter, Sailors at Newtarbat [*1763*], S.R.O. E746/80; *Petition, David Aitken Land Measurer at Newtarbat 1767*, S.R.O. E746/143/3; Sir G. S. Mackenzie, *A general view . . . of the counties of Ross and Cromarty*, p. 47.

2.70 A. Wight, *Present state of husbandry in Scotland*, 4(1), p. 235; Thomas Pennant, *A tour in Scotland 1769* (5th ed.; London, 1790), p. 186; W. Macgill, *Old Ross-shire and Scotland*, I, p. 187; Letter, Ebenezer Munro to Charles Robertson of Kindeace, Glasgow, 21st September, 1757, S.R.O. GD146/7; Letter, David Munro to Charles Robertson of Kindeace, Edinburgh, 9th July, 1759, S.R.O. GD146/11; Letter, Donald Macleod of Geanies to James Reoch Cartwright in Tain, Geanies, 6th Dec., 1792, S.R.O. GD146/15; *O.S.A.*, III, p. 392; IV, p. 294; XII, pp. 264-5.

2.71 10 Geo. III c 51. For the use made of this act in Easter Ross see *Registers of Improvement etc. made upon Lands held under settlements of Strict Entail*, S.R.O. SC34/18/1, SC25/67/1-2, SC34/23/1-4. The wording of these registers would suggest that the act in question was passed on the tenth of May 1768 but this in fact was the date of the first meeting of the Parliament which passed the 1770 act.

2.72. J. E. Handley, *Scottish farming in the eighteenth century*, pp. 149, 152.

2.73 A. Wight, *Present state of husbandry in Scotland*, 4(1), p. 233; Robert Southey, *Journal of a tour in Scotland in 1819* (London: Murray, 1929), p. 120; J. M. Bulloch, *The Families of Gordon of Invergordon, Newhall*, p. 13; W. Macgill, *Old Ross-shire and Scotland*, I, p. 291; Charles Fraser Mackintosh, *Letters of two centuries* (Inverness: Mackenzie, 1890), p. 235.

2.74 Sir G. S. Mackenzie, *A general view . . . of the counties of Ross and Cromarty*, p. 138; Sir John Sinclair, *General report of the agricultural state and political circumstances of Scotland* (Edinburgh, 1814), pp. 306-7; John Anderson, 'Essays on the present state of the Highlands & Islands of Scotland', *Prize Essays and Transactions of the Highland Society of Scotland*, New Series 8 (1831), p. 52.

2.75 R. Southey, *Journal*, p. 120; A. Wight, *Present state of husbandry in Scotland*, 4(1), p. 243.

2.76 *O.S.A.*, I, p. 274.

2.77 A. Wight, *Present state of husbandry in Scotland*, 4(1), p. 275; *Report, Genl. Inspector & Factor on Estates of Lovat and Cromarty to the Hon. Board of Annexed Estates* [*c. 1769*], S.R.O. E729/10/2; Sir J. Sinclair, *General view of the agriculture of the northern counties*, p. 69; *Accompt., David Aitken* [*to Charles Robertson of Kindeace*] 14 December, 1780, S.R.O. GD146/14.

2.78 Ian H. Adams, *Directory of former Scottish Commonties* (Edinburgh: Scottish

Record Society, 1971), pp. 207-8; *Plan of [the boundary between the lands of Meikle Allan belonging to Mr. Munro] 1761*, S.R.O., West Register House, RHP219.

2.79 A. Wight, *Present state of husbandry in Scotland*, 4(1), p. 235; R. Forbes, *Journals of the Episcopal Visitations of the Right Rev. Robert Forbes*, p. 219; *O.S.A.*, IV, p. 473; VI, p. 186; *View of the purchase agreed between William Baillie & Charles Robertson, 1751*, S.R.O. GD146/7; Sir J. Sinclair, *General view of the agriculture of the northern counties*, p. 38.

2.80 A. Wight, *Present state of husbandry in Scotland*, 4(1), pp. 250, 283.

2.81 Sir J. Sinclair, *General view of the agriculture of the northern counties*, pp. 58, 109; Sir G. S. Mackenzie, *A general view . . . of the counties of Ross and Cromarty*, p. 83.

2.82 Letter, David Munro to Charles Robertson of Kindeace, Edinburgh, 1756, S.R.O. GD146/11; Letter, David Munro to ? Charles Robertson of Kindeace, Edinburgh, 1757, S.R.O. GD146/11; Letter, Hugh Rose of Dam to Charles Robertson of Kindeace, Nigg, 1778, S.R.O. GD146/13; A. Wight, *Present state of husbandry in Scotland*, 4(1), pp. 266, 268; *Register of improvements made upon Lands . . . under . . . Strict Entail*, S.R.O. SC34/23/1.

2.83 *Minutes of the Presbytery of Chanonry*, 15th October, 1771, S.R.O. CH2/66/5; *Register of improvements made upon Lands . . . under . . . Strict Entail*, 1772, 1776-8, S.R.O. SC34/23/1.

2.84 A. Wight, *Present state of husbandry in Scotland*, 4(1), pp. 227, 233, 244, 247, 248, 256, 263, 265, 275-6, 281; Sir J. Sinclair, *General view of the agriculture of the northern counties*, p. 105; Letter, David Munro to Charles Robertson of Kindeace, Edinburgh, 4th January, 1757, S.R.O. GD146/11; R. Forsyth, *The beauties of Scotland*, 5, p. 220.

2.85 A. Wight, *Present state of husbandry in Scotland*, 4(1), pp. 239, 246, 256, 266, 284; *O.S.A.*, I, p. 261; *Register of improvements made upon Lands . . . under . . . Strict Entail, 1771-1775*, S.R.O. SC34/23/1; T. Pennant, *A tour in Scotland, 1769*, pp. 184-5; Sir J. Sinclair, *General view of the agriculture of the northern counties*, p. 40; Acknowledgement, Alex. Allison to Mr. Robertson of Kindeace, Rhives, 3rd December, 1793, S.R.O. GD146/8.

2.86 *Register of improvements made upon Lands . . . under . . . Strict Entail, 1775*, S.R.O. SC34/23/1; Sir J. Sinclair, *General view of the agriculture of the northern counties*, p. 41.

2.87 *Photograph of plan of the grounds and inclosures about Cromarty Castle and Hill 1753*, S.R.O., West Register House, RHP5498.

2.88 Letter, Roderick Macleod to Charles Robertson of Kindeace, Edinburgh, 24th June, 1778, S.R.O. GD146/13; R. Forbes, *Journals of the Episcopal Visitations of the Right Rev. Robert Forbes*, p. 218; Letter, Sir John Ross to William MacCulloch, Plymouth, 21st July, 1781, S.R.O. GD129/24/81.

2.89 A. Wight, *Present state of husbandry in Scotland*, 4(1), p. 236.

2.90 W. L. Wallace Brown, 'Alness in the eighteenth century', *Transactions of the Inverness Scientific Society and Field Club*, 6 (1899-1906), p. 25; *O.S.A.*, III, p. 9; V, pp. 205-6; XVII, p. 354.

2.91 Sir J. Sinclair, *General view of the agriculture of the northern counties*, p. 107; but for the earlier history of this nursery see *Petition, David Aitken Land Measurer at Newtarbat 1767*, S.R.O. E746/143/3.

2.92 Sir J. Sinclair, *General view of the agriculture of the northern counties*, p. 42; Letter, Sir John Ross to William MacCulloch, London, 13th April, 1776, S.R.O. GD129/24/81.

2.93 Letter, John Adam to Sir John Ross of Balnagown, Edinburgh, 16th January, 1762, S.R.O. GD129/7/7; Robert Grigor, 'Report on plantations of Pinus Sylvestris, forming part of the Forest of Balnagown, the property of Sir Charles Ross, Bart.', *Transactions of the Highland and Agricultural Society of Scotland*, New Series (1845-7), p. 121.

2.94 A. Wight, *Present state of husbandry in Scotland*, 4(1), pp. 234-5, 240, 263, 277; S. W. E. Vince, 'The Highlands of Scotland', in L. Dudley Stamp (ed.), *The land of Britain* (London: Geographical Publications, 1944), p. 582; *O.S.A.*, II, p. 559; IV, p. 290; XV, p. 619; Sir J. Sinclair, *General view of the agriculture of the northern counties*, p. 99.

2.95 A. Wight, *Present state of husbandry in Scotland*, 4(1), p. 237; *O.S.A.*, III, p. 10; XI, p. 335; XIV, p. 90; Sir J. Sinclair, *General view of the agriculture of the northern counties*, p. 22.

2.96 A. Wight, *Present state of husbandry in Scotland*, 4(1), pp. 258, 268; Sir J. Sinclair, *General view of the agriculture of the northern counties*, p. 16; *Political observations occasioned by the state of agriculture in the north of Scotland* (1756), p. 16.

2.97 A. Wight, *Present state of husbandry in Scotland*, 4(1), pp. 234, 241, 245, 253, 266; W. Macgill, *Old Ross-shire and Scotland*, I, p. 175.

2.98 A. Wight, *Present state of husbandry in Scotland*, 4(1), pp. 261-3; *O.S.A.*, I, p. 266; IV, p. 475; VI, pp. 194, 423.

2.99 Sir G. S. Mackenzie, *A general view . . . of the counties of Ross and Cromarty*, pp. 128-30; W. Macgill, *Old Ross-shire and Scotland*, I, p. 175; Letter, Sir John Ross to Lord Ankerville, Edinburgh, 10th May, 1779, S.R.O. GD129/7/11.

2.100 *Documents relative to the dearth and famine in Scotland in the year 1783, in consequence of the late harvest and loss of the potatoe crop* (London: H.M.S.O., 1846), Appendix 5, p. 6; *O.S.A.*, I, p. 280; III, pp. 13, 393; VI, p. 434; *View of the purchase agreed between William Baillie and Charles Robertson, 1751*, S.R.O. GD146/7; Letter, Donald Macleod of Geanies to James Reoch, Cartwright in Tain, 6th December, 1792, S.R.O. GD146/15.

2.101 *O.S.A.*, XVIII, p. 351; J. Macdonald, 'On the agriculture of the counties of Ross and Cromarty', p. 90, *Farmers Magazine*, Edinburgh, 1800-14; *Exchequer Fiars Prices, Ross, 1787-1825*, S.R.O. E848/1 (it should be noted that the Ross fiars prices before 1805 are no real indication of prices current in the area as they were calculated as two-thirds of the Fife fiars prices).

2.102 *N.S.A.*, 14, p. 464; 'Agricultural Intelligence Scotland, Ross-shire Quarterly Report', *Farmers Magazine*, 21 (1820), p. 118.

2.103 Letter, Sir John Ross to William MacCulloch, Plymouth, 22nd November, 1777, S.R.O. GD129/24/81.

2.104 G. & P. Anderson, *Guide to the Highlands and Islands (1850)*, p. 392; John Knox, *A view of the British Empire, more especially Scotland* (3rd ed.; London, 1785), p. 121.

2.105 A Ross-shire Farmer, 'Remarks on the Ross-shire resolutions concerning the Distilling Laws', *Farmers Magazine*, 8 (1807), pp. 175-6.

2.106 Sir G. S. Mackenzie, *A general view . . . of the counties of Ross and Cromarty*, pp. 140-1; Board of Agriculture, *Agricultural state of the kingdom in February, March and April 1816; being the substance of the replies to a circular letter* (London: Sherwood, Neely & Jones, 1816), p. 134.

2.107 *O.S.A.*, IV, pp. 294, 301, 474; XIX, p. 236; Sir G. S. Mackenzie, *A general view . . . of the counties of Ross and Cromarty*, p. 107; *N.S.A.*, 14, 27-28, 32.

2.108 J. Macdonald, 'On the agriculture of the counties of Ross and Cromarty', p. 77; Board of Agriculture, *Agricultural state of the kingdom*, p. 131.

2.109 Commissioners appointed to inquire into the state of the Municipal corporations in Scotland, *Local reports* (London: H.M.S.O., 1835), I, p. 189; II, pp. 422-4; N. Macrae, *The romance of a royal burgh*, pp. 224-5, 227-9, 232, 234-8, 242, 244-5, 247; *Tain Town Council minutes*, 20th April, 1787; 9th October, 1798; 28th October, 1812, S.R.O. B70/6/1.

2.110 J. Walker, *an economical history of the Hebrides*, I, p. 90; R. Forsyth, *The beauties of Scotland*, IV, p. 523; *Presbytery of Chanonry minutes*, 1st May, 1810, S.R.O. CH2/66/6.

2.111 Sir G. S. Mackenzie, *A general view . . . of the counties of Ross and Cromarty*, pp. 87, 296; *O.S.A.*, XII, pp. 251, 254; N. Macrae, *The romance of a royal burgh*, p. 181; *Scroll minutes of the Board of Trustees for fisheries manufactures & improvements in Scotland*, 8th June, 1796, S.R.O. NG1/2/3.

2.112 *O.S.A.*, IV, p. 301.

2.113 Sir G. S. Mackenzie, *A general view . . . of the counties of Ross and Cromarty*, p. 108; *O.S.A.*, VI, p. 187.

2.114 Sir G. S. Mackenzie, *A general view . . . of the counties of Ross and Cromarty*, pp. 87, 102.

2.115 *Ibid.*, p. 108.

2.116 *Ibid.*, p. 81; *O.S.A.*, XIV, p. 91.

2.117 'Essays on the improvement of the Highlands', *Farmers Magazine*, 7 (1806), p. 234; *O.S.A.*, XIV, p. 91; Sir G. S. Mackenzie, *A general view . . . of the counties of Ross and Cromarty*, p. 144.

2.118 *Ibid.*, pp. 146-8; *O.S.A.*, VI, p. 193.

2.119 *Ibid.*, IV, p. 294.

2.120 R. Forsyth, *The beauties of Scotland*, V, p. 219.

2.121 J. Macdonald, 'On the agriculture of the counties of Ross and Cromarty', p. 92; 'Agricultural Intelligence Scotland, Ross-shire Quarterly Report', *Farmers Magazine*, 7 (1806), p. 117; 'Agricultural Intelligence Scotland, Ross-shire Quarterly Report', *Farmers Magazine*, 16 (1815), p. 242.

2.122 *Ibid.*, 7 (1806), p. 118.

2.123 R. Maxwell, *Select transactions of the Society of Improvers*, p. XVIII; 'List of Members', *Highland Society prize essays and transactions* (2nd ed,; Edinburgh: Constable, 1812), I, pp. LXX-LXXXVIII.

2.124 Sir J. Sinclair, *General view of the agriculture of the northern counties*, pp. 67-8; *O.S.A.*, XI, p. 350.

2.125 Easter Ross Farming Society, *Minute books;* Easter Ross Farmers Club, *Minute book.*

2.126 James Barron, *The northern Highlands in the nineteenth century: newspaper index and annals* (3 vols.; Inverness: Carruthers, 1903-13), I, p. 50; Sir G. S.

Mackenzie, *A general view . . . of the counties of Ross and Cromarty*, pp. 332-3, 351; 'Agricultural Intelligence Scotland, Ross-shire Quarterly Report', *Farmers Magazine*, 14 (1813), p. 242.

2.127 *O.S.A.*, XVII, p. 341.

2.128 Sir G. S. Mackenzie, *A general view . . . of the counties of Ross and Cromarty*, p. 142; Petition of Mrs. Mackenzie of Cromartie and her Husband for Commuting the Multures of Meikle Allan 1803, S.R.O. GD71/220.

2.129 Sir J. Sinclair, *A general view of the agriculture of the northern counties*, p. 5.

2.130 Sir G. S. Mackenzie, *A general view . . . of the counties of Ross and Cromarty*, p. 105; 'Agricultural Intelligence Scotland, Ross-shire Quarterly Report', *Farmers Magazine*, 9 (1808), p. 535.

2.131 *Ibid.*, 10 (1809), p. 562; Sir John Sinclair, *General report of the agricultural state, and political circumstances of Scotland* (5 vols.; Edinburgh, 1814), I, p. 201.

2.132 A. Wight, *Present state of husbandry in Scotland*, 4(1), pp. 258, 271; 'Agricultural Intelligence Scotland, Ross-shire Quarterly Report', *Farmers Magazine*, 14 (1813), pp. 114, 504.

2.133 Sir G. S. Mackenzie, *A general view . . . of the counties of Ross and Cromarty*, p. 117; *O.S.A.*, VI, p. 420. Even as late as 1831 runrig was common on at least one major estate on the Black Isle; see *N.S.A.*, 14, p. 395.

2.134 Catherine Sinclair, *Scotland and the Scotch* (Edinburgh: Whyte, 1840), p. 333; Letter, James Rose to William Robertson of Kindeace, Edinburgh, 3rd November, 1792, S.R.O. GD146/15; Letter, James Rose to William Robertson of Kindeace, Edinburgh, 15th November, 1792, S.R.O. GD146/15; *Register of improvements made upon lands held under settlement of strict entail. Ross-shire-Tain*, S.R.O. SC34/23/1-4; H. Hamilton, *Economic History of Scotland*, pp. 203-4.

2.135 J. Mitchell, *Reminiscences of my life in the Highlands*, I, pp. 263-4; Alexander Mackenzie, *History of the Mackenzies* (Inverness: Mackenzie, 1894), pp. 343-4.

2.136 Board of Agriculture, *Agricultural state of the kingdom*, p. 132; 'Agricultural Intelligence Scotland, Ross-shire Quarterly Report', *Farmers Magazine*, 16 (1815), p. 508.

2.137 'Agricultural Intelligence Scotland, Ross-shire Quarterly Report', *Farmers Magazine*, 16 (1815), p. 118.

2.138 *Ibid.*, 14 (1813), p. 114; 16 (1815), pp. 242, 382; 17 (1816), p. 510; Rarichy Farm rent book, 1829, S.R.O. GD1/519.

2.139 G. & P. Anderson, *Guide to the Highlands and Islands (1850)*, p. 392; 'Agricultural Intelligence Scotland, Ross-shire Quarterly Report', *Farmers Magazine*, 21 (1820), pp. 505-6.

2.140 Great Britain, Commission for inquiring into the administration and practical operation of the poor laws in Scotland, *Report* (London: H.M.S.O., 1844), Appendix, II, pp. 2-3, 8, 12, 46.

2.141 J. Mitchell, *Reminiscences of my life in the Highlands*, I, pp. 214, 286; *Session Cases, Shaw V*, 1826-7, pp. 605-6; *N.S.A.*, 14, pp. 34, 48; Sir G. S. Mackenzie, *A general view . . . of the counties of Ross and Cromarty*, p. 51.

2.142 J. Anderson, 'Essay on the present state of the Highlands and Islands of Scotland', p. 44.

2.143 'Agricultural Intelligence Scotland, Ross-shire Quarterly Report', *Farmers Magazine*, 19 (1818), p. 118; 24 (1823), pp. 130, 503; 25 (1824), p. 94.

2.144 J. Barron, *The northern Highlands*, II, p. 28; III, pp. 41, 42, 45; R. Bain, *History of the Ancient Province of Ross*, p. 376.

2.145 'Agricultural Intelligence Scotland, Ross-shire Quarterly Report', *Farmers Magazine*, 19 (1818), p. 119; Commissioners of Inquiry into the collection and management of the revenue arising in Ireland; etc., *Fifth report* (London: H.M.S.O., 1823), Appendix 49, p. 130.

2.146 Commissioners of Inquiry into the collection and management of the revenue arising in Ireland; etc., *Fifth report*, Appendix 49, p. 130; Appendix 57, p. 137.

2.147 *Ibid.*, Appendix 57, p. 137; Appendix 58, p. 142.

2.148 *Ibid.*, Appendix 49, p. 130.

2.149 J. Barron, *The northern Highlands*, I, p. 185.

2.150 *N.S.A.*, 14, p. 322.

2.151 J. Barron, *The northern Highlands*, I, pp. 185, 250; 'Agricultural Intelligence Scotland, Ross-shire Quarterly Report', *Farmers Magazine*, 21 (1820), p. 380.

2.152 *Ibid.*, 21 (1820), pp. 380, 505; 25 (1824), p. 93; 26 (1825), p. 376; Great Britain, Select Committee appointed to inquire into the state of agriculture, *Third report* (London: H.M.S.O., 1836), p. 600.

2.153 *Ibid.*

2.154 *N.S.A.*, 14, p. 294; James Hooper Dawson, *An abridged statistical account of Scotland* (Edinburgh: Lizars, 1853), p. 869.

2.155 *N.S.A.*, 14, pp. 13, 33, 376.

2.156 George Houston, 'Agricultural statistics in Scotland before 1866', *Agricultural History Review*, 9 (1961), p. 94; 'Agricultural Intelligence Scotland, Ross-shire Quarterly Report', *Farmers Magazine*, 16 (1815), p. 242.

2.157 Joy Tivy, 'Easter Ross: a residual crofting area', *Scottish Studies*, 9 (1965), p. 72.

2.158 *N.S.A.*, 14, pp. 66-7, 374-6; George Anderson and Peter Anderson, *Guide to the Highlands and Islands of Scotland* (2nd ed.; Edinburgh: Tait, 1842), p. 541; I. H. Adams, *Directory of former Scottish commonties*, p. 205.

2.159 J. Macdonald, 'On the agriculture of the counties of Ross and Cromarty', pp. 118-9; *N.S.A.*, 14, pp. 60, 62, 67, 227, 294, 376-7.

2.160 *Ibid.*, pp. 53-4; Sir G. S. Mackenzie, *A general view . . . of the counties of Ross and Cromarty*, pp. 292, 296; *Abstract of the answers and returns made pursuant to Act 3 & 4 Vict. c.99, and 4 Vict. c.7* (London: H.M.S.O., 1843), pp. 662-3.

2.161 Robert Walker, 'Of 83 acres on the farm of Fyrish, Ross-shire', *Prize essays and transactions of the Highland and Agricultural Society of Scotland*, 13 (1841), pp. 242-3; James Ure, 'Of 44 acres 2 roods 23 poles on the farm of Easter and Wester Corntown, County of Cromarty', *Prize essays and transactions of the Highland and Agricultural Society of Scotland*, 13 (1841), pp. 516-9.

2.162 *N.S.A.*, 14, p. 19; 'Agricultural Intelligence Scotland, Ross-shire Quarterly Report', *Farmers Magazine*, 26 (1825), p. 90; C. Sinclair, *Scotland and the Scotch*, p. 333.

2.163 G. & P. Anderson, *Guide to the Highlands and Islands of Scotland* (1842), p. 487; J. Barron, *The Northern Highlands*, II, p. 278; Register of improvements made upon lands held under . . . strict entail. Ross-shire-Tain, S.R.O. SC34/21/1-5.

2.164 *N.S.A.*, 14, pp. 19, 48, 58, 293, 346, 395-6; Evander Maciver, *Memoirs of a Highland gentleman* (Edinburgh: Constable, 1905), p. 41; 'Plantations', *Prize essays and transactions of the Highland Society of Scotland*, 6 (1824), p. 259.

2.165 William Mackenzie, 'Report of improvements at Ardross', *Transactions of the Highland and Agricultural Society of Scotland*, N.S., 1857-9, pp. 137-8; *Abstract of the answers and returns made pursuant to Act 3 & 4 Vict. c.99 and 4 Vict. c.7* (London: H.M.S.O., 1843), pp. 662-3.

2.166 J. Knox, *A view of the British Empire (1785)*, p. 188; R. Forbes, *Journals of the Episcopal Visitations of the Right Rev. Robert Forbes*, p. 172; R. Pococke, *Tours in Scotland*, pp. 175, 181; John Knox, *A tour through the Highlands of Scotland and the Hebride Isles in 1786* (London: J. Walter, 1787), p. 114; *O.S.A.*, III, pp. 389, 391; IV, p. 290; XII, p. 248.

2.167 *O.S.A.*, XV, p. 623.

2.168 Replies for Donald Mackay, Andw. McAngus, Hugh Sutherland and John McAngus all ffishers in Hilltown and of Robert Bruce Aeneas McLeod of Cadboll and his curators. To the Answers for the Honourable Captain Charles Napier [1781], S.R.O. GD146/14; *O.S.A.*, III, p. 389; VI, p. 424.

2.169 Peter Frederick Anson, *Fishing boats and fisher folk on the east coast of Scotland* (London: J. M. Dent & Sons, 1930), p. 24; John Knox, *Observations on the northern fisheries* (London: J. Walter, 1786), p. 101; *O.S.A.*, XV, p. 627.

2.170 J. Knox, *Observations on the northern fisheries*, p. 105; Replies for Donald Mackay [*et al.*], S.R.O. GD146/14; *O.S.A.*, VI, p. 424.

2.171 James Cameron, 'Report on the sanitary condition and general economy of the town of Tain and the district of Easter Ross, made to the Poor Law Commissioners', in *Local reports on the sanitary condition of the labouring population of Scotland, in consequence of an inquiry directed to be made by the Poor Law Commissioners*, p. 325.

2.172 Donald A. Mackenzie, 'Cromarty dialect & folk lore', *Transactions of the Rymour Club*, 3 (1928), p. 77; *Judicial rental Cromarty, 1755*, S.R.O. E746/70; *Report by the Commissioners of the Annexed Estates, 1769*, S.R.O. E723/2.

2.173 *Judicial rental Cromarty, 1755*, S.R.O. E746/70; *O.S.A.*, VI, p. 424.

2.174 *O.S.A.*, XV, p. 627; J. Dunlop, *The British Fisheries Society, 1786-1893* (Edinburgh: J. Donald, 1978), p. 46.

2.175 E. Burt, *Letters from a gentleman in the North of Scotland*, I, p. 130; *O.S.A.*, VI, p. 196.

2.176 List of Subscribers in the Fishing Chamber of Inverness 1759, S.R.O. GD146/7; Alexander John Youngson, *After the Forty-Five* (Edinburgh: Edinburgh U.P., 1973), p. 104.

2.177 J. Dunlop, *The British Fisheries Society, 1786-1893*, p. 10.

2.178 Letter, Sailors at Newtarbat [1763], S.R.O. E746/80.

2.179 *O.S.A.*, III, p. 389; IV, p. 290; XV, p. 625.

2.180 Lewis McCulloch, *Observations on the herring fisheries upon the North & East coasts of Scotland* (London: W. Richardson, 1788), p. 16.

2.181 Sir G. S. Mackenzie, *A general view . . . of the counties of Ross and Cromarty*, p. 310; *N.S.A.*, 14, pp. 31, 34.

2.182 James Thomson, *The value and importance of the Scotch fisheries* (London: Smith, Elder & Co., 1849), pp. 14, 35; *Abstract of the answers and returns made pursuant to an act . . . for taking an account of the population of Great Britain, and of the increase or diminution thereof* (London: H.M.S.O., 1822), p. 532. Although impressment was not officially abolished, the end of the wars saw the release of many impressed sailors and a gradual changeover to a volunteer navy; see Alfred Hildesley, *The press gang* (London, 1925), pp. 29-30; G. J. Marcus, *A naval history of England; 2: the age of Nelson* (London: George Allen & Unwin, 1971), p. 458.

2.183 J. Thomson, *The value and importance of the Scotch fisheries*, p. 35; Robert Chambers, *The picture of Scotland* (Edinburgh: Tait, 1827), p. 321; *N.S.A.*, 14, pp. 14, 35.

2.184 J. Thomson, *The value and importance of the Scotch fisheries*, pp. 33, 35, 83; *N.S.A.*, 14, pp. 14, 35.

2.185 J. Thomson, *The value and importance of the Scotch fisheries, p. 35; N.S.A.*, 14, p. 35. The surplus won by the Nigg fishermen was hardly large enough to allow them to reinvest directly in larger boats but they may have had the same opportunities as the fishermen on the south coast of the Moray Firth who did become prosperous by reinvestment. (I am indebted to Malcolm Gray of Aberdeen University for this information on investment); Alexander Oswald Brodie, *Diary 1843-4*, p. 163, St Andrews University manuscript TA140. 38E43; J. Anderson, 'Essay on the present state of the Highlands and Islands of Scotland', p. 49; George Anderson and Peter Anderson, *Guide to the Highlands and Islands of Scotland* (London: Murray, 1834), p. 548.

2.186 *N.S.A.*, 14, p. 394; J. Anderson, 'Essay on the present state of the Highlands and Islands of Scotland', p. 51.

2.187 *N.S.A.*, 14, pp. 462-3; Central Board for the Relief of Destitution in the Highlands and Islands of Scotland, Edinburgh Section, *Third Report* (Edinburgh: Blackwood, 1848), p. 94.

2.188 *O.S.A.*, XI, p. 335.

2.189 N. Macrae, *The romance of a royal burgh*, pp. 151, 220, 225, 243, 247-9.

2.190 Tain Town Council, *Minutes*, 10th June, 1842, S.R.O., B70/6/4; *N.S.A.*, 14, p. 295.

2.191 James Cameron, 'Report on the sanitary condition and general economy of the town of Tain and the district of Easter Ross, made to the Poor Law Commissioners', p. 139.

3.1 A. Menzies, *Report, 1768* pp. 11, 12. S.R.O. E787/24.

3.2 *Accompts of Linen Cloth stamped in Scotland*, S.R.O. NG1/15/1.

3.3 Osgood Hanbury Mackenzie, *A hundred years in the Highlands* (London: Arnold, 1921), p. 38.

3.4 Letter to Alexander Mackenzie at Dingwall, 17th May, 1748, British Linen Company, *Letter copy book*, Bank of Scotland Archive; David Loch, *A tour through most of the trading towns and villages of Scotland* (Edinburgh, 1778), pp. 54-6; Robert Heron, *Scotland.described* (Edinburgh, 1797), p. 272.

3.5 Letter to Alexander Mackenzie at Dingwall, 17th May 1748, British Linen Company, *Letter copy book*, Bank of Scotland Archive; Board of Trustees for Fisheries, Manufactures & Improvements in Scotland, *Minutes*, 13th June 1755, 23rd January 1756, S.R.O. NG1/1/13; *To the Honble. The Commissionaries & Trustees upon the Annex'd Estates in Scotland. The petition of William Sandeman, Merchant in Perth, Edinburgh, 23rd January 1764*, S.R.O. E746/138/6; *The Petition and Memorial of John Montgomery. To the Right Honourable the Commissioners for Managing the Annex'd forfeited Estates in Scotland, 25th November, 1761*, S.R.O. E746/138/2.

3.6 Board of Trustees for Fisheries, Manufactures & Improvements in Scotland, *Minutes*, 21st February, 1755, 19th November, 1756, 29th July, 1757, 10th March, 1757, S.R.O. NG/1/1/13; 11th February, 1784, 18th February, 1784, S.R.O. NG1/1/24; Letter to John Reid at Tayne, 21st July 1748; Letter to William Anderson at Wick, 16th June, 1759; Letter to William Forsyth at Cromarty, 10th July, 1759; British Linen Company, *Letter copy books*, Bank of Scotland Archive.

3.7 *Petition To The Honble. Commissioners for the Annex'd Estates by William Forsyth at Cromarty*, Edinburgh, 3rd August, 1763, S.R.O. E746/138/4.

3.8 Letter to John Urquhart at Cromarty, 5th May, 1748; Letter to William Forsyth at Cromarty, 1st September, 1748; British Linen Company, *Letter copy book, Bank of* Scotland Archive; *Accompts of Linen Cloth stamped in Scotland*, S.R.O. NG1/15/1.

3.9 Letter to Alexander Mackenzie at Dingwall, 17th May, 1748, British Linen Company, *Letter copy book*, Bank of Scotland Archive; W. Macgill, *Old Ross-shire and Scotland*, I, p. 199; H. M. Meldrum, *Kilmuir Easter*, p. 74; Alexander Ross, 'The Munros of Culcairn', *Celtic Magazine*, 10 (1885), p. 559; A. G. R. Robertson, *The Lowland Highlanders* (Tain, 1972), p. 78.

3.10 H. Miller, *Tales and Sketches*, pp. 317-8; Letter to Robert Mackenzie, Commander of the *Batchelour*, 15th May, 1749; Letter to William Forsyth at Cromarty, 10th March, 1770; British Linen Company, *Letter copy book*, Bank of Scotland Archive; Board of Trustees for Fisheries, Manufactures & Improvements in Scotland, *Minutes*, 23rd January, 1756; 29th July, 1757, S.R.O. NG1/1/13.

3.11 See supra, note 3.6.

3.12 Letter, William Sandeman to Hary Barclay, Secretary to the Annexed Estates Office, Perth, 21st January, 1765, S.R.O. E746/94/4; A. Menzies, *Report, 1766*, p. 123, S.R.O. E729/8.

3.13 Letter, William Sandeman to Henry Barckly, Perth, 1st April, 1763, S.R.O. E746/94/1; *The petition and Memorial of John Montgomery. To the Right Honourable the Commissioners for Managing the Annex'd forfeited Estates in Scotland, 25th November, 1761*, S.R.O. E746/138/2.

3.14 Letter, William Sandeman to Hary Barclay, Secretary to the Annexed Estates Office, Perth, 21st January, 1765, S.R.O. E746/94/4; Letter, David Monro to Messrs. MacCulloch & Tod, Managers for the British Linen Company, Edinburgh, 10th May, 1750 (with reply), S.R.O. CH1/2/92.

3.15 A. Menzies, *Report, 1766*, p. 118, S.R.O. E729/8.

3.16 *Ibid.*, pp. 121-2; *O.S.A.*, II, p. 563.

3.17 A. Wight, *Present state of Husbandry in Scotland*, 4(1), p. 232; *O.S.A.*, VI, p. 433; XVII, p. 356.

3.18 *Accompts of Linen Cloth stamped in Scotland*, S.R.O. NG1/15/1.

3.19 James Mill, 'On the spinning of linen yarn in Ross, Caithness etc.', *Highland Society prize essays and transactions* (2nd ed.; Edinburgh: Constable, 1812), I, pp. 72-73.

3.20 *Accompts of Linen Cloth stamped in Scotland*, S.R.O. NG1/15/1.

3.21 Alexander Ross, 'The Munros of Culcairn', *Celtic Magazine*, 10 (1885), p. 559; Board of Trustees for Fisheries, Manufactures & Improvements in Scotland, *Minutes*, 13th June, 1755; 28th July, 1784, S.R.O. NG1/1/13, 24; Letter Lieut. Ken. Sutherland to Henry Barclay, Newtarbat, 23rd December, 1772, S.R.O. E746/81/1(1).

3.22 Letter, William Sandeman to Hary Barclay, Perth, 25th February, 1767,

S.R.O. E746/94/5(1); Letter, William Sandeman to Hary Barclay, Secretary to the Annexed Estates Office, Perth, 21st January, 1765, S.R.O. E746/94/4.

3.23 A. Wight, *Present state of Husbandry in Scotland*, p. 252; D. Loch, *A tour through most of the trading towns and villages of Scotland*, pp. 54-55.

3.24 A. Wight, *Present state of Husbandry in Scotland*, p. 252; *O.S.A.*, IV, p. 300.

3.25 *O.S.A.*, VI, p. 433; XV, p. 620; XVII, p. 356; Sir J. Sinclair, *General view of the agriculture of the northern counties*, pp. 63-4; Sir G. S. Mackenzie, *A general view . . . of the counties of Ross and Cromarty*, pp. 274, 347.

3.26 Sir J. Sinclair, *General view of the agriculture of the northern counties*, p. 64.

3.27 Board of Trustees for Fisheries, Manufactures & Improvements in Scotland, *Minutes*, 11th June, 1794; 13th February, 1799, S.R.O. NG1/2/3-4; W. Macgill, *Old Ross-shire and Scotland*, I, p. 199; Sir G. S. Mackenzie, *A general view . . . of the counties of Ross and Cromarty*, p. 335.

3.28 Sir G. S. Mackenzie, *A general view . . . of the counties of Ross and Cromarty*, p. 335; Board of Trustees for Fisheries, Manufactures & Improvements in Scotland, *Minutes*, 7th December, 1814, S.R.O. NG1/2/6.

3.29 *O.S.A.*, XV, p. 620.

3.30 *Accompts of Linen Cloth stamped in Scotland*, S.R.O. NG1/15/2. It should be noted that the post-war figures include, for the first time, the production of the Cromarty factory, though whether this was because of a change of fibre in Cromarty or merely an alteration in the method of recording is not clear.

3.31 Great Britain, Commission for inquiring into the administration and practical operation of the poor laws in Scotland, *Report*, Appendix, II, p. 7; J. Anderson, 'Essay on the present state of the Highlands and Islands of Scotland', p. 57; *N.S.A.*, 14, pp. 466-7; William Mackay Mackenzie, *Hugh Miller* (London: Hodder & Stoughton, 1905), p. 2.

3.32 Sir G. S. Mackenzie, *A general view . . . of the counties of Ross and Cromarty*, p. 335; D. Loch, *A tour through most of the trading towns and villages of Scotland*, pp. 54, 56; Board of Trustees for Fisheries, Manufactures & Improvements in Scotland, *Minutes*, 13th February, 1782; 8th June, 1796: S.R.O. NG/1/23; NG1/2/3.

3.33 Great Britain, Committee appointed to enquire into the illicit practices used in defrauding the revenue, *Second report, 1st March, 1784* (London: H.M.S.O., 1803), Appendix I, pp. 267-8.

3.34 *Ibid.*, pp. 264, 268; A. Wight, *Present state of husbandry in Scotland*, p. 238; *Report respecting the Scotch distillery duties. Ordered to be printed* 11th June 1798 (Readex Microcard), p. 373.

3.35 C. F. Mackintosh, *Antiquarian Notes*, p. 80.

3.36 *O.S.A.*, V, pp. 208, 210-1; A. Wight, *Present state of husbandry in Scotland*, p. 238; *Report respecting the Scotch distillery duties. Ordered to be printed 11th June 1798* (Readex Microcard), p. 375.

3.37 *O.S.A.*, I, p. 286; IV, p. 292; V, p. 211; VI, p. 188; XII, p. 265; XIV, p. 93; XV, p. 624; XVII, p. 351.

3.38 John Forbes, *Report upon the annexed estates of Lovat and Cromarty, 30th July, 1755*, p. 4, S.R.O. E729/1; W. Macgill, *Old Ross-shire and Scotland*, I, p. 119; Alexander John Youngson, *After the Forty-Five* (Edinburgh: Edinburgh U.P., 1973), p. 111.

3.39 *O.S.A.*, XVII, p. 352; *Report respecting the distilleries in Scotland etc. etc.*

Ordered to be printed 12th July 1799 (Readex Microcard), p. 29.

3.40 Sir J. Sinclair, *General view of the agriculture of the northern counties*, p. 65.

3.41 *O.S.A.*, XVII, p. 351.

3.42 *Report respecting the Scottish distillery duties. Ordered to be printed 11th June 1798* (Readex Microcard), p. 372.

3.43 A Ross-shire Farmer, 'Remarks on the Ross-shire resolutions concerning the distillery laws', *Farmers Magazine*, 8 (1807), p. 175.

3.44 *Report respecting the Scotch distillery duties. Ordered to be printed 11th June 1798* (Readex Microcard), p. 5.

3.45 *Ibid.*, p. 7; *54 Geo. III, c. 172.*

3.46 Board of Agriculture, *Agricultural state of the kingdom*, p. 133.

3.47 Commissioners of Inquiry into the collection and management of the revenue arising in Ireland, etc., *Fifth report*, Appendix 50, p. 131.

3.48 A Ross-shire Farmer, 'Remarks on the Ross-shire resolutions concerning the distillery laws', p. 176.

3.49 O. H. Mackenzie, *A hundred years in the Highlands*, p. 213.

3.50 J. Barron, *The northern Highlands in the nineteenth century*, II, pp. 3, 49.

3.51 Commissioners of Inquiry into the collection and management of the revenue arising in Ireland, etc., *Fifth report*, Appendix 57, p. 137.

3.52 J. Barron, *The northern Highlands in the nineteenth century*, I, pp. XXXII-XXXIII; 'Agricultural Intelligence Scotland, Ross-shire Quarterly Report', *Farmers Magazine*, 25 (1824), p. 94; 26 (1825), p. 89; Great Britain, Select Committee on petitions complaining of the additional duty on malt in Scotland, *Report* (London: H.M.S.O., 1821), p. 39; *Accounts relating to the distilleries in Scotland 1815-18* (London: H.M.S.O., 1818), p. 4; *I Geo. IV, c. 118: 3 Geo. IV, c. 52: 4 Geo. IV, c. 94.*

3.53 J. Barron, *The northern Highlands in the nineteenth century*, II, p. 49; N. Macrae, *The romance of a royal burgh*, p. 247.

3.54 *N.S.A.*, 14, pp. 233, 375.

3.55 R. W. Munro and J. Munro, *Tain through the centuries*, p. 128.

3.56 *N.S.A.*, 14, p. 295; Alfred Barnard, *The whisky distilleries of the United Kingdom* (Newton Abbot: David & Charles Reprints, 1969), p. 163.

3.57 A. Wight, *Present state of Husbandry in Scotland*, pp. 254-6; D. Loch, *A tour through most of the trading towns and villages of Scotland*, p. 55; H. Miller, *Tales and Sketches*, pp. 262-4.

3.58 *O.S.A.*, III, p. 398; Sir G. S. Mackenzie, *A general view . . . of the counties of Ross and Cromarty*, pp. 335, 346; *N.S.A.*, 14, p. 49; Great Britain, Commission for inquiring into the administration and practical operation of the poor laws in Scotland, *Report*, Appendix, III, pp. 387b, 396b.

3.59 Nigg W.R.I., *Nigg*, p. 44; *O.S.A.*, XIV, p. 96; R. Forsyth, *The beauties of Scotland*, 4, p. 527; J. Hunter, *The making of the crofting community*, pp. 16ff.

3.60 J. H. Dawson, *An abridged statistical account of Scotland*, p. 894; *N.S.A.*, 14, pp. 14-15, 49, 295, 326.

3.61 H. Miller, *Tales and Sketches*, p. 319.

3.62 J. Barron, *The northern Highlands in the nineteenth century*, II, pp. 74, 298-306; N.S.A., 14, pp. 228, 324; Sir G. S. Mackenzie, *A general view . . . of the counties of Ross and Cromarty*, p. 335; J. H. Dawson, *An abridged statistical account of Scotland*, p. 877.

3.63 A. O. Brodie, *Diary*, p. 164, St. Andrews University manuscript TA 140. B8E43; Roderick Maclean, 'Notes on the parish of Alness', *Transactions of the Gaelic Society of Inverness*, 14 (1887-8), p. 224; Letter, Sir Harry Munro of Foulis to John Mackenzie of Delvine, 1764, S.R.O. E727/45/6.

3.64 *O.S.A.*, XV, p. 613; J. Barron, *The northern Highlands in the nineteenth century*, I, p. XXIV; *The traveller's guide through Scotland* (3rd ed.; Edinburgh: Thomson, 1806), p. 502; John Adam, *Unto the Right Honourable the Lords of Council and Session, the Petition of John Adams, His Majesty's Master Mason for Scotland* (n.p., 1758), Signet Library Session Papers, 35, 33, pp. 2-3.

3.65 John Percival Day, *Public administration in the Highlands and Islands of Scotland* (London: London U.P., 1918), p. 326.

3.66 Tain Town Council, *Minutes*, 30th September, 1776; 29th September, 1777; 3rd June, 1796; 29th September, 1804, S.R.O. B70/6/1; N. Macrae, *The romance of a royal burgh*, p. 377.

3.67 Tain Town Council, *Minutes*, 25th June, 1777; 4th April, 1840, S.R.O. B70/6/1,4; R. W. Munro and J. Munro, *Tain through the centuries*, p. 93; C. G. Macdowall, *The Chanonry of Ross*, pp. 115-6.

3.68 Tain Town Council, *Minutes*, 7th November 1797, S.R.O. B70/6/1.

3.69 Tain Town Council, *Minutes*, 30th September, 1776; 29th September, 1788; 29th September, 1808; 22nd November, 1776; 27th July, 1778; 23rd September, 1780; 20th April, 1787, S.R.O. B70/6/1.

3.70 *Ibid.*, 20th April, 1787; 9th October, 1798; 28th October, 1812, S.R.O. B70/6/1; Commissioners appointed to inquire into the state of Municipal Corporations in Scotland, *Local reports*, I, p. 189; II, pp. 422-3.

3.71 George Pryde, *The Scottish burghs of barony in decline 1707-1908* (Glasgow, 1949), p. 49; Commissioners appointed to inquire into the state of Municipal Corporations in Scotland, *Local reports*, I, p. 162; Commissioners of Supply of the County of Cromarty, *Minutes*, 15th October, 1765, S.R.O. SC24/21/7.

3.72 Tain Town Council, *Minutes*, 27th December, 1841, S.R.O. B70/6/4; R. W. Munro and J. Munro, *Tain through the centuries*, pp. 92-4.

3.73 R. W. Munro and J. Munro, *Tain through the centuries*, p. 118.

3.74 *N.S.A.*, 14, p. 233.

3.75 *O.S.A.*, III, p. 397; Letter, Mr. Macleod of Geanies to Sir John Gordon of Invergordon, Calrossie, 24th September, 1780, S.R.O. GD235/7.

3.76 Tain Town Council, *Minutes*, 29th September, 1783; 29th September, 1784; 27th June, 1829, S.R.O. B70/6/1-2; A. O. Brodie, *Diary*, p. 135, St. Andrews University manuscript TA140.B8E43.

3.77 J. Mitchell, *Reminiscences of my life in the Highlands*, I, p. 43; John Stoddart, *Remarks on local scenery and manners in Scotland during the years 1799 and 1800* (2 vols; London: Miller, 1801), II, p. 89.

3.78 *N.S.A.*, 14, p. 26; Convention of the Royal Burghs of Scotland, *Records*, 5, p. 565; H. M. Meldrum, *Kilmuir Easter*, pp. 6, 8; Sir J. Sinclair, *General view of the agriculture of the northern counties*, p. 63; A. Ross, *Petition*, p. 14; Account, Charles Robertson Esq. of Kindeace to Gilbert Robertson merchant in Alness 1752-3, S.R.O. GD146/7.

3.79 Sir G. S. Mackenzie, *A general view . . . of the counties of Ross and Cromarty*, p. 277; *N.S.A.*, 14, pp. 233; 327.

3.80 J. Barron, *The northern Highlands in the nineteenth century*, I, pp. 185, 250.

3.81 Sir G. S. Mackenzie, *A general view . . . of the counties of Ross and Cromarty*, p. 277.

3.82 G. Pryde, *The burghs of Scotland*, pp. 76-9.

3.83 Sir John Gordon, *Pocket book 1754-9*, National Library of Scotland ms. 108.

3.84 *Ibid.*, p. 471.

3.85 *Ibid.*

3.86 *Register of Seisins; O.S.A.*, II, p. 561; Roderick Maclean, 'The parish of Rosskeen', *Transactions of the Gaelic Society of Inverness*, 12 (1885-6), p. 325.

3.87 John Forbes, *Report upon the annexed estates of Lovat and Cromarty . . . 30th July 1755*, p. 1, S.R.O. E729/1; Letter, W. Sandeman desiring assistance in carrying on linen trade, 1763, S.R.O. E746/94/1.

3.88 *Session Papers* v. 135, 1809, Appendix pp. 2-3, Advocates' Library, Edinburgh, (Photocopy in the possession of Mrs J. Durham).

3.89 R. Maclean, 'Notes on the parish of Alness', p. 219; R. Maclean, 'Notes on the parish of Kiltearn', p. 306; *N.S.A.*, 14, p. 62; G. S. M. Walker, *The parish of Resolis* (Resolis, 1958), p. 7.

3.90 A. O. Brodie, *Diary*, p. 178, St. Andrews University manuscript TA140.B8 E43; R. Southey, *Journal*, p. 118.

3.91 *Plan of the lands of Findon . . . surveyed in 1883-4 . . . and laid off in 1836, 1837*, S.R.O., West Register House, RHP3549.

3.92 G. & P. Anderson, *Guide to the Highlands and Islands* (1850), pp. 18, 390, 395.

3.93 R. Bain, *History of the Ancient Province of Ross*, p. 363.

3.94 *N.S.A.*, 14, p. 295; 'Sketch of a tour through the northern counties of Scotland, pt. IV', *Farmers Magazine*, 2 (1801), p. 420; J. Dunlop, *The British Fisheries Society, 1786-1893*, pp. 50-51, 61.

3.95 *O.S.A.*, III, p. 17; Sir G. S. Mackenzie, *A general view . . . of the counties of Ross and Cromarty*, p. 277; R. Heron, *Scotland described*, p. 272; Letter, Sir John Ross to William MacCulloch, Plymouth, 24th January, 1778, S.R.O. GD129/24/81; Account, Charles Robertson of Kindeace to George Miller, Merchant in Tain, 15th June, 1752, S.R.O. GD146/7; Account, Charles Robertson of Kindeace to Hugh Ross, silversmith in Tain, 23rd July, 1754, S.R.O. GD146/7.

3.96 W. Macgill, *Old Ross-shire and Scotland*, II, p. 106; Alexander Sutherland, *A summer ramble in the north Highlands* (Edinburgh: Hunter, 1825), p. 168; Tain Town Council, *Minutes*, 30th September, 1776; 28th May, 1793, S.R.O. B70/6/1; Discharged account, John Reid, Wigmaker, Dingwall, 25th April, 1776, S.R.O. GD146/7.

3.97 John Knox, *A view of the British Empire, more especially Scotland* (London, 1784), p. 17.

3.98 N. Macrae, *The romance of a royal burgh*, pp. 220-237; *Gross rental of the Barrony of Cromarty (1762)*, S.R.O. GD159/3/2(1).

3.99 A. Wight, *Present state of Husbandry in Scotland*, 4(1), p. 231; *Gross rental of the Barrony of Cromarty (1762)*, S.R.O. GD159/3/2(1).

3.100 *O.S.A.*, III, p. 396.

3.101 A. Wight, *Present state of Husbandry in Scotland*, 4(1), p. 258; *N.S.A.*, 14, pp. 225, 355; *O.S.A.*, III, p. 392, IV, p. 290.

3.102 *N.S.A.*, 14, pp. 15, 234; Receipt from Bank of Scotland Office, Tain, 7th July,

1798, S.R.O. GD146/8.

3.103 R. Southey, *Journal*, p. 118; N. Macrae, *The romance of a royal burgh*, pp. 252-3; J. Barron, *The northern Highlands in the nineteenth century*, II, p. 260; G. & P. Anderson, *Guide to the Highlands and Islands of Scotland* (1842), p. 485.

3.104 Tain Town Council, *Minutes*, 9th July, 1825; 18th June, 1839; 15th December, 1840, S.R.O. B70/6/2-4.

3.105 George Alexander Cooke, *A topographical description of the northern division of Scotland* (London: C. Cook, [1810]), p. 45; *Scotland delineated, or a geographical description of every shire in Scotland* (Edinburgh, 1791), p. 98; Abstract account book showing estimates and payments for various projects 1807 to circa 1825, pp. 92, 95, 101, 107, S.R.O. GD253/164; J. H. Dawson, *An abridged statistical account of Scotland*, p. 869.

3.106 Sir G. S. Mackenzie, *A general view . . . of the counties of Ross and Cromarty*, p. 335; *Petition of John Macintosh*, 14th December, 1784, S.R.O. E705/8/1(1); R. Pococke, *Tours in Scotland*, p. 175; H. Miller, *Tales and Sketches*, p. 320.

3.107 *O.S.A.*, XII, p. 261.

3.108 Commissioners for making roads and building bridges in the Highlands of Scotland, *Eighth report* (London: H.M.S.O., 1817), p. 31; Abstract account book showing estimates and payments for various projects 1807 to circa 1825, p. 107, S.R.O. GD253/164.

3.109 *N.S.A.*, 14, p. 467.

3.110 A. D. Brodie, *Diary*, p. 178, St Andrews University manuscript TA140.B8 E43.

3.111 Sir G. S. Mackenzie, *A general view . . . of the counties of Ross and Cromarty*, p. 277; *O.S.A.*, XII, p. 261; Commissioners for making roads and building bridges in the Highlands of Scotland, *Fourteenth report* (London: H.M.S.O., 1828), p. 53.

3.112 Sir J. Sinclair, *General view of the agriculture of the northern counties*, p. 63; Letter, Sir John Ross to William MacCulloch, Plymouth, 24th January, 1778, S.R.O. GD129/24/81; Tarbat Kirk Session, *Minutes*, 8th July, 1754, S.R.O. CH2/350/1; Letter to Charles Robertson of Kindeace, 2nd August, 1797, S.R.O. GD146/13.

3.113 H. Miller, *Tales and Sketches*, pp. 305, 319-20.

3.114 H. Miller, *My schools and schoolmasters*, pp. 12, 14, 18, 23.

3.115 Sir G. S. Mackenzie, *A general view . . . of the counties of Ross and Cromarty*, p. 335; *N.S.A.*, 14, p. 228; *O.S.A.*, III, p. 5.

3.116 H. Miller, *Trades and Sketches*, p. 320; J. H. Dawson, *An abridged statistical account of Scotland*, pp. 869-70.

3.117 James Hall, *Travels in Scotland* (2 vols, London: Johnson, 1807), II, p. 490; Sir G. S. Mackenzie, *A general view . . . of the counties of Ross and Cromarty*, p. 335.

3.118 J. H. Dawson, *An abridged statistical account of Scotland*, p. 869; Commissioners for making roads and building bridges in the Highlands of Scotland, *Eighth report*, p. 80.

3.119 *Accompts of linen cloth stamped in Scotland*, S.R.O. NG1/15/1-2.

3.120 Great Britain, Select committee appointed to inquire into the state of agriculture, *Third report*, p. 604.

3.121 Sir G. S. Mackenzie, *A general view . . . of the counties of Ross and*

Cromarty, p. 46; N. Macrae, *The romance of a royal burgh*, p. 169; H. Miller, *Tales and Sketches*, pp. 294-5; *O.S.A.*, IV, p. 297; VI, p. 429; XI, pp. 335, 350; XII, p. 277; *N.S.A.*, 14, pp. 72, 380, 398.

3.122 *N.S.A.*, 14, pp. 20, 32, 37, 63, 70.

3.123 Sir G. S. Mackenzie, *A general view . . . of the counties of Ross and Cromarty*, p. 335.

3.124 H. Miller, *Tales and Sketches*, p. 293; Discharged account of furniture by Mr. Cuthbert to Mr. Robertson, Milncraig, 3rd June, 1755, S.R.O. GD/146/7.

3.125 *N.S.A.*, 14, pp. 15, 33, 377; R. Bain, *History of the Ancient Province of Ross*, p. 366.

3.126 E. Burt, *Letters from a gentleman in the North of Scotland*, I, p. 246; A. Menzies, *Report, 1776*, pp. 136-7, S.R.O. E729/8.

3.127 J. Forbes, *Report upon the annexed estates of Lovat and Cromarty, 30th July 1755*, p. 4, S.R.O. E729/1; *Plan of the boundaries of the burgh of Tain, 1750*, S.R.O., West Register House, RHP275/3; Commissioners of Supply of the County of Cromarty, *Minutes*, 4th May, 1771, S.R.O. SC24/21/7; William Roy *et al.*, *The Military survey of Scotland, 1747-55* (National Library of Scotland photocopy of original in British Museum).

3.128 R. Forbes, *Journals of the Episcopal Visitations of the Right Rev. Robert Forbes*, p. 150.

3.129 J. S. Stephen, *The history of roads in the Highlands of Scotland in the eighteenth and nineteenth centuries* (Ph.D. thesis, Aberdeen University, 1936), p. 88; W. Macgill, *Old Ross-shire and Scotland*, I, p. 215; Sir J. Gordon, *Pocket-book*, p. 406, National Library of Scotland ms. 108.

3.130 J. S. Stephen, *The history of roads in the Highlands of Scotland*, pp. 88-9.

3.131 Presbytery of Chanonry, *Minutes*, 15th October, 1771, S.R.O. CH2/66/5; *Printed note on A.G.M. of Freeholders, J.Ps. & Commissioners of Supply of the County of Ross, 13th October, 1802*, S.R.O. GD129/25/86; *Act of the Justices of the Peace & Commissioners of Supply of the County of Ross. Met at Dingwall on the 22nd May, one thousand seven hundred and ninety three, . . . respecting roads, bridges & ferries* (Edinburgh, 1793), p. 3.

3.132 J. Knox, *A view of the British Empire* (1785), II, p. 478.

3.133 A. Wight, *Present state of Husbandry in Scotland*, 4(1), p. 266; Sir J. Sinclair, *General view of the agriculture of the northern counties*, p. 44.

3.134 R. Forsyth, *The beauties of Scotland*, 5, p. 221; Plan of the intended road from Portinliek alias Culrain to Dingwall . . . 1790, S.R.O., West Register House, RHP11591.

3.135 A. Wight, *Present state of Husbandry in Scotland*, 4(1), p. 270; Sir J. Sinclair, *General view of the agriculture of the northern counties*, p. 105; Letter, Roderick Macleod to Charles Robertson of Kindeace, Edinburgh, 10th May, 1774, S.R.O. GD146/13; Letter, Roderick Macleod to Charles Robertson of Kindeace, Edinburgh, 17th August, 1774, S.R.O. GD146/13.

3.136 Observations on the sketch & memorial given in by Geanies to the Tutors of Cadboll anent a new road, 1774, S.R.O. GD146/21.

3.137 R. Heron, *Scotland described*, (1797), p. 272; Letter, Donald Macleod of Geanies to Charles Robertson of Kindeace, Geanies, 9th April, 1777, S.R.O. GD146/13.

3.138 Commissioners of Supply for the County of Cromarty, *Minutes*, 30th April, 1768; 30th April, 1770, S.R.O. SC24/21/7.

3.139 *Memorial of George Munro of Poyntzfield to the Hon. the J.Ps & Commissioners of Supply for the Shire of Cromarty, 14th May, 1771*, S.R.O. SC24/21/7.

3.140 *Account of money received and laid out by Wm. Forsyth in purchasing tools for the roads in the County of Cromarty by orders of the Commissioners of Supply, Anno 1766 and 1769*, S.R.O. SC24/21/7.

3.141 The main roads were supposed to be gravelled from 1793 but this policy may not have been effectively pursued; see *Act of the Justices of Peace & Commissioners of Supply of the County of Ross. Met at Dingwall, on the 22nd May one thousand seven hundred and ninety three, . . . respecting roads, bridges & ferries*, p. 8; Sir J. Sinclair, *General view of the agriculture of the northern counties*, p. 45; A Ross-shire Farmer, 'On the assessment for roads in Ross-shire', *Farmers Magazine*, 15 (1814), p. 303.

3.142 Sir J. Sinclair, *General view of the agriculture of the northern counties*, p. 67; Presbytery of Chanonry, *Minutes*, 15th October, 1771, S.R.O. CH2/66/5.

3.143 J. Stoddart, *Remarks on local scenery and manners*, 2. p. 96; *Act of the Justices of Peace & Commissioners of Supply of the County of Ross. Met at Dingwall, on the 22nd May one thousand seven hundred and ninety three, . . . respecting roads, bridges & ferries*, p. 19.

3.144 Sir J. Sinclair, *General view of the agriculture of the northern counties*, p. 44.

3.145 N. Macrae, *The romance of a royal burgh*, p. 229; A. Menzies, *Report, 1766*, p. 137, S.R.O. E729/8; *O.S.A.*, I, p. 284; Letter, Colin Mackenzie, Factor of Cromarty to William Barclay, Esq., Secretary to the Board of Annexed Estates, Edinburgh, 2nd August, 1777, S.R.O. E727/34/10.

3.146 A Ross-shire Farmer, 'On the assessment for roads in Ross-shire', p. 303.

3.147 *O.S.A.*, I, p. 284: *Plan of the burgh lands of the estate of Tulloch, 1789*, S.R.O., West Register House, RHP1474.

3.148 In the early nineteenth century the landowners in Ross appear to have abused their control in order to pass on the costs of bridge repairs to their tenants through the commutation of statute labour but in the eighteenth century, in Cromarty at least, the funding of roads and bridges appears to have been kept separate; see Peter Patch & Co., *Sayings and doings in the counties of Ross and Cromarty and district of Ferintosh* (Inverness, 1824), p. 6; Commissioners of Supply of the County of Cromarty, *Minutes*, 27th April, 1775; 22nd June, 1775; S.R.O. SC24/21/7.

3.149 J. Macdonald, 'On the agriculture of the counties of Ross and Cromarty', p. 86.

3.150 Letter, Roderick Macleod to Charles Robertson of Kindeace, Edinburgh, 31st January, 1778, S.R.O. GD146/13.

3.151 A. Wight, *Present state of Husbandry in Scotland*, 4(1), p. 274; J. Macdonald, 'On the agriculture of the counties of Ross and Cromarty, p. 86; Sir J. Sinclair, *General view of the agriculture of the northern counties*, p. 22; A. Menzies, *Report, 1766*, p. 111, S.R.O. E729/8.

3.152 *O.S.A.*, I, p. 277; Sir J. Sinclair, *General view of the agriculture of the northern counties*, p. 22.

3.153 C. G. Macdowall, *The Chanonry of Ross*, p. 132.

3.154 Tain Town Council, *Minutes*, 27th July 1778, 17th January 1783, S.R.O. B70/6/1.

3.155 Leslie Gardiner, *Stage coach to John o' Groats* (London: Hollis & Carter, 1961), pp. 44-5.
3.156 Letter, ? Baillie George Miller to ? Mr. Robertson at Ardullie, Tain, 25th May, 1770, S.R.O. GD146/13.
3.157 Letter, Sir John Gordon of Invergordon to Charles Robertson of Kindeace, Invergordon, 8th February, 1773, S.R.O. GD146/13.
3.158 Letter, Roderick Macleod to Charles Robertson of Kindeace, Edinburgh, 25th September, 1779, S.R.O. GD146/13.
3.159 R. W. Munro and J. Munro, *Tain through the centuries*, p. 111; John Calder, *Diary*, 8th July, 1777, National Library of Scotland acc. 4156.
3.160 J. Stoddart, *Remarks on local scenery and manners*, 2, p. 95.
3.161 Commissioners for making roads and building bridges in the Highlands of Scotland, *Second report* (London: H.M.S.O., 1805), pp. 32-3.
3.162 Commissioners for making roads and building bridges in the Highlands of Scotland, *Fifth report* (London: H.M.S.O., 1811), pp. 18, 21.
3.163 *Abstract account book showing estimates and payments for various projects 1807 to circa 1825*, pp. 56, 88, 92, 95, 96, 98, S.R.O. GD253/164.
3.164 Commissioners for making roads and building bridges in the Highlands of Scotland, *Seventh report* (London: H.M.S.O., 1815), p. 1.
3.165 Commissioners for making roads and building bridges in the Highlands of Scotland, *Second report*, pp. 32-3; Trustees of the Third District of Roads (Ross and Cromarty), *Minutes 1807-25*, prefatory material, S.R.O. SC34/39/9.
3.166 Sir G. S. Mackenzie, *A general view . . . of the counties of Ross and Cromarty*, p. 270; 'Agricultural Intelligence Scotland, Ross-shire Quarterly Report', *Farmers Magazine*, 14 (1813), p. 243; A Ross-shire Heritor, 'On the assessment for roads in Ross-shire', *Farmers Magazine*, 15 (1814), p. 156.
3.167 'Agricultural Intelligence Scotland, Ross-shire Quarterly Report', *Farmers Magazine*, 14 (1813), p. 243.
3.168 Great Britain, Select Committee appointed to investigate the several acts, Public and Private, regulating the statute labour in Scotland, and the manner in which the conversion is exacted or levied and applied, in the several counties respectively, *Report* (London: H.M.S.O., 1836), Appendix, p. 84.
3.169 Commissioners for making roads and building bridges in the Highlands of Scotland, *Twenty second report* (London: H.M.S.O., 1836), p. 4; Trustees of the Third District of Roads (Ross and Cromarty), *Minutes 1807-25*, 14th October, 1812, S.R.O. SC34/29/9.
3.170 Trustees of the Third District of Roads (Ross and Cromarty), *Minutes 1807-25*, 8th September, 1817, S.R.O. SC34/29/9.
3.171 *N.S.A.*, 14, p. 50.
3.172 *Ibid.*, pp. 35, 49, 54.
3.173 J. S. Stephen, *The history of roads in the Highlands of Scotland*, p. 123.
3.174 *Letter book number 9, Repair of roads, 17th March, 1835 — 19th June, 1838*, p. 300, S.R.O. GD253/163.
3.175 J. Barron, *The northern Highlands in the nineteenth century*, I, pp. 14, 24.
3.176 *Ibid.*, I, pp. 166, 195; L. Gardiner, *Stage coach to John o' Groats*, p. 95.
3.177 L. Gardiner, *Stage coach to John o' Groats*, pp. 99-100; G. & P. Anderson, *Guide to the Highlands and Islands (1834)*, p. 553; G. & P. Anderson, *Guide to the*

Highlands and Islands (1842), p. 536.

3.178 *N.S.A.*, 14, p. 229; H. Miller, *My schools and schoolmasters*, p. 208; Taxes payable by Charles Munro of Meikle Allan, 1814, S.R.O. GD71/221.

3.179 J. Mitchell, *reminiscences of my life in the Highlands*, I, p. 258.

3.180 *O.S.A.*, XII, p. 251; Petition of John Macintosh, 14th December, 1784, S.R.O. E705/8/1(1); Commissioners for making roads and building bridges in the Highlands of Scotland, *Seventh report*, p. 57.

3.181 R. Southey, *Journal*, p. 121; Presbytery of Chanonry, *Minutes*, 6th May, 1766, S.R.O. CH2/66/5.

3.182 Presbytery of Chanonry, *Minutes*, 5th May, 1766, S.R.O. CH2/66/5; *O.S.A.*, III, p. 5.

3.183 R. Forbes, *Journals of the Episcopal Visitations of the Right Rev. Robert Forbes*, p. 151; Letter, Sir John Gordon of Invergordon to the Lord Advocate, Invergordon, 18th October, 1780, S.R.O. GD235/7.

3.184 Sir J. Sinclair, *General view of the agriculture of the northern counties*, pp. 46-7; A. Sutherland, *A summer ramble in the north Highlands*, pp. 77, 87; J. Barron, *The northern Highlands in the nineteenth century*, I, pp. 24, 46.

3.185 R. Southey, *Journal*, p. 167.

3.186 A. Sutherland, *A summer ramble in the north Highlands*, p. 88.

3.187 Commissioners for making roads and building bridges in the Highlands of Scotland, *Third report*, (London H.M.S.O., 1807), p. 32.

3.188 N. Macrae, *The romance of a royal burgh*, pp. 175, 246; J. Anderson, 'Essay on the present state of the Highlands and Islands of Scotland', p. 57; *Abstract account book showing estimates and payments for various projects 1807 to circa 1825*, pp. 92, 95, 101, 103, 107.

3.189 *Reminiscences of a Dingwall centenarian: the late Mrs Mackenzie, Inchvanie, by a friend* (Inverness, 1908), p. 10.

3.190 R. Southey, *Journal*, p. 118.

3.191 *N.S.A.*, 14, pp. 20, 378; J. H. Dawson, *An abridged statistical account of Scotland*, p. 891; Tain Town Council, *Minutes*, 25th September, 1839, S.R.O. B70/6/4.

3.192 John Adam, *Unto the Right Honourable the Lords of Council and Session, the Petition . . .*, pp. 2-3.

3.193 J. Barron, *The northern Highlands in the nineteenth century*, I, pp. XXV, 3.

3.194 *Ibid.*, II, p. 112; *N.S.A.*, 14, p. 15. Even before the introduction of steam there may have been a weekly service in operation; see N. Macrae, *The romance of a royal burgh*, p. 175.

3.195 J. Anderson, 'Essay on the present state of the Highlands and Islands of Scotland', p. 57; Letter to Robert Mackenzie, Commander of the *Batchelour*, Edinburgh, 15th May, 1749, British Linen Company, *Letter copy book*, Bank of Scotland Archive.

3.196 'Agricultural Intelligence Scotland, Ross-shire Quarterly Report', *Farmers Magazine*, 12 (1811), p. 128; 'Agricultural Intelligence Scotland, Ross-shire Quarterly Report', *Farmers Magazine*, 21 (1820), p. 505.

3.197 O. H. Mackenzie, *A hundred years in the Highlands*, p. 6.

3.198 J. Barron, *The northern Highlands in the nineteenth century*, III, pp. XLII, 68; J. Macdonald, 'On the agriculture of the counties of Ross and Cromarty,' p. 88.

3.199 T. B. Lang, *An historical summary of the Post Office in Scotland*, p. 11.

3.200 Sir G. S. Mackenzie, *A general view . . . of the counties of Ross and Cromarty*, p. 277; Francis Ronaldson, *Journal book 1786-1814*, pp. 48-9, National Library of Scotland ms 10687.

3.201 F. Ronaldson, *Journal book 1786-1814*, p. 13, National Library of Scotland ms 10687; Commissioners for making roads and building bridges in the Highlands of Scotland, *Eighth report*, p. 68; J. H. Dawson, *An abridged statistical account of Scotland*, pp. 873-97; Tain Town Council, *Minutes*, 3rd August, 1836, S.R.O. B70/6/3.

4.1 *Rental of estate of Balnagown 1777*, S.R.O. GD129/31/118.

4.2 *Copy rental of the parish of Fearn, 1751*, S.R.O. GD71/273; *Copy rental of the parish of Fearn, 1792*, S.R.O. GD71/273. During this period the rental of the whole parish of Fearn which included part of the Balnagown estate as well as all of Meikle Allan increased slightly.

4.3 The figures quoted for the 1790s, 1815 and, infra, for 1853 refer only to the rental for the parishes of Kiltearn, Rosskeen, Dingwall, Kilmuir, Tarbat, Resolis, Killearnan, Alness, Tain, Fearn, Rosemarkie and Nigg. Figures for the other five parishes are not available for all three dates. While the totals correspond by and large with national figures for the same periods, individual parish figures for the 1790s and 1815 are not necessarily correct and should be treated with some caution. The conclusions on the value of improvement must remain tentative, therefore. *O.S.A.*, I, p. 273; II, p. 563; III, pp. 11, 393; IV, p. 293; VI, pp. 188, 422; XI, p. 339; XIII, p. 15; XIV, p. 94; XVII, p. 346; XIX, p. 237; *Scotland. A district arrangement of the 970 parishes* (n.p., n.d.).

4.4 J. H. Dawson, *An abridged statistical account of Scotland*, p. XXVIII; J. E. Handley, *The agricultural revolution in Scotland*, p. 242.

4.5 *Valuation Roll for the County of Ross, 1855-6*, S.R.O. VR115/1-3; *Valuation Roll for the County of Cromarty, 1855-6*, S.R.O. VR115/4.

4.6 A. Wight, *Present state of husbandry in Scotland*, 4(1), p. 233; E. Maciver, *Memoirs of a Highland gentleman*, p. 41; Duncan Warrand, *Some Mackenzie pedigrees* (Inverness: Carruthers, 1965), pp. 78-9.

4.7 *Williamson's Directory for the City of Edinburgh, Canongate, Leith and Suburbs . . . 1774 . . . 1775* (Edinburgh: Williamson, 1774), pp. 62, 82; *Williamson's Directory for the City of Edinburgh, Canongate, Leith and Suburbs . . . 1784 . . . 1785* (Edinburgh: Williamson, 1784), pp. 58, 75; Supplement, p. 9; Receipt, 1777, S.R.O. GD199/31.

4.8 Sir John Gordon, *Pocket book 1754-9*, National Library of Scotland ms 108.

4.9 'Agricultural Intelligence Scotland, Ross-shire Quarterly Report', *Farmers Magazine*, 21 (1820), pp. 505-6; Great Britain, Commission for inquiring into the administration and practical operation of the poor laws in Scotland, *Report*, Appendix, IV, pp. 386a-398a; G. & P. Anderson, *Guide to the Highlands and Islands of Scotland (1834)*, pp. 504-6.

4.10 A. Wight, *Present state of husbandry in Scotland*, 4(1), pp. 242, 247, 269; Sir G. S. Mackenzie, *A general view . . . of the counties of Ross and Cromarty*, pp. 68-72; D. Aitken, *Plan of the Estate and Barrony of Findon*, S.R.O., West Register House, RHP3513; *A plan of part of the ye Lands of Ankervil and Meikle Allan . . . 1759*, S.R.O., West Register House, RHP239.

4.11 R. Forbes, *Journals of the Episcopal Visitations of the Right Rev. Robert Forbes*, p. 172.

4.12 John Nightingale, 'The threat to Cromarty', *Country Life*, 162 (1977), pp. 338-40.

4.13 Sir John Gordon, *Pocket book 1754-9*, pp. 469-70, National Library of Scotland ms 108; A. Wight, *Present state of husbandry in Scotland*, 4(1), p. 248.

4.14 Letter, John Adam to Sir John Ross of Balnagown, Edinburgh, 28th January, 1762, S.R.O. GD129/7/7; W. Macgill, *Old Ross-shire and Scotland*, I, p. 175.

4.15 Arthur Bolton, *The architecture of Robert and James Adam (1758-1794)* (London: Country Life, 1922), II, p. 7.

4.16 Letter, Sir John Ross to MacCulloch, Edinburgh, 24th April, 1780, S.R.O. GD129/24/81.

4.17 Great Britain, Scottish Development Department, *List of buildings of Architectural or Historic Interest, Ross and Cromarty, Cromarty Landward Area*, December 1965: *Resolis*, December 1965; Letter, John Adam to Sir John Ross of Balnagown, Edinburgh, 28th January, 1762, S.R.O. GD129/7/7; W. Macgill, *Old Ross-shire and Scotland*, I, pp. 48-9. I am indebted to the Secretary of the Scottish Georgian Society, Highland Branch, Mrs Maclean, for the information on Newhall.

4.18 Great Britain, Scottish Development Department, *List of buildings of Architectural or Historic Interest, Ross and Cromarty, Kilmuir Easter*, August 1966: *Resolis*, December 1965; *Tarbat*, August 1966; 'Agricultural Intelligence Scotland, Ross-shire Quarterly Report', *Farmers Magazine*, 7 (1806), p. 119; Robert Carruthers, *The Highland Notebook; or sketches and anecdotes* (Edinburgh: Black, 1843), p. 288; William Mackenzie, 'Report of improvements at Ardross', p. 132; E. Maciver, *Memoirs of a Highland gentleman*, p. 52.

4.19 Letter, Capt. Archibald Robertson to John Henderson, joiner, Invergordon, 1766, S.R.O. GD146/7; W. Macgill, *Old Ross-shire and Scotland*, I, pp. 139-41.

4.20 *Copy inventory of the late Mr. Munro of Allan's House ffurniture & Labouring Stocking at Meikle Allan*, 16th December, 1767, S.R.O. GD71/252.

4.21 *Inventory of Household Furniture etc. etc. in Allan House — Taken 8th May, 1842*, S.R.O. GD71/254.

4.22 H. Miller, *Tales and sketches*, pp. 294-5; *O.S.A.*, III, p. 398; IV, p. 297; VI, p. 429; XVII, p. 353.

4.23 W. Macgill, *Old Ross-shire and Scotland*, I, p. 201; *O.S.A.*, XI, p. 350.

4.24 *Petition for Sir John Gordon, Bart. and other Proprietors of the County of Ross*, 8th August, 1774, S.R.O. E746/148(1).

4.25 Nigg W.R.I., *Nigg*, p. 13.

4.26 Discharged Account Charles Robertson of Kindeace to Geo. Miller in Tain, May 26th, 1761, S.R.O. GD146/7.

4.27 *Ibid.*: Account, Mrs. Ross to Mrs. Robertson, Inverness, 7th October, 1779, S.R.O. GD146/8.

4.28 Discharged account, Kindeass Robeson to Alexander Ross, 3rd August, 1780, S.R.O. GD146/8.

4.29 J. Barron, *The northern Highlands in the nineteenth century*, II, p. 198; E. Maciver, *Memoirs of a Highland gentleman*, pp. 51-2; A. Mackenzie, *History of the Munros of Fowlis*, pp. 138-9; Sir Charles Elphinstone Adam, *View of the political state of Scotland in the last century* (Edinburgh: Douglas, 1887), p. 86; Donald Sage,

Memorabilia Domestica (Wick: W. Rae, 1889), pp. 66, 378; Duncan Forbes, *Some Kindeace Letters* (Dingwall: Ross, 1896), p. 1; *The dictionary of national biography* (22 vols; London: Oxford University Press, 1967-8), XX, p. 43.

4.30 Sir W. Fraser, *The Earls of Cromartie*, II, pp. 243-4; *Dictionary of national biography*, XX, p. 43; LIV, p. 368; LVIII, p. 43.

4.31 James Playfair, *Geographical and statistical description of Scotland* (2 vols; Edinburgh: Constable, 1819), I, p. 214.

4.32 *O.S.A.*, I, p. 296; II, p. 562; III, pp. 11, 393; IV, pp. 294, 476; V, p. 211; VI, pp. 191, 430; XI, p. 343; XII, pp. 258, 260; XIII, p. 18; XIV, p. 95; XV, p. 632; XVII, p. 355; XIX, p. 238; J. H. Dawson, *An abridged statistical account of Scotland*, pp. 873-97.

4.33 Sir J. Sinclair, *General view of the agriculture of the northern counties*, p. 26.

4.34 Hew Scott, *Fasti Ecclesiae Scoticanae: the succession of ministers in the parish churches of Scotland, from the Reformation, A.D. 1560, to the present time. New edition . . . Edited by William S. Crockett and Francis Grant* (9 vols; Edinburgh: Oliver & Boyd, 1915-61), VII, pp. 27, 56.

4.35 Commissioners for inquiring into the opportunities of Public Religious Worship, and means of Religious Instruction, and the Pastoral Superintendance afforded to the people of Scotland, *3rd Report* (London: H.M.S.O.), 1837, pp. 1-5; Appendix I, Table II, pp. 40-1; Table III, pp. 28-31; Table VII, pp. 66-9.

4.36 Sir G. S. Mackenzie, *A general view . . . of the counties of Ross and Cromarty*, p. 29; *O.S.A.*, VI, pp. 191, 430; Letter, George Balfour to Charles Robertson of Kindeace, Tarbat, 23rd January, 1780, S.R.O. GD146/14.

4.37 Commissioners for inquiring into the opportunities of Public Religious Worship, and means of Religious Instruction, and the Pastoral Superintendance afforded to the people of Scotland, *3rd Report*, Appendix I, Table II, pp. 40-1; Table III, pp. 28-31; Table VII, pp. 66-9.

4.38 *N.S.A.*, 14, pp. 36, 38, 309, 327; *O.S.A.*, II, p. 562; III, p. 11; IV, pp. 295, 476; V, p. 212; XI, p. 344, XII, p. 270; XIX, p. 238.

4.39 *N.S.A.*, 14, pp. 51, 70, 230, 276, 296, 327, 357, 363, 396, 467.

4.40 Great Britain, Scottish Development Department, *List of buildings of Architectural or Historic Interest, Ross and Cromarty, Alness*, May 1966; *Fortrose and Rosemarkie*.

4.41 E. Maciver, *Memoirs of a Highland gentleman*, pp. 36, 39; H. Miller, *My schools and schoolmasters*, p. 507; Commissioners of Inquiry into the collection and management of the revenue arising in Ireland, etc., *Fifth report*, Appendix 57, p. 137.

4.42 E. Maciver, *Memoirs of a Highland gentleman*, pp. 43-5.

4.43 *O.S.A.*, III, p. 7; A. Sutherland, *A summer ramble in the north Highlands*, p. 168.

4.44 Great Britain, Commission for inquiring into the administration and practical operation of the poor laws in Scotland, *Report*, Part II, Appendix, p. 50.

4.45 *O.S.A.*, III, p. 16.

4.46 *N.S.A.*, 14, p. 234.

4.47 J. Hall, *Travels in Scotland*, II, p. 488.

4.48 H. Miller, *My schools and schoolmasters*, p. 345; W. Macgill, *Old Ross-shire and Scotland*, I, p. 156; R. W. Munro and J. Munro, *Tain through the centuries*, p. 111.

4.49 R. Southey, *Journal*, p. 118.

4.50 Beriah Botfield, *Journal of a tour through the Highlands of Scotland during the summer of MDCCCXXIX* (Norton Hall, 1880), p. 101.

4.51 Elizabeth Isabella Spence, *Letters from the North Highlands during the summer 1816* (London: Longman, 1817), p. 148.

4.52 *O.S.A.*, III, p. 13; VI, p. 433; Sir J. Sinclair, *General view of the agriculture of the northern counties*, p. 50. In the absence of detailed statistics, judgments such as these must be based on general impressions.

4.53 *O.S.A.*, XVII, p. 343; Sir J. Sinclair, *General view of the agriculture of the northern counties*, p. 50.

4.54 *Ibid;* Sir G. S. Mackenzie, *A general view . . . of the counties of Ross and Cromarty*, pp. 73-4; R. Forsyth, *The beauties of Scotland*, IV, p. 522.

4.55 Sir J. Sinclair, *General view of the agriculture of the northern counties*, p. 77.

4.56 *Ibid.*, p. 76; J. Macdonald, 'On the agriculture of the counties of Ross and Cromarty', p. 88.

4.57 Sir J. Sinclair, *General view of the agriculture of the northern counties*, p. 76.

4.58 *Ibid.*, p. 51. As late as 1809 there was only one farm on the Balnagown estates in Easter Ross with more than fifty acres arable but by 1855, the largest nine farms, all but one rented at over £200, were worth seventy per cent of the total rental; see *Plans of the Estate of Balnagown lying in the Parishes of Killmuir, Loggie, Fearn, Eddertown and Kincardine . . . 1808*, S.R.O., West Register House, RHP13299; *Valuation Roll for the County of Ross 1855-6*, S.R.O. VR115/1-3.

4.59 Clericus, 'On farm houses in Ross-shire', *Farmers Magazine*, 7 (1806), p. 217.

4.60 G. & P. Anderson, *Guide to the Highlands and Islands (1850)*, p. 392.

4.61 Sir G. S. Mackenzie, *A general view . . . of the counties of Ross and Cromarty*, p. 74; *O.S.A.*, VI, p. 192.

4.62 *O.S.A.*, III, p. 397; VI, p. 192; XV, p. 629; *Unto the Honble. the Commissioners for managing the annexed Estates in Scotland . . . The Petition of George Hosack, Donald Munro and Robert Hendry, Masons . . . 1st February, 1782*, S.R.O. E746/137/5(1); *Register of Improvements made upon Lands held under Settlement of Strict Entail, Ross-shire-Tain*, S.R.O. SC34/23/1.

4.63 *N.S.A.*, 14, pp. 225, 307.

4.64 H. Miller, *My schools and schoolmasters*, pp. 153, 158, 164, 191-2, 239.

4.65 *Ibid.*, p. 191.

4.66 *Ibid.*, pp. 191-2.

4.67 Sir G. S. Mackenzie, *A general view . . . of the counties of Ross and Cromarty*, p. 83; N. Macrae, *The romance of a royal burgh*, p. 181; *O.S.A.*, I, p. 279; VI, p. 423; Sir J. Sinclair, *General view of the agriculture of the northern counties*, pp. 36-7; *J. Walker, An economical history of the Hebrides*, I, pp. 90-91; R. Bain, *History of the Ancient Province of Ross*, p. 363; *N.S.A.*, 14, pp. 33, 66-68; 222, 292; Great Britain, Commission for inquiring into the administration and practical operation of the poor laws in Scotland, *Report*, Appendix, II, pp. 2, 21.

4.68 W. Mackenzie, 'Report of improvements at Ardross', pp. 136-9; *N.S.A.*, 14, pp. 53-4, 311-2; *O.S.A.*, I, p. 288; Great Britain, Commission for inquiring into the administration and practical operation of the poor laws in Scotland, *Report*, Appendix, II, pp. 2-3, 9, 23.

4.69 *O.S.A.*, I, p. 279; III, pp. 13, 397; IV, p. 478; *N.S.A.*, 14, pp. 294, 307, 377; Sir

J. Sinclair, *General view of the agriculture of the northern counties*, p. 37; T. Pennant, *A Tour in Scotland, 1769*, p. 186; *Unto the Honble. the Commissioners for managing the annexed Estates in Scotland . . . The Petition of George Hosack, Donald Munro and Robert Hendry, Masons . . . 1st February, 1782*, S.R.O. E746/137/5(1); *Register of Improvements made upon Lands held under Settlement of Strict Entail, Ross-shire-Tain, 1807-8*, S.R.O. SC34/23/1; Great Britain, Commission for inquiring into the administration and practical operation of the poor laws in Scotland, *Report*, Appendix, IV, pp. 386a-398a.

4.70 Sir G. S. Mackenzie, *A general view . . . of the counties of Ross and Cromarty*, p. 296; *N.S.A.*, 14, pp. 222, 376; J. Barron, *The northern Highlands in the nineteenth century*, II, p. 53.

4.71 Sir J. Sinclair, *General view of the agriculture of the counties of Ross and Cromarty*, pp. 76, 79.

4.72 *O.S.A.*, III, p. 9; IV, p. 475; XII, p. 265; XIV, p. 92; Sir G. S. Mackenzie, *A general view . . . of the counties of Ross and Cromarty*, pp. 163, 185; J. Macdonald, 'On the agriculture of the counties of Ross and Cromarty', pp. 87-8; H. Miller, *My schools and schoolmasters*, p. 264.

4.73 J. H. Dawson, *An abridged statistical account of Scotland*, p. 871.

4.74 J. Cameron, *Report on the sanitary condition and general economy of the town of Tain and the district of Easter Ross, made to the Poor Law Commissioners*, pp. 326-7.

4.75 G. & P. Anderson, *Guide to the Highlands and Islands of Scotland* (1842), p. 23.

4.76 Central Board for the Relief of Destitution in the Highlands and Islands of Scotland, Edinburgh Section, *Third report* (Edinburgh: Blackwood, 1848), p. 93.

4.77 *N.S.A.*, 14, p. 68; J. Macdonald, 'On the agriculture of the counties of Ross and Cromarty', pp. 86-7; Great Britain, Commission for inquiring into the administration and practical operation of the poor laws in Scotland, *Report*, Appendix, II, pp. 3, 9, 13, 21, 50; *Labour book for Tarlogie, Morangie & Culcairn, 1829*.

4.78 A. Wight, *Present state of husbandry in Scotland*, 4(1), p. 287; Sir J. Sinclair, *General view of the agriculture of the northern counties*, pp. 38, 104; Sir G. S. Mackenzie, *A general view . . . of the counties of Ross and Cromarty*, pp. 227-8; J. Cameron, *Report on the sanitary condition and general economy of Tain and the district of Easter Ross, made to the Poor Law Commissioners*, p. 323.

4.79 A. Wight, *Present state of husbandry in Scotland*, 4(1), p. 286; J. H. Dawson, *An abridged statistical account of Scotland*, p. 871; Sir G. S. Mackenzie, *A general view . . . of the counties of Ross and Cromarty*, p. 226; Sir J. Sinclair, *General view of the agriculture of the northern counties*, p. 36; *O.S.A.*, I, pp. 278-9; XII, p. 276; XV, p. 629; *N.S.A.*, 14, pp. 61, 225, 377.

4.80 A. Wight, *Present state of husbandry in Scotland*, 4(1), p. 287; *O.S.A.*, VI, p. 423; J. H. Macdonald, 'On the agriculture of the counties of Ross and Cromarty', p. 88; Great Britain, Commission for inquiring into the administration and practical operation of the poor laws in Scotland, *Report*, Appendix, II, pp. 11, 13.

4.81 *O.S.A.*, VI, p. 192; *N.S.A.*, 14, pp. 33, 225, 294.

4.82 J. Cameron, *Report on the sanitary condition and general economy of Tain and the district of Easter Ross, made to the Poor Law Commissioners*, p. 324.

4.83 *Ibid.*, p. 325.

4.84 N. Macrae, *The romance of a royal burgh*, p. 349; Great Britain, Commission for inquiring into the administration and practical operation of the poor laws in Scotland, *Report*, Appendix, II, p. 22; Rosalind Mitchison, 'The making of the old Scottish Poor Law', *Past and Present*, No. 63 (1974), pp. 58-93; *O.S.A.*, I, pp. 280-1; IV, p. 476.

4.85 R. Mitchison, 'The making of the old Scottish Poor Law', pp. 58-93; Kiltearn Kirk Session, *Minutes*, S.R.O. CH2/569/3; Tarbat Kirk Session, *Minutes*, S.R.O. CH2/350/1-2; Great Britain, Commissioners for inquiring into the administration and practical operation of the poor laws in Scotland, *Report*, p. V; Tain Town Council, *Minutes*, 3rd January, 1799; 7th July 1840, S.R.O. B70/6/1, 4.

4.86 Kiltearn Kirk Session, *Minutes*, 27th September, 1770; 25th August, 1771; 6th May, 1777; 27th July, 1778; 15th November, 1793; 2nd September, 1798; 4th January, 1838; S.R.O. CH2/569/3; Tarbat Kirk Session, *Minutes*, 24th December, 1750; 25th November, 1751; 16th June, 1752; 22nd June, 1768, S.R.O CH2/350/1; Tain Kirk Session, *Minutes*, 19th September, 1794, S.R.O. CH2/349/2.

4.87 *O.S.A.*, I, p. 280; IV, p. 295; Synod of Ross, *Minutes*, 9th October, 1754, S.R.O. CH2/312/4.

4.88 Great Britain, Commission for inquiring into the administration and practical operation of the poor laws in Scotland, *Report*, Appendix, II, pp. 3, 11; Synod of Ross, *Minutes*, 9th October, 1754; 19th April, 1757; 15th April, 1800; 21st April, 1801, S.R.O. CH2/312/4-5.

4.89 *O.S.A.*, XII, p. 257; Great Britain, Commission for inquiring into the administration and practical operation of the poor laws in Scotland, *Report*, Appendix, II, pp. 3, 7, 51; R. Forbes, *Journals of the Episcopal Visitations of the Right Rev. Robert Forbes*, p. 277.

4.90 Central Board for the Relief of Destitution in the Highlands and Islands of Scotland, Edinburgh Section, *Third report* (Edinburgh: Blackwood, 1848), pp. 93-9; Tarbat Kirk Session, *Minutes*, 28th July, 1783, S.R.O. CH2/350/1; J. Macdonald, 'On the agriculture of the counties of Ross and Cromarty', pp. 88-9.

4.91 Great Britain, Commission for inquiring into the administration and practical operation of the poor laws in Scotland, *Report*, Appendix, II, p. 13.

4.92 Kiltearn Kirk Session, *Minutes*, S.R.O. CH2/569/3; Tarbat Kirk Session, *Minutes*, S.R.O. CH2/350/1-2; Kilmuir Easter Kirk Session, *Minutes*, S.R.O. CH2/429/1; Tain Kirk Session, *Minutes*, S.R.O. CH2/349/2-3; Sir G. S. Mackenzie, *A general view . . . of the counties of Ross and Cromarty*, pp. 282, 287.

4.93 Great Britain, Commission for inquiring into the administration and practical operation of the poor laws in Scotland, *Report*, Appendix, II, pp. 3, 5, 22, 30; Tarbat Kirk Session, *Minutes*, 7th June, 1754; 28th July, 1783, S.R.O. CH2/350/1; Scotland, Church of Scotland, General Assembly, Committee on the management of the poor in Scotland, *Report*, p. 13.

4.94 Great Britain, Commission for inquiring into the administration and practical operation of the poor laws in Scotland, *Report*, Appendix, II, pp. 30, 50.

4.95 Tain Kirk Session, *Minutes*, 22nd September, 1808, S.R.O. CH2/349/3;

4.96 Synod of Ross, *Minutes*, 16th April, 1766, S.R.O. CH2/312/5; Tarbat Kirk Session, *Minutes*, 23rd January, 1780; 6th November, 1805, S.R.O. CH2/350/1; Presbytery of Dingwall, *Minutes*, 19th July, 1826, S.R.O. CH2/92/9.

4.97 Tarbat Kirk Session, *Minutes*, 9th February, 1842, S.R.O. CH2/350/2; H.

Miller, *My schools and schoolmasters*, pp. 176-9, 400-3; *Labour book for Tarlogie, Morangie & Culcairn, 1829.*

4.98 *O.S.A.*, XI, p. 344. There was a regular credit balance in the Tarbat poor fund in the mid-eighteenth century and even as late as 1838 Kiltearn Kirk Session, which tended to be parsimonious in its charitable duties, had substantial capital reserves; see Tarbat Kirk Session, *Minutes*, 16th June, 1752, S.R.O. CH2/350/1; Kiltearn Kirk Session, *Minutes*, 4th January, 1838, S.R.O. CH2/569/3.

4.99 Great Britain, Commission for inquiring into the administration and practical operation of the poor laws in Scotland, *Report*, Appendix, II, p. 28.

4.100 *O.S.A.*, I, p. 281; R. Bain, *History of the Ancient Province of Ross*, p. 386; 'Agricultural Intelligence Scotland, Ross-shire Quarterly Report', *Farmers Magazine*, 24 (1832), p. 130; 'Agricultural Intelligence Scotland, Ross-shire Quarterly Report', *Farmers Magazine*, 25 (1824), p. 94. There was a 25 per cent rise in the numbers on the Tain poor roll in the decade after 1782 as compared with a similar period before that date; see Tain Kirk Session, *Minutes*, S.R.O. CH2/349/2-3; J. Macdonald, 'On the agriculture of the counties of Ross and Cromarty', p. 89.

4.101 Great Britain, Commission for inquiring into the administration and practical operation of the poor laws in Scotland, *Report*, Appendix, II, pp. 3, 10, 13, 21.

4.102 *Ibid.*, Appendix, II, pp. 2, 3, 4, 28, 46; Scotland, Church of Scotland, General Assembly, Committee on the management of the poor in Scotland, *Report*, p. 5; *N.S.A.*, 14, p. 36; Commission for inquiring into the opportunities of Public Religious Worship and means of Religious Instruction, and the Pastoral Superintendence afforded to the people of Scotland, *4th Report*, Appendix I, p. 301.

4.103 Kiltearn Kirk Session, *Minutes*, S.R.O. CH2/569/3; Tain Kirk Session, *Minutes*, S.R.O. CH2/349/2-3; Tarbat Kirk Session, *Minutes*, S.R.O. CH2/350/1-2; Great Britain, Commission for inquiring into the administration and practical operation of the poor laws in Scotland, *Report*, Appendix, II, p. 47.

4.104 Tain Kirk Session, *Minutes*, 4th September, 1810, S.R.O. CH2/349/3; Sir G. S. Mackenzie, *A general view . . . of the counties of Ross and Cromarty*, pp. 285, 287; *O.S.A.*, III, p. 12; XII, p. 271; XIV, pp. 95-6.

4.105 *N.S.A.*, 14, pp. 17, 297-8, 397; Great Britain, Commission for inquiring into the administration and practical operation of the poor laws in Scotland, *Report*, Appendix, II, pp. 3, 5; V, pp. 387c-398c.

4.106 Presbytery of Dingwall, *Minutes*, 25th November, 1840, S.R.O. CH2/92/9; Great Britain, Commission for inquiring into the administration and practical operation of the poor laws in Scotland, *Report*, Appendix, II, pp. 5, 9, 11.

4.107 *Ibid.*, Appendix, II, pp. 3, 8, 22, 28, 51, 54.

4.108 *Ibid.*, Appendix, II, p. 6; J. P. Day, *Public administration in the Highlands*, p. 80; Great Britain, Board of Supervision for the relief of the Poor in Scotland, *First annual report* (Edinburgh: H.M.S.O., 1847), pp. 35-6.

4.109 J. P. Day, *Public administration in the Highlands*, p. 53.

4.110 R. W. Munro and J. Munro, *Tain through the centuries*, p. 123; G. & P. Anderson, *Guide to the Highlands and Islands* (1850), p. 394; Henry Dunning Macleod, *The results of the operation of the poor house system in Easter Ross* (Inverness, 1851), p. 4.

4.111 J. Barron, *The northern Highlands in the nineteenth century*, III, p. 127; Great Britain, Board of Supervision for the relief of the Poor in Scotland, *First annual report*, pp. 35-6; Central Board for the Relief of Destitution in the Highlands and Islands of Scotland, Edinburgh Section, *Third report*, pp. 93-4; H. D. Macleod, *The results of the operation of the poor house system in Easter Ross*, p. 7.

5.1 F. Forbes and W. J. Anderson, 'Clergy lists of the Highland district, 1732-1828', *Innes Review*, 17 (1966), pp. 129-184.

5.2 James Gray Kyd, *Scottish population statistics*, Scottish History Society Publications, 3rd Series, No. 43 (Edinburgh: Scottish History Society, 1952), p. 61; James Darragh, 'The Catholic population of Scotland since the year 1680', *Innes Review*, 4 (1953), p. 59. There were almost certainly some unrecorded Catholics in 1851; see *Census of Great Britain 1851, Religious Worship and Education. Scotland Report and Tables* (London: H.M.S.O., 1854), p. 18.

5.3 R. Forbes, *Journals of the Episcopal Visitations of the Right Rev. Robert Forbes*, pp. 16, 66, 68, 103, 122-4, 126-8, 131-2.

5.4 *Ibid.*, p. 273; John Kennedy, *The days of the fathers in Ross-shire* (New ed., Inverness: G. Young, 1895) p. 198.

5.5 J. Macinnes, *The Evangelical Movements in the Highlands*, p. 33.

5.6 *N.S.A.*, 14, pp. 62, 357, 379.

5.7 R. Forbes, *Journals of the Episcopal Visitations of the Right Rev. Robert Forbes*, pp. 172-3, 276, 279.

5.8 R. Forbes, *Journals of the Episcopal Visitations of the Right Rev. Robert Forbes*, pp. 157, 217-9; G. & P. Anderson, *Guide to the Highlands and Islands (1834)*, p. 26; Charles John Shore, 2nd Baron Teignmouth, *Sketches of the coasts and islands of Scotland* (2 vols, London: Parker, 1836), p. 79.

5.9 Tarbat Kirk Session, *Minutes*, 10th September, 1750, S.R.O. CH2/350/1.

5.10 C. Macnaughton, *Church life in Ross and Sutherland*, p. 264.

5.11 *Ibid.*, pp. 187, 267, 293-4, 381; Presbytery of Dingwall, *Minutes*, 5th February, 1783; 20th March, 1828; 4th May, 1831, S.R.O. CH2/92/8-9; Presbytery of Chanonry, *Minutes*, 15th December, 1772; 7th May, 1776, S.R.O. CH2/66/5; Kilmuir Easter Kirk Session, *Minutes*, 11th October, 1771; 19th July, 1781, S.R.O. CH2/429/1.

5.12 Tain Town Council, *Minutes*, S.R.O. B70/6/3-4: Presbytery of Dingwall, *Minutes* S.R.O. CH2/92/17-21.

5.13 Tain Town Council, *Minutes*, 11th March, 1841; S.R.O. B70/6/4.

5.14 Presbytery of Dingwall, *Minutes*, 26th March, 1834, S.R.O. CH2/92/9.

5.15 *O.S.A.*, XII, p. 257; *Origines Parochiales Scotiae*, II(2), pp. 481, 501, 522, 537, 551, 552; John Nightingale, 'The threat to Cromarty', p. 340.

5.16 R. W. Munro and J. Munro, *Tain through the centuries*, p. 104; Commissioners for inquiring into the opportunities of Public Religious Worship, and means of Religious Instruction, and the Pastoral Superintendance afforded to the people of Scotland, *4th Report* (London: H.M.S.O., 1838), Appendix I, pp. 296-7.

5.17 H. Scott, *Fasti Ecclesiae Scoticanae*, VII, p. 8.

5.18 Kiltearn Kirk Session, *Minutes*, S.R.O. CH2/569/3; Tarbat Kirk Session, *Minutes*, S.R.O. CH2/350/1-2.

5.19 Tarbat Kirk Session, *Minutes*, 7th July, 1754; 22nd June, 1779, S.R.O. CH2/350/1.

5.20 W. Macgill, *Old Ross-shire and Scotland*, I, p. 55.

5.21 Tarbat Kirk Session, *Minutes*, 21st October, 1751, S.R.O. CH2/350/1.

5.22 *Ibid.*, 30th April, 1753; 6th March, 1758.

5.23 *Ibid.*, 25th April, 1803; 7th May, 1804; 15th May, 1809, 19th June, 1809; 23rd April, 1810.

5.24 *Labour book for Tarlogie, Morangie and Culcairn, 1829.*

5.25 *Ibid.*

5.26 R. Forbes, *Journal of the Episcopal Visitations of the Right Rev. Robert Forbes*, pp. 157, 217-9, 226, 276.

5.27 *Unto the very Reverend the Synod of Ross. The complaint of William Urquhart of Meldrum Esq., patron of the Parish of Cromarty, et al.*, Dingwall, 14th April, 1752, S.R.O. CH1/2/95.

5.28 J. Hall, *Travels in Scotland*, II, p. 491-3.

5.29 *O.S.A.*, XIX, p. 240.

5.30 D. Sage, *Memorabilia Domestica*, p. 351.

5.31 *Ibid.*, p. 352; G. & P. Anderson, *Guide to the Highlands and Islands of Scotland (1842)*, p. 489; Synod of Ross, *Minutes*, 19th April, 1808, S.R.O. CH2/312/6.

5.32 H. Miller, *My schools and schoolmasters*, pp. 408-9; *An account of the present state of religion throughout the Highlands of Scotland* (Edinburgh, 1827), pp. 19-28, 39-42.

5.33 *O.S.A.*, I, p. 296.

5.34 J. Macinnes, *The Evangelical Movements in the Highlands*, p. 28; *N.S.A.*, 14, p. 71. The number of parishes whose patronage was held by the Crown varied from time to time. The figure quoted is derived from the Old Statistical Account and includes not only those patronages assigned to the Crown in that work but also the Cromartie estate patronages which were held by the Crown until 1784; see *O.S.A.*, I, p. 296; II, p. 562; III, p. 393; IV, pp. 295, 476; VI, p. 191; XI, p. 344; XII, pp. 257, 270; XIII, p. 18; XVII, p. 354; J. H. Dawson, *An abridged statistical account of Scotland*, pp. 873-97; J. Playfair, *Geographical and statistical description of Scotland*, I, p. 214.

5.35 H. Scott, *Fasti Ecclesiae Scoticanae, VII, pp. 2. 5; Cromarty Settlement case papers*, S.R.O. CH1/2/95; Synod of Ross, *Minutes*, 3rd October, 1750, S.R.O. CH2/312/4.

5.36 C. Macnaughton, *Church life in Ross and Sutherland*, pp. 208-39.

5.37 John Noble, *Religious life in Ross* (Edinburgh: Thin, 1909), p. 85.

5.38 C. Macnaughton, *Church life in Ross and Sutherland*, pp. 299-300; H. Scott, *Fasti Ecclesiae Scoticanae*, VII, pp. 2, 15; Presbytery of Dingwall, *Minutes*, 27th March, 1816; 27th June, 1816, S.R.O. CH2/93/21.

5.39 D. Sage, *Memorabilia Domestica*, p. 346; C. Macnaughton, *Church life in Ross and Sutherland*, pp. 350, 363-70, 374, 376, 380; Presbytery of Dingwall, *Minutes*, 26th March, 1834; 6th February, 1839: 4th March, 1840; 31st April, 1841, S.R.O. CH2/92/9; Synod of Ross, *Minutes*, 20th April, 1841, S.R.O. CH2/312/6; *An account of the present state of religion throughout the Highlands of Scotland*, p. 43.

5.40 J. Macinnes, *The Evangelical Movements in the Highlands*, pp. 92-5; William Mackelvie, *Annals of the United Presbyterian Church* (Edinburgh: Oliphant & Co., 1873), p. 255.

5.41 *O.S.A.*, XV, p. 624; *N.S.A.*, 14, p. 396.

5.42 H. Miller, *My schools and schoolmasters*, p. 408; J. Haldane, *et al.*, *Journal of a tour through the Northern Counties of Scotland . . . in autumn, 1797* (2nd ed.; Edinburgh, 1798), pp. 80-5.

5.43 Presbytery of Dingwall, *Minutes*, 20th March, 1838, S.R.O. CH2/92/9.

5.44 W. Mackelvie, *Annals of the United Presbyterian Church*, p. 261.

5.45 J. H. Dawson, *An abridged statistical account of Scotland*, p. 890.

5.46 *Ibid.*, pp. 873-97; H. Scott, *Fasti Ecclesiae Scoticanae*, VII, pp. 6, 13, 16, 19, 28, 43, 47, 57, 59, 64, 66, 69, 73, 76; J. Barron, *The northern Highlands in the nineteenth century*, III, p. 55; *Parochial schoolmasters (Scotland), Return to an address of the . . . House of Commons . . . 1854* (London: H.M.S.O., 1854), p. 44.

5.47 Great Britain, Commission for inquiring into the administration and practical operation of the poor laws in Scotland, *Report*, Appendix, II, pp. 28-30.

5.48 J. Forbes, *Report*, p. 2, S.R.O. E729/1; Great Britain, Select Committee appointed to inquire into the state of Education in Scotland, *Answers made by schoolmasters in Scotland to queries circulated in 1838* (London: H.M.S.O., 1841), I, pp. 267-78.

5.49 Donald J. Withrington, 'The S.P.C.K. and Highland schools in mid eighteenth century', *Scottish Historical Review*, 41 (1962), p. 89.

5.50 *O.S.A.*, XVII, p. 357.

5.51 *Ibid.*, III, p. 397; N. Macrae, *The romance of a royal burgh*, pp. 222-223, 240, 243; C. G. Macdowall, *The Chanonry of Ross*, p. 167; Tain Town Council, *Minutes*, 11th February, 1779, S.R.O. B70/6/1; W. Macgill, *Old Ross-shire and Scotland*, II, p. 111.

5.52 D. J. Withrington, 'The S.P.C.K. and Highland schools in mid eighteenth century', p. 95; Society for Propagating Christian Knowledge, *Register of Society's schools*, pp. 200-1, 206-7, S.R.O. GD95/9/1; The Society in Scotland for Propagating Christian Knowledge, *An account of the funds, expenditure and general management of the affairs of the Society* (Edinburgh, 1796), Appendix, pp. 7-8, 23. While the schools on the first patent gave a basic standard education with a strong emphasis on religion, those erected on the second patent concentrated on teaching sewing and spinning to girls; see John Mason, 'Scottish Charity Schools of the eighteenth century', *Scottish Historical Review*, 33 (1954), p. 11.

5.53 Presbytery of Chanonry, *Minutes*, 17th June, 1794, S.R.O. CH2/66/5; J. Mitchell, *Reminiscences of my life in the Highlands*, I, p. 43.

5.54 R. W. Munro and J. Munro, *Tain through the centuries*, pp. 105-8; *Royal charter, List of subscribers, state of funds, etc. etc. of the Tain Academy* (London, (1810).

5.55 J. Barron, *The northern Highlands in the nineteenth century*, I, p. 42; C. G. Macdowall, *The Chanonry of Ross*, p. 165; *Royal Charter, list of subscribers . . . of the Tain Academy*, pp. 17-26; Presbytery of Chanonry, *Minutes*, 17th June, 1794, S.R.O. CH2/66/5; Tain Town Council, *Minutes*, 8th August, 1842, S.R.O. B70/6/4; *The traveller's guide through Scotland (1806)*, p. 501.

5.56 J. Barron, *The northern Highlands in the nineteenth century*, III, p. 31; Presbytery of Chanonry, *Minutes*, 17th June, 1805; 17th September, 1805; 29th March, 1808, S.R.O. CH2/66/6; Great Britain, Commission for inquiring into the administration and practical operation of the poor laws in Scotland, *Report*, Appendix, II, p. 51.

5.57 *N.S.A.*, 14, p. 298.

5.58 *Ibid.*, p. 62; H. Miller, *My schools and schoolmasters*, p. 129; Presbytery of Chanonry, *Minutes*, 18th June, 1844, S.R.O. CH2/66/7.

5.59 Presbytery of Dingwall, *Minutes*, 1st May, 1806, S.R.O. CH2/92/19; Inverness, Society for the education of the poor in the Highlands, *Moral statistics* (Inverness, 1826), pp. 19-20.

5.60 Inverness, Society for the education of the poor in the Highlands, *Moral statistics*, pp. 20, 22; Appendix pp. XLV, ff.

5.61 *Ibid.*, p. 68; J. H. Dawson, *An abridged statistical account of Scotland*, pp. 873-97; J. P. Day, *Public administration in the Highlands*, pp. 146-8; Church of Scotland, General Assembly, Education Committee, *Report*, 1847, p. 21, S.R.O. CH1/2/198.

5.62 *N.S.A.*, 14, p. 379; Great Britain, Commission for inquiring into the administration and practical operation of the poor laws in Scotland, *Report*, Appendix, II, p. 8.

5.63 *N.S.A.*, 14, p. 16; Tain Town Council, *Minutes*, 6th April, 1846, S.R.O. B70/6/4.

5.64 Tain Town Council, *Minutes*, 27th January, 1789, S.R.O. B70/6/1; *O.S.A.*, XII, p. 273.

5.65 H. Miller, *My schools and schoolmasters*, p. 39; *N.S.A.*, 14, pp. 16, 56, 231, 278, 358, 378, 397; Inverness, Society for the education of the poor in the Highlands, *Moral statistics*, p. 22; Presbytery of Chanonry, *Minutes*, 2nd February, 1802, S.R.O. CH2/66/5; Great Britain, Select Committee on the Poor Laws, 1818, *Third report* (London: H.M.S.O., 1818), Appendix, p. 38.

5.66 Great Britain, Select Committee appointed to inquire into the state of education in Scotland, *Answers made by schoolmasters in Scotland to queries circulated in 1838*, I, pp. 684-6, 689-91, 694-5, 699-702, 705-6, 708; II, pp. 267-78.

5.67 H. Miller, *My schools and schoolmasters*, p. 45; Presbytery of Chanonry, *Minutes*, 2nd February, 1802, S.R.O. CH2/66/5; Presbytery of Dingwall, *Minutes*, 26th November, 1783; 29th November, 1797; 26th December, 1826, S.R.O. CH2/92/8-9, 18; John Gibson, 'Report on the schools within the Presbyteries of Tongue and Tain, 1842', in Great Britain, Privy Council, Committee of Council on Education, *Minutes*, (London: H.M.S.O., 1844), p. 668.

5.68 H. Miller, *My schools and schoolmasters*, pp. 45, 129; Presbytery of Dingwall, *Minutes*, 1st November, 1837, S.R.O. CH2/92/9.

5.69 R. W. Munro and J. Munro, *Tain through the centuries*, pp. 107-8; Presbytery of Chanonry, *Minutes*, 17th June, 1805, 29th March, 1808, S.R.O. CH2/66/6.

5.70 Patrick Butter, *Journal of a visit to the schools of the Society in Scotland for Propagating Christian Knowledge*, 1824, pp. 135-60, S.R.O. GD95/9/3; *Notes of a visit to Society schools in Inverness-shire and Ross-shire in summer 1836*, pp. 15-20, S.R.O. GD95/14/29; The Society in Scotland for Propagating Christian Knowledge, *An account of the funds . . . of the Society*, p. 30; J. Tawse, *Reports of visits to the schools of the S.P.C.K.*, p. 106, S.R.O. GD95/9/4.

5.71 H. Miller, *My schools and schoolmasters*, pp. 27-8; Great Britain, Select Committee on Education in Scotland, *Answers made by schoolmasters in Scotland to queries circulated in 1838*, I, pp. 684-6, 689-91, 694-5, 699-702, 705-6, 708.

5.72 Great Britain, Select Committee on Education in Scotland, *Answers made by schoolmasters in Scotland to queries circulated in 1838*, I, pp. 684-6, 689-91, 694-5, 699-702, 705-6, 708.

5.73 D. Sage, *Memorabilia Domestica*, p. 30.

5.74 Inverness, Society for the education of the poor in the Highlands, *Moral statistics*, pp. 16-18; H. Hunter, *A brief history of the Society in Scotland for Propagating Christian Knowledge in the Highlands and Islands*, p. 41; J. Mason, 'Scottish Charity Schools of the eighteenth century', p. 8.

5.75 Inverness, Society for the education of the poor in the Highlands, *Moral statistics*, pp. 19-21; William Mackay, 'Education in the Highlands in the olden times', *Celtic Monthly*, 14 (1905-6), p. 183.

5.76 John Anderson, *Prize essay on the state of society and knowledge in the Highlands of Scotland, particularly in the northern counties* (Edinburgh: William Tait, 1827), p. 109.

5.77 J. Gibson, 'Report on the schools within the Presbyteries of Tongue and Tain, 1842', p. 673.

5.78 *O.S.A.*, XI, p. 346; *Royal charter, list of subscribers . . . of the Tain Academy.*

5.79 N. Macrae, *The romance of a royal burgh*, p. 251.

5.80 H. Miller, *My schools and schoolmasters*, p. 43.

5.81 J. Gibson, 'Report on the schools within the Presbyteries of Tongue and Tain, 1842', pp. 658-9.

5.82 Although schoolhouses for parish teachers became obligatory only after 1803, they were frequently provided before that date but the standard of accommodation was fairly miserable; see Presbytery of Dingwall, *Minutes*, 4th May, 1791, S.R.O. CH2/92/17; W. Macgill, *Old Ross-shire and Scotland*, II, p. 117; *Expense of building the schoolhouse of Fearn*, 1794, S.R.O. GD71/469; John Tawse *et al.*, *Reports of visits to the schools of the S.P.C.K.* pp. 21-2, S.R.O. GD95/9/4; J. Gibson, 'Report on the schools within the Presbyteries of Tongue and Tain, 1842', p. 659.

5.83 J. Gibson, 'Report on the schools within the Presbyteries of Tongue and Tain, 1842', p. 660; R. W. Munro and J. Munro, *Tain through the centuries*, p. 107.

5.84 W. Macgill, *Old Ross-shire and Scotland*, II, p. 110; *O.S.A.*, I, p. 285; III, p. 396; XV, p. 633; *To The Right Honourable The Commissioners of The Annexed Estates — The petition of the Magistrates and Town Council of the Burgh of Fortrose, Fortrose*, 1st October, 1770, S.R.O. E787/16/1; Presbytery of Dingwall, *Minutes*, 30th November, 1808, S.R.O. CH2/92/20.

5.85 H. Miller, *My schools and schoolmasters*, p. 49.

5.86 *O.S.A.*, XI, p. 348; *N.S.A.*, 14, p. 298; Presbytery of Chanonry, *Minutes*, 2nd February, 1802, S.R.O. CH2/66/5; Disbursements on account of Mr. J. Robertson, Fortrose, July 22nd, 1794, S.R.O. GD146/8; W. Macgill, *Old Ross-shire and Scotland*, II, p. 133; *Scotland, Education enquiry, Abstract of the answers and returns*, pp. 659, 661.

5.87 *N.S.A.*, 14, pp. 62, 71, 231, 328, 346, 379, 397.

5.88 Great Britain, Select Committee appointed to inquire into the state of Education in Scotland, *Answers made by schoolmasters in Scotland to queries circulated in 1838*, I, pp. 684-6, 689-91, 694-5, 699-702, 705-6, 708.

5.89 Sir G. S. Mackenzie, *A general view . . . of the counties of Ross and Cromarty*, p. 351; H. Hunter, *A brief history of the Society in Scotland for Propagating Christian Knowledge in the Highlands and Islands*, p. 76; Society for Propagating Christian Knowledge, *Register of Society's schools*, pp. 20-1, 206-7; Great Britain, Select Committee appointed to inquire into the state of Education in Scotland, *Answers made by schoolmasters in Scotland to queries circulated in 1838*, pp. 684-6, 689-91, 694-5,

699-702, 705-6, 708; The Society in Scotland for Propagating Christian Knowledge, *An account of the funds . . . of the Society*, p. 31.

5.90 Inverness, Society for the education of the poor in the Highlands, *Moral statistics*, p. 20; Presbytery of Chanonry, *Minutes*, 2nd February, 1802, S.R.O. CH2/66/5; Great Britain, Select Committee appointed to inquire into the state of Education in Scotland, *Answers made by schoolmasters in Scotland to queries circulated in 1838*, I, pp. 684-6, 689-91, 694-5, 699, 702, 705-6, 708.

5.91 *Unto the Honourable ye Commissioners on ye Annexed Forfeited Estates, The Petition of us undersubscribers part of ye King's Cottingers on the Estate of Cromartie att Newtarbatt*, 25th April, 1765, S.R.O. E746/135/2; *Copy report, Act & Commission, Robertson against Ross of Easterfearn . . . 1755*, S.R.O. GD71/173/14; Acknowledgement, Wm. & Finlay Munro, Dykers, to Kindeace, 8th July, 1793, S.R.O. GD146/8.

5.92 Kiltearn Kirk Session, *Minutes*, 27th October, 1772; 3rd May, 1774, S.R.O. CH/569/3; *Mandate from the Parish of Alness to Mr. Colin Mackenzie*, August, 1770; S.R.O. CH/2/112; J. Macinnes, *The Evangelical Movements in the Highlands*, p. 64.

5.93 *Judicial rental, Cromarty, 1755*, S.R.O. E746/70; *Copy Report, Act & Commission, Robertson against Ross of Easterfearn . . . 1755*, S.R.O. GD/173/14.

5.94 *N.S.A.*, 14, pp. 231, 310, 328; Inverness, Society for the education of the poor in the Highlands, *Moral statistics*, pp. 54, 64-5.

5.95 *N.S.A.*, 14, p. 297; Presbytery of Chanonry, *Minutes*, 29th March, 1831, S.R.O. CH2/66/7.

5.96 Great Britain, Commission for inquiring into the administration and practical operation of the poor laws in Scotland, *Report*, Appendix, II, p. 9; Great Britain, Select Committee appointed to enquire into the Education of the Poor, *A digest of parochial returns* (3 vols, London: H.M.S.O., 1819), III, pp. 1427-31; *Scotland, Education enquiry, Abstract of the answers and returns*, pp. 637, 649, 657; Scotland, Church of Scotland, General Assembly, Committee on the management of the poor in Scotland, *Report* (London: H.M.S.O., 1839), p. 13; The Society in Scotland for Propagating Christian Knowledge, *An account of the funds . . . of the Society, p.* 33.

5.97 Inverness, Society for the education of the poor in the Highlands, *Moral statistics*, pp. 54, 64-5.

5.98 *N.S.A.*, 14, p. 323; *Scotland, Education enquiry, Abstract of the answers and returns*, pp. 649, 657; The Society in Scotland for Propagating Christian Knowledge, *An account of the funds . . . of the Society*, p. 33.

5.99 Scotland, Education enquiry, *Abstract of the answers and returns*, pp. 636-62.

5.100 Great Britain, Select Committee appointed to inquire into the state of Education in Scotland, *Answers made by schoolmasters in Scotland to queries circulated in 1838*, I, pp. 684-6, 689-91, 694-5, 699-702, 705-6, 708; II, pp. 267-78.

5.101 *Scotland, Education enquiry, Abstract of the answers and returns*, pp. 636-62; The Society in Scotland for Propagating Christian Knowledge, *An account of the funds . . . of the Society*, Appendix, pp. 7-8, 23; *Reports on Society in Scotland for Propagating Christian Knowledge schools at Davidstoun, 1778 and Inver, 1779*, S.R.O. CH1/2/121.

5.102 D. Forbes, *Some Kindeace letters*, p. 5; A. Mackenzie, *History of the Munros of Fowlis*, pp. 138-9.

5.103 D. Sage, *Memorabilia Domestica*, pp. 30-2; Account, Charles Robertson of

Kindeace, Esq., to John Straith, Nairn, 30th April, 1788, S.R.O. GD146/8; Hugh Miller, 'The story of a parish school', *The Witness*, 27th March, 1850.

5.104 Mr. John Robertson, Student in the Academie of Fortrose to James Grigor, Shoemaker, Fortrose, 29th October, 1793, S.R.O. GD146/8; *To The Right Honourable The Commissioners of The annexed Estates — The petition of the Magistrates and Town-council of the Burgh of Fortrose, Fortrose*, 1st October, 1770, S.R.O. E787/16/1; Alexander Mackenzie and Alexander Macbain, *History of the Mathesons* (Stirling: Mackay, 1900), pp. 46, 53; William Taylor, *Researches into the history of Tain earlier and later* (Tain: Ross, 1882), p. 98.

5.105 Charles Robertson of Kindeace's eldest son, for example, was educated in Edinburgh while a younger brother went to Fortrose academy; see Mr. John Robertson, Student in the Academie of Fortrose to James Grigor, Shoemaker, Fortrose, 29th October, 1793, S.R.O. GD146/8; Letter, Roderick Macleod to Charles Robertson of Kindeace, 15th November, 1780, S.R.O. GD146/14; Letter, John MacGilvray to Charles Robertson of Kindeace, Eton, 2nd August, 1777, S.R.O. GD146/13; Alexander Mackenzie, 'Sir Kenneth S. Mackenzie of Gairloch, Bart.', *Celtic Magazine*, 6 (1881), p. 28; John Bateman, *The great landowners of Great Britain and Ireland* (London: Harrison & Sons, 1878), pp. 17, 266, 268, 298, 356.

5.106 C. Macnaughton, *Church life in Ross and Sutherland*, p. 301; Presbytery of Dingwall, *Minutes*, 26th November, 1800; 27th November, 1811; 24th June, 1812; 29th March, 1815; 2nd August, 1815, S.R.O. CH2/92/19-20.

5.107 W. Macgill, *Old Ross-shire and Scotland*, I, p. 67.

5.108 *O.S.A.*, V, p. 216.

5.109 Synod of Ross, *Minutes*, 10th April, 1751; 22nd April, 1773; 20th April, 1784; 15th April, 1794, S.R.O. CH2/312/4-5.

5.110 Tain Kirk Session, *Minutes*, 27th August, 1778; 30th August, 1781; 19th September, 1794, S.R.O. CH2/349/2-3; Synod of Ross, *Minutes*, 21st April, 1767, S.R.O. CH2/312/4.

5.111 A. Mackenzie and A. Macbain, *History of the Mathesons*, pp. 46-7, 53; J. Bateman, *The great landowners of Great Britain and Ireland*, p. 356; D. Sage, *Memorabilia Domestica*, pp. 32-3; H. Scott, *Fasti Ecclesiae Scoticanae*, VII, pp. 2-76; J. M. Bulloch, *The Families of Gordon of Invergordon, Newhall*, pp. 59-60; H. Tayler, *History of the family of Urquhart*, pp. 256, 259; A. Mackenzie, *History of the Munros of Fowlis*, pp. 138-9; Synod of Ross, *Minutes*, S.R.O. CH2/312/4-5; Letter, David Munro to Charles Robertson of Kindeace, Clelands Yds nr Edinburgh, 14th October, 1761, S.R.O. GD146/12; Letter, R. B. Aeneas Macleod to Charles Robertson of Kindeace, Glasgow, 7th August, 1780, S.R.O. GD146/14.

5.112 C. Macnaughton, *Church life in Ross and Sutherland*, pp. 257, 329; Synod of Ross, *Minutes*, 19th March, 1707; 8th October, 1707, 4th April, 1710, 12th April, 1732, S.R.O. CH312/1, 3; Donald Maclean, 'Highland libraries in the eighteenth century', *Transactions of the Gaelic Society of Inverness*, 31 (1922-4), pp. 70-96.

5.113 W. Macgill, *Old Ross-shire and Scotland*, I, p. 71; H. Miller, *My schools and schoolmasters*, pp. 28-30, 49, 51-2, 55; J. Macinnes, *The Evangelical Movements in the Highlands*, p. 69; Hugh Miller, *Scenes and legends of the North of Scotland* (Edinburgh: Nimmo, 1885), p. 377; Society for Propagating Christian Knowledge, *Register of Society's Schools*, pp. 200-1, 206-7; Letter, Roderick Macleod to Charles Robertson of Kindeace, Edinburgh, 6th June, 1778, S.R.O. GD146/13.

5.114 J. Barron, *The northern Highlands in the nineteenth century*, I, p. 192; II, p. 29; *N.S.A.*, 14, p. 232; J. H. Dawson, *An abridged statistical account of Scotland*, p. 894; J. Anderson, 'Essay on the present state of the Highlands and Islands of Scotland', pp. 29-30.

5.115 *N.S.A.*, 14, p. 278; Ian R. M. Mowat, 'Literacy, libraries and literature in 18th and 19th century Easter Ross', *Library History*, 5 (1979), pp. 1-10.

5.116 James Cameron, 'Report on the sanitary condition and general economy of the town of Tain and the district of Easter Ross, made to the Poor Law Commissioners', p. 331.

5.117 *Ibid.*, p. 18.

5.118 R. W. Munro and J. Munro, *Tain through the centuries*, p. 107; James William Hudson, *History of adult education* (London: Longman, 1851), pp. 235-6; H. D. Macleod, *The results of the operation of the poor house system in Easter Ross*, title page.

5.119 Gordon Donaldson, *Scottish Historical Documents* (Edinburgh: Scottish Academic Press, 1970), p. 174; Inverness, Society for the education of the poor in the Highlands, *Moral statistics*, p. 17.

5.120 E. Burt, *Letters from a gentleman in the North of Scotland*, I, p. 41; *The Highlands of Scotland in 1750*, p. 125.

5.121 N. Macrae, *The romance of a royal burgh*, pp. 220 ff.; The heritors and elders of Avoch, *Answers to the Reasons for the Transportation of Mr. Alexr. Fraser from the Parish of Avoch to the Burgh and Parish of Taine — Humbly offered to the Very Reverend the Presbytery of Chanonry, Rosemarkie, 20th March, 1750*, S.R.O. CH1/2/92; Discharged Account Charles Robertson of Kindeace to Geo. Miller in Tain, 26th May, 1761, S.R.O. GD146/7; Tain Town Council, *Minutes*, S.R.O. B70/6/1; A. Menzies, *Report, 1768*, pp. 11-12, S.R.O. E787/24.

5.122 J. Forbes, *Report*, p. 2, S.R.O. E729/1.

5.123 R. Forbes, *Journals of the Episcopal Visitations of the Right Rev. Robert Forbes*, p. 156; D. A. Mackenzie, 'Cromarty dialects and folk lore', pp. 75-77; R. Heron, *Scotland described (1797)*, p. 274; *O.S.A.*, I, p. 291; II, pp. 562-3; III, p. 18; IV, pp. 298, 477; XII, p. 267; John Calder, *Diary*, 23rd March, 1776, National Library of Scotland acc. 4156.

5.124 *O.S.A.*, II, pp. 562-3; VI, pp. 430-1; XIX, p. 340; J. Macinnes, *The Evangelical Movements in the Highlands*, pp. 246-7.

5.125 John Walker, *Report concerning the State of the Highlands and Islands*, 1771, S.R.O. CH1/2/113.

5.126 *Ibid.*

5.127 *N.S.A.*, 14, pp. 11-12.

5.128 *Ibid.*, pp. 27, 30; Presbytery of Chanonry, *Minutes*, 29th March, 1831; 26th April, 1836, S.R.O. CH2/66/7.

5.129 Inverness, Society for the education of the poor in the Highlands, *Moral statistics*, pp. 51-4, 64-5. The main English areas in this calculation are considered to be the eastern Black Isle parishes of Avoch, Rosemarkie and Cromarty and the two semi-burghal parishes of Tain and Dingwall. Only in the eastern Black Isle were English speakers actually in a majority.

5.130 *N.S.A.*, 14, pp. 30, 56, 67, 222-3, 272, 292, 306, 322-3, 344-5, 375; J. Macdonald, 'On the agriculture of the counties of Ross and Cromarty', p. 77; P. Butter,

Journal, 1824, p. 155, S.R.O. GD95/9/3.

6.1 J. Tivy, 'Easter Ross: a residual crofting area', p. 64.

6.2 A. J. Youngson, *After the Forty-Five*, pp. 4-10; G. Donaldson, *Scottish Historical Documents*, pp. 101-2; William Croft Dickinson, *Scotland from the earliest times to 1603* (London: Nelson, 1961), pp. 8-10.

6.3 Andrew Charles O'Dell and Kenneth Walton, *The Highlands and Islands of Scotland* (London: Nelson, 1962 (1963), pp. 4-56; *O.S.A.*, X, pp. 545, 551-6, 560-1.

6.4 A precedent for recognising an intermediate zone was established in 1797 when the existing Highland district was split into two for excise purposes; see Great Britain, Committee upon the distilleries in Scotland, *Report. Ordered to be printed 11th June, 1798* (London: H.M.S.O., 1803), p. 320.

6.5 W. C. Dickinson, *Scotland from the earliest times to 1603*, p. 8; John S. Kellie, *A history of the Scottish Highlands, Highland clans and Highland regiments* (2 vols., Edinburgh: Fullarton, 1879), I, pp. 1-2.

6.6 M. Gray, *The Highland Economy 1750-1850*, pp. 52, 140, 222-8; Malcolm Gray, 'The abolition of runrig in the Highlands of Scotland', *Economic History Review* N.S. 5 (1952), p. 52; Malcolm Gray, 'Economic welfare and money income in the Highlands 1750-1850', *Scottish Journal of Political Economy*, 2 (1955), p. 47; Malcolm Gray '[Review article]', *Scottish Historical Review*, 53 (1974), p. 95.

6.7 One author, writing a short popular history of Tain, has succinctly identified the issue in the title of his work; see A. G. R. Robertson, *The Lowland Highlanders.*

6.8 M. Gray, *The Highland Economy 1750-1850*, pp. 3-54.

6.9 Eric R. Cregeen, *Argyll estate instructions: Mull, Morvern, Tiree 1771-1805*, Publications of the Scottish History Society, 4th series, 1 (Edinburgh: Scottish History Society, 1964), XVII-XVIII; Philip Gaskell, *Morvern transformed* (Cambridge: Cambridge University Press, 1968), p. 3.

6.10 P. Gaskell, *Morvern transformed*, pp. 1-13; Robert James Adam, *Papers on Sutherland estate management*, Publications of the Scottish History Society, 4th series, 8-9 (2 vols.; Edinburgh: Scottish History Society, 1972), I, pp. 16, 32; John Horne, *The county of Caithness* (Wick: W. Rae, 1907), pp. 49-54, 117-20.

6.11 For the purposes of this comparison lowland Caithness is taken to include the parishes of Bower, Cannisbay, Dunnet, Halkirk, Olrig, Thurso, Watten and Wick, but as with Easter Ross the parish boundaries are only an approximate guide to the geographical and historical realities. For the areas of the parishes concerned see W. & A. K. Johnston, *Gazetteer of Scotland.*

6.12 R. J. Adam, *Papers on Sutherland estate management*, I, p. XII; P. Gaskell, *Morvern transformed*, p. 12.

6.13 M. Gray, *The Highland Economy 1750-1850*, pp. 124-8, 133-6, 141-2, 151, 187-9; P. Gaskell, *Morvern transformed*, pp. 23-6.

6.14 R. J. Adam, *Papers on Sutherland estate management*, I, pp. X-XII, LIX.

6.15 Eric R. Cregeen, 'The tacksmen and their successors', *Scottish Studies*, 13 (1969), pp. 93-144; R. J. Adam, *Papers on Sutherland estate management*, I, pp. 18-9; P. Gaskell, *Morvern transformed*, pp. 8, 13.

6.16 Rosalind Mitchison, *Agricultural Sir John* (London: Bles, 1962), p. 3; John E. Donaldson, *Caithness in the 18th century* (Edinburgh: Moray Press, 1938), pp. 39, 106.

6.17 *The Highlands of Scotland in 1750*, p. 20.

6.18 *Ibid.*, pp. 19-23; P. Gaskell, *Morvern transformed*, pp. 2-3.

6.19 Isabel Frances Grant, *The Macleods. The history of a clan 1200-1956* (London: Faber & Faber, 1959), pp. 582-5.

6.20 Sir W. Fraser, *The Earls of Cromartie*, I, p. XXIII; D. Warrand, *Some Mackenzie pedigrees*, p. 56.

6.21 R. Maclean, 'Notes on the parish of Kiltearn', p. 309.

6.22 P. Gaskell, *Morvern transformed*, pp. 8, 10, 18-20; R. J. Adams, *Papers on Sutherland estate management*, I, pp. 16, 32.

6.23 M. Gray, *The Highland Economy 1750-1850*, p. 31; Royal Commission on the Ancient and Historical Monuments of Scotland, *Argyll. An inventory of the ancient monuments. Volume 2, Lorn* (Edinburgh: Royal Commission on the Ancient and Historical Monuments of Scotland, 1975), pp. 281-4.

6.24 P. Gaskell, *Morvern transformed*, pp. 8, 47, 49.

6.25 R. J. Adams, *Papers on Sutherland estate management*, I, pp. LX, CII.

6.26 *The Highland Economy 1750-1850*, pp. 61-6, 107, 124-9, 139, 144-5; P. Gaskell, *Morvern transformed*, pp. 8, 26.

6.27 R. J. Adams, *Papers on Sutherland estate management*, I, pp. XXXVIII, LXXXIII; P. Gaskell, *Morvern transformed*, pp. 7-8, 25.

6.28 Ian Grimble, *The trial of Patrick Sellar* (London: Routledge & Kegan Paul, 1962), p. 17; R. J. Adams, *Papers on Sutherland estate management*, I, p. 33; P. Gaskell, *Morvern transformed*, pp. 20-1, 54; M. Gray, *The Highland Economy 1750-1850*, pp. 170-3.

6.29 I. Grimble, *The trial of Patrick Sellar*, p. 15; P. Gaskell, *Morvern transformed*, pp. 22-4.

6.30 P. Gaskell, *Morvern transformed*, pp. 10, 49; R. J. Adams, *Papers on Sutherland estate management*, I, pp. LX, 25.

6.31 R. Mitchison, *Agricultural Sir John*, pp. 190, 195; J. E. Donaldson, *Caithness in the 18th century*, p. 56.

6.32 J. Horne, *The county of Caithness*, pp. 157-80; Malcolm Gray, 'Organisation and growth in the east-coast herring fishing 1800-1885', in Peter L. Payne, *Studies in Scottish business history* (London: Frank Cass & Co., 1967), pp. 188-9

6.33 R. Mitchison, *Agricultural Sir John*, pp. 28, 191; J. Horne, *The county of Caithness*, pp. 150-2.

6.34 R. Mitchison, *Agricultural Sir John*, p. 195; J. Horne, *The county of Caithness*, p. 54.

6.35 Sir G. S. Mackenzie, *A general view . . . of the counties of Ross and Cromarty*, p. 333.

6.36 In the early eighteenth century Munro of Culrain, whose estates lay on the western borders of Easter Ross, was cited as a good example of a Highland chieftain; see E. Burt, *Letters from a gentleman in the north of Scotland*, II, pp. 105-6. Even towards the end of the nineteenth century there were eight parishes in which a majority of the population habitually spoke Gaelic; see *Ninth decennial census of the population of Scotland taken 4th April, 1881* (2 vols; London: H.M.S.O., 1882), vol. 1, p. 101.

6.37 Inverness, Society for the education of the poor in the Highlands, *Moral statistics*, pp. 51-3, 64-5.

6.38 J. E. Donaldson, *Caithness in the 18th century*, p. 40.

6.39 J. Macinnes, *The Evangelical Movements in the Highlands*, p. 28; Owen

Lattimore, *Studies in frontier history* (London: Oxford University Press, 1962), pp. 470-91.

6.40 E. Burt, *Letters from a gentleman in the North of Scotland*, I, pp. 40, 180-1; *The Highlands of Scotland in 1750*, p. 125.

6.41 A. Menzies, *Report*, 1768, p. 1, S.R.O. E787/24.

6.42 *Ibid.*, p. 11.

6.43 J. Forbes, *Report*, pp. 3-4, S.R.O. E729/1; Letter, Roderick Macleod to Charles Robertson of Kindeace, Edinburgh, 2nd August, 1780, S.R.O. GD146/14.

6.44 R. Forsyth, *The beauties of Scotland*, 5, p. 211.

6.45 H. Miller, *My schools and schoolmasters*, p. 95. Anyone who stands at Cromarty, or, even better, at Nigg across the firth, must be struck immediately by the physical differences between the immediate environs and the hill country to the west.

6.46 J. Anderson, 'Essay on the present state of the Highlands and Islands of Scotland', p. 22.

6.47 Adrian N. L. Hodd, *Agricultural change in the Carse of Gowrie 1750-1875* (unpublished Ph.D. thesis, Dundee University, 1974).

6.48 The Gaelic congregation at Cromarty was only dissolved in 1918; see H. Scott, *Fasti Ecclesiae Scoticanae*, VII, p. 8.

6.49 Quite apart from the obedience imposed by sanctions of one sort or another, the traditions of loyalty commented upon by early eighteenth century observers such as Burt continued to operate well after 1750.

6.50 J. Hall, *Travels in Scotland*, II, pp. 488-9; 'Sketch of a tour through the northern counties of Scotland', pt. IV, pp. 420-1.

6.51 Laurence James Saunders, *Scottish democracy, 1815-1840* (Edinburgh: Oliver & Boyd, 1950), pp. 259-60.

6.52 H. Miller, *Tales and Sketches*, p. 309; A. Menzies, *Report, 1766*, p. 106-7, S.R.O. E729/8.

6.53 H. Miller, *Tales and Sketches*, pp. 293, 306, 325; Commissioners of Supply for the County of Cromarty, *Minutes*, 8th June, 1787, S.R.O. SC24/21/7.

6.54 Such close relationships were standard throughout Britain in the pre-industrial era; see Peter Laslett, *The world we have lost* (London: Methuen, 1965), pp. 4-12.

6.55 *N.S.A.*, 14, pp. 320-2, 325.

6.56 H. Scott, *Fasti Ecclesiae Scoticanae*, VII, pp. 27, 56.

6.57 R. Bain, *History of the Ancient Province of Ross*, p. 341; Kenneth J. Logue, *Popular disturbances in Scotland 1780-1815* (Edinburgh: John Donald, 1979), pp. 58ff.

6.58 R. Bain, *History of the Ancient Province of Ross*, p. 384; J. Barron, *The northern Highlands in the nineteenth century*, III, pp. 126-8; K. J. Logue, *Popular disturbances in Scotland 1780-1815*, pp. 30, 43.

6.59 'Sketch of a tour through the northern counties of Scotland', pt. IV, p. 421; Sir W. Fraser, *The Earls of Cromartie*, I, pp. 247-50.

6.60 *O.S.A.*, XII, p. 265.

6.61 Letter, David Munro to ? Charles Robertson of Kindeace, Edinburgh, 1758, S.R.O. GD146/11; Letter, David Munro to Charles Robertson of Kindeace, Edinburgh, 15th September, 1759, S.R.O. GD146/11; *Survey & measure of Meikle Allan pr Alex Sangster*, 1756, S.R.O. GD71/182.

6.62 Letter, Sir John Gordon of Invergordon to Charles Robertson of Kindeace, Invergordon, 1771, S.R.O. GD146/13; Letter, Roderick Macleod to Charles Robertson of Kindeace, Edinburgh, 1778, S.R.O. GD146/3.

6.63 Peter May, *Papers on Peter May land surveyor 1749-1793*, edited by Ian H. Adams (Edinburgh: Scottish History Society, 1979), Scottish History Society Publications, 4th series, 15, pp. xiii-xiv.

6.64 Walt Whitman Rostow, *The stages of economic growth* (Cambridge: Cambridge University Press, 1969), pp. 26-7.

6.65 H. Miller, *My schools and schoolmasters*, pp. 2, 37, 55, 246; D. Sage, *Memorabilia Domestica*, p. 366.

6.66 A. Wight, *Present state of Husbandry in Scotland*, 4(1), pp. 237-8, 283; W. Macgill, *Old Ross-shire and Scotland*, II, p. 54.

6.67 J. Anderson, 'Essay on the present state of the Highlands and Islands of Scotland', p. 52.

6.68 J. E. Handley, *Scottish farming in the eighteenth century*, pp. 149-52; D. Warrand, *Some Mackenzie pedigrees*, p. 129.

6.69 Sir J. Sinclair, *General view of the agriculture of the northern counties*, p. 125; 'Sketch of a tour through the northern counties of Scotland', pt. IV, p. 421.

6.70 H. Hamilton, *Economic history of Scotland*, pp. 320-2.

6.71 T. C. Smout, [Review of Stein Tveite, Jord og Gjerning (Kristiansund, 1959)], *Scottish Historical Review*, 53 (1974), pp. 69-76.

6.72 Sir G. S. Mackenzie, *A general view . . . of the counties of Ross and Cromarty*, pp. 138, 351.

6.73 C. J. Shore, 2nd Baron Teignmouth, *Sketches of the coasts and islands of Scotland*, II, p. 71.

6.74 *O.S.A.*, IV, p. 294; VI, p. 187; R. Bain, *History of the Ancient Province of Ross*, pp. 352-3.

6.75 It is not possible to make the case statistically, but a comparison of the mid-nineteenth century valuation rolls with earlier estate records reveals quite clearly that the native tenantry were badly squeezed in the first half of the nineteenth century; see, for example, *Abstract rental shewing the gross rents payable in kind from the . . . Estate of Balnagown . . . 1809*, S.R.O. GD/129/31/14; *Rental of estate of Balnagown, 1777*, S.R.O. GD129/31/118; *Valuation Roll for the County of Ross 1855-6*, S.R.O. VR115/1-3.

6.76 Although tenants had been rackrented and subjected to considerable pressure and had been individually liable to eviction, there had been no general threat to their possession of the land despite lack of tenure.

6.77 *N.S.A.*, 14, p. 325.

6.78 *The Highlands of Scotland in 1750*, p. 18; *Rental of estate of Balnagown, 1777*, S.R.O. GD129/31/118; R. Forsyth, *The beauties of Scotland*, 5, p. 267; *The dictionary of national biography*, XVII, pp. 269-71.

6.79 R. Bain, *History of the Ancient Province of Ross*, p. 335.

6.80 Sir G. S. Mackenzie, *A general view . . . of the counties of Ross and Cromarty*, p. 21; A. Wight, *Present state of Husbandry in Scotland*, 4(1), p. 243; *Plan of the farm and policy of Novar . . . 1777*, S.R.O., West Register House, RHP10671; John Lettice, *Letters on a tour through various parts of Scotland in the year 1792* (London: Cadell, 1794), p. 341.

6.81 P. Gaskell, *Morvern transformed*, pp. 30-1; E. Richards, 'Patterns of Highland discontent', pp. 75-114.

6.82 H. Miller, *Tales and Sketches*, pp. 262-71.

6.83 Letter, Roderick Macleod to Charles Robertson of Kindeace, Edinburgh, 2nd August, 1780, S.R.O. GD146/14; Letter, Sir John Gordon of Invergordon to the Lord Advocate, Invergordon Castle, 3rd August, 1780, S.R.O. GD235/7; Ian G. Lindsay, *Inveraray and the Dukes of Argyll* (Edinburgh: Edinburgh University Press, 1973).

6.84 H. Miller, *Tales and Sketches*, p. 265.

6.85 A. J. Youngson, *After the Forty-Five*, pp. 178-94.

6.86 R. Southey, *Journal*, p. 120; Alexander M. Ross, *History of the clan Ross* (Dingwall: North Star, 1932), p. 40.

6.87 *N.S.A.*, 14, p. 34.

6.88 'Agricultural Intelligence Scotland, Ross-shire Quarterly Report', *Farmers Magazine*, 14 (1813), p. 243.

6.89 It should be stressed again that no claim is being made that substantial investment would inevitably have brought prosperity, although the rise of industry in such a city as Aberdeen is surely sufficient proof that an area did not always need mineral wealth to succeed. What is suggested is that the creation of a prosperous industry, however temporary, can help a region to cope more successfully with changing circumstances. If the tobacco lords of Glasgow had spent an even greater proportion of their wealth on personal expenditure rather than investing it in cotton, would their descendants have had the chance to exploit the local mineral wealth in the nineteenth century?

6.90 T. C. Smout, 'Scottish landowners and economic growth 1650-1850', *Scottish Journal of Political Economy*, 11 (1964), pp. 228-9. The obvious difficulties facing industrial development in a rural area are all too clearly seen in the failure of David Urquhart of Braelangwell's ventures; see Sir G. S. Mackenzie, *A general view . . . of the counties of Ross and Cromarty*, p. 335; *N.S.A.*, 14, p. 49.

6.91 List of Subscribers in the Fishing Chamber of Inverness 1759, S.R.O. GD146/7; Eric Richards, 'Structural change in a regional economy: Sutherland and the Industrial Revolution 1780-1830', *Economic History Review*, 26 (1973), pp. 68-73.

6.92 Jane Jacobs, *The economy of cities* (London: Jonathan Cape, 1970), pp. 21, 122, 180-2.

6.93 Great Britain, Board of Supervision for the relief of the poor in Scotland, *First annual report* (Edinburgh: H.M.S.O., 1847), pp. 35-6.

6.94 Arnold Joseph Toynbee, *A study of history. Abridgement of volumes I-VI by D. C. Somervell* (London: O.U.P., 1946), pp. 48-163.

6.95 R. Mitchison, *Agricultural Sir John*, p. 83.

6.96 E. Maciver, *Memoirs of a Highland gentleman*, pp. 51-2.

6.97 *N.S.A.*, 14, p. 322.

6.98 J. Cameron, *Report on the sanitary condition and general economy of the town of Tain and the district of Easter Ross, made to the Poor Law Commissioners*, p. 333.

6.99 E. R. Cregeen, *Argyll estate instructions*, p. XXI.

6.100 T. C. Smout, 'Scottish landowners and economic growth 1650-1850', p. 234; T. C. Smout, *A history of the Scottish people 1560-1830* (London: Collins 1970), pp. 280-360.

Bibliography

1 Guides to the literature

Adams, Ian H. *Descriptive list of plans in the Scottish Record Office.* 3 vols.; Edinburgh: H.M.S.O., 1966-74.

Black, George F. *A list of works relating to Scotland.* New York: New York Public Library, 1916.

Craigie, James. *A bibliography of Scottish education before 1872.* London: University of London Press, 1970.

Edinburgh Public Libraries. *Scottish family histories: a list of books for consultation in the Reference Library, George IV Bridge.* 3rd ed.; Edinburgh: Libraries and Museums Committee, 1958.

Great Britain, Parliament, House of Commons. *Catalogue of parliamentary reports, and a breviate of their contents: arranged under heads according to the subjects. 1696-1834.* London: H.M.S.O., 1834.

Great Britain, Parliament, House of Commons. *General index to the accounts and papers, reports of commissioners, estimates etc. etc. Printed by order of the House of Commons, or presented by Command: 1801-52.* London: H.M.S.O., 1853.

Great Britain, Parliament, House of Commons. *General index to the reports of select committees, printed by order of the House of Commons: 1801-1852.* London: H.M.S.O., 1853.

Hancock, Philip David. *A bibliography of works relating to Scotland, 1916-1950.* 2 vols.; Edinburgh: Edinburgh University Press, 1959-60.

Higgs, Henry. *Bibliography of economics 1751-1775.* Cambridge: Cambridge University Press. 1935.

The Kress Library of Business and Economics. *Catalogue.* 2 vols.; Boston (Mass.): Baker Library, 1940, 1957.

'List of articles on Scottish history published during the year 1959—'. *Scottish Historical Review,* 39 (1960—).

'List of publications on the economic (and social) history of Great Britain and Ireland'. *Economic History Review,* New series, 1 (1948-9—).

Macdougall, Ian. *An interim bibliography of the Scottish working class movement and of other labour records held in Scotland.* Edinburgh: Scottish Committee, Society for the Study of Labour History, 1965.

Matheson, Cyril. *A catalogue of the Publications of Scottish Historical and kindred Clubs and Societies . . . 1908-27.* Aberdeen: Milne and Hutchinson, 1928.

Marwick, William Hutton. 'Bibliography of Scottish economic history'. *Economic History Review*, 3 (1931-2), pp. 117-37.

Mitchell, Sir Arthur. *List of travels and tours in Scotland 1296-1900*. Edinburgh, 1902.

Mitchell, Sir Arthur and Cash, Caleb George. *A contribution to the bibliography of Scottish topography*. Scottish History Society Publications, 2nd series, XIV. 2 vols.; Edinburgh: Scottish History Society, 1917.

National Library of Scotland. *Catalogue of manuscripts acquired since 1925. 7 vols.;* Edinburgh: H.M.S.O., 1938-68 [Vols. IV-VII in Typescript].

National Library of Scotland. *Scottish topography supplement* [in typescript].

Paton, Henry M. 'Record sources for Scottish church history'. *Records of the Scottish Church History Society*, 5 (1935), pp. 103-16.

Records of the Church of Scotland preserved in the Scottish Record Office and General Register Office, Register House, Edinburgh. Scottish Record Society Publications, 94. Glasgow: Scottish Record Society, 1967.

Scott, William Robert. *Scottish economic literature to 1800*. Glasgow: William Hodge and Company, 1911.

Scottish Record Office. *Source List 1. National record sources for local history*. [Typescript].

Scottish Record Office. *Source List 2. National record sources for economic history*. [Typescript].

Scottish Record Office. *Source List 5. Source list of material on communications in Scottish Record Office*. [Typescript].

Scottish Record Office. *Source List 25. Official records and local history*. [Typescript].

Scottish Record Office. *Source List 26. The Highlands and Islands*. [Typescript].

Stuart, Margaret. *Scottish family history: a guide to works of reference on the history and genealogy of Scottish families*. Edinburgh: Oliver & Boyd, 1930.

Terry, Charles Sanford. *A catalogue of the Publications of Scottish Historical and kindred Clubs and Societies . . . 1780-1908*. Glasgow: James Maclehose and Sons, 1909.

2 Manuscript sources

(a) Bank of Scotland—
British Linen Company. *Scots letter books 1748-1808;* N.R.A. 0273.

(b) National Library of Scotland—
British Fisheries Society. *Extracts of letters addressed to Deputy Governor of The British Fisheries Society for extending the Fisheries;* ms. 2619.
Brown, George. *Journal 1799-1815;* ms. 3271.
Brown, Peter. *Journal 1815-18;* ms. 3272.
Calder, Reverend John, of Rosskeen. *Diary 1775-82.* acc. 4156.
Gordon, Sir John. *Pocket book;* ms. 108.
Mackenzie of Delvine papers; ms. 1101-1530.
Macleod of Geanies papers; acc. 5340.

(c) St Andrews University Library—
Brodie, Alexander Oswald. *Diary 1843;* ms. TA140; B8E43.

(d) Scottish Record Office—

(i) Burgh records

Tain Town Council. *Minutes 1773-1847;* B70/6/1-4.

(ii) Church records

Church of Scotland, General Assembly. *Assembly papers, main series;* CH1/2/92-205.

Synod of Ross. *Minutes 1750-1876;* CH2/312/4-6.

Presbytery of Chanonry. *Minutes 1762-1846;* CH2/66/5-7.

Presbytery of Dingwall. *Minutes 1774-1855;* CH2/92/8-10, 17-21.

Kilmuir Easter Kirk Session. *Minutes 1771-1840;* CH2/429/1.

Kiltearn Kirk Session. *Minutes 1770-97, 1817-46;* CH2/569/3.

Tain Kirk Session. *Minutes 1762-1828;* CH2/349/2-3.

Tarbat Kirk Session. *Minutes 1750-1957;* CH2/350/1-2.

(iii) Estate papers

Gordon of Invergordon; GD235/7.

Munro of Allan; GD71.

Rarichy farm rent book 1783-1834; GD1/519.

Robertson of Kindeace; GD146.

Ross of Balnagown; GD129.

Ross of Cromarty; GD1/481, GD159.

Ross of Pitcalnie; GD199.

Warrand of the Bught; GD23.

(iv) Exchequer records

Forfeited Estates papers; E700-E788.

Exchequer Fiars prices 1708-1894; E5/5, E848/1-3.

Shop tax, window tax; E326/4/2.

Highland roads and bridges papers; E330, E416.

(v) Industrial records

Accompts of linen cloth stamped in Scotland; NG1/15/1-2.

Board of Trustees for Fisheries, Manufactures & Improvements in Scotland, *Minutes;* NG1/1/11-39, NG1/2/1-3.

(vi) Miscellaneous papers

D. & J. H. Campbell, W.S. papers; GD253/150-179.

Society in Scotland for Propagating Christian Knowledge records; GD95.

(vii) Plans

Outline plan of the Estate of Cromarty 1825; GD6393.

Plan of farm of Kirktoun in Kiltearn [*actually Resolis*] [*1782?*]; RHP1472.

Plan of part of ye lands of Ankervil and Meikle Allan . . . 1759. Surveyed & planed [*sic*] *by Alexander Sangster;* RHP 239.

Plan of part of the estate of Flowerburn proposed to be feued by Roderick G. Mackenzie Esq. [*circa 1850*]; RHP 1464.

Plan of the burgh lands of the estate of Tulloch . . . 1789; RHP 1474.

Plan of the controverted marches betwixt Lady Erskine's lands of Wester Kessock, Kilmuir & Easter Sligo [*circa 1800*]; RHP 117/3.

Plan of the Davoch of Davidstoun 1748; RHP 5494.

Plan of the Estate and Barrony of Findon, the property of Sir Roderick

Mackenzie of Scatwell . . . David Aitken 1769; RHP 3513.
A plan of the Estate of Cromarty. The property of Lord Elibank . . . 1764; RHP 1046.
Plan of the Estate of Findon . . . 1849; RHP 3680.
Plan of the Estate of Mountgerald . . . the property of Captain Mackenzie . . . 1850; RHP 3544.
A plan of the Estate of Tulloch . . . David Aitken fecit 1763; RHP 1473.
Plan of the Estate of Tulloch . . . 1827; RHP 1475.
Plan of the farm and policy of Novar . . . 1777; RHP 10671.
Plan of the grounds and inclosures about Cromarty Castle & Hill . . . 1753; RHP 5498.
Plan of the Hill of Nigg as divided 1763; RHP 680.
Plan of the intended road from Portinliek alias Culrain to Dingwall . . . 1790; RHP 11591.
Plan of the lands of Drumcudden. The property of Captain Hugh Robert Duff of Muirtoun . . . 1796; RHP 1469.
Plan of the lands of Findon . . . Surveyed in 1833-4 . . . & laid off in 1836, 1837; RHP 3549.
Plans of the boundaries of the burgh of Tain 1750; RHP 275/1-3.
Plans of the Estate of Balnagown lying in the parishes of Killmuir, Loggie, Fearn, Eddertoun and Kincardine . . . 1808; RHP 13299.
Reduced plan of the survey of the Commons of Milbuy, Cromarty etc. . . . 1816; RHP 4045.
Sketch of Ardmeanach, being the portion of the Milbuie assigned by the Court of Session to the Burgh of Fortrose 1849; RHP 1452.
Sketch of the lands of Ardmeanach . . . the property of John Stevenson Esq. . . . 1830; RHP 1451.

(viii) Sheriff Court records

Cromarty	SC24
Dingwall	SC25
Tain	SC34

(ix) Valuation Rolls
Ross valuation book 1756; E901/28/1.
Valuation book of the county of Cromarty 1802; E901/10/2.
Valuation book of the County of Nairn 1802; E901/23/4.
Valuation book of the County of Ross 1802; E901/28/2.
Valuation of the county of Cromarty as settled by the Commissioners of Supply . . . 25th May, 1765; SC24/21/7.
Valuation roll for the County of Cromarty 1855-6; VR115/4.
Valuation roll for the County of Ross 1855-6; VR115/1-3.

(e) Others—

(i) Mr. and Mrs. W. Gill, Auchintoul Farm, Invergordon, Ross-shire.
Arabella Farm Labour Book 1831-2.
Culcairn Farm Labour Book 1830.
Labour Book for Tarlogie, Morangie & Culcairn 1829.
Tarlogie Farm Labour Book 1830-2.

(ii) Mrs. R. Mackenzie, Tain Museum
Easter Ross Farmers' Club. *Minute book.*
Easter Ross Farming Society. *Minute books.*

3 Reports and Theses etc.

Aberdeen University Library, Printed papers on legal processes.

(a) Commissioners and trustees of annexed estates, *Answers for the Commissioners . . ., David Ross, Multurer of the Mills of Milntown, & Colin Mackenzie, factor on the forfeited estate of Cromarty; to the petition of Captain Alexander Ross, etc.*, 19th February, 1777.

(b) Munro, George, *et al., Information . . . against John Inglis, Merchant in Edinburgh, pursuer & Robert Fraser of Phopachy, one of the defenders*, 22nd December, 1768.

(c) Munro, George, *et al., Objections for George Munro of Culcairn, and his curators, and others . . . to the process of Cessis bonorum pursued at the instance of John Ross, late factor on the forfeited estate of Mulderg*, 8th March, 1769.

(d) Munro, Sir Harry, *et al., Information . . . against Captain John Ross of Balnagown*, 30th July, 1768.

(e) Ross, Alexander, *Information . . . against Master Charles Ross, second lawful son to George, Lord Ross, and his curators, defenders*, 6th December, 1739.

(f) Ross, Alexander, *Petition of Captain Alexander Ross of Calrossie, Roderick MacCulloch of Glastullich, Charles Monro of Allan & David Ross of Priesthill*, 29th January, 1777.

(g) Ross, Charles, *Petition of Colonel Charles Ross, second son of the late David Ross, Esq. of Inverchassley*, 19th February, 1765.

(h) Ross, John, *Information . . . against the heirs and creditors of the deceased David MacCulloch of Mulderg, defenders*, 30th July, 1768.

(i) Ross, John, *Petition . . . and answers . . . to the objections for George Munro of Culcairn*, 9th March, 1769.

(j) Ross, Munro, *Petition unto the Right Honourable the Lords of Council & Session*, 5th August, 1761.

Edinburgh, College of Art, School of Town and Country Planning, *The burgh of Cromarty report*, 1962.

Hodd, Adrian N. L., *Agricultural change in the Carse of Gowrie 1750-1875*. Unpublished Ph.D. thesis, Dundee University, 1974.

Stephen, J. S., *The history of roads in the Highlands of Scotland in the eighteenth and nineteenth centuries*. Unpublished Ph.D. thesis, Aberdeen University, 1936.

Thompson, A. R., *An enquiry into the reading habits of the working classes in Scotland from 1830-40*. Unpublished B.Litt. thesis, Glasgow University, 1961-2.

4 Government publications

(a) Census
1801 (PP 1801 VI; 1801-2VI, VII).
1811 (PP 1812 XI).
1821 (PP 1822 XV).

1831 (PP 1833 XXXVI-XXXVIII).
1841 (PP 1843 XXII, XLIX).
1851 (PP 1852-3 LXXXVI; 1854 LII).

(b) Miscellaneous

Accounts relating to the distilleries in Scotland 1815-18 (PP 1818 XIV).

Accounts relating to wash and worts distilled in Scotland (PP 1822 XXI).

Documents relative to the dearth and famine in Scotland in the year 1783, in consequence of the late harvest and loss of the potato crop (PP 1846 XXXVII).

Privy Council, Committee on Education, *Minutes*, 1843. London: H.M.S.O., 1844.

Scottish Development Department, *Lists of buildings of Architectural or Historic Interest, Ross and Cromarty*, 1965-8.

Stills licensed & revenue collected 1813-18 (PP 1819 XV).

(c) Reports etc., of Commissions and Commissioners

Commission for inquiring into the administration and practical operation of the poor laws in Scotland, *Report* (PP 1844 XX-XXI, XXIII-XXVI).

Commission of inquiry into the condition of the crofters and cottars in the Highlands and Islands of Scotland, *Report* (PP 1884 XXXII-XXXVI).

Commissioners appointed to inquire into the state of municipal corporations in Scotland, *General report and local reports* (PP 1835 XXIX; 1836 XXIII, XXIX, XXXIII).

Commission for inquiring into the opportunities of Public Religious Worship, and means of Religious Instruction, and the Pastoral Superintendence afforded to the people of Scotland, *Third, fourth and ninth reports* (PP 1837-8 XXXIII; 1839 XXVI).

Commissioners for making roads and building bridges in the Highlands of Scotland, *Reports, etc.* (PP 1803-4 V; 1805 III; 1807 III; 1809 IV; 1810-11 IV; 1812-13 V; 1813-14 III; 1814-15 III; 1817 IX; 1821 X, XVI; 1824 IX; 1825 XV; 1826 XI; 1826-7 VII; 1828 IX; 1829 V; 1830 XV; 1830-1 IV; 1831-2 XXIII; 1833 XVII; 1834 XL; 1835 XXXVI; 1836 XXXVI; 1837 XXXIII; 1837-8 XXXV; 1839 XV; 1840 XXVIII; 1841 XII; 1842 XXV; 1843 XXIX; 1844 XXXI; 1845 XXVI; 1846 XXIII; 1847 XXXIII; 1847-8 XXXVII; 1849 XXVII).

Commissioners for the Herring Fishery, *Reports 1822-3* (PP 1824 IX; 1825 XV).

Commissioners of Inquiry into the collection and management of the revenue arising in Ireland; etc., *Fifth, sixth, eleventh, twelfth and twentieth reports* (PP 1823 VII; 1825 XIII-XIV; 1828 XIII; 1830 XIII).

(d) Reports etc., of Committees and Select Committees

Committee appointed to consider the laws, relative to the distilleries in Scotland, *Report, 12th July, 1799* (PP 1803 XI).

Committee appointed to enquire into the state of the British fisheries and into the most effectual means for their improvement and extension, *First, second and third reports, 1785; First, second, third and fourth reports, 1786* (PP 1803 X).

Committee appointed to examine the matters contained in several papers, which were presented to the House upon the 21st of February last, relative to the distilleries in Scotland etc., *Report, 11th June, 1798* (PP 1803 XI).

Committee on illicit practices used in defrauding the revenue, *Second report, 1st March, 1784* (PP 1803 XI).

Committee on petitions from the Royal Burghs, *Report* (PP 1821 VIII).

Committee on petition of the Royal Burghs of Scotland, respecting the providing of jails, *Report* (PP 1818 VI).

Committee on the survey of the coasts etc. of Scotland, *Second and fourth reports* (PP 1802-3 IV).

Committee to whom the several petitions from the Royal Burghs of Scotland, together with the several accounts and papers relating to the internal government of the said Royal Burghs were referred, *Report, 1793* (PP 1819 VI).

Select Committee appointed to consider the past and present state of the law of Church Patronage in Scotland, and to inquire how far that system is in accordance with the constitution and principles of the Church of Scotland, and conducive to its usefulness and prosperity, *Report* (PP 1834 V).

Select Committee appointed to inquire into the state of agriculture, *Third report* (PP 1836 VIII).

Select Committee appointed to inquire into the state of education in Scotland, *Answers made by schoolmasters in Scotland to queries circulated in 1838* (PP 1841 XIX).

Select Committee appointed to inquire into the state of education in Scotland, *Report, 1838* (PP 1837-38 VII).

Select Committee appointed to investigate the several acts, Public and Private, regulating the statute labour in Scotland, and the manner in which the conversion is exacted or levied and applied in the several counties respectively, *Report* (PP 1836 XVIII).

Select Committee on emigration, Scotland, *First and second reports* (PP 1841 VI).

Select Committee on petitions complaining of the additional duty on malt in Scotland, *Report* (PP 1821 VIII).

Select Committee on sale of corn, *Report* (PP 1834 VII).

Select Committee on Scotch entails, *Report and second report* (PP 1828 VII).

Select Committee on the Poor Laws, *Third report* (PP 1818 V).

Select Committee to inquire into the education of the poor, *Digest of parochial returns* (PP 1819 IX).

Select Committee to whom the several petitions from the Royal Burghs of Scotland were referred, *Report* (PP 1819 VI).

(e) Reports etc., miscellaneous

Board of Supervision for the relief of the poor in Scotland, *First, second, third and fourth annual reports* (PP 1847 XXVIII; 1847-48 XXXIII; 1849 XXV; 1850 XXVII).

Cameron, James, 'Report on the sanitary condition and general economy of the town of Tain and the district of Easter Ross, made to the Poor Law Commissioners', in *Local reports on the sanitary condition of the labouring population of Scotland, in consequence of an inquiry directed to be made by the Poor Law Commissioners*, pp. 311-334 (PP H.L. 1842 XXVIII).

Church of Scotland, General Assembly, Committee on the management of the poor in Scotland, *Report* (PP 1839 XX).

Church of Scotland, General Assembly, Committee on the mode of striking the fiars of the date 1830 and 1831, *Report* (PP 1834 XLIX).

Highland and Agricultural Society of Scotland, *Report . . . to the Board of Trade on the agricultural statistics of Scotland for the year 1854* (PP 1854-5 XLVII).

Report respecting the Scotch distillery duties (PP 1797-8 XXI).

Report upon the boundaries of the several cities, burghs and towns in Scotland in respect to the election of members to serve in parliament (PP 1831-2 XLII).

Telford, Thomas, *A survey and report of the coasts and central Highlands of Scotland* (PP 1802-3 III).

(f) Returns to questionnaires etc.

An account showing the state of the establishment for parochial education in Scotland (PP 1826 XVIII).

Education enquiry, Scotland. *Abstract of the answers and returns 1834* (PP 1837-8 VII).

Parochial schoolmasters (Scotland). Return to an address of the . . . House of Commons (PP 1854 LIX).

Proprietors of lands (Scotland). Return to an address of the . . . House of Commons . . . 1855 (PP 1854-5 XLVII).

A return of the rents of all turnpike gates in each county in Scotland for the last three years preceding Whitsunday 1835 (PP 1836 XLVII).

5 Books and articles

An account of the present state of religion throughout the Highlands of Scotland. Edinburgh, 1827.

Act of the Justices of Peace & Commissioners of Supply of the County of Ross. Met at Dingwall, on the 22nd May one thousand seven hundred and ninety three, . . . respecting roads, bridges & ferries. Edinburgh, 1793.

Adam, Sir Charles Elphinstone. *View of the political state of Scotland in the last century.* Edinburgh: Douglas, 1887.

Adam, John. *Unto the Right Honourable the Lords of Council and Session, the Petition of John Adams, His Majesty's Master Mason for Scotland.* [Edinburgh?, 1758] Signet Library Session Paper, 35, 33.

Adam, Margaret I. 'Eighteenth century Highland landlords and the poverty problem'. *Scottish Historical Review*, 19 (1921-2), pp. 1-20.

Adam, Robert James. *Papers on Sutherland estate management 1802-16.* Scottish History Society Publications, 4th series, 8-9. Edinburgh: Scottish History Society, 1972.

Adams, Ian H. *Directory of former Scottish commonties.* Scottish Record Society Publications, New series, 2. Edinburgh: Scottish Record Society, 1971.

'Agricultural Intelligence Scotland. Ross-shire quarterly reports'. *Farmers' Magazine*, 1 (1800)-26 (1825).

Anderson, George and Anderson, Peter. *Guide to the Highlands and Islands of Scotland.* London: Murray, 1834.

—— 2nd ed. Edinburgh: Tait, 1842.

—— 3rd ed. Edinburgh: A. & C. Black, 1850.

Anderson, John. 'Essay on the present state of the Highlands and Islands of Scotland'. *Prize essays and Transactions of the Highland Society of Scotland*, 8 (1831), pp. 16-62.

—— *Prize essay on the state of society and knowledge in the Highlands of Scotland, particularly in the northern counties.* Edinburgh: William Tait, 1827.

Anderson, Rev. John. *Calendar of the Laing Charters.* Edinburgh: Thin, 1899.

Anderson, Mark Louden. *A history of Scottish forestry.* Edinburgh: Nelson, 1967.

Annand, A. McK. 'Major General Lord Macleod . . . 73rd Macleod's Highlanders'. *Journal of the Society for Army Historical Research*, 37 (1959), pp. 21-7.

Anson, Peter Frederick. *Fishing boats and fisher folk on the east coast of Scotland.* London: J. M. Dent & Sons, 1930.

Bain, Robert. *History of the Ancient Province of Ross, the County Palatine of Scotland. From the earliest to the present time.* Dingwall: Pefferside Press, 1899.

Barnard, Alfred. *The whisky distilleries of the United Kingdom.* Newton Abbot: David & Charles Reprints, 1969.

Barron, James. *The northern Highlands in the nineteenth century: newspaper index and annals.* 3 vols.; Inverness: Carruthers, 1903-13.

Bateman, John. *The great landowners of Great Britain and Ireland.* London: Harrison & Sons, 1878.

Blackie, John Stuart. *The Scottish Highlanders and the land laws.* London: Chapman and Hall, 1885.

Board of Agriculture. *Agricultural state of the kingdom in February, March and April, 1816; being the substance of the replies to a circular letter.* London: Sherwood, Neely & Jones, 1816.

Bolton, Arthur. *The architecture of Robert and James Adam (1758-1794).* 2 vols.; London: *Country Life*, 1922.

Bond, Elizabeth. *Letters of a village governess, descriptive of rural scenery and manners, with anecdotes of Highland children etc.* 2 vols.; London, 1814.

Botfield, Beriah. *Journal of a tour through the Highlands of Scotland during the summer of MDCCCXXIX.* Norton Hall, 1830.

Boutcher, William. *A treatise on forest trees.* Edinburgh: 1775.

Bowley, A. L. 'Agricultural wages in Scotland'. *Journal of the Royal Statistical Society*, 62 (1899), pp. 140-51.

Brown, John. *The testimony of experience of the utility and necessity of Sabbath schools.* Edinburgh, 1826.

Brown, Peter Hume. *Early travellers in Scotland.* Edinburgh: David Douglas, 1891.

Brown, W. L. Wallace. 'Alness in the eighteenth century'. *Transactions of the Inverness Scientific Society and Field Club*, 6 (1899-1906), pp. 18-25.

Bulloch, John Malcolm. *The Families of Gordon of Invergordon, Newhall, also Ardoch, Ross-shire, and Carroll, Sutherland.* [Dingwall]: Ross-shire Printing & Publishing Co., 1906.

[Burt, Edward]. *Letters from a gentleman in the North of Scotland to his friend in London, containing the description of a capital town in that northern country . . . likewise an account of the Highlands, with the customs and manners of the Highlanders.* 2 vols., 2nd ed., London: Pottinger, 1759. (Reprinted Edinburgh: John Donald, 1974).

Campbell, John. *A full particular description of the Highlands of Scotland . . .* London, 1752.

Campbell, Hugh Fraser. *Highland reconstruction.* Glasgow: Maclaren, 1920.

Campbell, Roy Hutcheson. *Scotland since 1707.* Oxford: Blackwell, 1965.

Carruthers, Robert. *The Highland notebook; or, sketches and anecdotes.* Edinburgh: Black, 1843.

Central Board for the Relief of Destitution in the Highlands and Islands of Scotland, Edinburgh Section. *Third report.* Edinburgh, Blackwood, 1848.

Chambers, Robert. *The picture of Scotland.* Edinburgh: Tait, 1827.

Church of Scotland. *A collection of all the papers published in relation to the scheme for augmenting the stipends of the established clergy of Scotland.* Edinburgh, 1751.

Church of Scotland, General Assembly. *Acts of the General Assembly 1638-1842.* Edinburgh: Edinburgh Printing & Publishing Co., 1843.

Church of Scotland, General Assembly, Committee on Education. *Educational statistics of the Highlands & Islands of Scotland.* Edinburgh: J. & D. Collie, 1833.

Clericus. 'On farm houses in Ross-shire'. *Farmers' Magazine,* 7 (1806), p. 217.

Clew, Kenneth R. *The Dingwall canal.* [Tadworth: The author, 1975].

Clough, Monica, 'Making the most of one's resources: Lord Tarbat's development of Cromarty Firth', *Country Life,* 162 (1977), pp. 856-8.

Comparative aspects of Scottish and Irish economic and social history 1600-1900, edited by L. M. Cullen and T. C. Smout. Edinburgh: John Donald, 1977.

Convention of the Royal Burghs of Scotland. *Records of the Convention of the Royal Burghs of Scotland.* 7 vols.; Edinburgh: W. Paterson, 1870-1918.

Cooke, George Alexander. *A topographical description of the northern division of Scotland.* London: C. Cook [1810?].

Cordiner, Charles. *Antiquities and scenery of the North of Scotland.* London, 1780.

Cregeen, Eric Radcliffe. *Argyll Estate Instructions, Mull, Morvern, Tiree, 1771-1805.* Scottish History Society Publications, 4th Series, vol. 1. Edinburgh: Scottish History Society, 1964.

—— 'The tacksmen and their successors'. *Scottish Studies,* 13 (1969), pp. 93-144.

Cromartie, Earl of. *A Highland history.* Berkhamsted: Gavin Press, 1979.

Cruden, Stewart. *The Scottish Castle.* Edinburgh: Nelson, 1960.

Cruickshank, James B. 'The Black Isle, Ross-shire'. *Scottish Geographical Magazine,* 77 (1961), pp. 3-14.

Curle, Cecil L. 'The chronology of the early Christian monuments of Scotland'. *Proceedings of the Society of Antiquaries of Scotland,* LXXIV (1939-40), pp. 60-115.

Darragh, James. 'The Catholic population of Scotland since the year 1680'. *Innes Review,* 4 (1953), pp. 49-59.

Dawson, James Hooper, *An abridged statistical account of Scotland.* Edinburgh: Lizars, 1853.

Day, John Percival. *Public administration in the Highlands and Islands of Scotland.* London: London University Press, 1918.

Dean, Irene F. M. *Scottish spinning schools.* London: London University Press, 1930.

Dempster, George. *A discourse, containing the proceedings of the Society for extending Fisheries and improving the sea coasts of Great Britain, and thoughts on the present emigration from the Highlands.* London: Wilkie & Debrett, 1789.

Devine, T. M. 'Sources of capital for the Glasgow tobacco trade, ca. 1740-1780'. *Business History,* 16 (1974), pp. 115-29.

—— 'The rise and fall of illicit whisky making in northern Scotland, 1780-1840'. *Scottish Historical Review*, 54 (1975), pp. 155-77.

Dick, William. 'Report on the improvements of waste land on the farm of Parkton in the parish of Killearnan . . . belonging to Col. H. D. Baillie of Redcastle, M.P.' *Transactions of the Highland and Agricultural Society of Scotland*, New series, 1845-7, pp. 18-9.

Dickinson, William Croft. *Scotland from the earliest times to 1603*. London: Nelson, 1961.

The dictionary of national biography. 22 vols.; London: Oxford University Press, 1967-8.

Documents connected with the question of reform in the royal burghs of Scotland. Edinburgh: Black, 1819.

Donaldson, Gordon. *Scottish Historical Documents*. Edinburgh: Scottish Academic Press, 1970.

Donaldson, James. *Modern agriculture; or the present state of husbandry in Great Britain*. 4 vols.; Edinburgh, 1795-6.

Donaldson, John Edward. *Caithness in the 18th century*. Edinburgh: Moray Press, 1938.

Donnachie, Ian. *A history of the brewing industry in Scotland*. Edinburgh: John Donald, 1979.

Dunlop, Jean. 'The British Fisheries Society: 1787 questionnaire'. *Northern Scotland*, 2 (1974-7), pp. 37-55.

—— *The British Fisheries Society, 1786-1893*. Edinburgh: John Donald, 1978.

Duns, John. 'Notes on Easter Ross'. *Proceedings of the Society of Antiquaries of Scotland*, 21 (1887), pp. 165-9.

Durie, Alastair J. 'Linen spinning in the north of Scotland'. *Northern Scotland*, 2 (1974-7), pp. 13-36.

—— *The Scottish linen industry in the eighteenth century*. Edinburgh: John Donald, 1979.

Easson, David Edward. *Medieval Religious Houses, Scotland*. London: Longmans, Green & Co., 1957.

Edinburgh, Society for the Support of Gaelic Schools. *Fourteenth-Seventeenth Annual Reports*. Edinburgh, 1825-8.

Emery, F. V. 'A geographical description of Scotland prior to the Statistical Accounts'. *Scottish Studies*, 3 (1959), pp. 1-16.

'Essays on the improvement of the Highlands'. *Farmers Magazine*, 7 (1806), p. 234.

Ewing, William. *Annals of the Free Church of Scotland, 1843-1900*. 2 vols.; Edinburgh: T. & T. Clark, 1914.

'Excursion to Alness and Strathrory'. *Transactions of the Inverness Scientific Society and Field Club*, 2 (1880-83), pp. 317-23.

'Excursion to the Black Isle'. *Transactions of the Inverness Scientific Society and Field Club*, 2 (1880-83), pp. 236-43.

'Excursion to the Black Isle'. *Transactions of the Inverness Scientific Society and Field Club*, 4 (1889-95), pp. 268-74.

'Extract of a letter from a Gentleman on a tour through the North of Scotland, dated Ross-shire, July 24'. *Farmers Magazine*, 7 (1806), pp. 387-8.

F. N. R. 'McCullochs of Plaids, Kindeace & Glastullich'. *Scottish Antiquary*, 5

(1891), pp. 58-66.

Fairhurst, Horace. 'Scottish clachans'. *Scottish Geographical Magazine*, 76 (1960), pp. 67-76.

Ferguson, William. 'Dingwall burgh politics and the parliamentary franchise in the 18th century'. *Scottish Historical Review*, 38 (1959), pp. 89-108.

—— 'The Urquharts of Cromarty'. *Scottish Genealogist*, 6 (1959), pt. 2, pp. 16-18; pt. 3, pp. 1-14.

Fergusson, James. '"Making Interest" in Scottish County elections'. *Scottish Historical Review*, 26 (1947), pp. 119-33.

Forbes, Duncan. *Some Kindeace letters*. Dingwall: Ross, 1896.

—— 'Report of improvement of waste ground'. *Transactions of the Highland and Agricultural Society of Scotland*, New series, 1853-5, pp. 99-110.

Forbes, F. and Anderson, W. J. 'Clergy lists of the Highland district, 1732-1828'. *Innes Review*, 17 (1966), pp. 129-84.

Forbes, Robert. *Journals of the Episcopal Visitation of the Right Rev. Robert Forbes, M.A. of the dioceses of Ross and Caithness . . . with a history of the episcopal church in the diocese of Ross . . . and a memoir of Bishop R. Forbes. Edited and compiled by the Rev. J. B. Craven.* London: Skeffington & Son, 1886.

Forman, Sheila. *Scottish country houses and castles*. Glasgow: Collins, 1971.

Forsyth, Robert. *The beauties of Scotland*. 5 vols.; Edinburgh: Constable, 1805-8.

Foster, Joseph. *Members of Parliament, Scotland*. 2nd ed.; London: Hazell, Watson & Viney, 1882.

Fraser, Hugh C. *The land statistics of the Shires of Inverness, Ross and Cromarty in the year 1871*. Inverness: *Advertiser* Office, 1872.

Fraser, Sir William. *The Earls of Cromartie: their kindred, country and correspondence*. 2 vols.; Edinburgh, 1876.

Gailey, R. Alan. 'Agrarian improvement and the development of enclosure in the South West Highlands of Scotland'. *Scottish Historical Review*, 42 (1963), pp. 103-25.

—— 'The evolution of Highland rural settlement'. *Scottish Studies*, 6 (1962), pp. 155-77.

—— 'The peasant houses of the Southwest Highlands of Scotland: Distribution, parallels and evolution'. *Gwerin*, 3 (1962), pp. 227-242.

Gardiner, Leslie. *Stage coach to John o' Groats*. London: Hollis & Carter, 1961.

Gaskell, Philip. *Morvern transformed*. Cambridge: Cambridge University Press, 1968.

Geddes, Arthur. 'Scotland's Statistical Accounts of Parish, County & Nation 1790-1825 and 1835-1845'. *Scottish Studies*, 3 (1959), pp. 17-29.

—— and Forbes, John. 'Rural communities of Ferm-Toun and Baile in the Lowlands and Highlands of Aberdeenshire, 1696'. *Aberdeen University Review*, 32 (1948), pp. 98-104.

Genealogy of the families of Douglas of Mulderg and Robertson of Kindeace with their descendants. Dingwall, 1895.

Goldie, Frederick. *A short history of the Episcopal church in Scotland*. London: S.P.C.K., 1951.

Graham, Henry Grey. *The social life of Scotland in the 18th century*. 2 vols.; London, 1899.

Grant, Isabel Frances. 'The Highland openfield system'. *Geographical Teacher*, 13

(1925-6), pp. 480-88.

— *The Macleods. The history of a clan 1200-1956.* London: Faber & Faber, 1959.

— 'The social effects of the agricultural reforms and enclosure movement in Aberdeenshire'. *Economic History*, 1 (1926-9), pp. 89-116.

Gray, Malcolm. 'The abolition of runrig in the Highlands of Scotland'. *Economic History Review*, New series, 5 (1952), pp. 46-57.

— 'Economic welfare and money income in the Highlands 1750-1850'. *Scottish Journal of Political Economy*, 2 (1955), pp. 47-63.

— *The fishing industries of Scotland 1790-1914: a study in regional adaptation.* Aberdeen University Studies, 155. Oxford: Oxford University Press for Aberdeen University Press, 1978.

— *The Highland Economy 1750-1850.* Edinburgh: Oliver & Boyd, 1957.

— 'The Highland potato famine of the late 1840s'. *Economic History Review*, 2nd series, 7 (1954-5), pp. 357-68.

— 'The kelp industry in the Highlands and Islands'. *Economic History Review*, 2nd series, 4 (1951-2), pp. 197-210.

— 'Organisation and growth in the East coast Herring Fishing 1800-1885'. In Payne, Peter Lester (ed.), *Studies in Scottish business history.* London: Cass, 1967, pp. 187-216.

— '[Review article]'. *Scottish Historical Review*, 53 (1974), p. 95.

— 'Settlement in the Highlands, 1750-1950: the documentary and the written record'. *Scottish Studies*, 6 (1962), pp. 145-54.

Grigor, Robert. 'Report on publications of Pinus Sylvestris forming part of the Forest of Balnagown, the property of Sir Charles Ross, Bart'. *Transactions of the Highland and Agricultural Society of Scotland*, New series, 1845-7, pp. 120-34.

Grimble, Ian. *The trial of Patrick Sellar.* London: Routledge & Kegan Paul, 1962.

Haldane, Archibald Richard Burdon. *The drove roads of Scotland.* Edinburgh: Nelson, 1952.

— *New ways through the glens.* Edinburgh: Nelson, 1962.

— *Three centuries of Scottish posts.* Edinburgh: Edinburgh University Press, 1971.

Haldane, J. *et. al.*, *Journal of a tour through the Northern counties of Scotland . . . in autumn, 1797.* 2nd ed.; Edinburgh, 1798.

Hall, James. *Travels in Scotland.* 2 vols.; London: Johnson, 1807.

Hamilton, Henry. 'Economic growth in Scotland 1720-70'. *Scottish Journal of Political Economy*, 6 (1959), pp. 85-98.

— *An Economic History of Scotland in the eighteenth century.* Oxford: Clarendon Press, 1963.

— *The industrial revolution in Scotland.* Oxford: Clarendon Press, 1932.

Handley, James Edmund. *The agricultural revolution in Scotland.* Glasgow: Burns, 1963.

— *Scottish farming in the eighteenth century.* London: Faber & Faber, 1953.

Hay, George. *The architecture of Scottish Post-Reformation Churches 1560-1843.* Oxford: Clarendon Press, 1957.

Heron, Robert. *Scotland described.* Edinburgh, 1797. 3rd ed.; Edinburgh, 1806.

Higgins, J. P. P. and Pollard, Sidney. *Aspects of capital investment in Great Britain, 1750-1850.* London: Methuen, 1971.

Highlander. *The present conduct of the chieftains and proprietors of lands in the*

Highlands of Scotland, towards their clans and people, considered impartially. N.p., 1773.
The Highlands of Scotland in 1750. Edinburgh: Blackwood, 1898.
Hildesley, Alfred. *The press gang.* London, 1925.
Hodd, Adrian N. L. 'Runrig on the eve of the agricultural revolution in Scotland'. *Scottish Geographical Magazine,* 90 (1974), pp. 130-133.
Home, John. *The county of Caithness.* Wick: W. Rae, 1907.
Houston, George. 'Agricultural statistics in Scotland before 1866'. *Agricultural History Review,* 9 (1961), pp. 93-7.
—— 'Farm labour in Scotland, 1800-50'. *Bulletin of the Society for the Study of Labour History,* 11 (1965), pp. 10-13.
—— 'Labour relations in Scottish agriculture before 1870'. *Agricultural History Review,* 6 (1958), pp. 27-41.
Houston, J. M. 'Village planning in Scotland 1745-1845'. *The Advancement of Science,* 5 (1948), pp. 129-32.
Hudson, James William. *History of adult education.* London: Longman, 1851.
Hunter, Henry. *A brief history of the Society in Scotland for Propagating Christian Knowledge in the Highlands and Islands and of the Correspondent Board in London.* London, 1795.
Hunter, James. 'The emergence of the crofting community 1798-1843: the religious contribution'. *Scottish Studies,* 18 (1974), pp. 95-116.
—— *The making of the crofting community.* Edinburgh: John Donald, 1976.
Inverness, Society for the education of the poor in the Highlands. *Moral statistics.* Inverness, 1826.
Jacobs, Jane. *The economy of cities.* London: Jonathan Cape, 1970.
Johnston, Thomas. *The history of the working classes in Scotland.* Glasgow: Forward Publishing Co., 1923.
Johnston, W. and A. K. *Gazetteer of Scotland.* Edinburgh: Johnston, 1937.
Kay, George. 'The landscape of improvement. A case study of agricultural change in North East Scotland'. *Scottish Geographical Magazine,* 78 (1962), pp. 100-11.
Kellie, John S. *A history of the Scottish Highlands, Highland clans and Highland regiments.* 2 vols.; Edinburgh: Fullarton, 1879.
Kennedy, John. *The days of the fathers in Ross-shire.* New ed.; Inverness: G. Young, 1895.
Kirby, D. P. 'Bede and the Pictish Church'. *Innes Review,* XXIV (1973), pp. 6-25.
Knox, John. *Observations on the northern fisheries.* London: J. Walter, 1786.
—— *A tour through the Highlands of Scotland and the Hebride Isles in 1786.* London: J. Walter, 1787.
—— *A view of the British Empire, more especially Scotland.* London, 1784. 3rd ed., 2 vols.; London, 1785.
Kyd, James Gray. *Scottish population statistics.* Scottish History Society Publications, 3rd series, 43. Edinburgh: Scottish History Society, 1952.
Lang, Thomas Bamford. *An historical summary of the Post Office in Scotland, compiled from authentic records.* Edinburgh, 1856.
Laslett, Peter. *The world we have lost.* London: Methuen, 1965.
Lattimore, Owen. *Studies in Frontier History. Collected papers 1928-1958.* London: Oxford University Press, 1962.

Lebon, J. H. G. 'The beginnings of the agrarian and industrial revolution in Ayrshire'. In Stamp, Laurence Dudley and Wooldridge, S. W. (eds.). *London essays in geography*. London: Longmans Green & Co., 1951.

Lettice, John. *Letters on a tour through various parts of Scotland in the year 1792.* London: Cadell, 1794.

Lindsay, Ian G. and Cosh, Mary. *Inveraray and the Dukes of Argyll.* Edinburgh: Edinburgh University Press, 1973.

'List of members'. *Prize essays and transactions of the Highland Society of Scotland,* 1 (2nd ed.; 1812), pp. LXX-LXXXVIII.

'List of members'. *Transactions of the Highland and Agricultural Society of Scotland,* New series, 1849-51, pp. LXV-CXXI.

A list of persons concerned in the rebellion transmitted to the Commissioners of Excise by the several supervisors in Scotland in obedience to a general letter of the 7th May, 1746, and a supplementary list with evidence to prove the same. Scottish History Society Publications, 8. Edinburgh: Constable, 1890.

Loch, David. *Curious and entertaining letters concerning the trade and manufactures of Scotland.* 3rd ed.; Edinburgh, 1754.

—— *Essays on the trade, commerce, manufactures and fisheries of Scotland.* Edinburgh, 1775.

—— *A tour through most of the trading towns and villages of Scotland.* Edinburgh, 1778.

Lochhead, Marion Cleland. *Episcopal Scotland in the nineteenth century.* London: Murray, 1966.

Logue, Kenneth J. *Popular disturbances in Scotland, 1780-1815.* Edinburgh: John Donald, 1979.

McCulloch, Lewis. *Observations on the herring fisheries upon the North & East coasts of Scotland.* London: W. Richardson, 1788.

Macdonald, Donald & Polson, A. *The book of Ross; and Sutherland and Caithness by A. Polson. Descriptive, historical and antiquarian notes.* Dingwall, 1931.

Macdonald, Donald Farquhar. *Scotland's shifting population 1770-1850.* Glasgow: Jackson, 1937.

Macdonald, James. 'On the agriculture of the counties of Ross and Cromarty'. *Transactions of the Highland and Agricultural Society of Scotland,* 4th series, 9 (1877), pp. 67-209.

Macdonald, Jessie and Gordon, Anne. *Down to the sea.* Aberdeen, 1971.

Macdonald, Roderick. 'Catholics in the Highlands in the 1760s'. *Innes Review,* 16 (1965), pp. 218-20.

—— 'The Highland district in 1764'. *Innes Review,* 15 (1964), pp. 140-50.

Macdowall, Charles George. *The Chanonry of Ross.* Fortrose, 1963.

Macfarlane, Walter. *Geographical Collections relating to Scotland.* Scottish History Society Publications, 51-3. 3 vols.; Edinburgh: Scottish History Society, 1906-8.

Macgill, William. *Old Ross-shire and Scotland as seen in the Tain and Balnagown documents.* 2 vols.; Inverness: Northern Counties Newspaper Company, 1909.

Macinnes, John. *The Evangelical Movements in the Highlands of Scotland, 1688-1800.* Aberdeen: Aberdeen University Press, 1951.

[Macintosh, William]. *An essay on ways and means for inclosing, fallowing, planting . . . Scotland: and that in sixteen years at farthest.* Edinburgh: Freebairn,

1729.

Maciver, Evander. *Memoirs of a Highland gentleman.* Edinburgh: Constable, 1905.

Mackay, William. 'Education in the Highlands in the olden times'. *Celtic Monthly,* 14 (1905-6), pp. 131-4, 155-6, 173-5, 182-5.

Mackelvie, William. *Annals of the United Presbyterian Church.* Edinburgh: Oliphant & Co., 1873.

[Mackenzie, Alexander]. *View of the political state of Scotland at the late general election.* Edinburgh: Ainslie, 1790.

Mackenzie, Alexander, F.S.A.Scot. *The Highland clearances.* Inverness: A. & W. Mackenzie, 1883.

—— *History of the Mackenzies.* Inverness: Mackenzie, 1894.

—— *History of the Munros of Fowlis.* Edinburgh: Mackenzie, 1898.

—— 'The late Duncan Davidson of Tulloch'. *Celtic Magazine,* 6 (1881), pp. 486-7.

—— 'Sir Kenneth Mackenzie of Gairloch, Bart.' *Celtic Magazine,* 6 (1881), pp. 26-34.

—— and Macbain, Alexander. *History of the Mathesons.* Stirling: Mackay, 1900.

Mackenzie, Donald A. 'Cromarty dialects and folk lore'. *Transactions of the Rymour Club,* 3 (1928), pp. 75-82.

Mackenzie, Sir Francis. *Hints for the use of Highland tenants and cottagers.* Inverness, 1838.

Mackenzie, Sir George Steuart. *A general view of the agriculture of the counties of Ross and Cromarty.* London, 1810.

—— 'Letter . . . concerning the price of labour'. *Farmers Magazine,* 5 (1804), p. 43.

—— *Letter to the proprietors of land in Ross-shire.* Inverness, 1803.

—— 'On the distilleries of the Lowlands and Highlands'. *Farmers Magazine,* 8 (1807), pp. 375-9.

Mackenzie, Sir Kenneth S. 'Changes in the ownership of land in Ross-shire, 1756-1853'. *Transactions of the Gaelic Society of Inverness,* 12 (1885-6), pp. 293-324.

—— 'Military roads in the Highlands'. *Transactions of the Inverness Scientific Society and Field Club,* 5 (1895-7), pp. 364-84.

Mackenzie, Osgood Hanbury. *A hundred years in the Highlands.* London: Arnold, 1921.

Mackenzie, William. 'Report of improvements at Ardross'. *Transactions of the Highland and Agricultural Society of Scotland,* New series, 1857-9, pp. 137-38.

Mackenzie, William Cook. *The Highlands in 1747.* N.p., 1922?

Mackenzie, William Mackay. *Cromarty: its old chapels and parish church.* Edinburgh: Scottish Ecclesiological Society, 1905.

—— *Hugh Miller.* London: Hodder & Stoughton, 1905.

—— 'The old sheriffdom of Cromarty. Repr. from the Northern Chronicle, Inverness'. *Transactions of the Gaelic Society of Inverness,* 30 (1924), pp. 329-59.

—— '[Review article]'. *Scottish Historical Review,* 26 (1947), pp. 168-78.

—— 'The royal burgh of Cromarty and the breaking of the burgh'. *Transactions of the Gaelic Society of Inverness,* 31 (1927), pp. 289-325.

Mackinnon, K. M. 'The school in Gaelic Scotland'. *Transactions of the Gaelic Society of Inverness,* 47 (1971-2), pp. 374-91.

Mackintosh, Charles Fraser. *Antiquarian notes: A series of papers regarding families and places in the Highlands.* Inverness, 1865.

—— *Letters of two centuries.* Inverness: Mackenzie, 1890.

Maclean, Donald. 'Highland libraries in the eighteenth century'. *Transactions of the Gaelic Society of Inverness*, 31 (1922-4), pp. 69-79.

—— 'The Presbytery of Ross and Sutherland — 1693-1700'. *Records of the Scottish Church History Society*, 5 (1935), pp. 251-61.

Maclean, Roderick. 'Notes on the parish of Alness'. *Transactions of the Gaelic Society of Inverness*, 14 (1887-8), pp. 217-32.

—— 'Notes on the parish of Kiltearn'. *Transactions of the Gaelic Society of Inverness*, 15 (1888-9), pp. 302-10.

—— 'The parish of Rosskeen'. *Transactions of the Gaelic Society of Inverness*, 12 (1885-6), pp. 324-39.

Macleod, Henry Dunning. *The results of the operation of the poor house system in Easter Ross*. Inverness, 1851.

Macleod, M. L., *et al. 3 centuries of falsehood exposed . . .* Golspie, 1970.

Macmillan, Mona. *Sir Henry Barkly, Mediator and moderator*. Cape Town, 1970.

Macnaughton, Colin. *Church life in Ross and Sutherland from the Revolution, 1688, to the present time. Compiled chiefly from the Tain Presbytery records*. Inverness: Northern Counties Newspaper Co., 1915.

Macpherson, Alexander. *Glimpses of church and social life in the Highlands in the olden times*. Edinburgh: Blackwood, 1893.

Macrae, Norman. *The Romance of a Royal Burgh. Dingwall's story of a thousand years*. Dingwall: North Star, 1923.

Malcolm, Charles Alexander. *The history of the British Linen Bank*. Edinburgh, 1950.

Marcus, G. J. *A naval history of England, 2: The age of Nelson*. George Allen & Unwin, 1971.

Martin, John R. *The church chronicles of Nigg*. [N.p., 1967].

Marwick, William Hutton. *Mechanics Institutes in Scotland*. London: Sidgwick & Jackson, 1934.

Mason, John. 'Conditions in the Highlands after the '45'. *Scottish Historical Review*, 26 (1947), pp. 134-46.

—— 'Scottish Charity Schools of the eighteenth century'. *Scottish Historical Review*, 33 (1954), pp. 1-13.

Maxwell, Robert. *Select transactions of the Society of Improvers in the Knowledge of Agriculture in Scotland*. Edinburgh, 1743.

Maxwell, S. 'Highland dress and tartan in the Ross of Pitcalnie papers'. *Costume*, 10 (1976), pp. 49-52.

May, Peter. *Papers on Peter May land surveyor 1749-1793*, edited by Ian H. Adams. Scottish History Society Publications, 4th series, 15. Edinburgh: Scottish History Society, 1979.

Mechie, Stewart. *The church and Scottish social development, 1780-1870*. London: Oxford University Press, 1960.

Meldrum, Helen Myers. *Kilmuir Easter. The history of a Highland parish*. Inverness: R. Carruthers & Sons, 1935.

Mill, James. 'On the spinning of linen yarn in Ross, Caithness, etc.' *Prize essays and transactions of the Highland Society of Scotland*, 1 (2nd ed., 1811), pp. 62-79.

Miller, Hugh. *My schools and schoolmasters*. Edinburgh: Nimmo, 1869.

—— *Scenes and legends of the North of Scotland*. Edinburgh: Nimmo, 1885.

—— *Tales and Sketches.* Edinburgh: Black, 1863.

—— 'The story of a Parish school'. *The Witness,* 27th March, 1850, p. [2].

Mitchell, Joseph. *Reminiscences of my life in the Highlands (1883): A reprint with a new introduction, corrigenda and index by Ian Robertson.* 2 vols.; Newton Abbot: David & Charles Reprints, 1971.

Mitchison, Rosalind. *Agricultural Sir John.* London: Bles, 1962.

—— 'The making of the old Scottish Poor Law'. *Past and Present,* No. 63 (1974), pp. 58-93.

—— 'The movements of Scottish grain prices in the seventeenth and eighteenth centuries'. *Economic History Review,* 2nd series, 18 (1965), pp. 278-91.

Moir, Donald G. 'Statute labour roads. The first phase'. *Scottish Geographical Magazine,* 73 (1957), pp. 101-10.

Morgan, Valerie. 'Agricultural wage rates in later 18th century Scotland'. *Economic History Review,* 2nd series, 24 (1971), pp. 181-200.

Mowat, Ian R. M. 'Literacy, libraries and literature in 18th and 19th century Easter Ross'. *Library History,* 5 (1979), pp. 1-10.

'Muir of Ord market'. *Transactions of the Gaelic Society of Inverness,* 33 (1925-27), pp. 137-9.

Munro, Robert William and Munro, Jean. *Tain through the centuries.* Tain: Tain Town Council, 1966.

Neill, Patrick. *On Scottish gardens & orchards.* N.p., n.d.

The new picture of Scotland. Perth: Morison, 1807.

The New Statistical Account of Scotland by the ministers of the respective parishes, under the superintendence of a Committee of the Society for the benefit of the sons and daughters of the Clergy. 15 vols.; Edinburgh & London: W. Blackwood & Sons, 1845.

Nicholson, Ranald G. *Scotland: The later middle ages.* Edinburgh History of Scotland, 2. Edinburgh: Oliver & Boyd, 1974.

Nigg Women's Rural Institute. *The parish of Nigg.* Aberdeen, [1967].

Nightingale, John, 'The threat to Cromarty'. *Country Life,* 157 (1977), pp. 338-40.

Noble, John. *Religious life in Ross.* Edinburgh: Thin, 1909.

Observations on the manner in which the liberal offer of government to assist the county of Ross in building bridges and making roads has been received by certain individuals of that county. Inverness, 1804.

O'Dell, Andrew Charles. 'A century of coal transport — Scotland 1742-1842'. In Stamp, Laurence Dudley and Wooldridge, S.W. (eds.). *London essays in geography.* London: Longmans Green & Co., 1951.

—— 'A view of Scotland in the middle of the eighteenth century'. *Scottish Geographical Magazine,* 69 (1958), pp. 58-63.

—— and Walton, Kenneth. *The Highlands and Islands of Scotland.* London: Nelson, 1962 (1963).

Origines Parochiales Scotiae. 2 vols.; Edinburgh: Lizars, 1850-55.

P. 'Cursory remarks on the present state of agriculture and rural economy of the Highlands, and made in the latter end of May, and beginning of June, 1807'. *Farmers Magazine,* 8 (1807), pp. 500-18.

Patch, Peter, & Co. *Sayings and doings in the counties of Ross and Cromarty and district of Ferintosh.* Inverness, 1824.

Pennant, Thomas. *A tour in Scotland 1769.* 5th ed., London, 1790.

Phillipson, Nicholas Tindall & Mitchison, Rosalind (eds.). *Scotland in the age of improvement.* Edinburgh: Edinburgh University Press, 1970.

Plant, Marjorie. *'Clothes and the eighteenth century Scot'.* *Scottish Historical Review*, 27 (1948), pp. 1-24.

—— *The domestic life of Scotland in the eighteenth century.* Edinburgh: Edinburgh University Press, 1952.

'Plantations'. *Prize essays and transactions of the Highland Society of Scotland*, 6 (1824), pp. 258-60.

Playfair, James. *Geographical and statistical description of Scotland.* 2 vols; Edinburgh: Constable, 1819.

Pococke, Richard. *Tours in Scotland 1747, 1750, 1760.* Scottish History Society Publications, 1. Edinburgh: Scottish History Society, 1887.

Political observations occasioned by the state of agriculture in the north of Scotland. N.p., 1756.

Polson, Alexander. *Easter Ross.* Tain: Macpherson, 1914.

Prebble, John. *The lion in the north. A personal view of Scotland's history.* London: Secker and Warburg, 1971.

Pryde, George. *The burghs of Scotland, a critical list.* London: Oxford University Press, 1965.

——*The Scottish burghs of barony in decline 1707-1908.* Glasgow, 1949.

Ramsay, Alexander. *History of the Highland and Agricultural Society of Scotland.* Edinburgh: Blackwood, 1879.

Registers of Seisins [Ross 1781-1860]. [N.p., n.d.].

Reid, Francis Nevile. *The Earls of Ross and their descendants.* Edinburgh, 1894.

Reminiscences of a Dingwall centenarian: the late Mrs Mackenzie, Inchvanie, by a friend. Inverness, 1908.

'Report on the depressed state of the agriculture of the United Kingdom'. *Farmers Magazine*, 22 (1821), pp. 325-44.

'Review of a general survey of the counties of Ross and Cromarty'. *Farmers Magazine*, 11 (1810), pp. 217-52.

Richards, Eric. 'How tame were the Highlanders during the clearances?' *Scottish Studies*, 17 (1973), pp. 35-50.

—— *The Leviathan of wealth.* London: Routledge & Kegan Paul, 1973.

—— 'Patterns of Highland Discontent'. In Quinault, T. and Stevenson, J. (eds.). *Popular Protest and Public Order: Six studies in British History 1790-1920.* London: George Allen & Unwin, 1974, pp. 75-114.

—— 'Structural change in a regional economy: Sutherland and the Industrial Revolution 1780-1830'. *Economic History Review*, 26 (1973), pp. 63-76.

Robertson, A. G. R. *The Lowland Highlanders.* Tain, 1972.

Ross, A. *Ross-shire, past and present; ecclesiastical, antiquarian and traditional notes.* Invergordon, n.d.

Ross, Alexander. 'The Munros of Culcairn'. *Celtic Magazine*, 10 (1885), pp. 495-506, 559-66.

—— 'The Munros of Milntown'. *Celtic Magazine*, 10 (1885), pp. 49-56, 103-12, 151-58, 230-7.

—— 'Old Highland roads'. *Transactions of the Gaelic Society of Inverness*, 14 (1887-8), pp. 172-93.

Ross, Alexander M. *History of the clan Ross.* Dingwall: *North Star*, 1932.

Ross, Walter. *The present state of the distillery of Scotland.* Edinburgh: Martin & McDowall, 1786.

A Ross-shire Farmer. 'Remarks on the Ross-shire resolutions concerning the Distillery Laws'. *Farmers Magazine*, 8 (1807), pp. 174-80.

—— 'On the assessment for roads in Ross-shire'. *Farmers Magazine*, 15 (1814), pp. 300-4.

A Ross-shire Heritor. 'On the assessment for roads in Ross-shire'. *Farmers Magazine*, 15 (1814), pp. 155-9.

Rostow, Walt Whitman, *Stages of economic growth.* Cambridge: Cambridge University Press, 1969.

Royal charter, list of subscribers, state of funds, etc. etc. of the Tain Academy. London, 1810.

Ryder, M. L. 'Sheep and clearance in the Scottish Highlands'. *Agricultural History Review*, 16 (1968), pp. 155-8.

Rymer, L. 'The Scottish kelp industry'. *Scottish Geographical Magazine*, 90 (1974), pp. 142-52.

Sage, Donald. *Memorabilia Domestica.* Wick: W. Rae, 1889.

Saunders, Laurence James. *Scottish democracy, 1815-1840.* Edinburgh: Oliver and Boyd, 1950.

Scotland. *A district arrangement of the 970 parishes.* N.p., n.d.

Scotland delineated, or a geographical description of every shire in Scotland. Edinburgh, 1791.

Scott, Hew. *Fasti Ecclesiae Scoticanae: the succession of ministers in the parish churches of Scotland, from the Reformation, A.D. 1560, to the present time. New edition . . . edited by William S. Crockett and Francis Grant.* 9 vols.; Edinburgh: Oliver & Boyd, 1915-61.

Scottish Record Society. *Calendar of Writs of Munro of Foulis, 1299-1823.* Scottish Record Society Publication 71. Edinburgh: Scottish Record Society, 1940.

Sinclair, Catherine. *Scotland and the Scotch.* Edinburgh: Whyte, 1840.

Sinclair, Sir John. *An account of the systems of husbandry adopted in the more improved districts of Scotland.* 2nd ed., 2 vols.; Edinburgh: J. Ballantyne & Co., 1813.

—— *General report of the agricultural state and political circumstances of Scotland.* 5 vols.; Edinburgh, 1814.

—— *General view of the agriculture of the northern counties and islands of Scotland.* London, 1795.

—— *The Statistical Account of Scotland; drawn up from the communications of the ministers of the different parishes.* 21 vols.; Edinburgh, 1791-99.

'Sketch of a tour through the northern counties of Scotland, pt. IV'. *Farmers Magazine*, 2 (1801), pp. 417-29.

Smith, Annette Macfarlane. 'The administration of the Forfeited Annexed Estates 1752-1784'. In Barrow, Geoffrey W. S. (ed.). *The Scottish tradition: Essays in honour of Ronald Gordon Cant.* Edinburgh: Scottish Academic Press, 1974, pp. 198-210.

Smout, T. C. *A history of the Scottish people 1560-1830.* London: Collins, 1970.

—— '[Review of Stein Tveite, Jord og Gjerning (Kristiansund, 1959)]'. *Scottish Historical Review*, 53 (1974), pp. 69-76.

—— 'Scottish Landowners and economic growth, 1650-1850'. *Scottish Journal of*

Political Economy, 11 (1964), pp. 218-34.

—— and Fenton, Alexander. 'Scottish agriculture before the improvers'. *Agricultural History Review*, 13 (1965), pp. 73-93.

The Society in Scotland for Propagating Christian Knowledge. *An account of the funds, expenditure and general management of the affairs of the Society.* Edinburgh, 1796.

—— *A summary account of the rise and progress of the Society in Scotland for Propagating Christian Knowledge.* Edinburgh: Society in Scotland for Propagating Christian Knowledge, 1783.

Southey, Robert. *Journal of a tour in Scotland in 1819.* London: Murray, 1929.

Spence, Elizabeth Isabella. *Letters from the north Highlands, during the summer 1816.* London: Longman, 1817.

Stewart, Alexander. *Memoirs of the late Rev. Alexander Stewart, D.D., one of the ministers of Canongate, Edinburgh. To which are subjoined a few of his sermons.* 2nd ed. Edinburgh: W. Oliphant, 1822.

Stewart, David. *Sketches of the character, manners and present state of the Highlanders of Scotland.* 2 vols.; Edinburgh, 1822. (Reprinted Edinburgh: John Donald, 1977).

Stoddart, John. *Remarks on local scenery and manners in Scotland during the years 1799 and 1800.* 2 vols.; London: Miller, 1801.

Sutherland, Alexander. *A summer ramble in the north Highlands.* Edinburgh: Hunter, 1825.

Symon, James Alexander. *Scottish farming: Past and present.* Edinburgh: Oliver & Boyd, 1959.

Tayler, Henrietta. *History of the family of Urquhart.* Aberdeen: Aberdeen University Press, 1946.

Taylor, George, and Skinner, Andrew. *Taylor & Skinner's Survey & Maps of the Roads of North Britain or Scotland.* London, 1776.

Taylor, William. *Researches into the history of Tain earlier and later.* Tain: Ross, 1882.

Teignmouth, Charles John Shore, 2nd Baron. *Sketches of the coasts and islands of Scotland.* 2 vols.; London: Parker, 1836.

Telford, Thomas. *Life of Thomas Telford, civil engineer, written by himself* [*with a folio atlas*]. 2 vols.; London, 1838.

Third, Betty M. W. 'Changing landscape and social structure in Scottish Lowlands as revealed by eighteenth century estate plans'. *Scottish Geographical Magazine*, 71 (1955), pp. 83-93.

Thom, W. 'Journal of a Tour in the North of Scotland'. *New Agricultural & Commercial Magazine*, 1 (1811), pp. 282-85.

Thomson, James. *The value and importaace of the Scotch fisheries.* London: Smith, Elder & Co., 1849.

Thomson, William Aird. *Preaching Christ crucified indispensible in a faithful minister of the gospel.* Edinburgh, 1823.

Tivy, Joy. 'Easter Ross: a residual crofting area'. *Scottish Studies*, 9 (1965), pp. 64-84.

Toynbee, Arnold Joseph. *A study of history. Abridgement of volumes I-VI* by D. C. Somervell. London: Oxford University Press, 1946.

The traveller's guide through Scotland. 3rd ed.; Edinburgh: Thomson, 1806.

Turnock, David. 'Small farmers in north Scotland: an exploration in historical geography'. *Scottish Geographical Magazine*, 91 (1975), pp. 164-81.

Ure, James. 'Of 144 acres 2 roods 23 poles on the farm of Easter and Wester Corntown, County of Cromarty'. *Prize essays and transactions of the Highland and Agricultural Society of Scotland*, 13 (1841), pp. 516-9.

Vince, S. W. E. 'The Highlands of Scotland'. In Stamp, Laurence Dudley (ed.). *The land of Britain*. London: Geographical Publications 1 (1944), pp. 423-669.

Walker, G. S. M. *The parish of Resolis*. Resolis, 1958.

Walker, John. *An economical history of the Hebrides and Highlands of Scotland*. 2 vols.; Edinburgh, 1808.

Walker, Robert. 'Of 83 acres on the farm of Fyrish, Ross-shire'. *Prize essays and transactions of the Highland and Agricultural Society of Scotland*, 13 (1841), pp. 242-3.

Warrand, Duncan. *Some Mackenzie pedigrees*. Inverness: Carruthers, 1965.

Watson, William John. *Place names of Ross and Cromarty*. Inverness: Northern Counties Printing and Publishing Co., 1904.

Webb, R. R. 'Literacy among the working classes in nineteenth century Scotland'. *Scottish Historical Review*, 33 (1954), pp. 100-14.

Wheeler, Philip Theodore. 'Landownership and the crofting system in Sutherlandshire since 1800'. *Agricultural History Review* 14 (1966), pp. 45-56.

Whyte, Ian D., 'The growth of periodic market centres in Scotland 1600-1707'. *Scottish Geographical Magazine*, 95 (1979), pp. 13-26.

Wight, Andrew. *Present state of Husbandry in Scotland. Extracted from reports made to the commissioners of the annexed estates*. 4 vols.; Edinburgh, 1778-84.

Wilkie, T. *The representation of Scotland*. Paisley: Wilkie, 1895.

Williamson's *Directory for the City of Edinburgh, Canongate, Leith and Suburbs . . .* 1773 . . . 1774 — 1794-96. Edinburgh, 1774-94.

Withrington, Donald J. 'The S.P.C.K. and Highland schools in mid-eighteenth century'. *Scottish Historical Review*, 41 (1962), pp. 89-99.

Wood, John Philip. *The antient and modern state of the Parish of Cramond*. Edinburgh: Peter Hill, 1794.

Youngson, Alexander John. *After the Forty-Five*. Edinburgh: Edinburgh University Press, 1973.

—— 'Alexander Webster and his "Account of the number of people in Scotland in the year 1755"'. *Population Studies*, 15 (1961), pp. 198-200.

Appendix I
Maps

MAP 1

THE NORTHERN HIGHLANDS

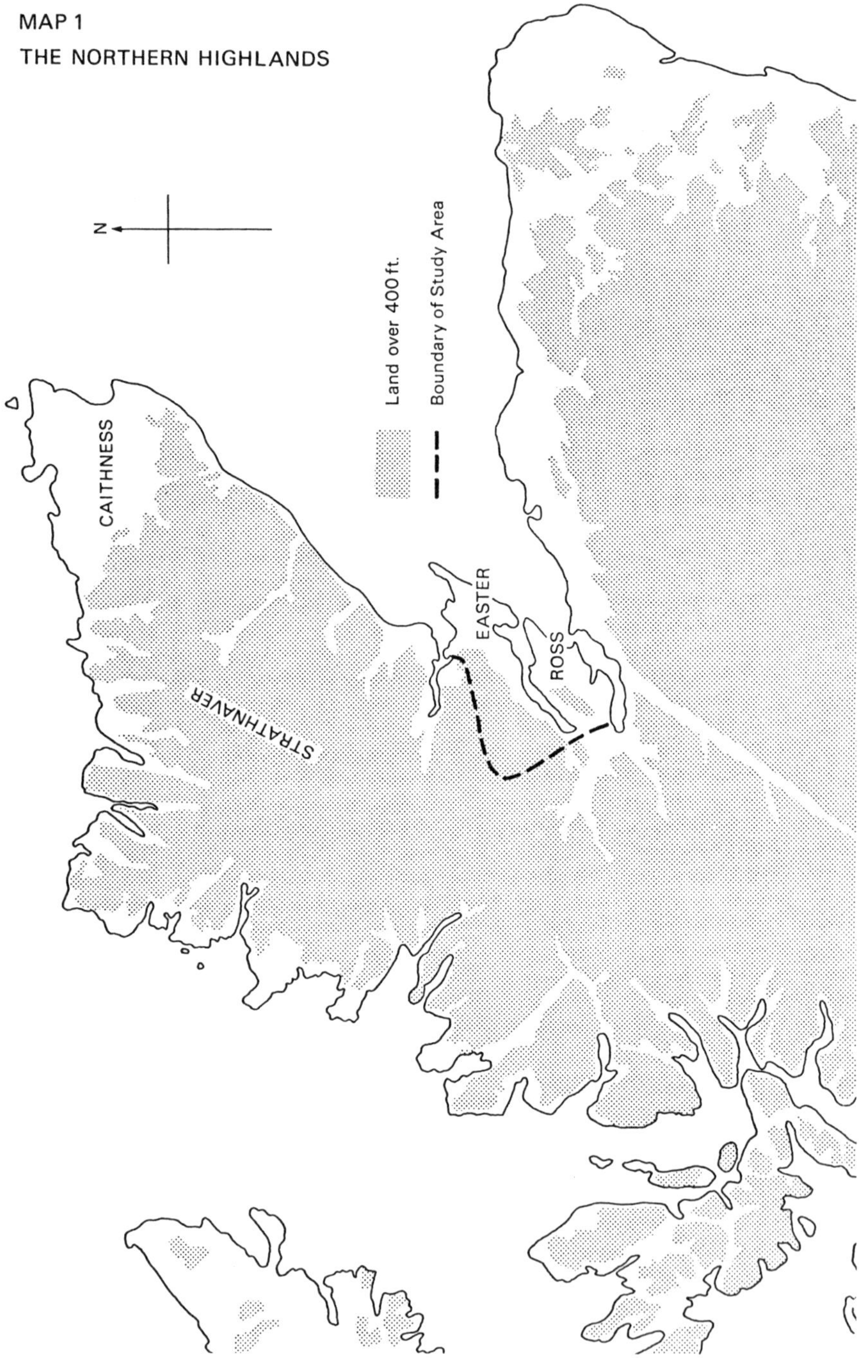

MAP 2
COMMUNICATIONS

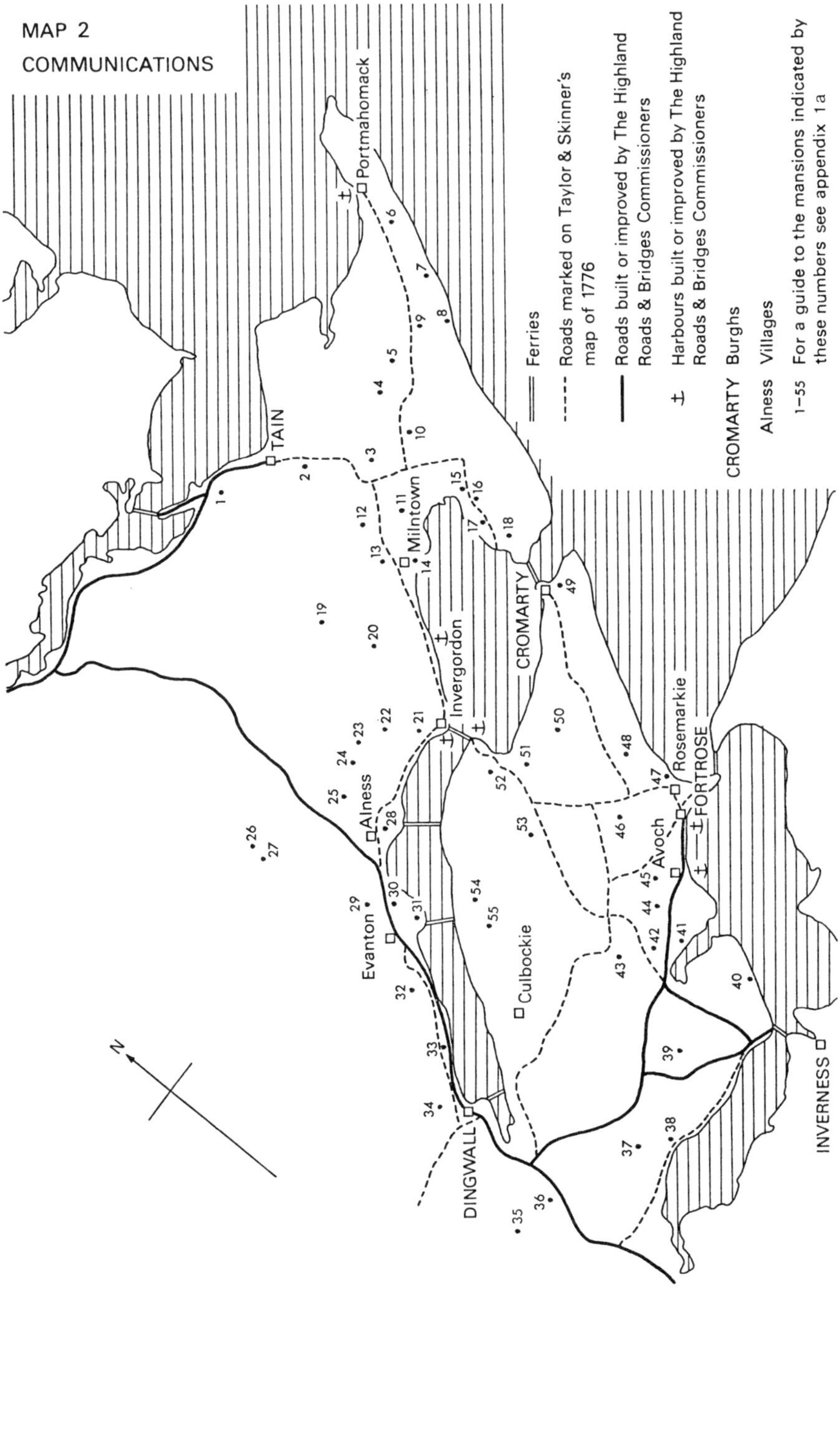

MAP 3
EASTER ROSS PARISHES

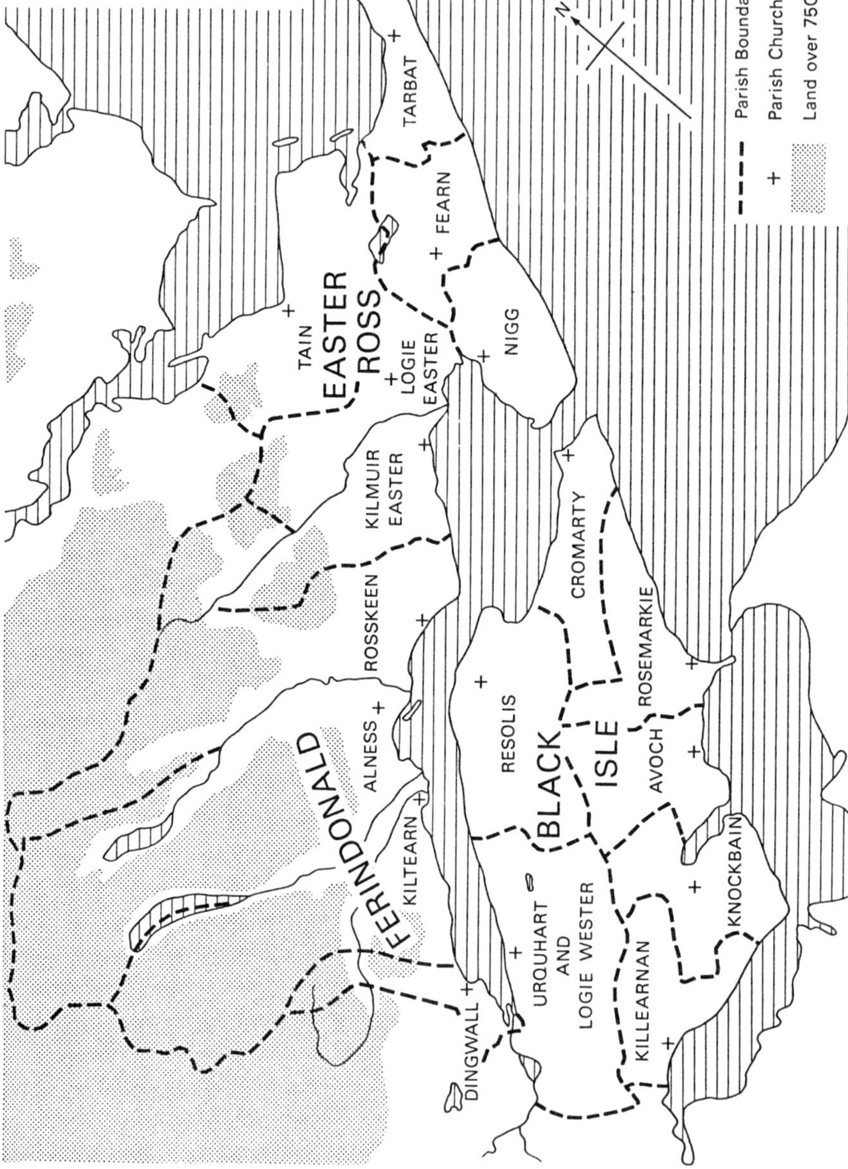

Appendix Ia

List of principal mansions indicated on Map 2, Appendix I. Where the name of the mansion is uncertain, the name of the estate has been given.

1. Tarlogie
2. Aldie
3. Calrossie
4. Mounteagle
5. Rhynie
6. Little Tarrel (Rockfield)
7. Geanies
8. Cadboll
9. Pitkerry
10. Meikle Allan
11. Shandwick
12. Glastullich
13. Balnagown
14. Tarbat
15. Meikle Kindeace (Bayfield)
16. Pitcalnie
17. Nigg
18. Pitcalzean
19. Scotsburn
20. Kindeace
21. Invergordon
22. Kincraig
23. Newmore
24. Culrain
25. Milncraig
26. Ardross
27. Lealty
28. Teaninich
29. Novar
30. Culcairn
31. Balcony
32. Foulis
33. Mountgerald
34. Tulloch
35. Brahan
36. Conon
37. Kilcoy
38. Redcastle
39. Allangrange
40. Drynie
41. Bennetsfield
42. Suddie
43. Belmaduthy
44. Rosehaugh
45. Avoch
46. Raddery
47. Kincurdy
48. Flowerburn
49. Cromarty
50. Udol
51. Ardoch (Poyntzfield)
52. Newhall
53. Braelangwell
54. Drumcudden
55. Kinbeachie

Appendix II
Population Statistics

(a) Parish populations 1755-1851

Parish	1755	1801	1811	1821	1831	1841	1851
Alness	1090	1072	1038	1270	1437	1269	1240
Avoch	1457	1476	1560	1821	1956	1931	2029
Cromarty	2096	2208	2413	2649	2901	2662	2727
Dingwall	1030	1418	1500	2031	2124	2100	2364
Fearn	1898	1528	1508	1654	1695	1914	2122
Killearnan	945	1131	1390	1371	1479	1643	1794
Kilmuir Easter	1095	1703	1559	1381	1551	1486	1437
Kilmuir Wester	600	—	—	—	—	—	—
Kiltearn	1570	1525	1552	1454	1605	1436	1538
Knockbain	—	1859	1766	1973	2139	2565	3005
Logie	850	1031	928	813	934	1015	965
Nigg	1261	1443	1349	1436	1404	1426	1457
Resolis	1371	1067*	1168	1201	1470	1549	1551
Rosemarkie	1140	1289	1312	1571	1799	1719	1776
Rosskeen	1958	2074	2390	2581	2916	3222	3699
Suddie	699	—	—	—	—	—	—
Tain	1870	2277	2384	2861	3078	3128	3574
Tarbat	1584	1343	1379	1625	1809	1826	2151
Urquhart	2590	4430	4174	2822	2864	2997	3153
Easter Ross	25164	28874	29370	30514	33161	33888	36582

*A later estimate

Sources — J. G. Kyd, *Scottish Population Statistics;* Census reports.

(b) Habitual Gaelic speakers as a percentage of the total population

Parish	1826	1881
Alness	85.72	46.95
Avoch	5.70	7.63
Cromarty	8.88	14.98
Dingwall	41.87	27.29
Fearn	94.08	69.50
Killearnan	93.43	52.69
Kilmuir	77.82	45.20
Kiltearn	86.18	54.91
Knockbain	87.08	57.39
Logie	88.77	52.72
Nigg	82.36	60.30
Resolis	55.06	42.20
Rosemarkie	4.94*	4.86
Rosskeen	—	33.71
Tain	67.08	33.77
Tarbat	96.59	66.24
Urquhart	95.43	71.89
Easter Ross	67.90	42.65

*The Inverness Society for the education of the poor in the Highlands figures for the parish of Rosemarkie are actually 13 families understanding English best and 250 families understanding Gaelic best, but in the light of other evidence (discussed in chapters four and five) it is clear that these figures have been accidentally transposed.

Sources—Inverness, Society for the education of the poor in the Highlands, Moral statistics; Ninth decennial census of the population of Scotland, report.

Appendix III

Property ownership 1756-1855

(a) Easter Ross estates in 1756[1]

Name of major estate, or estate from which territorial title, if any, derived	Value of land in each parish		Total valuation	Owner
Newtarbat	Kilmuir, Logie		£4288. 8. 4	Crown
Invergordon	Tarbat	£1972.13. 4		
	Rosskeen	£1180		
	Resolis	£ 193. 3. 6	£3345.16.10	Sir John Gordon
Cadboll	Fearn	£1201. 9. 6		
	Tain	£ 918. 3.10½		
	Nigg	£ 206		
	?	£ 165.10		
	Tarbat	£ 50		
	Rosemarkie	£ 16.10	£2557.13. 4½	Roderick Macleod
Scatwell	Urquhart	£1233		
	Avoch	£1058		
	Resolis	£ 100	£2391	Sir Lewis Mackenzie
Balnagown	Kilmuir	£ 679		
	Nigg	£ 676		
	Fearn	£ 520.15		
	Logie	£ 426	£2301.15	Sir James Ross
Obsdale	Alness	£ 871.10		
	Kiltearn	£ 802.17. 6		
	Rosskeen	£ 401.10	£2075.17. 6	Duncan Munro's heirs
Cromarty	Cromarty		£1826. 9	John Urquhart
Redcastle	Killearnan	£ 822.15		
	Knockbain	£ 669	£1491.15	Rory Mackenzie

Names of major estate, or estate from which territorial title, if any, derived	Value of land in each parish		Total valuation	Owner
Newhall	Resolis		£1451.12. 6	William Gordon
Rosehaugh	Rosemarkie	£1096. 3. 6		
	Avoch	£ 306.10	£1402.13. 6	James Stuart Mackenzie
Inverchassley	Nigg	£ 627		
	Tain	£ 450		
	Logie	£ 127		
	Fearn	£ 102.11. 2	£1306.11.2	David Ross
Ferintosh	Urquhart		£1200	? Forbes
Findrassie	Rosemarkie		£1060.15	John Leslie
Foulis	Kiltearn		£1025. 2	Sir Harry Munro
Kilcoy	Knockbain	£ 607.12. 8		
	Killearnan	£ 295		
	Urquhart	£ 107. 5	£1009.17. 8	Colin Mackenzie
Mulderg	Fearn		£ 953. 3. 7	? Margaret McCulloch
Kilravock	Nigg		£ 896. 5. 8	Hugh Rose
Allangrange	Killearnan	£ 452.10		
	Knockbain	£ 300		
	Rosemarkie	£ 110.10	£ 863	George Mackenzie
Aldie	Tain	£ 600.10		
	Tarbat	£ 188.10		
	Fearn	£ 64. 9	£ 853. 9	William Ross
Ardoch	Resolis	£ 410		
	Rosemarkie	£ 373.17. 8	£ 783.17. 8	Adam Gordon
—	Urquhart	£ 580		
	Dingwall	£ 165	£ 745	Lady Kincraig
Inchcoulter	Alness	£ 380		
	Kiltearn	£ 341	£ 721	George Mackenzie
Ardross	Rosskeen		£ 670.10	John Mackenzie
Newmore	Rosskeen	£ 450		
	Kilmuir	£ 175	£ 625	Heirs of John Munro
Novar	Alness	£ 616	£ 616	George Munro
Glasstullich	Logie	£ 348		
	Fearn	£ 266.18. 6	£ 614.18. 6	Roderick McCulloch
Easter Arboll	Tarbat		£ 575	Col. Urquhart
Geanies	Tarbat		£ 546. 7	Hugh Macleod

Names of major estate, or estate from which territorial title, if any, derived	Value of land in each parish		Total valuation	Owner
Pitcalnie	Nigg	£ 317.10		
	Tarbat	£ 225	£ 542.10	Alex. Ross
Auchnagairn	Tarbat	£ 486	£ 486	Duncan Fraser
Kilmuir	Knockbain		£ 457. 8. 4	Heirs of Capt. Hugh Fraser
Teaninich	Alness		£ 449	Hugh Munro
Pitkerry	Nigg	£ 401. 3		
	Fearn	£ 45. 6	£ 446. 9	George Ross
—	Avoch	£ 379		
	Rosemarkie	£ 50	£ 429	Lady Belmaduthy
Scotsburn	Logie	£ 207		
	Fearn	£ 183.13. 4		
	Kilmuir	£ 30.10	£ 421. 3. 4	Simon Mackenzie
Belmaduthy	Avoch	£ 250		
	Knockbain	£ 162	£ 412	? Mackenzie
Meikle Kindeace	Nigg		£ 404	Duncan Ross
Bennetsfield	Avoch	£ 213		
	Knockbain	£ 181.10	£ 394.10	John Matheson
Milncraig	Rosskeen		£ 390	James Cuthbert
Tulloch	Dingwall		£ 384.19	Kenneth Bain
Mountgerald	Kiltearn		£ 383.10	Heirs of Colin Mackenzie
Culrain	Rosskeen		£ 380. 5	George Munro
Seaforth	Dingwall	£ 200		
	Rosemarkie	£ 136	£ 336	Kenneth Mackenzie
Kincraig	Rosskeen	£ 234.10		
	Kilmuir	£ 81	£ 315.10	John Mackenzie
Delny	Kilmuir		£ 312	Alex. Bayne
Culcairn	Kiltearn	£ 203		
	Alness	£ 92.10	£ 295.10	Heirs of Capt. George Munro
Suddie	Knockbain		£ 278.10	Kenneth Mackenzie
Avoch	Avoch		£ 274.17. 2	John Mackenzie
Drynie	Knockbain		£ 269. 8. 4	George Graham
Culliss	Nigg		£ 267.14. 4	James Rose
Easterfearn	Fearn	£ 207. 8. 6		

Names of major estate, or estate from which territorial title, if any, derived	Value of land in each parish		Total valuation	Owner
	Tain	£ 60	£ 267. 8. 6	Easterfearn Creditors
Coull	Alness		£ 254.10	Albert Munro
—	Dingwall		£ 250	Lady Chisholm
Calrossie	Logie	£ 151.15		
	Tain	£ 84	£ 235.15	Thomas Ross
Little Tarrel	Tarbat		£ 233.19	Thomas Mackenzie
Pitcalzean	Nigg	£ 215		
	Alness	£ 12	£ 227	James Fraser
Greenhill	Cromarty		£ 219	David Urquhart ?
Muirtown	Knockbain		£ 213. 6.10	? Mackenzie
Braelangwell	Resolis		£ 204	Charles Urquhart
Kinrive	Kilmuir	£ 196		
	Rosskeen	£ 5	£ 201	William Baillie
Inchfuir	Kilmuir		£ 200.10	John Martin
Over Cambuscurry	Tain	£ 110		
	Tarbat	£ 84	£ 194	Roderick Dingwall
—	Alness		£ 185.10	Duncan Simson
Auchnacloich	Fearn		£ 175.17. 6	Robert Ross
Dam	Nigg		£ 162.16	Thomas Gair
—	Rosemarkie		£ 162.16	Heirs of Hugh Baillie
Drumhall	Cromarty		£ 155.16	John Davidson
Mounteagle	Fearn		£ 155. 1	John Urquhart
Priesthill	Kilmuir		£ 142	David Ross
Udol	Cromarty		£ 140. 5	William Anderson
Kincurdy	Rosemarkie		£ 134.15	Andrew Miller
Kiltearn	Kiltearn		£ 132	Alex. Munro
—	Rosemarkie		£ 128. 5	Heirs of Duncan Forbes
Kinnock	Rosemarkie		£ 120	Bernard Mackenzie
Meikle Allan	Fearn		£ 118	David Munro
Milntown	Kiltearn		£ 112	John Munro
Kinbeachy	Resolis		£ 100. 0. 4	? Urquhart
Culbo	Resolis		£ 100	? Mackenzie
Pitlundy	Knockbain		£ 90	? Mackenzie

Names of major estate, or estate from which territorial title, if any, derived	Value of land in each parish	Total valuation	Owner
Gairloch	Urquhart	£ 90	Sir Alex. ? Mackenzie
Killichoan	Kiltearn	£ 82.10	John Munro
—	Rosemarkie	£ 70.13. 4	Heirs of Alex. Ross
—	Fearn ?	£ 70	Donald Ross
Neilston	Cromarty	£ 62	John Clunes
Drumcudden	Resolis	£ 55. 3	William Duff
Knockmuir	Avoch	£ 49.19. 2	John Mackenzie
Shandwick	Fearn	£ 49	Heirs of William Ross
—	Rosemarkie	£ 38. 6. 8	M'Ever's heirs
Langlands	Cromarty	£ 37. 7. 6	Alex. Davidson
Teanaird	Kiltearn	£ 34	William Munro
Culniskee	Kiltearn	£ 33.10	David Bethune
Pitcalzean	Nigg	£ 32	David Reoch
Lealty	Alness	£ 30	? Munro
—	Rosemarkie	£ 27	Heirs of George Houston
—	Rosemarkie	£ 25.15	George Jamieson
—	Cromarty	£ 22.11	Henry Davidson
Drums of Fearn	Fearn	£ 20	Heirs of Baillie Donald Ross
—	Rosemarkie	£ 18. 2. 6	John Mackenzie
?	Cromarty ?	£ 16.10	?
—	Cromarty	£ 12. 8	Alex. Mitchell
—	Cromarty	£ 10.12. 6	Thos. Lindsay's representative
Haugh	Cromarty	£ 6.10	Robert Gordon
Navity	Cromarty	£ 4.16	Donald Williamson
—	Cromarty	£ 3. 7. 6	Hugh Macleod & Jas. Williamson
—	Cromarty	£ 3. 4	? Junor
—	Cromarty	£ 0.12	John McCulloch
—	Cromarty	£ 0.10	Alex. Simpson's widow

Sources—Valuation Rolls.

NOTES:

1. The valuations are those of the mid-seventeenth century and are not, therefore, reliable but they do give some indication of the relative sizes of properties and of the range of values. In this and the succeeding tables burgh properties, glebes and mortified lands have been omitted.

2. Where the major property of the landlord lay outside Ross or Cromarty the name of the largest estate within these counties is given except when properties did not have a clear name. In all other cases the territorial designation is given.

3. The valuation for Newtarbat is actually that for all the Cromartie estates in Ross and Cromarty. Newtarbat itself was probably a middle ranking estate.

4. The valuation for Ferintosh is derived from the Nairn valuation roll of 1802 but is unlikely to be substantially different from the 1756 figure.

(b) Easter Ross estates in 1802[1]

Name of major[2] estate, or estate from which territorial title, if any, derived	Value of land in each parish		Total valuation	Owner
Cadboll	Tarbat	£2168.13. 4		
	Fearn	£1367		
	Rosskeen	£1180		
	Tain	£1167		
	Nigg	£ 119	£6001.13. 4	Robert B. A. Macleod
Newtarbat	Kilmuir, Logie		£4358. 8. 4[3]	Mrs. Moira Hay Mackenzie
Balnagown	Kilmuir	£1467.10		
	Nigg	£ 676		
	Logie	£ 426		
	Fearn	£ 332.10. 6	£2902. 0. 6	Sir Charles Ross
Scatwell	Avoch	£1687		
	Urquhart	£1034		
	Resolis	£ 100		
	Rosemarkie	£ 50	£2871	Sir Roderick Mackenzie
Cromarty	Cromarty	£2428. 4. 8½		
	Nigg	£ 381. 5	£2809. 9. 8½	Alex. Ross
Geanies	Tarbat	£1832. 7. 6		
	Fearn	£ 336. 2	£2168. 9. 6	Donald Macleod
Foulis	Kiltearn		£2139. 9. 6	Sir Hugh Munro
Flowerburn	Rosemarkie		£1951. 6	Roderick Mackenzie
Shandwick	Nigg	£1791		

Names of major estate, or estate from which territorial title, if any, derived	Value of land in each parish		Total valuation	Owner
	Logie	£ 127	£1918	James Cockburn Ross
Redcastle	Killearnan	£ 822.15		
	Knockbain	£ 679	£1501.15	James Grant
Newmore	Tain	£ 600.10		
	Rosskeen	£ 450		
	Tarbat	£ 188.10		
	Kilmuir	£ 175		
	Fearn	£ 64. 9	£1478. 9	William Ross Munro
Culcairn	Alness	£ 893.10		
	Rosskeen	£ 289		
	Kiltearn	£ 203	£1385.10	Duncan Munro
Kilcoy	Killearnan	£ 740. 9. 8		
	Knockbain	£ 584. 3. 2	£1324.12.10	Charles Mackenzie
Ferintosh	Urquhart		£1200	Arthur Forbes
Newhall	Resolis		£1139.15. 6½	Charles Lockhart
Findrassie	Rosemarkie		£1060.15	John Leslie
Mulderg	Fearn		£1002. 3. 7	John Anderson
Tulloch	Dingwall	£ 799.19		
	Kiltearn	£ 82.10	£ 882. 9	Henry Davidson
Allangrange	Knockbain	£ 752.10		
	Rosemarkie	£ 110.10	£ 863	John Mackenzie
Glastullich	Logie	£ 499.15		
	Fearn	£ 275.17. 6		
	Tain	£ 84	£ 859.12.6	Hugh Rose Ross
Novar	Alness	£ 796.10	£ 796.10	Sir Hector Munro
Teaninich	Alness		£ 779	Hugh Munro
Gairloch	Urquhart		£ 777. 5	Sir Hector Mackenzie
Inchcoulter	Alness	£ 380		
	Kiltearn	£ 341	£ 721	Anne Mackenzie Grieve
Ardross	Rosskeen		£ 670.10	Murdo Mackenzie
Braelangwell	Resolis		£ 651. 1. 8½	David Urquhart
Avoch	Avoch		£ 581. 7. 2	George Mackenzie
Milncraig	Rosskeen	£ 502.10		
	Fearn	£ 20	£ 522.10	David Ross

Names of major estate, or estate from which territorial title, if any, derived	Value of land in each parish	Total valuation	Owner
Drynie	Knockbain	£ 518. 3. 4	Charles Graham
Inverchassley	Tain	£ 450	David Ross
Scotsburn	Logie £ 207 Fearn £ 183.13. 4 Kilmuir £ 30.10	£ 421. 3. 4	Roderick Mackenzie
Poyntzfield	Resolis	£ 410	George G. Munro
Bayfield	Nigg	£ 404	William Mackenzie
Bennetsfield	Avoch £ 213 Knockbain £ 181.10	£ 394.10	Colin Matheson
Mountgerald	Kiltearn	£ 383.10	Colin Mackenzie
Culrain	Rosskeen	£ 380. 5	George Munro
Meikle Allan	Fearn	£ 325. 8. 6	Charles Munro
Pitcalnie	Nigg	£ 317.10	Munro Ross
Kincraig	Rosskeen £ 234.10 Kilmuir £ 81	£ 315.10	John Mackenzie
Suddie	Knockbain	£ 278.10	John R. Mackenzie
Nigg	Nigg	£ 249.16	Walter Ross
Little Tarrel	Tarbat	£ 234	Allan Robertson
Pitcalzean	Nigg £ 215 Alness £ 12	£ 227	? Fraser
Seaforth	Dingwall	£ 200	Francis Mackenzie, Lord Seaforth
Pitlundy	Resolis £ 100 Knockbain £ 90	£ 190	George Mackenzie
Rhynie	Fearn	£ 166.18. 6	William Rose
Belmaduthy	Knockbain	£ 162	Mrs. Martha Mackenzie
Mounteagle	Fearn	£ 155. 1	John Urquhart
Udol	Cromarty	£ 140. 5	Alex. Anderson
Kincurdy	Rosemarkie	£ 134.15	Andrew Miller
Kinbeachy	Resolis	£ 100. 0. 4	John Urquhart
Gowanhead	Rosemarkie	£ 70.13. 4	Michael Miller
—	Rosemarkie	£ 58. 7. 8	Hugh Maclean
Drumcudden	Resolis	£ 55. 3	H. R. Duff

Names of major estate, or estate from which territorial title, if any, derived	Value of land in each parish	Total valuation	Owner
Newton	Avoch	£ 49.19. 2	Mrs. Ann Mackenzie
Wellfield	Rosemarkie	£ 34.19. 6	James Fowler
Pitcalzean	Nigg	£ 32	John Mackenzie
Lealty	Alness	£ 30	Finlay Munro
—	Rosemarkie	£ 25.15	Widow Hood
—	Rosemarkie	£ 24. 1	Donald Junor
—	Rosemarkie	£ 18. 2. 6	Kenneth Mackenzie
—	Rosemarkie	£ 11.18.10	Joe. Millar
—	Rosemarkie	£ 7. 5. 2	Jas. Moir
Chancellor's Croft	Rosemarkie	£ 6.16. 6	Jas. Grigor
Kindeace	Rosskeen	£ 5	William Robertson
Navity	Cromarty	£ 4.16	William Williamson
—	Rosemarkie	£ 3. 8. 2	Donald Watson
—	Cromarty	£ 3. 7. 6	Hugh Macleod's heirs
—	Cromarty	£ 3. 4	Jeremiah Joyner
—	Rosemarkie	£ 2. 6. 1	Kenneth Leitch
—	Rosemarkie	£ 1.10. 8	Jas. Wilson
—	Rosemarkie	£ 1.10. 8	John Mackeddy
—	Rosemarkie	£ 1. 5. 7	John Davidson
—	Rosemarkie	£ 0.17	George Aird

Sources—Valuation Rolls.

NOTES:

1. See (a) note 1.
2. See (a) note 2.
3. See (a) note 3.

(c) **Easter Ross estates in 1855**[1]

Names of major[2] estate, or estate from which territorial title, if any, derived	Value of land in each parish		Total valuation	Owner
Cadboll	Fearn	£2995.10		
	Rosskeen	£2444. 2. 3		
	Tarbat	£1777.15. 6		
	Tain	£ 798.12. 1		
	Kilmuir	£ 309.13. 6	£8325.13. 4	R. B. A. Macleod
Cromarty	Cromarty	£3916.10. 2		
	Rosskeen	£ 897. 6		
	Nigg	£ 459	£5272.16. 2	George W. H. Ross
Balnagown	Logie	£2649. 0. 4		
	Kilmuir	£ 969. 9. 8		
	Nigg	£ 810.12.10		
	Fearn	£ 463. 3. 6		
	Tain	£ 58.15. 8	£4951. 2	Sir Charles Ross
Novar	Alness	£3248.12		
	Kiltearn	£ 889. 4	£4137.16	Hugh A. J. Munro
Kilcoy	Knockbain	£2555.18		
	Killearnan	£1465.18	£4021.16	Charles Mackenzie
Redcastle	Killearnan	£2650.15		
	Knockbain	£1300. 5	£3951	Col. H. D. Baillie
Scatwell	Avoch	£2824.16		
	Knockbain	£ 719. 8		
	Rosemarkie	£ 349.18	£3894. 2	Sir James J. R. Mackenzie
Foulis	Kiltearn		£3057. 5	Sir Charles Munro
Ferintosh	Urquhart		£2758. 6	Arthur Forbes
Shandwick	Nigg	£2076. 4. 5		
	Logie	£ 434.19	£2511. 3. 5	Miss ? Willemena Ross
Ardross	Rosskeen	£2272.14. 7		
	Alness	£ 120	£2392.14. 7	Alex. Matheson
Geanies	Tarbat	£1808. 8.10		
	Fearn	£ 431. 0. 9		
	Tain	£ 49.18. 9	£2289. 8. 4	W. H. Murray
Glastullich	Tain	£1381.14		
	Rosskeen	£ 668		
	Fearn	£ 234.16. 9	£2284.10. 9	Major ? Rose

Names of major estate, or estate from which territorial title, if any, derived	Value of land in each parish		Total valuation	Owner
Newhall	Resolis		£2048. 9. 6	John A. Shaw Mackenzie
Findon	Urquhart	£1832. 3		
	Resolis	£ 210.11	£2042.14	Lewis M. Mackenzie
Tulloch	Dingwall	£1793.14		
	Kiltearn	£ 196	£1989.14	Duncan Davidson
Sutherland	Kilmuir	£1211. 2. 2		
	Logie	£ 611.16		
	Tain	£ 94.15. 9	£1917.13.11	George Granville Leveson Gower, Duke of Sutherland
Allangrange	Knockbain		£1202.14	James F. Mackenzie
Gairloch	Urquhart		£1195.14	Sir Kenneth Mackenzie
Newmore	Rosskeen		£1157.17. 8	F. M. Gillanders
Meikle Allan	Fearn			
	Tain		£1122	David Munro
Teaninich	Alness		£1114.18	Lt. General? Munro
Drynie	Knockbain		£1055.17	Paul Graham
Avoch	Avoch			
	Resolis		£ 973.17	Alex. G. Mackenzie
Kindeace	Kilmuir		£ 854. 7. 4	Major ? William Robertson
Westfield	Nigg		£ 841. 7. 8	T. L. R. Murray
Kincraig	Rosskeen			
	Kilmuir		£824.17. 2	Executors of late Major ? Mackenzie
Aldie	Tain			
	Tarbat			
	Fearn		£ 807. 9. 9	George Mackenzie Ross
Ethie	Rosemarkie		£ 694.10	Evan Baillie of Dochfour
Flowerburn	Rosemarkie		£ 671.13	Roderick G. Mackenzie
Balintraid	Kilmuir		£ 623. 3. 2	Thos. Ogilvie

Names of major estate, or estate from which territorial title, if any, derived	Value of land in each parish	Total valuation	Owner
Seaforth	Dingwall	£ 616. 3	Hon. Mrs. S. Mackenzie
Raddery	Rosemarkie	£ 612.18	Henry M. Fowler
Mountgerald	Kiltearn	£ 603.10	Col. Simon F. Mackenzie
Swordale	Kiltearn	£ 561.12	John Munro
Bennetsfield	Avoch Dingwall	£ 488.8	Sir Jas. Matheson of the Lews
Pitcalnie	Nigg	£ 488	George Ross
Balcony	Kiltearn	£ 350	Mrs. Catherine Munro
Rhynie	Fearn	£ 350	Trustees of late Wm. Rose
Bayfield	Nigg	£ 348. 9	Wm. Humphrey
Weavis	Kiltearn	£ 300	Frederick Ward
Bogbain	Tain	£ 290	Trustees of Bogbain
Little Tarrel	Tarbat	£ 251.14	Andrew Munro
Mounteagle	Fearn	£ 245. 1	Trustees of late Wm. Robertson
Drumcudden	Resolis	£ 216.18	Colin Lyon Mackenzie
Kincurdy	Rosemarkie	£ 210. 8	Colin M. Millar
Kinbeachy	Resolis	£ 176.11	Thomas Urquhart
Balnabeen	Urquhart	£ 150	Donald Mackenzie
Hartfield	Tain	£ 120	David Ross
Knockbreck	Tain	£ 103.15	John Dalrymple
Moorfarm	Tain	£ 102. 5	David Ross
North Glastullich	Tain	£ 94. 4	Malcolm Fraser
Tainaharn	Urquhart	£ 74	James Ure's representatives
Rosemount	Tain	£ 67	Trustees of late Geo. Murray
Ardmeanach	Rosemarkie	£ 50	J. M. Fraser
Highfield	Tain	£ 40	R. Matheson

Names of major estate, or estate from which territorial title, if any, derived	Value of land in each parish	Total valuation	Owner
Pentlands	Tain	£ 24	Mrs. Murray
Knockrash	Kiltearn	£ 16	Murdo Cameron
Lamington	Tain	£ 13.15	Mrs. Stewart
Hawkhill	Rosemarkie	£ 13	Patrick Maclean
Alcaig	Urquhart	£ 12	Donald Mackenzie
Balblair	Resolis	£ 11.17	James Campbell
St Vincent	Tain	£ 10	Donald Mackay
Culdeach	Avoch	£ 10	Rev. Peter Ferries
Newton of Kinkell	Urquhart	£ 9	William Forbes
Woodside	Tain	£ 8	F. James
Mineralbank	Tain	£ 7.10	D. Vass
Newton of Kinkell	Urquhart	£ 5	Donald Macdonald
Morangie	Tain	£ 4.10	D. M. Mackenzie executors
Platcock	Rosemarkie	£ 1.10	Mrs. ? Watson
Hill of Fortrose	Rosemarkie	£ 0.15	Donald Ross

Sources—Valuation Rolls.

NOTES:

1. This table gives the real value of property in 1855, excluding burgh properties, glebes and mortified lands.
2. See (a) note 2.

Index

References to Ross-shire and Easter Ross (referring to the whole area covered by this book rather than the more specific district of that name) have been omitted from the index.